Introduction

A Message from Barbara Weltman...

EVERYONE WANTS TO ACHIEVE a level of financial security to pay bills, have a cushion in the bank against unforeseen expenses and the promise of an even better future. To achieve this, follow a simple three-step process:

▶ **Step 1—Get information.** You must understand how to accumulate the funds you'll need for your financial obligations and dreams—buying a home, sending children to college, retiring, supporting parents, travel and more. You must also learn how to protect your assets so that your wealth won't be eroded by taxes, inflation, creditors, catastrophe or death.

▶ **Step 2—Make a plan.** Once you've gained insight into what it takes to get ahead financially, you need to formulate a plan. Your plan will be composed of numerous ideas that move you toward your goals. There's no single financial plan for everyone; yours must meet your individual needs and desires. A financial plan for a single person won't be the same as a plan for a married couple. Those with dependent children or aging parents have distinct responsibilities and financial concerns. Some people want to live in luxury or retire young, while others are satisfied with more modest achievements. Your plan must fit who you are and what you want to accomplish. And your plan must adapt to changes you experience (the addition or loss of a family member, a sudden windfall or unforeseen financial loss, relocation, job changes, litigation) as well as changes in the economy (increased inflation, ups and downs of interest rates, stock market swings).

▶ **Step 3—Take action.** After you've put together a plan for the things you want or need to do, you must act on your decisions. If you don't act, you've effectively elected inaction. For example, assume you have cash sitting in a money market fund. You are deciding whether to invest in (A) a stock, (B) a bond or (C) a mutual fund. If you *don't* act to invest in A, B or C, you've effectively decided to continue earning the rate of return that the money market fund is paying.

Some people leap into Steps 2 and 3 without having first completed Step 1—gaining a good understanding of financial options and consequences. No matter what your level of financial sophistication, you can always learn something new. This book presents you with proven money ideas that you can incorporate into your financial plans and implement to increase and protect your wealth. Some ideas may seem basic but they can be helpful nonetheless.

This book not only gives you the information you need to understand your options but also provides you with strategies—ideas for action identified with the symbol " ★ ." These strategies explain how to go about doing things, including the advantages to be gained, and the disadvantages that may result.

Some people spend their lives stuck on Step 1, always gathering information but never doing anything about it. Others may proceed to Step 2, putting plans together but never implementing them. There's nothing in this book that can *make* you take Step 3 and act on your plans. But I hope that by learning how to do things, seeing how simple certain approaches can be and understanding the consequences of inaction, you'll be motivated to get started and take action now.

Because I have a tax background I tend to look for the tax implications of every money decision. As a result, I've sprinkled tax considerations throughout the book to alert you to tax opportunities and pitfalls that may result from the actions you take (or don't take). But I want to emphasize that your financial decisions should be guided by your overall goals. Taxes are only one factor to be considered in your decision-making and should not be the only driving force for your actions.

How to use this book

This book is designed to broaden your knowledge of financial matters and provide you with suggestions on how to implement your plans. Whether you're a financial novice or a seasoned professional, you're sure to find new ideas and strategies to help you keep your financial house in order. Each chapter focuses on a different facet of your financial life—including banking, investing in the stock market, saving money in retirement plans and handling debt. Concentrate on those chapters of particular interest to you, in areas where you want the most help. But don't overlook the chapters on subjects you think you understand; they may contain ideas and suggestions that will benefit you.

This book provides numerous telephone numbers and web sites to help you access more information. In 2003, nearly 57% of all US households (and more than three-quarters of those earning more than $50,000 a year) had access to the Internet at home or elsewhere—through computers, devices such as Web TV, personal digital assistants (PDAs such as the Palm Pilot) and even cell phones—that's more than the number of households with cable TV! That's nearly 150 million Americans. But if you don't yet have this home access, you can easily obtain it at your local library or through neighborhood schools, which are now usually "wired" for Internet access. *One word of caution:* Web addresses can change, so listings in the book that were operational at the time of publication may be different or out of date when you try to access them. My apologies for any inconvenience.

Keep in mind that the material contained in this book is designed to provide overall information on a topic—not accounting, legal or investment advice. Your individual financial situation requires a critical look at the material, and actions you take should be tailored for your particular needs. Consult a financial professional for answers to your specific questions.

I'd like to thank my husband, Malcolm Katt, who provided not only technical assistance on financial topics but also personal encouragement and support.

February 2007   Barbara Weltman

Contents

About the Author

A noted attorney and financial expert in Westchester, New York, Barbara Weltman is eminently qualified to write a guide to financial planning for Bottom Line readers.

In addition to an extensive law practice in taxation, trusts and estates, small business planning and elder law, she has written many best-selling personal finance books, including *J.K. Lasser's Small Business Taxes, The Complete Idiot's Guide to Starting a Home-Based Business, The Complete Idiot's Guide to Starting an eBay Business* and *The Complete Idiot's Guide to Making Money after You Retire.*

As a highly respected and sought-after commentator on tax and small business issues, she has appeared on national media, including the *Today* show, *CNN, CNBC* and nationwide radio stations. Ms. Weltman also lectures extensively and gives courses to financial professionals and consumers alike, and is a contributor to *Bottom Line/Personal.*

A former editor for the J.K. Lasser Tax Institute, now President of BWideas.com Inc. and publisher of *Barbara Weltman's Big Ideas for Small Business*®, a free monthly online newsletter **(www.barbaraweltman.com)**, Barbara Weltman contributes her expertise to educational and community activities.

What wealth is really all about

"If you can count your money, you don't have a billion dollars." —J. Paul Getty

THE OLD ADAGE that money can't buy happiness may be true, but it's also true that money can go a long way in helping you achieve what you seek. Wealth can enable you to do many things not otherwise possible—obtain a secure financial future in which you know you can cover your basic needs, provide financial help to family and friends, give to charities, travel, try new things and more.

Financially speaking, the term *wealth* is an everyday word that means having an abundance of money and material possessions. But what does the term mean to you? Is it a dollar amount—$1 million, $10 million or more? Does wealth mean freedom to do the things you want? Or does it mean added work and responsibility, such as monitoring investments, making decisions and looking after your financial affairs?

What would it take to make you feel wealthy? Are you already wealthy? You may have more assets on hand to provide for your financial well-being than you imagine. You may be overlooking certain assets, such as a company-provided retirement plan or an eventual inheritance.

This chapter covers basic information about wealth—what it is and where it comes from. It helps you to appraise your current wealth, set short- and long-term financial goals, and to examine how Social Security benefits fit into your financial plans.

WHAT IS WEALTH AND WHERE DOES IT COME FROM?

Wealth comprises not only cash but also assets of every kind. Below is a listing of common assets you may own. When you think about your property, consider what it's worth today. This is called "fair market value"—that is, the cash you would receive if you sold the property to a willing buyer in an arm's-length transaction (a transaction involving two strangers).

▶ **Art and other collectibles.**

▶ **Bank accounts** (savings and checking accounts, certificates of deposit and money market accounts).

▶ **Business interests** (ownership in a sole proprietorship, partnership, limited liability company or corporation).

▶ **Car, boat, motor home.**

▶ **Home** (your principal residence as well as vacation property).

▶ **Investment property** (such as rental properties or land).

▶ **IRAs** (including IRA rollovers and Roth IRAs).

▶ **Jewelry and silver flatware.**

▶ **Life insurance policies** that build up a cash surrender value.

▶ **Personal items** (furniture, books, clothing, etc.).

▶ **Qualified retirement plan accounts** (for example, 401(k) accounts).

▶ **Stocks, bonds and mutual funds.** You may hold a stock certificate or other evidence of ownership directly or through an account with a brokerage firm or mutual fund.

▶ **Inheritance.** You may also be sitting on a potential inheritance that will bring you money or property in the future. For example, your father may have died, leaving his estate in trust for the benefit of your mother. You'll inherit your share of what remains in his estate when your mother dies, as well as your share of your mother's own estate.

Gaining wealth

Wealth can come to you in a number of ways. You can earn money through your labor and use your compensation to acquire assets. This may be a slow process, requiring you to set aside money so that, over time, you'll have what's needed to buy the items you want. If you own a business, its value adds to your wealth, and you can turn that into cash by selling your interest. You can receive a onetime windfall, perhaps even without any action on your part—an inheritance, a lottery win, an insurance settlement or a court award. And your wealth can increase through the appreciation of assets. For example, if you bought a stock several years ago for $10 a share and the same stock is now selling for $90 a share, you've increased your wealth from this asset by 800%!

Of course, don't lose sight of the fact that wealth can disappear just as quickly. Poor planning, bad investments, lawsuits and catastrophic illness can easily wipe out a lifetime of accumulated wealth.

NET WORTH

Net worth refers to what you're worth at any given time, balancing out all of your assets (the things you own) against all of your liabilities (the debts you owe). The excess of your total assets over your total liabilities is your net worth.

A net worth statement is a snapshot of the details of your financial holdings at a particular point in time. Having a net worth statement allows you to assess where you stand financially, and it is one of the items used by a bank when making a decision on a loan application.

Net worth statement for   (your name)   (date)

Assets	
Art and collectibles	$
Bank accounts: Acct. No.	$
Acct. No.	$
Acct. No.	$
Business interests	$
Car, boat, motor home	$
Home	$
Investment property	$
IRA accounts (including IRA rollovers and Roth IRAs)	
Acct. No.	$
Acct. No.	$
Acct. No.	$
Jewelry and silver flatware	$
Life insurance cash surrender value	$
Personal items (furniture, books, clothing, etc.)	$
Qualified retirement plan accounts: 401(k) plan account	$
Other (e.g., 403(b) annuity)	$
Stocks, bonds, mutual funds	$
Other assets	$
Total assets	$
Liabilities	
Car loan	$
Credit card debt	$
Home mortgage: Acquisition debt	$
Home-equity loan	$
Life insurance loans	$
Retirement account loans	$
Student loans	$
Other liabilities	$
Total liabilities	$
Net worth (total assets minus total liabilities)	$

Prepare your net worth statement at the end of each year. This will allow you to see not only what you own and owe, but also whether your financial strategies are working. Why? Because you can compare your current net worth statement with the one you prepared for the prior year to see whether your wealth has increased. If you don't use a year-end date for your net worth statements, use your birthday or some other memorable date, such as the April tax filing date. However, it's probably easier if you use a year-end date, because financial institutions and pension plans provide you with year-end statements listing the value of your accounts on December 31.

Net worth statement for ____ (your name) ____ (date)

Assets

Art and collectibles	$
Bank accounts: Acct. No.	$
Acct. No.	$
Acct. No.	$
Business interests	$
Car, boat, motor home	$
Home	$
Investment property	$
IRA accounts (including IRA rollovers and Roth IRAs)	
Acct. No.	$
Acct. No.	$
Acct. No.	$
Jewelry and silver flatware	$
Life insurance cash surrender value	$
Personal items (furniture, books, clothing, etc.)	$
Qualified retirement plan accounts: 401(k) plan account	$
Other (e.g., 403(b) annuity)	$
Stocks, bonds, mutual funds	$
Other assets	$
Total assets	$

Liabilities

Car loan	$
Credit card debt	$
Home mortgage: Acquisition debt	$
Home-equity loan	$
Life insurance loans	$
Retirement account loans	$
Student loans	$
Other liabilities	$
Total liabilities	$
Net worth (total assets minus total liabilities)	$

When you list items on your net worth statement, use their fair market value (or as close as you can come to it)—that is, what you would get for the items if you were to sell them to a third party. Do not reduce the items by any debt on them; the debt is listed separately in the liability portion of your net worth statement.

If you're married, you may wish to prepare a joint net worth statement with your spouse. In this case, it's advisable to use four columns (your items, your spouse's items, your joint items and the combination of similar items) so you'll know what you're worth as a couple. The worksheet on page 4 is an example of a joint net worth statement that you can adapt to your own personal use.

There is no set format for a net worth statement. You may modify the statement to include special assets you may own, such as a boat. You may use separate schedules for certain assets, such as a listing of stocks, bonds and mutual funds. Then enter only the total on your net worth statement.

Alternate ways to prepare your net worth statement

If you use commercial software (such as *Quicken*®) to pay your bills, balance your checkbook and keep track of investments, you can also use it to prepare a net worth statement. Simply follow the software's instructions. The advantage of using such software is that the statement virtually prepares itself. Since you've already told the program your assets and liabilities, it compiles the net worth statement for you.

Or you may wish to complete a net worth statement online. The advantage of using an online statement is that it automatically totals your net worth. *Example:*

▶ American Public Media **(http://marketplacemoney.publicradio.org/toolbox/calculators/Net Worth.html)**

▶ Chittenden Bank **(www.chittenden.com/wealth-management/resource-center/networth-calculator.html)**

▶ iFigure **(www.ifigure.com/money/budget/budget.htm)** for links to various net calculators

▶ LaSalle's Financial Resource Center **(www.netletter.net/lasalle_resourcecalculators/worth.html)**

Where you stand in comparison with the rest of the country

Now that you know your net worth, what does the figure mean to you? The fact that in 2006 *Forbes* listed 793 billionaires probably doesn't mean much to you. According to a Federal Reserve Board report, the median net worth of Americans was $93,100 in 2004, the latest year for which statistics are published. (Median essentially means the person in the middle—i.e., that there were the same number of Americans with greater net worth and the same number with lower net worth.) And, given the rise in real estate values, it's been estimated that there are more than 8.9 million Americans who are millionaires—their net worth exceeds $1 million, which accounts for about 7% of all American households! How do you compare with the median figures?

Unfortunately, these numbers don't tell the entire story. Net worth generally increases with age. Older Americans have a higher net worth on average than younger Americans.

Why you should know your net worth

More than a point of curiosity, if you know your net worth, you can take a proactive role in your financial future.

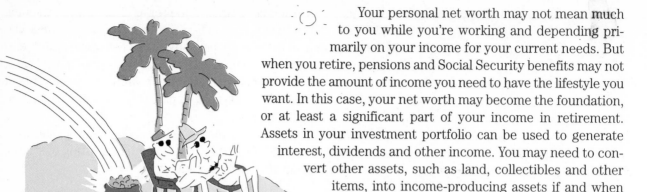

Your personal net worth may not mean much to you while you're working and depending primarily on your income for your current needs. But when you retire, pensions and Social Security benefits may not provide the amount of income you need to have the lifestyle you want. In this case, your net worth may become the foundation, or at least a significant part of your income in retirement. Assets in your investment portfolio can be used to generate interest, dividends and other income. You may need to convert other assets, such as land, collectibles and other items, into income-producing assets if and when you need added income. Remember that liabilities you still owe—for example, a home mortgage, car payments and credit card debt—will continue to be a drain on your income.

As a rule of thumb, expect your net worth to be able to produce about 5% to 8% annually. So, if your net worth is $1 million, anticipate an annual income from it of about $50,000 to $80,000 per year.

Still, this figure may be misleading, because not every asset is a productive income-generating asset. For example, your home may be a substantial portion of your net worth, but while you live there, no income will be realized from it. However, if you sell your home and invest the proceeds in securities that pay interest or dividends, this portion of your net worth becomes productive and returns income to you.

Social Security won't make you rich

If you're already collecting Social Security, you know this to be true. If you're a GenXer, you probably don't think about what Social Security will do for you in the distant future, and you may not believe you'll ever see a penny from the Social Security system. But if you are middle-aged and not yet retired, you need to be realistic about the role Social Security benefits will play in your financial picture. This is especially true for the 78 million baby boomers poised to start collecting full benefits in 2012.

The Social Security Administration (SSA, **www.socialsecurity.gov**) estimates that Social Security benefits replace about 40% of earnings for the average retiree. However, you may not be average and your benefits may not represent a significant monthly portion of the income you need to maintain the lifestyle you want.

Social Security basics

You may be eligible to collect Social Security benefits, but do not expect this income to enable you to live a comfortable retirement. The average monthly Social Security benefit payable in 2007 is just $1,044, and the maximum benefit is $2,116. Benefits adjust annually for inflation, but adjustments have been modest and may not keep up with your personal cost-of-living increases each year.

What's more, if you retire before your full retirement age (the age at which you can receive full retirement benefits), your benefits will be permanently reduced. The full retirement age set by the SSA is increasing in steps to age 67, as shown on the following chart.

Age for full retirement benefits

Year of birth	Full retirement age as set by SSA
1937 and earlier	65
1938	65 and 2 months
1939	65 and 4 months
1940	65 and 6 months
1941	65 and 8 months
1942	65 and 10 months
1943 through 1954	66
1955	66 and 2 months
1956	66 and 4 months
1957	66 and 6 months
1958	66 and 8 months
1959	66 and 10 months
1960 and later	67

Early retirement benefits

Even though the traditional retirement age is 65, you may receive benefits at age 62. Your benefits are permanently reduced in comparison to what you would have received at your full retirement age. The chart below shows this reduction. According to the House Ways and Means Committee's *Green Book for 1998*, about 60% of all workers choose to commence benefits at age 62, and the average age for retirement is 63.5 years old.

Year of birth	Monthly % reduction	Total % reduction if retiring at age 62
1937 and earlier	.555	20.00
1938	.548	20.83
1939	.541	21.67
1940	.535	22.50
1941	.530	23.33
1942	.525	24.17
1943 through 1954	.520	25.00
1955	.516	25.84
1956	.512	26.66
1957	.509	27.50
1958	.505	28.33
1959	.502	29.17
1960 and later	.500	30.00

As I've said, opting for early retirement *permanently* reduces your Social Security benefits by a formula based on the number of months you retire before your expected retirement age. If you retire up to 36 months early, the benefit is reduced by ⅝ of 1% for the first 36 months and ⁵⁄₁₂ of 1% for each additional month.

> **Example:** Someone born in 1945 who turns 62 in 2007 and opts for early retirement at age 62 would have Social Security benefits permanently reduced by 25%. So, if benefits at 66 would have been $1,200 a month, taking retirement at 62 reduces benefits to $900 a month. (Refer to chart on page 7 or visit **www.socialsecurity.gov/retire2/agereduction.htm**.)

Unless your birthday is on the first or second day of the month, Social Security eligibility commences the month following the triggering date (e.g., age 62; 65 years, two months).

Delaying the start of benefits can mean a bonus

For each year past full retirement age that you wait before collecting Social Security, you receive additional benefits, depending on when you were born, as follows:

Year of birth	Annual bonus
1931–1932	5.0%
1933–1934	5.5%
1935–1936	6.0%
1937–1938	6.5%
1939–1940	7.0%
1941–1942	7.5%
1943 and later	8.0%

> **Example:** You were born in 1942 and turn 65 years, 10 months in 2007. If you wait until you're 70 to start receiving benefits, you would get a bonus of 37.5%. So, if benefits at full retirement age would have been $1,500 a month, you would start your benefits at age 70 at $2,063 a month.

When should you start to take benefits?

Does it pay to wait until your full retirement age or even until age 70 to be eligible for bonus benefits? Unless you can be sure you'll live to Methuselah's age, probably not.

Shrewd move: Start benefits as early as possible and receive benefits for a longer period of time. Consider the following:

> **Example:** Your full retirement age is 65 years, 10 months. By starting benefits at age 62, you'll collect for an additional three years and 10 months. Even though your benefits are permanently reduced, it's estimated that you would have to collect to age 78 to reach the break-even point, where the total benefits collected are the same regardless of when you retired. After that point, you would be ahead by having waited until the full retirement age.

When you look at your future goals, don't forget to consider the "time value" of money, having early use of your money and investing it. For example, if you didn't have to spend your benefits for living expenses and were able to invest them, you would certainly come out ahead by taking benefits early. Depending on your investment return, you would probably always make the right choice for growth and income.

But if you choose to receive benefits before age 65 and continue to earn income through a job or self-employment, your benefits will be reduced by $1 for each $2 of earnings over the annual limit ($12,960 in 2007). So, if you plan to earn more than the limit after age 62, wait until you retire or reach 65, whichever comes first, to start benefits. (In the year you turn age 65, before attaining full retirement age, benefits are reduced by $1 for each $3 over the earnings limit, which is $2,870 per month in 2007.)

No additional bonus accrues after age 70. If you haven't yet started to take your benefits, start doing so at 70. As long as you keep working, benefits can be adjusted if you earn more now than you did in earlier years.

Projecting your benefits

For planning purposes, you should know what you can expect in Social Security benefits. The Social Security Administration helps you by providing a personal earnings and benefits statement annually, about three months before your birthday. The statement shows what you've earned throughout your life as well as what your benefits will be at age 62, at full retirement age and at 70, based on your earnings history and an assumption of your life span. If you fail to receive your statement, ask the SSA for Form SSA-7004, *Request for Social Security Statement*, at 800-772-1213 or go to **www.socialsecurity.gov**.

Check your statement carefully. It's a good indication of what benefits you can expect to receive, and you can integrate this information into your financial plans. Make sure that your recorded earnings and the Social Security and Medicare taxes are correct. Correct errors immediately, as it's difficult to do so three years after errors appear.

You can also make your own projection of benefits using a Social Security Retirement Planner calculator from the SSA Web site at **www.socialsecurity.gov/retire2**. The calculator lets you vary assumptions—your earnings, when you'll commence benefits—so you get a more precise projection.

Applying for benefits

Benefits don't start automatically on a specific birthday. You must apply for benefits within four months of the date you plan to start collecting (for example, if you're 61 years and nine months and want benefits to start at age 62). Apply for benefits at any SSA office; you'll find a local office listed in your area phone book, or call 800-772-1213.

You can also apply for benefits online (**www.socialsecurity.gov** and click on "Apply for Retirement Benefits"). The online application starts the process by supplying your information to the SSA. You will need to go in person to your local SSA office to furnish necessary documents, such as your birth certificate, and to sign your application.

Taxes on benefits

Even though you earned your benefits by paying Social Security taxes, you may have to pay federal income taxes on your benefits when you receive them. Thus, the real value—what you actually have to spend in your retirement years—is reduced accordingly. The tax determination is based on "provisional income"—your other income, plus tax-free interest from municipal bonds and one-half of Social Security benefits. Benefits may be tax free and wholly excluded from income, or they may be included in income at the rate of 50% or 85%.

▶ **Benefits are tax free** if your provisional income is no more than $25,000 if you're single or $32,000 if you're married filing jointly. If you're married and file a separate return (and don't live apart from your spouse for the entire year), 85% of your benefits are automatically included in your income.

▶ **50% of your benefits are included in income** if your provisional income is more than $25,000 but no more than $34,000 if you're single, or more than $32,000 but no more than $44,000 if you're married filing jointly.

▶ **85% of your benefits are included in income** if your provisional income is more than $34,000 if you're single, more than $44,000 if you're married filing jointly or if you have any income if you're married filing separately (and don't live apart from your spouse for the entire year).

> **Example:** Assume you receive $1,200 a month in benefits, you're in the 35% tax bracket (federal and state combined) and 85% of your benefits are included in income. Your gross benefits for the year are $14,400, but you have only $10,116 (after tax) to spend. Your benefits are effectively reduced by 30% (85% includable benefits x 35% tax bracket).

Whether or not your benefits are subject to federal income tax, they may be subject to state income tax. At present, 26 of the 41 states (and the District of Columbia) with an income tax exempt Social Security benefits. They are taxable in the following states—Colorado, Connecticut, Iowa, Kansas, Minnesota, Missouri, Montana, Nebraska, New Mexico, North Dakota, Rhode Island, Utah, Vermont, West Virginia and Wisconsin.

SETTING GOALS

It's unfortunate that most people don't make savings or investment plans or set financial goals. They are reactive, living off what they produce, rather than proactive, designing strategies that lead to increased wealth.

It's shrewd to have financial goals for several reasons:

▶ **The process of setting goals makes you focus on your money,** often serving as a wake-up call to get your financial house in order.

▶ **Creating a game plan makes it easier to move ahead.** When your strategy is established all you have to do is follow it.

Long-term financial goals (to be achieved in two years or more) generally differ according to one's stage of life. For example, goals for many people age 25 to 45 may include buying a home, saving for a child's education or starting a business. Those age 45 and older may be saving for retirement at the usual retirement age of about 65, but might include funding a child's or grandchild's education, starting a business or planning a new career. Those already retired might want to generate more income from their assets and protect these assets in case of catastrophic medical conditions.

Short-term goals (to be achieved within a year or two) may not be as age-dependent. For example, anyone might set a short-term financial goal of buying a big-screen TV or new car, taking a vacation or paying for cosmetic surgery.

Whether you consider a goal as short-term or long-term depends on when you expect to achieve it. For example, a goal of building up a down payment for a home might be short- or long-term, depending on the amount of the down payment and how much you can regularly save.

Make a wish list of your short-term and long-term financial goals. Include everything you *think* you want or need at this time; you can always decide later to forgo some of them.

My financial goals

Short-term goals	Long-term goals
1.	1.
2.	2.
3.	3.
4.	4.
5.	5.

Obviously, the sooner you start working toward your goals, the easier it will be to achieve them. People who wait until their 50s to focus on retirement planning leave themselves only a decade or so to reach their targets. It's shrewd to start retirement planning at the same time you begin your work life, even though retirement may seem far off. Early focus on retirement planning gives you a longer savings period, and requires less effort to reach your target.

Fixing the dollars

One of the most difficult aspects of setting financial goals is estimating the costs. What's the cost of a child's education? How much is needed for a comfortable retirement income? If you're saving for a private college, you may need $120,000 to $200,000 or more. If you're anticipating attendance at a state university, then a goal of $50,000 may be sufficient, depending on your child's age and your state of residence. But you need to project some monetary amount in order to structure a savings/ investment plan to meet your goals.

▶ **Impact of inflation.** Something that costs $1,000 today may cost $1,500 at some future date. *Reason:* Inflation erodes the buying power of the dollar. Even with modest inflation, something we've had for the past several years, a dollar will lose buying power over time. The historic rate of inflation has been about 3% annually. To illustrate how you may need to adjust your goals to take inflation into account, the following chart shows the amount of money needed at different inflation rates to maintain your buying power.

EASY ST

What you'll need to equal the buying power of $50,000

Years from today	3% inflation rate	4% inflation rate
5	$ 56,272	$ 58,493
10	65,239	71,166
15	75,629	86,584
20	87,675	105,342
25	101,640	128,165
30	117,828	155,933

Source: American Society of Chartered Life Underwriters and Chartered Financial Consultants

Setting strategies for achieving goals

Once you fix a goal and put a dollar amount on it, how do you reach it? What do you need to save weekly, monthly, etc.? How quickly do your investments have to grow? Some people save as much as they can each month and see how that accumulates over time. Realistically, this approach may not provide sufficient savings to meet intended goals, and often there's no money left over at the end of the month to save. And even if some funds are earmarked for savings, the amount may fall short of what's needed to meet your goals.

A shrewder strategy is to back into your savings requirements by looking at your financial goals. You can determine how much you'll need to set aside and how much that money must earn in order to achieve your goals within the time limits you've targeted. Strategies for saving money and investing it are discussed throughout the book.

To determine the savings required to meet your goals, try one of many financial calculators available online. You set the parameters; for example, name your goal and what you think you can earn annually on your money (for example, 8%). The program calculates what to set aside each month, and what to invest at your expected return rate to reach your goal.

Online financial calculators for making projections

▶ General savings calculators:
www.choosetosave.org/calculators
www.dinkytown.net
www.betterbudgeting.com/budgetingtools.htm
www.fool.com/calcs/calculators.htm

▶ College savings calculators:
www.usatoday.com/money/perfi/calculators/calculator.htm, then click on "Savings"
www.finaid.org/savings/calculators.phtml
www.troweprice.com, then type in "College Savings Calculator" in the search box

▶ Retirement savings calculators:
www.usatoday.com/money/perfi/calculators/calculator.htm
www.dinkytown.net
www.retirementcalcs.com
www.finance.cch.com/tools/calcs.asp
www.bloomberg.com/analysis/calculators/retire.html
www.smartmoney.com/retirement

2

Working with financial experts

"In the multitude of counselors, there is safety." —PROVERBS

THE TASK OF HANDLING MONEY, making investments, protecting assets from creditor claims and planning for the future can be daunting for many individuals. The sheer range of issues is enormous. What's more, some people simply hate numbers. Others are overwhelmed by the amount of information available or don't have time to process it. Still others don't understand what's necessary for effective money management. There's an army of financial professionals ready to help.

Depending on your level of financial sophistication, wealth and what advice you want, you may need to work with more than one financial professional at a time. If you're looking for a comprehensive financial plan, you may work with a financial planner, stockbroker or accountant. You'll probably work with a planner or stockbroker to implement the investment suggestions and an attorney to follow up on any necessary legal documents. If you're contemplating the purchase of certain investment property, you'll probably work with an accountant and an attorney to put the deal together. Financial professionals can make sure that you don't overlook critical matters, such as changes in the law or new financial products and services that can impact your wealth.

This chapter explains how to work with different advisers to achieve your financial goals. It also tells you how to locate them.

WHAT FINANCIAL PROFESSIONALS CAN AND CANNOT DO FOR YOU

Finances are a complex subject, and it's shrewd to get professional help. A financial professional can provide information to make informed decisions about your money. He or she may raise concerns or questions that you may have overlooked. And the professional can help make projections and suggest strategies. Ultimately, however, you must make your own decisions and are responsible for the consequences.

It makes sense to turn to a financial professional when:

▶ **You need information** about investments, taxes, insurance products, asset protection or other specialized areas.

▶ **You are confused** about the information you already have.

▶ **You need some perspective** on your options. This is especially important following major life cycle events, such as the birth of a child or the death of a spouse, when emotions can easily cloud rational action.

You may have a particular financial issue, like evaluating the pros and cons of a new type of investment or protecting your assets when starting up a business. You may require a broader range of assistance, such as devising and implementing a comprehensive financial plan.

You should only engage someone to whom you feel comfortable divulging personal information. You need to have a high level of trust that the advice you receive is both expert and in your best interest.

But don't expect a financial professional to be responsible for your decision-making. Only you know what you want; these are your financial goals. Only you know what type of risk you can handle. Only you will suffer the financial consequences of bad decisions.

WHO IS A FINANCIAL PROFESSIONAL?

Many people claim to be financial professionals, and some may even have a string of initials following their name to tout their qualifications. You need to understand what those letters mean and find the type of professional who can best address your issues.

No single financial professional can handle all of your money management needs which require different types of expertise. For example, attorneys may draw up trusts or powers of attorney to be used in managing your assets, but they don't provide investment advice. You may turn to an accountant for questions on tax issues but defer to an insurance agent for your life insurance needs. There may be some overlap in the areas of help that professionals can provide. For example, most financial professionals can provide assistance with estate planning considerations.

People without any particular credentials may call themselves financial planners. Certain professionals, such as CPAs and attorneys, hold a state license in order to practice their profession, and stockbrokers must hold securities licenses in each state where they trade for a customer on the national exchanges. Although neither federal nor state law requires "financial planners" to pass any exams or hold any licenses in order to claim expertise in the field, it is possible to find proficient experts with the credentials to prove it. The chart on page 15 shows the different types of financial professional designations and what each one means.

You can't always rely on designations to ensure competence. A particular string of letters after a name isn't a guarantee of expert assistance. At the same time, financial planners who lack any particular designation may still have expertise to offer. It's up to you to assess the competence of the professionals you consult. Here is a listing of many of the designations you may run into.

Designations for financial professionals

Designation	What it means
AAMS	Accredited asset management specialist—designation awarded by the College for Financial Planning upon completing a 4-month program.
CEBS	Certified employee benefits specialist—designation from the International Foundation of Employee Benefit Plans at The Wharton School at the University of Pennsylvania upon completing a $2\frac{1}{2}$- to 3-year program.
CFA	Chartered financial analyst—designation from the Association of Investment Management Research, Charlottesville, VA, following completion of exams taken in three successive years, which are administered only to those meeting certain educational and experience requirements.
CFP	Certified financial planner—designation from the College for Financial Planning, Denver, CO, following completion of an eight-course, off-campus curriculum.
ChFC	Chartered financial consultant—designation from the American College, Bryn Mawr, PA, following completion of an eight-course, off-campus curriculum.
CIC	Chartered investment counselor—designation from the Investment Counsel Association of America, New York, NY, awarded to CFPs who meet certain professional requirements to serve as investment counselors.
CIMA	Certified investment management analyst—designation from the Investment Management Consultants Association, Denver, CO, upon completing a one-week course and meeting certain professional requirements.
CIMC	Certified investment management consultant—designation from the Investment Management Consultants Association to members who have more experience than AIMCs.
CLU	Chartered life underwriter—a designation for life insurance agents noting completion of an eight-course curriculum.
CPA	Certified public accountant—designation awarded after passing an exam administered by the American Society of CPAs and meeting certain minimum work requirements (although the CPA must also hold a state license to practice accounting within a particular state).
Esq.	Attorney—a state licensed lawyer.
LLM	Master of legal letters—a postgraduate degree that attorneys may hold. Most with this designation have that degree in the area of taxation.
MSFS	Master of science in financial services—a graduate degree granted by the American College.
PFS	Personal financial specialist—designation for CPAs who've completed a special program.
RFC	Registered financial consultant—designation given after an 18-month program from the International Association of Registered Financial Consultants.
RFP	Registered financial planner—designation from the Registered Financial Planners Institute given to those who meet certain minimum academic and work experience requirements.

Checklist for selecting your financial professional

Here are some questions to ask:

▶ **What is the professional's education and experience?**

▶ **What do you expect the professional to help you with?**

▶ **What fees or other costs can you expect?**

▶ **What type of client does the professional usually service?** Your money management needs may be too small or too big for this particular professional to handle properly.

▶ **Will the professional be doing the work personally** or will a junior associate be handling things?

▶ **What's the personal investment philosophy of the professional** (conservative, aggressive) and does it jibe with yours?

▶ **Has the professional ever had any regulatory problems?** Are there any now pending?

FINANCIAL PLANNERS

Financial planners come in two varieties: Those who have special designations or degrees attesting to certain competency in the field and those who simply label themselves as planners and may or may not have any expertise in the field.

Finding a financial planner

Obviously, the best way to find a financial planner is by personal recommendation. If you don't have one, you can use the following resources for locating a planner. Check with your local Better Business Bureau or your state attorney general to see whether the planner you've found has had any complaints filed against him or her.

Resources for finding a financial planner

Resource	What you'll find
American Institute of Certified Public Accountants (AICPA), 888-777-7077, **www.aicpa.org**	Member organization with a special section for those who have received the PFS designation.
The Financial Planning Association (FPA), 800-322-4237, **www.fpanet.org**	Member organization providing listing of financial planners with the CFP designation.
The National Association of Personal Financial Advisors (NAPFA), 800-366-2732, **www.napfa.org**	Member organization for fee-only financial planners.

Fees

Financial planners have three types of fee structure:

▶ **Fee-only planners** charge for their time and advice regardless of your subsequent actions. The fee may be an hourly rate or a flat fee for a particular service, like creating a comprehensive financial plan. For ongoing services, you may be charged a fee based on your assets or income.

▶ **Commission-based planners** don't charge for advice but receive commissions on your investments. This arrangement seems simple, but it raises the issue of biased advice.

▶ **Fee-plus-commission planners** require you to pay a fee for the preparation of a comprehensive financial plan plus commissions on any products you buy or sell through them.

STOCKBROKERS

Stockbrokers are investment advisers licensed by the Securities and Exchange Commission (SEC) (a federal agency) and state securities regulators to sell various investment products. Brokers do not display their licenses but must have them in order to sell the products.

Different types of stockbrokers offer differing levels of service. Brokers are paid entirely on commission. You can view your accounts online and, in some cases, execute trades electronically without speaking to a broker. Brokerage firms fall into three general categories:

▶ **Full-service brokers** offer a complete range of investment products, including proprietary products (such as mutual funds created and sold exclusively by the brokerage firm). Full-service brokers may be separate brokerage firms (part of national chains or regional or local boutiques) or banks' brokerage firm subsidiaries. *Examples of full-service brokers:* Banc of America Investment Services; Merrill Lynch; Wachovia Securities.

▶ **Discount brokers** charge lower fees (typically 40% less than full-service brokers). Typically, you get less advice but have access to a broad range of investment products. *Examples of discount brokers:* Fidelity; TD Ameritrade.

▶ **Deep-discount brokers** are essentially order takers who buy and sell at your instructions but offer no personalized investment advice. *Example:* E*Trade.

Directory of brokerage firms

Firm	Telephone	Web site
Banc of America Investment Services	800-822-2222	www.baisidirect.com
Charles Schwab	866-855-9102	www.schwab.com
E*Trade	800-387-2331	www.etrade.com
Fidelity	800-544-6666	www.fidelity.com
Merrill Lynch	800-MERRILL	www.ml.com
Morgan Stanley	800-688-6896	www.morganstanley.com
Muriel Siebert and Co.	800-872-0444	www.msiebert.com
Smith Barney Citigroup	800-221-3636	www.smithbarney.com
TD Ameritrade	800-454-9272	www.tdameritrade.com
UBS	800-221-3260	http://financialservicesinc.ubs.com/Home
Wachovia Securities	866-798-7982	www.wachovia.com (click on "Investing")

Which type of broker is for you?

If you need advice to guide you with investment choices, a full-service firm might be your best bet. Or, you can save money by buying or selling online or through a deep-discount broker, provided you've done your own research.

You can, of course, use different brokers for different purposes—for example, a full-service broker for investment guidance and an online one for your own stock picks. The downside here is the burden of tracking investments in different places, instead of having all investments appear on one statement.

 Strategy: *If you do your own online trading but also use a full-service broker, tell your broker about your other investments. This is the only way a broker can have a full picture of your holdings and give meaningful investment suggestions.*

Resolving problems

If you have a problem with your account and/or your broker, act immediately to correct the situation. For account problems, first speak with your broker. Speak with your broker's supervisor—the branch manager or other supervisor—to resolve problems with your broker or unresolved account problems.

If these steps are not satisfactory, talk to the firm's compliance department. Put your complaint in writing. If you don't get a response within 30 days, contact the Office of Investor Education and Assistance at the U.S. Securities and Exchange Commission **(www.sec.gov)**. You'll want to forward copies of all your correspondence.

Investors can also lodge complaints against brokers with the National Association of Securities Dealers, Inc. (NASD). Arbitration proceedings can—and in most cases must—be used to resolve problems that aren't settled to your satisfaction by the firm.

 Strategy: *Check a particular broker's employment record through the NASD Regulation Public Disclosure Program by accessing **www.nasdr.com/2000.htm** or calling the Public Disclosure Hotline at 800-289-9999.*

INSURANCE PROFESSIONALS

Insurance agents are licensed by the state to sell insurance. Because insurance is part of your financial picture, you need to deal with an insurance professional to make sure you have the protection you want and need.

Types of insurance professionals

There are two types of insurance professionals. An *insurance agent* sells insurance for one insurance company (such as Allstate or State Farm). An *insurance broker* can sell products for more than one company.

Insurance professionals don't charge a fee for their services. Instead, they earn their money by receiving commissions on the insurance products you buy from them.

To find an insurance agent, recommendations from family, friends or neighbors may be helpful. But if you don't have any recommendations, contact the insurance company you're interested in for a referral to an agent in your area. You can also find listings of insurance agents and brokers in your phone directory.

ACCOUNTANTS

Accountants are numbers experts. Some people rely on their accountants for tax return preparation. Others use accountants for a wide range of financial tasks, like tax planning, budgeting and helping to make major financial decisions, such as whether they can afford a bigger house or have enough money to retire.

There are:

▶ **Certified public accountants (CPAs)**—accountants who have passed the licensing requirements of the American Institute of CPAs.

▶ **Public accountants (PAs)**—those holding accounting degrees but who don't have the CPA designation.

▶ **Enrolled agents (EAs)**—those persons licensed by the US government to represent taxpayers.

Finding an accountant

As with any professional, the best way to find one is through personal recommendation. If you already use a business accountant, you may want this person to handle your personal matters as well. But sometimes you may want to use a different accountant for your personal financial advice. Discuss his or her qualifications for this task. For a referral:

▶ **To find a CPA,** contact your state society of CPAs (listed in the phone directory). Also check with the American Institute of CPAs at **www.aicpa.org/consumer+information/Find+a+CPA** for a listing of members in your area. Or search the CPA Directory by city and state at **www.cpadirectory.com**.

▶ **To find a tax professional** (CPA, accountant or enrolled agent), contact the National Society of Accountants (**www.nsacct.org**) or the National Association of Tax Professionals (**www.taxprofessionals.com**).

Fees

Accountants generally charge an hourly rate for their services. This rate varies widely in different parts of the country and for different levels of expertise.

Some accountants may charge a flat fee for a specific service, like the preparation of your tax return.

Make sure you understand the fee structure before you engage the accountant. If he or she neglects to bring up the subject, you must ask about the charges for the services you want.

Personality

You expect competence and good communication from your accountant. But think about your approach to financial matters, especially taxes. Does your tax personality match the accountant's approach?

Accountant-client privilege

Are your disclosures to your accountant confidential? Can your accountant be forced to testify against you in court? Generally, these disclosures aren't privileged. There's only limited protection for exchanges between you and your accountant and most other tax professionals authorized to practice before the IRS.

What's protected: Disclosures you make to your accountant are protected in noncriminal (civil) federal tax matters. *Caution:* Only disclosures made after July 22, 1998, have this protection.

What's not protected: Disclosures you make to your accountant in the course of ordinary tax return preparation aren't protected. Other unprotected areas:

- ▶ **State tax matters** (unless the state creates a special privilege).
- ▶ **Federal criminal tax matters.**
- ▶ **Matters before other federal agencies,** such as the SEC.
- ▶ **Communications** heard or witnessed by third parties.

 Strategy: Engage an attorney to handle any questionable tax matters for you. If your attorney hires an accountant to assist him or her, communications become confidential under the attorney-client privilege.

ATTORNEYS

Attorneys are professionals who handle legal matters. Whatever you disclose to an attorney remains confidential, adding a level of comfort to discussions of financial matters. In your finances, attorneys can play an important role in key areas:

- ▶ **Asset management.** To make sure that assets can be managed and invested when someone becomes incapable or incapacitated, an attorney can draft suitable powers of attorney and trusts.

- ▶ **Asset protection.** Attorneys can advise on the use of trusts and asset transfers to protect assets from the claims of creditors (including spouses in the midst of a divorce). For instance, elder law attorneys can advise on asset transfer strategies that will protect the family while not preventing eligibility for Medicaid.

- ▶ **Tax planning.** Attorneys who specialize in the area of taxation can advise on strategies for tax savings. Such attorneys may hold an advanced degree in taxation (such as an LLM degree in taxation).

- ▶ **Estate planning.** Attorneys can draft wills and trusts to ensure that assets are distributed as desired after a person's death. They can also integrate these documents with tax-saving strategies.

- ▶ **Starting a business.** Attorneys can advise on the best way to set up the business for personal asset protection and to accomplish your business objectives.

- ▶ **Reviewing contracts.** If you undertake any major financial obligation—home renovations, time-share purchases, pre-funded funeral arrangements, etc.—attorneys can review your responsibilities under the terms of the contract.

- ▶ **Handling criminal matters,** including charges of tax fraud.

Finding an attorney

If you don't have a personal referral to an attorney, find one by contacting your state or local bar association. Look in the *Martindale-Hubbell Law Directory* in your local library or online at **www.lawyers.com**. Other online directories of attorneys include:

- ▶ American Bar Association (**www.abanet.org**)

▶ Attorney Find (**www.attorneyfind.com**)

▶ Martindale.com (**www.martindale.com**)

▶ Respond.com (**www.respond.com**)

Interviewing an attorney

Hiring a professional is like any job interview. You need
to find out:

▶ **Experience.** How long has the attorney been in
practice? Where is he or she licensed to practice law? What areas of the law does the attorney have expertise in or concentrate in?

▶ **Who's working on your matter?** Do your issues get delegated to a paralegal? Junior associate?
Or does the attorney handle it himself or herself?

▶ **How will you be billed?**

▶ **Also consider whether you have a rapport with the attorney.** You'll be discussing personal
and often sensitive information, so you need someone you have confidence in and are comfortable with.

Fees

Attorneys generally charge an hourly rate for their services. An initial consultation may be free, but be sure
to determine this before you make an appointment. Attorneys' rates vary widely in different parts of the country (for example, an attorney in one area may charge $150 per hour for the same type of assistance for which
another attorney charges $600 an hour). The fees also vary according to the attorney's degree of expertise
and the complexity of your work. Associate attorneys and paralegals should bill at lower rates.

Some attorneys may charge a flat rate for a particular type of service—for example, $150 for preparing
a will or $3,000 for preparing a living trust. They may charge an hourly rate for reviewing a home improvement
contract. In personal injury cases, or when settling an estate, attorneys will usually charge a fixed percentage
of the estate's assets or of the recovery from a personal injury suit.

Before you engage an attorney to do any work for you, make sure you understand the fee structure—
what it is and when you are required to make payments. For example, you may be required to pay a retainer,
an up-front payment that acts as a deposit. If the attorney uses up the retainer, you'll have to make further
payment, but if the work is finished more quickly than anticipated, you'll get a refund of any part of the
retainer not spent. Also, the attorney's hourly rate generally does not include "extras" such as the cost of
photocopying and faxing.

 Strategy: *Have the attorney put the fee and billing arrangements in writing before
you engage him or her to work for you. This will avoid any confusion later on.*

3

Banking

"*A penny saved is more than a penny gained.*" —SCOTTISH PROVERB

BANKING ACTIVITIES FOR MOST PEOPLE are the nuts and bolts of their financial lives. On a daily, weekly or monthly basis, bank accounts process money that comes in, such as paychecks, stock dividends, Social Security benefits and interest from bonds and savings accounts, and they disburse money to pay bills and satisfy debts. Banks also store valuables in safe-deposit boxes, provide a source of borrowing for buying a home, car or other needs and a means for amassing savings.

Banks and their accounts come in many shapes and sizes. Knowing your options and the best type of account can help you better manage your finances and save money.

This chapter explains your banking options today—from your neighborhood savings and loan association to an online banking Web site. It also alerts you to potential problems you may be unaware of, such as fees that can trip you up, and advises on how to handle banking problems.

CHOOSING A BANK

Today many types of financial institutions are commonly referred to as banks. The distinctions among them have become blurred for consumers, as most provide checking accounts, loans and other identical services. However, each type of bank has unique services to offer as well, and checking accounts can vary greatly from one type of bank to another. The four main categories of banks include:

▶ **Savings and loan associations.** These are consumer-oriented banks, many of which are still regional or local institutions. They specialize in offering home mortgages and other consumer-type services.

▶ **Commercial banks.** These business-oriented banks also provide consumer services. There are large money-center banks, such as Bank of America **(www.bankofamerica.com)**, JPMorgan Chase **(www.jpmorganchase.com)** and Citibank **(www.citibank.com)**, that have a national network. Smaller commercial banks operate regionally, usually specializing in business financing needs.

▶ **Credit unions.** Similar to savings and loan associations, credit unions offer their members check-writing, personal loan and other consumer-type services.

▶ **Online options.** The newest type of banking, these are financial portals for handling checking-type functions. Other types of banks may offer certain online service options, such as checking account balances or paying bills with your home computer. But online banks are exclusively "clicks, no bricks"—you don't deal with a person unless there's a problem you can't resolve online.

Tips on finding the best bank for you

Generally, smaller is better. These banks may offer better customer service for individual depositors than larger institutions do. Also, look for:

▶ **Banking hours.** Some banks have certain evening hours and may be open on Saturdays, a convenience you may want or need.

▶ **Branches.** See if your bank has a branch office near your home or place of work. This will make your funds more accessible.

▶ **Services.** Make sure the bank offers the services you require—for example, ATM access.

▶ **Charges for services.** Before you put your money into a bank, make sure you're fully acquainted with the fees you'll pay for various services.

CREDIT UNIONS—A BANKING ALTERNATIVE

Credit unions are like bank "clubs," since only members are allowed to use their services. Companies and some government agencies may establish credit unions—nonprofit banks—for their employees as well as employees' family members. Unaffiliated individuals can also join a credit union by simply completing a membership application (for example, through the USAlliance Federal Credit Union at **www.usalliance.org**). As of September 2004 there were about 9,500 credit unions nationwide with more than 86 million depositors.

What credit unions can and cannot offer

Credit unions can provide the basic banking services most individuals seek—checking accounts, savings accounts, credit and debit cards, car loans and home mortgages. Because they are consumer-oriented non-profit organizations, they tend to keep their fees low.

Credit unions may not offer you all the services you want from a bank, such as safe-deposit boxes or online account access. More important, they may not necessarily offer the highest rates on savings accounts.

To find a credit union in your area which you may be eligible to join, contact the Credit Union National Association (**www.cuna.org**, 800-356-9655).

CHEAPER CHECKING

For most people, checking accounts act as a clearinghouse for their money. Salary income, dividends and interest, and Social Security benefits are deposited into the account. Then bills are paid by writing checks or authorizing automatic debiting of the account.

Checking accounts vary widely from one banking institution to another. To avoid problems and unnecessary fees, make sure you understand the following:

▶ **Minimum balance requirements.** Some accounts require you to keep a certain amount of money in the account and failure to do so can trigger extra charges. Minimum balances generally are figured on an average daily basis. You need not have that minimum in the account *every* day of the month as long as the average balance is met over that period. For example, if your minimum balance requirement is $1,000 and you dip down to $900 for five days of the month, you'll meet your minimum by simply making sure your account tops $1,100 for at least five days.

▶ **How long it takes for checks to clear.** Generally, banks have uniform clearance standards. Federal and state checks generally clear within a day, as do checks drawn on the same bank branch, certified checks, postal money orders and the first $100 on any check. In-state checks take a little longer—typically two days for local checks and three business days for deposits through ATMs, while out-of-state checks can take up to five business days. Some deposits can take up to 30 days to clear—such as foreign checks, deposits in new accounts and certain large deposits. Understand your bank's clearance policy. If you try to draw on funds before they are available, you will pay added charges.

 Strategy: Don't play the float (the time between when a check is written and when funds are withdrawn from the account to satisfy the check amount) anymore. Under a federal law called "Check 21," banks now process checks electronically, completely eliminating the time it takes to clear from your account. This law does not *speed up the time your deposits will clear.*

▶ **Fees.** The bank may charge fees for a variety of services, including monthly charges, per-check charges, fees for bounced checks (politely referred to as "returned" checks) and ATM access fees. Look for ways to minimize your monthly costs. For example, if your bank charges for withdrawing money from an ATM machine, it will save you money to visit your bank in person and cash a check—a no-fee transaction. It's shrewd to avoid banks that charge for inquiring about account balances or for inactivity.

 Strategy: Avoid interest-bearing checking accounts that require high minimum balances but don't pay high interest rates. Instead, put your additional balance into another interest-bearing account, like a money market fund that earns a greater return.

Banking fees for the average consumer can run several hundred dollars a year. Consider the following ways of reducing your banking fees:

▶ **Linking accounts.** You may qualify for lower fees by linking together multiple accounts in the same bank. If you have a checking and savings account, by linking them you may satisfy minimum balance requirements even if one account drops below a stand-alone minimum.

▶ **Senior discounts.** If you are 50 or older, your bank may offer special senior citizen checking or other discounts. Ask whether you qualify for any special accounts.

▶ **New depositors.** Banks try to lure new money by offering special breaks for new depositors. If you intend to take advantage of this offer by transferring funds, make sure that all outstanding checks have cleared and other obligations have been satisfied (for example, overdraft withdrawals have been repaid) before you make any transfers.

Overdraft privileges

You may be allowed to exceed your account balance to cash a check. Overdraft privileges, offered by about 2,500 institutions, are essentially bank loans up to a fixed dollar limit. You must apply for overdraft privileges as you would for any loan. Then, according to your income, credit history and other factors, a limit will be fixed (such as $1,000, $2,500 or $5,000). There's no charge to you for having overdraft privileges in place. But you're charged interest on any portion which you actually draw upon. What's more, the interest you pay isn't tax deductible if it's incurred to cover your living expenses or other personal non–business-related items.

The advantage of overdraft privileges is to prevent problems in tight cash situations. For example, you need to pay a bill before the date when you expect the check to clear. Using overdraft privileges avoids bouncing a check, which can cost you as much as $25 and worse, cause problems with your creditors. When the check clears, you pay off the portion of the overdraft line to limit your interest charges. Overdraft privileges are crucial in light of "Check 21" banking changes.

The disadvantages of overdraft privileges are the same as with any debt. There's a borrowing cost (typically, the rate on money used through overdraft privileges fluctuates and the bank notifies you of changes in the interest rate). Some consumers have a tendency to abuse the credit opportunity and thereby pile on debt.

TYPES OF BANK ACCOUNTS

Generally, there are two major types of accounts—savings accounts and checking accounts. Interest is paid on the funds in a savings account. You can access the funds without penalty but usually have to present a passbook or make a personal visit to the bank to make a withdrawal.

Checking accounts generally do not pay interest—although there are some interest-bearing checking accounts—but you may draw on the account penalty-free simply by writing a check against the account. NOW (negotiable order of withdrawal) accounts are interest-paying checking accounts. If you opt for a NOW account, make sure you understand the minimum balance requirements and how interest is credited. The best arrangement pays interest on a day-of-deposit to a day-of-withdrawal basis.

There are special types of bank accounts that you may want or need. Be sure to understand your options so you can set up the account that best meets your needs.

If you plan to use the bank account for asset management—in case you can't get to the bank or can't handle your money, you can let someone else run your account via these methods:

▶ **Joint accounts.** You can name someone—your spouse, adult child or a friend—as joint owner of your account, even if you're the only one putting money into the account. Your joint owner has full authority over the funds and can use them for your benefit if you can no longer manage your money. There are no special fees for setting up the account, and you can terminate the joint ownership anytime you want simply by changing the title of the account. The disadvantage of joint accounts is your inability to control the actions of your joint owner. That person, having full and unrestricted access to the account, can use the funds against your wishes.

▶ **Convenience accounts.** Some states allow for joint ownership purely for asset management purposes. A joint account is set up and labeled as a convenience account, allowing the joint owner to manage the money in the account. By law, the agent does not become the owner of the account automatically upon your death, but you can bequeath what remains in the account to the joint owner.

▶ **Power of attorney (POA).** You can set up the account in your name alone but give someone else the authority to act as your agent (also called an attorney-in-fact). Sign the bank's power of attorney form to designate the person you want in this role. (If you already have an account, you can sign the designation form at any time and don't need to set up a new account.) The agent has no ownership interest in the account. But, as in the case of a joint account, there is no means of preventing the agent from mishandling the money.

Strategy: Sign the bank's POA form even if you have a separate comprehensive power of attorney. Although banks generally are required to accept a personal POA, they are reluctant to do so. If you've already signed the bank's POA form, you'll save your agent the trouble of persuading a bank to accept your own POA.

If you want to use the bank account as a will substitute so that funds remaining in your account pass automatically at your death to an heir, set up the account with a specific title. Here are your choices:

▶ **Joint accounts.** Joint accounts serve an asset management function by allowing a joint owner to write checks for your benefit while you're alive, and they allow funds to pass automatically at death to the surviving joint owner.

▶ **Totten trusts.** More than a century ago, New York created this special type of bank account to allow people of modest means to create a legacy without any legal complication or expense. Essentially, funds remaining in the account at the depositor's death pass automatically to a named beneficiary.

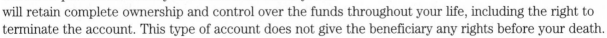

▶ **In trust for...accounts.** These are accounts set up in your name alone, with the notation that upon your death the funds pass automatically to a named beneficiary. You will retain complete ownership and control over the funds throughout your life, including the right to terminate the account. This type of account does not give the beneficiary any rights before your death.

ATMS—USES AND ABUSES

In today's electronic age, what could be better than a machine that dispenses cash? Americans love ATMs—using them more than seven billion times a year!

ATMs (automatic teller machines) let you access funds in your checking and/or savings account virtually any time of the day or night, seven days a week. For convenience, it can't be beat. You can often use your ATM overseas, avoiding the need for costly travelers' checks.

But for financial management purposes, exercise caution. The main drawback to using ATMs for cash withdrawals is cost. Nearly 80% of banks charge for making withdrawals and about 40% charge for making deposits through ATMs. What's more, you may be charged extra for using a machine not owned by your bank—as much as $2 or more per transaction. And fees for using ATMs are on the rise.

To minimize or avoid fees, consider these simple strategies:

▶ **Find accounts that provide for no-cost ATM access** or for a set number of free accesses per month (such as four no-charge withdrawals).

▶ **Use ATMs only at your bank** (or branches of your bank) to avoid higher charges for using the ATMs of other banks.

▶ **Make larger withdrawals** to cut down on access frequency (and fee charges).

▶ **Cash checks at teller windows** to avoid fees altogether.

 Strategy: Select a personal identification number (PIN) for accessing your ATM that can't easily be guessed. Don't use your birthday, Social Security number, street address or other number clearly associated with you. Then keep your PIN number well guarded. Don't carry it in your wallet with your ATM card!

ONLINE BANKING

Online banking offers new convenience, higher interest rates on savings certificates and lower fees for most transactions. According to the Online Banking Report by eMarketer in May 2006, 58% of U.S. households now utilize Web banking and the figure could rise to 62% by 2010. However, before you transfer funds from your neighborhood bank to an online bank, consider both the benefits and the drawbacks:

Advantages...

▶ **Convenience.** You have access to account information 24 hours a day, seven days a week. You can see whether checks have cleared and whether ATM withdrawals have been posted correctly, and transfer funds from one account to another. You can set up online payments for recurring bills, such as a mortgage or car loan, and schedule automatic transfers of funds to cover these recurring bills.

▶ **Cost savings.** You save on postage and on the time required to write checks and keep your records. If you regularly mail 10 payments a month, you would save more than $50 in postage annually. And there's little or no cost for using online banking, as the software usually is provided free of charge. However, there may be charges for certain online services, such as bill paying.

▶ **Financial management.** Online banking can be integrated with your other financial activities. You can have your online banking information automatically included in your personal finance software data.

Disadvantages...

▶ **Service.** If you have a problem, it's often difficult to find a live person to talk to.

▶ **Insurance.** Not all online banks have FDIC insurance for deposits. Don't put money into an online bank without checking its FDIC coverage.

▶ **Security.** Although online bank sites are secured sites designed to protect your privacy, there is always a risk that hackers can access your personal information. Banks use a variety of methods to ensure your privacy, such as firewalls to prevent information from moving from the bank past a gatekeeper and data encryption to scramble personal information so that it's difficult to read. Passwords or personal identification numbers (PINs) prevent access to account information without your personal code.

To search for an online bank, go to:

▶ Bankrate.com **(www.bankrate.com)**

Online banking options from neighborhood banks

You don't have to use an e-bank to obtain the convenience of online banking. Most banks—Bank of America, JPMorgan Chase, Citibank, etc.—now allow customers to access their accounts online. These online services allow you to:

▶ **Check your balance and recent account transactions.**

▶ **Pay bills.**

▶ **Transfer funds between your accounts.**

BANK INVESTMENT PRODUCTS

Today, despite our growing sophistication with investments, there are still more than $1 trillion held in low-interest passbook savings accounts. According to one study, 58% of passbook and money market account holders didn't know their interest rate and 30% didn't believe there was a difference between the rate paid on a passbook account and a CD.

Although funds in passbook accounts are completely safe (to the extent of FDIC protection explained in Chapter 23), it's wrong to believe you can't lose money in these accounts. When the rate of inflation and taxes on interest are factored in, you lose money every day you continue to keep funds in these so-called investment vehicles. While it may make sense to keep a small "emergency" fund—one to six months of income needed to meet your basic living expenses—safely in a passbook account, don't expect to build your financial future on this savings product. Look beyond passbook accounts.

The line between banking and investments has blurred, and it's now possible to obtain investment products through your bank. Banks continue to offer traditional bank investment products, like CDs and money market funds, in addition to passbook savings accounts.

In addition, banks sell stocks, bonds, Treasury bills, mutual funds, annuities and other investment products. But these investment products aren't FDIC-protected. They enjoy the same protection afforded products purchased through brokerage firms—SIPC insurance (financial protections are discussed in Chapter 23). Investments in Treasuries don't need separate protection; the interest and principal is guaranteed by the full faith and credit of the federal government.

Strategy: Consider linking your bank account to your bank's brokerage account. This will make it easy to pay for investment products and to credit your bank account with sales proceeds, dividends, interest from bonds and other investment money.

Certificates of deposit (CDs)

Certificates of deposit are time-sensitive savings instruments that commit a certain amount of funds for a set length of time—for example, $5,000 for two years—earning a fixed rate of interest. The longer the term of the CD, the greater the interest rate you'll receive. However, the spread between interest on a 12-month CD and a 60-month CD may be only ½ of 1%.

The interest rate may depend on the amount of money you put into the CD. You may get a higher rate for investing $25,000 than you would for a $5,000 CD.

If you cash in your CD prior to the maturity date, you'll pay a penalty, forfeiture of a certain amount of interest, depending on how early you cash in the CD. For example, you may forfeit three months' interest on a 12-month CD and as much as 18 months' interest on a 60-month CD. *Note:* Forfeiture of interest may be waived on a CD held in an IRA or other retirement plan account if you withdraw funds to satisfy minimum distribution requirements (see Chapter 9).

Strategy: Split your funds among multiple CDs. You may be able to earn the same interest rate on the varying maturities, but staggering maturity dates assures you of ongoing liquidity. You'll have access to funds on a regular basis (as each CD matures) without the need to take an early withdrawal and forfeit interest.

To locate high-yield CDs that are FDIC-insured, check online at:

▶ Federally Insured Savings Network (**www.fisn.com**)

Bank CDs vs. brokered CDs (CDs sold by brokerage firms): Brokerage firms offer brokered CDs that may earn higher interest than your local bank's rate. If funds are needed prior to the CD's maturity, they can be sold at a market rate.

*Strategy: Beware of the many current CD scams—long-term CDs (10 to 20 years) being sold primarily to the elderly. **Problem:** Withdrawal before maturity can result in the loss of up to 30% of principal. If you want information about a questionable brokered CD or think that you have already been scammed, contact the SEC (**www.sec.gov**).*

Large CDs: If you plan to put more than $100,000 into CDs, you obviously risk losing FDIC protection (which runs only to $100,000 for each bank in which you have funds as explained in Chapter 23). But you can with Certificate of Deposit Account Registry Service (CDARS), you can obtain up to $5 million in deposit insurance coverage. Over 600 participating banks effectively spread your funds to maximize your coverage (**see www.cdars.com**).

Money market funds

Banks may offer money market funds similar to those sold by mutual fund companies. Deposits pay a fluctuating rate of interest. Compare the bank's interest rate on money market funds with interest offered by mutual fund money market accounts.

Funds in bank money market funds may be accessible through check-writing. In contrast to CDs, they are completely liquid because you can make withdrawals at any time penalty free. Generally, there are minimum deposit requirements—such as $2,500—to open up a money market fund.

For transferring funds to higher-yielding investment products, see Chapters 5 through 7.

USING SAFE-DEPOSIT BOXES

Banks may have safe-deposit vaults in which they rent boxes to depositors. Annual rental fees depend on the size of the box.

Advantages: A safe-deposit box gives you a secure place to store your valuables, such as stock certificates, savings bonds, jewelry and other precious items. You can store important documents—birth certificates, death certificates, divorce decrees, titles to cars, real estate deeds. Don't store a will in a safe-deposit box; the box can be sealed upon the owner's death. Instead, keep the will in a home safe or with the attorney who drafted it.

You can deduct the cost of safe-deposit box rental as a miscellaneous itemized deduction if you use the box to store stock certificates and other investments. *Caution:* Claiming a deduction for a safe-deposit box alerts the IRS to its existence. When an owner dies, the IRS will want to see these investments listed on the stock owner's estate tax return.

Disadvantages: Contents are not FDIC-insured. Thefts from safe-deposit boxes do occur on rare occasions. In some cases, you may be able to obtain bank protection for some of your valuables by requesting a "safekeeping receipt" in your box (it won't cover stocks and bonds). A bank officer will itemize the contents —at the cost of your privacy—and provide you with a receipt. Should loss occur, the bank would have to make good on the value of the contents.

 Strategy: Always insure the contents of your box. Ask whether your homeowner's insurance will cover items in the box. You may be able to put an off-premises rider on your existing policy, or you may need a separate policy.

Other disadvantages include:

▶ **Access** is only during banking hours, so you can't get your jewelry on a Saturday night.

 Strategy: Use a private safe-deposit box instead of one at your local bank. These private companies generally offer greater access and even better security protection for contents. And some private boxes come with automatic contents coverage— up to $10,000—and the opportunity for additional coverage at a modest cost.

▶ **In some states, such as New York,** safe-deposit boxes are sealed upon the owner's death. A court order is needed to open the box in this case, severely limiting access.

Strategy: *Check whether your state seals a safe-deposit box on an owner's death. If not, then obtain a box with someone else—a spouse, an adult child or another trusted person. If your state law seals the box on the owner's death, then hold your safe-deposit box in the name of a corporation or limited liability company. Even if an owner dies, the box will not be sealed.*

HANDLING BANKING PROBLEMS

If you have a problem at your bank—for example, an error in your monthly statement or a check that is miscredited—try to resolve it at your branch level. Speak with the manager for fast action. For example, if the bank bounces one of your checks in error, the bank should not only make good on your funds but also write to your creditor apologizing for its error and any problems it may have caused you. The bank should also inform credit-reporting bureaus of its mistake.

Don't ignore unexplained charges or adjustments. Question any items you don't understand; they simply may be wrong. Demand that disputed debits be credited to your account and other items be corrected.

If attempts at the branch fail, go up the ladder to the bank's headquarters. And if further efforts on your part don't work, contact your state's banking commissioner.

 Strategy: *Switch banks after you've resolved your problem. This will avoid further difficulties with the same institution.*

Bank failures

In the 1980s, many banks that had made imprudent loans were in danger of folding. Banks failed, were taken over by larger ones or helped along by the federal government. Through this banking trauma, depositors with FDIC insurance coverage slept more soundly than others. The FDIC is a federal agency that provides insurance protection for accounts in participating banks and credit unions nationwide. There are, however, limits on coverage, and not every banking institution carries this protection. For more information about FDIC insurance, see Chapter 23, "Financial Protection."

 Strategy: *Look for the FDIC logo displayed at your bank, or ask whether the bank is an FDIC member bank. Don't assume that every bank has FDIC coverage.*

Some states also offer protection against failing state banks. However, the coverage may be well below the federal protection. And, in contrast to federal payments that are made immediately, it may take considerable time to collect from state funds.

4

Insurance

❝ *...whatever happens, I've kept my insurance up.* **❞**

—EDGAR LEE MASTERS

THE BEST-LAID FINANCIAL PLANS can easily be undermined by sudden disaster—an accident, death, illness, natural catastrophe, acts of terrorism, or even a lawsuit. I have seen people lose hard-earned money and long-held investments in a single moment.

Fortunately, you can obtain financial protection and peace of mind by carrying the right kinds of insurance. True, insurance is often costly, and you may be one of the lucky people who never have a claim. But consider what assets you would lose if you don't carry the insurance and, tragically, disaster of any kind does happen. You may not need every type of insurance discussed in this chapter. But I suggest that you review it all to see where your needs lie and learn about cost-effective ways of obtaining the appropriate protection.

This chapter discusses the types of disasters or other occurrences which you may need to protect against and what type of insurance to buy. You'll find out how to shop for insurance and traps to avoid in insurance protection.

WHAT IS INSURANCE?

Insurance—for your health, your home, your car or other needs—is a form of financial protection that shifts the risk of loss to a larger pool that is able to bear the risk of loss, something you can't do on your own.

The insurance industry is a state-regulated one. Companies must meet state-set requirements to sell insurance within that state. Some states set stricter standards than others. Generally, however, most state standards are sufficient to protect consumers for any liabilities under their policies.

Check an insurance company's financial soundness and other factors as they are rated by certain independent companies. These companies provide rating reports, which reflect their opinion about the financial strength or weakness of an insurance company. These ratings services include:

▶ **A.M. Best Company** (**www.ambest.com**, 908-439-2200)

▶ **Duff & Phelps** (**www.duffllc.com**, 212-450-2800)

▶ **Moody's** (**www.moodys.com**, 212-553-1653)

▶ **Standard and Poor's** (**www.standardandpoors.com**, 800-400-4303 or 212-438-7280)

▶ **The Street.com Ratings** (**www.weissratings.com**, 800-289-9222)

 Strategy: If you have any questions about a particular carrier, contact your state insurance department.

When buying any insurance, shop around. Premiums can vary greatly from company to company. Just make sure you're comparing similar coverage and that the coverage offered for a stated premium by one company is the same as that offered by another carrier.

 Strategy: Don't buy coverage you don't need or don't want. To make sure you're buying only the coverage you need, check the itemized coverage included in each policy you review.

There are different ways to shop for coverage:

▶ **You can work with an insurance agent or broker**—an insurance professional—who may be able to provide guidance or raise issues you might otherwise overlook. Insurance professionals are explained in Chapter 2.

▶ **You may also be able to purchase insurance directly from an insurance company** (for example, GEICO sells car insurance directly to the public) or through an insurance broker (for example, Quotesmith). You can find insurance companies, brokers and agents in your area through Life and Health Underwriters, Inc. (**www.lhui.com**).

 Strategy: Whichever method you use to buy insurance, you may wish to do online comparison shopping to see what rates are offered.

Here are some places to look:

▶ E-insure (**www.einsure.com**, 312-372-7400)

▶ Insweb (**www.insweb.com**, 916-853-3300)

▶ Quick Quote (**www.quickquote.com**, 800-867-2404)

▶ Quicken.com Insurance (**www.quicken.com/insurance**, 800-811-8766)

Strategy: *Always pay premiums on time to prevent any lapse in coverage. Some insurance, such as life insurance, may have a 30-day grace period for premiums. Other types of coverage do not have similar grace periods. You could lose your coverage by not paying on time.*

To learn about insurance in general and to keep up on insurance developments, check out:

▶ Insurance Information Institute (**www.iii.org**, 212-346-5500)

▶ Insure.com (**www.insure.com**, 800-556-9393)

▶ Insurance.com (**www.insurance.com**, 866-533-0227)

LIFE INSURANCE

The primary purpose of life insurance is to provide a death benefit to the policy's beneficiary. The proceeds can be used to replace income lost due to the insured's death, as well as to pay death-related costs, such as funeral expenses, probate costs and death taxes. In the case of a business owner, the proceeds may be needed to fund business-buyout obligations on an owner's death.

Life insurance can also serve certain ancillary purposes:

▶ **Source of a loan.** The owner of the policy can borrow against its cash surrender value, usually at attractive interest rates.

▶ **Source of funds to cover long-term-care expenses.** Some policies allow the death benefit to be accelerated and claimed if the insured becomes terminally or chronically ill. The proceeds can be used to cover the cost of long-term care or for any other purpose.

Taking your life insurance inventory

You may have coverage that you've overlooked. In addition to policies you've purchased, coverage may be provided to you—for example, by your employer. Check the following sources:

▶ **Employer-paid coverage** (group-term or split-dollar).

▶ **Coverage through a credit card** used to purchase air travel when death results from a plane crash.

▶ **Benevolent associations.**

▶ **Trade and professional associations.**

Use the following chart to list your coverage:

My life insurance coverage

Face value	Ins. co./policy no.	Policy owner	Beneficiary	Other info
$				
$				
$				
$				
$				
$				
$				

How much life insurance to carry

How much insurance do you have? How much insurance do you need? There's no simple answer. It depends on your reason for having the insurance.

▶ **To provide income for your family** (income replacement). If you are the primary wage earner, you need coverage sufficient to generate the income that would be lost on your death. If you are a home-maker, you need to have sufficient coverage to generate the income required to pay for the services you currently perform (housekeeping, child care, etc.).

Rule of thumb: Buy a policy worth five to eight times your annual income. For example, if you earn $75,000, you'll want insurance to be between $375,000 and $600,000 to ensure that income will continue for your family. In determining your exact income replacement needs, you'll fine-tune the five to eight times factor by other considerations— the length of time the money will be needed (for example, you need substantial sums if you have young children but only modest amounts if you're elderly), the rate of return you can earn on the insurance proceeds and the percentage of income you want to replace (generally 60% to 75% of your income).

▶ **To provide liquidity for your estate.** According to the Federated Funeral Directors of America, the average cost of a funeral today is over $6,500 in 2004, not counting cemetery property. To settle an estate, administrative costs—attorney's fees, court costs, etc.—generally run around 5% of the value of the estate; thus, if you leave an estate of $2 million, expect your administrative costs to run around $100,000. Finally, there's Uncle Sam's cut of your estate—which can amount to 45% of your estate's value in 2007. If you want to replace what's lost through taxes, one way is to buy insurance to fill the void.

 Strategy: If you use life insurance to pay for death-related expenses, have an irrevo-cable life insurance trust own the policy to keep the proceeds out of your estate. Otherwise, life insurance proceeds will be reduced by death taxes—up to 45% in 2007. See Chapter 20 for irrevocable life insurance trusts.

▶ **To follow through on a buyout of business interest agreement.** If you co-own a business, you may be obligated to buy out the interests of your co-owners when they die. This will prevent the business from falling into the hands of outsiders and provide funds for the deceased owner's family. Your co-owners, in turn, will carry insurance to fund their obligation to buy out your interest in the event of your death.

Use the worksheet on the following page to estimate your income replacement and other needs:

Estimating the insurance coverage for income replacement and your other needs

Total up your needs	
Income replacement	$
Death-related expenses (funeral, estate taxes, administrative costs)	$
College fund for children	$
Other needs	$
Subtract what you already have	
Assets	$
Existing insurance	$
Total insurance coverage needed	$

Example: Assume you're a 55-year-old widow, with grown children and an estate of about $2 million. Assume that you have no income replacement needs and don't need any college fund for your children. If you want to leave your children $2 million, you'll need to make up for what's lost in funeral costs (about $5,000), estate administration costs (about $100,000) and death taxes (about $400,000). If you have no other insurance and want to fully preserve your assets, you'll need insurance coverage of $505,000.

Types of life insurance

There are two main categories of life insurance—nonpermanent and permanent coverage. Nonpermanent insurance is term insurance, which provides a fixed benefit payable on the death of the insured (though, for a slightly higher annual premium, there is a guaranteed money-back payment at the end of the term). Generally, premiums for term insurance escalate with age. Premiums soar as the insured passes middle age. But premiums may be fixed ("level") for a set period. For example, a level-premium five-year or 10-year renewable term policy would fix the premium payments for that five- or 10-year period.

Types of permanent insurance, which include death benefits and an investment element, are:

▶ **Whole life.** This type of policy has a premium that's fixed for the life of the insured. Thus, the younger the insured when the policy commences, the lower the premiums for the rest of his or her life. The policy builds up a cash value that can be used as a source of borrowing, provide a greater death benefit, or pay premiums or be recouped if the policy is surrendered. This cash value is based on a guaranteed minimum rate of return (which is usually a very modest 3% to 4%), plus additional returns if the company's investments are more profitable.

▶ **Universal life.** Like whole life, this policy is intended to build up a cash value. However, the owner may vary the premium payments after the first year—paying less (as long as the policy's value is sufficient to cover the cost of the term coverage) or more to be used as a form of investment.

▶ **Variable life.** A form of universal life, this type of policy lets the owner determine how the premium will be invested (for example, pick from a menu of mutual fund options).

▶ **Second-to-die insurance** insures the lives of a husband and wife but pays benefits only on the death of the second spouse to die. It is intended to cover taxes due on the death of the surviving spouse. The policy can be structured as a whole life, universal life or even a variable life policy.

Which type of life insurance should you carry to meet your income replacement, estate liquidity or business buyout needs? There's no single answer:

▶ **If you know you're going to need insurance for a limited time only** (for example, to cover your family income needs until your children complete college), you may want only term insurance. It's the least costly policy for the most coverage. And if you buy a five-year or 10-year renewable term policy, you lock in the premiums for a set period and are guaranteed coverage for the renewal periods even if your health changes.

▶ **If you want coverage to provide liquidity for your estate,** consider a form of permanent insurance. You'll hope to carry the policy for many years. Term coverage becomes too costly as you move beyond middle age. Couples may opt for a second-to-die policy—a less costly form of permanent insurance that will cover estate tax and other costs when the second spouse dies.

▶ **If you are required to buy out the business interest of a partner,** you'll probably want to carry a form of permanent insurance, because the date when you'll need the coverage is not known.

Shrewder shopping for life insurance

Once you know what amount of coverage you need and are familiar with the types of policies available, you can become a savvy consumer. Here are some key dos and don'ts in shopping for a policy:

Strategy: Do buy only the coverage you need. Don't let an agent or broker convince you to purchase coverage that doesn't meet your needs. The agent may be more interested in his or her commission than in your needs. Commissions on permanent insurance can equal 10 times those on term coverage.

Strategy: Don't rely on policy examples based on unreasonable assumptions. If you're buying permanent insurance, the company may project how the policy will perform, based on interest rate assumptions. Because the policy will probably be in force for many years, through good and bad economic times, don't believe exaggerated figures. Over a 30- or 40-year period, an 8% or 10% return may be unrealistic and inflate your expectations. Ask for illustrations at varying interest rates—4%, 6% and 8%.

Strategy: Don't be induced by a high guaranteed first-year rate. Again, think long term and look carefully at the long-term guaranteed rate.

Strategy: Don't pay for riders that you don't need. For example, you'll pay a higher premium for a policy with a disability rider. But if you have disability insurance (which provides income in case of disability and can be used to pay your life insurance premiums), you don't need this rider.

Strategy: Do agree to make annual premium payments. Fees for monthly, quarterly or semiannual premium payments can be avoided with annual payments.

You can buy directly from certain companies. They allow you to comparison shop for insurance and offer low-load policies (because there are no commissions involved).

▶ Ameritas Life Insurance Corp. (**www.ameritas.com**, 800-745-1112)

▶ Insure.com (**www.insure.com**, 800-556-9393)

▶ Term4Sale® from Compulife® Software, Inc. (**www.term4sale.com**, 800-798-3488)

▶ USAA (**www.usaa.com**, 800-531-8111)

You may be eligible for low-cost group coverage through a trade association or other group. For example, those age 50 and older who belong to the American Association of Retired Persons (AARP) can buy member coverage.

You can buy through an insurance agent or broker (see Chapter 2 for an explanation of the difference). However, because health is a big factor in fixing premiums, consider working with an insurance broker who can shop around for the lowest premium based on your health history. Major insurance companies offer life insurance policies. There are many choices:

▶ Guardian Life Insurance (**www.guardianlife.com**, 866-425-4542)

▶ John Hancock (**www.johnhancock.com**, 800-732-5543)

▶ MassMutual Financial Group (**www.massmutual.com**, 800-272-2216)

▶ MetLife (**www.metlife.com**, 800-638-5433)

▶ New York Life Insurance (**www.newyorklife.com**, 800-710-7945)

▶ Northwestern Mutual Financial Network (**www.nmfn.com**, 800-388-8123)

▶ State Farm Life Insurance (**www.statefarm.com**, 877-734-2265)

▶ The Hartford (**www.thehartford.com**, 800-833-5575)

▶ UNIFI Companies (**www.unificompanies.com**, 800-745-1112)

▶ UnumProvident Corporation (**www.unumprovident.com**, 877-322-7222)

 Strategy: Don't buy policies you don't need. Although you may need to carry a certain amount of life insurance, don't carry policies that provide coverage only under special circumstances and may cost more for the same coverage than standard policies.

▶ **Accident life insurance.** This coverage pays benefits only if death is accidental; there are no benefits payable if death is the result of an illness or other medical condition. Why bet that death will happen in this way? If life insurance coverage is needed, explore the standard options above.

▶ **Air-travel life insurance.** This coverage is not really cost-effective. It's usually sold in air terminals and through credit cards used to buy airline tickets to cover a crash-related death. The odds of dying in an airplane crash are small compared with the cost of the coverage. But if the credit card company gives you a minimum amount of this coverage without additional charge (called automatic flight insurance—for example, $50,000 for American Express Gold Card Members), you don't have to turn it down.

▶ **Credit insurance.** This coverage pays your credit card debt or other loans when you die. Typically, the amount of the coverage decreases annually as the loans are repaid. But the cost of this coverage is high compared with the amount of term insurance that can be purchased for the same premiums.

▶ **Mortgage insurance.** This is a type of credit insurance that covers the loan balance in case of the homeowner's death; it decreases annually as the loan balance is reduced. Again, standard, nondecreasing coverage may be preferable and less costly.

Better borrowing against your policy

If the insurance policy has built up sufficient cash value, the owner can borrow against this amount, usually at attractive interest rates.

Advantages: An easy and quick source of borrowing. Typically you can have your check in a day or two. The interest rate may be lower than on bank or credit card loans. Further, you have complete flexibility in repayment. You can repay as much or as little as you want, any time you want. You can pay interest only, or interest plus principal. If there is sufficient cash value in the policy, you don't even have to make interest payments to keep the policy in force.

Disadvantages: Any loan amount outstanding on the death of the insured reduces the proceeds payable to the beneficiary. This can undermine the very reason you bought the policy.

Switching policies the right way

You may own a policy that does not give you the return you expect. Or you can obtain a return at more favorable rates through another policy. You can exchange these policies on a tax-free basis (called a 1035 exchange after the section in the Internal Revenue Code that created it). To make the exchange, simply complete the paperwork provided by the insurer so that the funds are transferred directly between companies (no check is disbursed to you). Make sure you understand the ramifications of such an exchange to avoid any problems; the company may be required by state law to list them for you.

What you can exchange tax free

Old insurance	New insurance
Life insurance	Life insurance; endowment policy annuity
Endowment policy	Endowment policy (provided that regular payments begin no later than they would have under the old policy); annuity
Annuity	Annuity

What you can't exchange tax free

Old insurance	New insurance
Life insurance	Life insurance with a different insured
Endowment policy	Life insurance; endowment policy with a different beginning payment date
Annuity	Life insurance; endowment policy

Strategy: *If the policy has been in effect for a long time, it may not make sense to exchange it.* Reason: *Permanent insurance generally is front-loaded; that is, the commissions and fees have already been paid. A new policy would start the obligation all over again.* Alternative: *Keep the old coverage and purchase additional new coverage if desired.*

Policy loans

An outstanding loan on a policy doesn't prevent you from making a tax-free exchange. However, added care is required. You must be sure that the loan balance carries over to the new policy.

Strategy: *Don't surrender the policy and use the cash surrender value to buy new coverage. This is purely for the agent's convenience to avoid paperwork necessary to make tax-free exchanges of insurance products.* Exception: *When the insurance company is insolvent or in conservatorship, rehabilitation or a similar state proceeding, you may make a tax-free exchange that includes a surrender if you use the proceeds to buy a new policy within 60 days of the disbursement.*

What to do with unneeded policies

If you own a life insurance policy that's no longer needed for the purpose for which it was purchased (for example, you bought it to provide income protection for your family, but now you're widowed and your children are grown), you may want to stop paying premiums. You have several choices on how to benefit from the policy:

Strategy: *Cash it in. Permanent insurance, such as whole life and universal life, may have a cash surrender value that's payable to you.*

Strategy: *Donate it. Give the policy to your alma mater or other charity. Claim a current income tax deduction for your donation. You may also take deductions for cash contributions to enable the charity to pay the premiums.*

Strategy: *Let the policy pay for itself to provide an additional inheritance for children or others. Instead of paying premiums, use the cash built up on the policy for this purpose. Convert the policy to a paid-up policy (perhaps reducing the death benefit to ensure that the cash value will carry the policy for your life expectancy).*

Strategy: *Sell the policy. Viatical settlement providers—companies that buy life insurance policies or broker them to third parties—pay a portion of the policy's death benefit in exchange for the policy. The shorter the life expectancy of the insured, the greater the payment (for example, an insured who is expected to die within a year may receive 60% of the death benefit as payment for selling the policy). The buyer collects the proceeds when the insured dies. Contact the Life Insurance Settlement Association (**www.lisassociation.org**, 407-894-3797).*

INSURING YOUR HOME

Whether you own or rent your home, you should carry homeowner's insurance or renter's insurance. Make sure the amount of coverage is sufficient to protect you against two types of loss:

▶ **Personal property protection**—reimbursement if your property is damaged or destroyed as a result of a fire, storm or other casualty.

▶ **Liability protection**—coverage for personal injury claims made by visitors.

Make sure your coverage is sufficient

If your homeowner's insurance fails to insure at least 80% of the value of your home, you effectively become a co-insurer in case of loss. For example, if your home's value is $251,000 and you insure it for only $200,000 (which is less than 80% of its value) and suffer a loss, the insurance company need only cover its percentage of the loss. So if you have $10,000 in damages, your policy will pay only $8,000 (you're the coinsurer for 20% of the loss in this case).

Also make sure your liability protection is high enough. Standard coverage, typically $100,000, may not be sufficient for most people. Increase coverage under your homeowner's policy to $300,000 or even $500,000. Supplement your homeowner's coverage with an umbrella policy (discussed later in this chapter).

 Strategy: Cut the cost of coverage by increasing your deductible. For example, your policy may have a $500 deductible per occurrence. If you increase the deductible to $1,000, you may cut your premiums by as much as 15% annually.

Check exclusions in the policy—events not covered—to address specific concerns. For example, ask your agent whether an exclusion for "acts of war" would include terrorist attacks. Also understand special deductibles that may apply to your policy. For example, despite a general $1,000 deductible, your policy may have a separate one for severe hurricanes of 3% of the value of the dwelling unit. Thus, if your home's value is $400,000 and the roof blows off, you bear the first $12,000 of cost (3% of $400,000).

Ordinary coverage versus replacement value

Ordinary coverage provides a fixed dollar amount of property protection. Replacement value coverage obligates the insurer to compensate for the amount necessary to bring the property to its pre-casualty condition. Replacement value coverage is more expensive because it affords greater protection. However, not all insurers offer this option. If you have ordinary coverage, review your limits annually to make sure you are fully insured. Ordinary coverage may cover your loss plus up to 25% (you're still considered to be fully insured and don't risk coinsurance exposure). So, for example, if your home is insured for $300,000, you can receive reimbursement of up to $375,000 ($300,000 plus 25%). Alternately, you can put an inflation guard on your policy to adjust it automatically as inflation increases. Just make sure the inflation index relates to housing prices and is not the general CPI (since housing prices have escalated considerably more than the general cost of living).

Upgrades

You may need to adjust your homeowner's coverage or buy a supplementary policy in certain situations to avoid risk of loss. Review your current policy's limits and exclusions for the following items or events. If they are not covered, you may be able to obtain coverage with a rider to your current policy or with a separate policy.

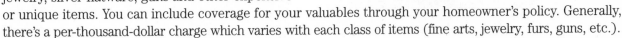

▶ **Expensive items.** Homeowner's policies generally have modest limits on coverage for jewelry, silver flatware, guns and other expensive or unique items. You can include coverage for your valuables through your homeowner's policy. Generally, there's a per-thousand-dollar charge which varies with each class of items (fine arts, jewelry, furs, guns, etc.).

▶ **Special architectural details.** Generally, insurance coverage is figured on the cost of building a plain-vanilla home on a square footage basis. If your home has special features—built-in cabinets, stained glass windows, parquet floors—you may need additional coverage. This is also true if you have special shrubbery or landscaping features.

▶ **Flood zone.** If you're located in a flood zone, your homeowner's policy won't cover damage resulting from a flood. You'll need separate flood insurance available through a federal insurance program (contact the National Flood Insurance Program at **www.fema.gov/business/nfip**, 800-638-6620). Your policy may exclude coverage for earthquake damage, but your insurer may be required by state law to offer such coverage. This may be very expensive but may be worth the cost to you.

▶ **Home office.** If you work from home, will your homeowner's policy cover you for loss of property (for example, fire damage to your office and equipment) and provide liability protection against injury to business visitors? Consider upgrading your coverage for specific needs (e.g., home office, flood zone, antiques). Whether you amend your homeowner's policy to cover your home office or obtain a separate policy depends on your business. For example, if you have only occasional business visitors, a rider to your homeowner's policy may suffice. If you have expensive equipment and/or frequent visitors, you may want a separate policy.

▶ **Home rental.** If you rent out your home, your standard policy may not cover all your possible losses. You may need to adjust your policy for "all risk" or "special peril" to protect for property damage and theft as well as rent-related liability losses.

▶ **Identity theft protection.** This coverage can provide reimbursement for the expenses of repairing your credit if your identity is stolen. See p. 314.

Discounts

Homeowner's coverage can be costly, especially as you increase the extent of coverage. To reduce your premiums, take advantage of any discounts to which you may be entitled:

▶ **Multiple policy discounts.** If you have your car insurance with the same carrier as your homeowner's policy, you may be eligible for a multiple policy discount (*Range:* 3%–5%).

▶ **Special homeowner's equipment.** Discounts generally apply if the home has a burglar alarm (*Range:* 2%–5%), deadbolts (*Range:* 2%–5%), smoke alarm (*Range:* 2%–5%) or a sprinkler system (*Range:* 15%–20%).

▶ **Homeowner characteristics.** You may be eligible for discounts just because you're you—for example, if there are no smokers in the home or if the residents are 55 or older.

Renter's insurance

As a tenant, you don't need to insure against damage or destruction of the building. But you do want protection for losses to interior items (cabinetry, carpeting, etc.) as well as your personal items. You also want liability protection against personal injury to visitors. Renter's insurance has a very modest liability limit (typically $25,000), which can be increased to $100,000 or more for a small premium charge. Like homeowners, premiums for renters can be cut by increasing the deductible.

Title insurance

When you buy a home, you may purchase insurance to protect your title to property. If you finance the purchase through a mortgage, the lender will require you to purchase this coverage for its protection.

Strategy: You may want to carry owner's title insurance, which can be combined with the lender's insurance. (In some areas, the seller pays for this coverage to protect the buyer.) This insurance obligates the carrier to defend you against any claims relating to your title in the property. There's a one-time charge for the coverage, which is, effectively, permanent. If a claim arises after you've sold the home, you still have protection. Hold onto your old policy.

ADDING COVERAGE WITH UMBRELLA POLICIES

If you have substantial assets or income to protect, think about how rampant lawsuits are today. To obtain protection for personal injury claims, consider supplementing your homeowner's and car insurance with an umbrella policy. The umbrella policy picks up where the liability protection under your other policies leaves off. For example, your homeowner's policy may provide protection for up to $300,000 for personal injury sustained on your premises by nonresidents. A $1 million umbrella policy would provide protection from $300,000 up to $1 million.

The cost of umbrella coverage is relatively modest (about $300 or less a year for $1 million in coverage, or $1,200 for $5 million in coverage). Make sure that all of your policies are coordinated. For example, the umbrella coverage may require you to increase your homeowner's limits or your car insurance limits.

Check on the extent of coverage for special situations provided by your umbrella policy.

▶ **Does it cover your actions as a board member?** If you serve as an officer on the board of a nonprofit organization, you might want protection for your actions in this capacity. Generally the organization carries directors' and officers' liability protection (a D & O policy). If it does not (and perhaps, even if it does), you'll want your umbrella policy to provide D & O protection.

▶ **Does it cover occurrences related to a second home?** Make sure the policy covers your vacation home. If your second home is rental property, you may need separate protection.

DISABILITY COVERAGE

People under age 50 are much more likely to become disabled than to die; at age 40, it's three and a half times more likely. Unless you're independently wealthy, you'll want insurance to provide sufficient income if you can no longer work. Don't rely on Social Security disability payments to fill the gap. Monthly benefits are no higher than those payable for old age (see Chapter 1). Social Security disability benefits are payable only if you are totally and permanently disabled and you can no longer perform *any* type of work.

You may have disability coverage through an employer. If the employer pays the premiums, it's a non-taxable benefit. However, if you ever collect on the policy, the payments will be taxable. On the other hand, if you purchase the policy yourself, you can't deduct the premiums, but any benefits you receive are tax free. If your employer pays for the policy, coverage terminates when you leave the company—unless you have the option to pick up the policy yourself.

How much coverage do you need?

A disability policy replaces income which you would lose if you became incapable of working. If you're retired, you don't need such a policy, since you don't rely on earned income to pay your bills. But if your investment income and other resources don't generate sufficient income to cover your monthly expenses, have a disability policy to provide benefits in case you become disabled.

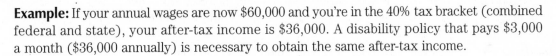

Rule of thumb: If you pay for the policy (so that benefits are tax free), you need a policy that provides 60% of your current, taxable income.

> **Example:** If your annual wages are now $60,000 and you're in the 40% tax bracket (combined federal and state), your after-tax income is $36,000. A disability policy that pays $3,000 a month ($36,000 annually) is necessary to obtain the same after-tax income.

Paying for disability coverage

The cost of disability coverage varies with age, medical condition, the definition of "disabled" and the exclusion period (the time—30 days, 60 days, 90 days or 180 days—between the onset of the disability and the commencement of benefits). To estimate cost, figure that a $50,000 policy for a 40-year-old with no health problems might now cost about $2,000 annually.

You can lower the cost of coverage by:

▶ **Buying coverage through a group** (such as a professional or trade association).

▶ **Extending the exclusion period** (the longer you wait to collect—say, 90 days instead of 30 days—the lower the premiums). The recommended exclusion period is 60 or 90 days.

> **Strategy:** *Make sure your policy will pay sufficient benefits if you're unable to perform your current job, not only if you are unable to perform any type of work. Don't buy a policy that refers to the Social Security Administration's definition of disability, which means unable to perform any work at all.*

Other features to look for in a disability policy

Make sure the policy is noncancelable by the insurance company and guaranteed renewable so that premium costs remain fixed to age 65. You may also want a policy (or a rider on the policy) that pays benefits in case of partial (residual) disability. For example, if you are able to work only a limited schedule, you may be entitled to benefits as long as your earnings have dropped by a certain amount (such as by 20% of pre-disability income).

Also check on how long the policy extends. Some policies end at age 65 when you are entitled to full Social Security benefits. But if you expect to continue working past the normal retirement age, you'll want a policy that continues to work for you (until age 70 or 75).

CAR INSURANCE

Whether you own or lease a car, you need to carry insurance to protect yourself in case of accidents and other claims. Car insurance consists of four types of coverage:

▶ **Damage to someone else's property** (for example, damage to another driver's car).

▶ **Bodily injury.** This provides coverage for injury to other parties. In states with "no fault" laws, your insurance provides coverage for injury to you.

▶ **Comprehensive coverage.** This provides protection if your car is stolen or damaged other than in an accident.

▶ **Collision.** This coverage will restore your car in the event of an accident. If the car is beyond fixing (i.e., the insurance company considers it a total loss), you'll receive compensation for its value (as determined by the insurance company).

You *must* carry coverage for the first three types of liability. State law mandates minimum coverage amounts (for example, $10,000 per injured person in the car and a total of $25,000 for persons outside the car).

You *may* opt to buy collision coverage. It's generally a good idea to carry collision coverage (unless the car is so old—generally 10 years or more—that it doesn't pay to do so).

 Strategy: Carry more than the minimum coverage to avoid personal liability for excess injuries. Make sure that if you have an umbrella policy, the coverage amounts are coordinated.

Note: Personal property stolen from your car is not covered by your car insurance policy. Your homeowner's personal property floater covers your personal property from theft in this case.

 Strategy: Consider increasing car insurance coverage. For example, you may want glass protection (called "full glass coverage") to cover the cost of replacing broken glass without any deductible. A policy may also cost more if it includes towing charges for breakdowns or accidents and car rental costs incurred while the car is being repaired. Don't take this coverage if you belong to an auto club that provides such coverage—you would be paying twice for the same protection.

Strategy: Reduce the cost of coverage by increasing your deductible. Increasing the deductible from $250 to $500 may cut premiums by as much as 30% (although the typical range is 15%–20%). You'll be responsible for small problems. You can also reduce premiums by qualifying for discounts.

 Strategy: To keep premium costs down, avoid making small claims under your policy. Although the total of these amounts may exceed your deductible and therefore be covered, they may trigger premium increases upon renewal.

Discounts

You can lower the cost of coverage if you qualify for certain discounts offered by your carrier. Ask which of these discounts apply to you:

▶ **Multiple car discounts.** If you insure more than one car with the same company, you may be entitled to a discount (*Range:* 10%–25%).

▶ **Multiple policy discounts.** If you have your homeowner's policy with the same company, you may be entitled to a discount (*Range:* 3%–5%).

▶ **Special equipment discounts.** If your car has certain equipment, you're entitled to a discount. Special equipment includes antilock brakes, air bags, special alarm systems and passive restraints.

▶ **Driver education discounts.** If you take a special driver's education course, you may be entitled to a flat rate discount. For example, in New York, the discount is $39 per year for three years; then you must repeat the course for further discounts. Mature drivers' courses are especially important for those age 75 and older who may otherwise pay 5%–15% additional cost. You can find a mature drivers' course near you by contacting the AARP (**www.aarp.org/statepages**, 888-OUR-AARP; 800-687-2277).

▶ **Limited driving.** If your car is used less than a certain number of miles per year (typically 7,500), there may be a discount. If you're insuring a car for your child, the cost of coverage (not really a discount) will be lowered if an adult is listed as the primary driver and your child as an occasional driver. If your child is a good student, there may be a discount for this status. When your child goes away to school (more than 100 miles from home) and the car remains on your premises, there may be a college student discount (*Range:* 10%–15%).

Shopping for coverage

There are several ways to find the best policy for you. In some cases, you can go directly to the insurer. Direct policy writers include:

▶ Amica (**www.amica.com**, 800-242-6422), if you have a perfect, or almost perfect, driving record

▶ GEICO (**www.geico.com**, 800-861-8380)

▶ USAA (**www.usaa.com**, 800-531-8111), provided a family member has been in the military

You can find coverage through an insurance agent who sells policies from such companies as Allstate, Nationwide and State Farm.

 Strategy: *If you already have car insurance but want to switch—you're unhappy with the service you've received or think you can find lower premiums—start your comparison shopping about six months before your policy expires. Don't drop your existing coverage until you have new insurance in place.*

MEDICAL INSURANCE

A lthough many people have medical insurance through an employer, their spouse's or partner's employer or under a government program, the US Census Bureau estimated that in 2004, there were 45 million Americans with no medical insurance at all. These people may have high out-of-pocket costs for even routine medical care, only part of which may be tax deductible, and they face the daunting prospect that a serious accident or illness could wipe out their life savings. But there are options available for finding and buying affordable health coverage.

Traditional health insurance

The most expensive coverage allows the greatest freedom of choice in the doctors you use and the medical procedures they select. Typically, you pay for costs up to a set dollar amount or annual deductible. Then insurance pays 80% of covered benefits after that; you pay the other 20%.

Employer-provided health coverage is discussed in Chapter 13.

Health maintenance organizations (HMOs)

These organizations require you to go through a gatekeeper—your primary-care physician—to obtain referrals to most specialists within the HMO network of doctors. Services and procedures generally must be preapproved. But if you follow procedures, 100% of expenses are covered (after a small co-payment, such as $10 or $15 per doctor's visit).

Using an HMO avoids the need to submit claims to an insurance company for reimbursement.

Preferred provider organizations (PPOs)

These organizations are similar to HMOs except you don't need to have a primary-care physician act as a "gatekeeper" to approve referrals to specialists. At your option, you can see any doctor within the PPO system.

Buying individual health coverage

If you don't have coverage through your or your spouse's employer—free or subsidized coverage—and you don't yet qualify for Medicare, buy health coverage on your own.

▶ **COBRA coverage.** If you've left employment, been divorced from someone who had employer-provided coverage or have reached the age of majority and are no longer covered by a parent's employer policy, you can opt to pay the group-health insurance rate, plus a small administrative fee. COBRA is a federal law that requires employers who regularly employ 20 or more workers to offer continuation coverage under these circumstances. You can have the same coverage you previously had or can choose any coverage available to existing employees. However, COBRA coverage generally extends only 18 months following the triggering event.

 Strategy: Buy individual coverage when COBRA coverage lapses, unless you or your spouse have coverage through a new employer. Don't let coverage lapse or you will have an exclusion period for preexisting conditions that will delay coverage of old conditions.

▶ **Professional and trade associations.** These associations offer individual coverage to their members at group health insurance rates. The type of coverage may vary—from fee-for-service to HMO-type plans.

▶ **State programs.** Your state may offer health care coverage if you meet certain requirements (for example, you fall below a set income level or you're a small-business owner who covers employees). For example, New York has Healthy NY, a modestly-priced health insurance program for the uninsured (866-432-5849 or **www.ins.state.ny.us/website2/hny/english/hny.htm**).

▶ **Individual coverage.** The most costly alternative for purchasing traditional medical insurance is buying it on your own, not through an employer or group. However, if you have no other options, individual coverage may be necessary to protect you from financial disaster due to health-related expenses.

 Strategy: To keep costs down, buy a "high-deductible health plan," a policy that is designed to cover catastrophic medical needs (i.e., amounts above a high deductible) and make tax-deductible contributions to a health savings account (HSA). The HSA allows funds to grow tax-deferred and can be tapped tax free to cover out-of-pocket medical expenses.

Medicare

This is a federal program of health coverage for those age 65 and older who have worked for the required period to qualify for free coverage or who agree to pay for this coverage. In general, Medicare Part A covers the cost of hospital stays and Part B covers doctors' bills and certain other outpatient costs. As of this time, only a limited amount of prescription drug costs is covered by Medicare.

▶ **Obtaining coverage.** Coverage isn't automatic. You must file an application with the Social Security Administration (SSA). To find your local SSA office, call 800-772-1213 or check **www.socialsecurity.gov**. *Caution:* Even if you opt for early Social Security benefits, you can't start Medicare coverage until age 65. On the other hand, if you delay collection of Social Security benefits, you can still apply for Medicare at age 65.

 Strategy: Apply for Medicare as soon as you are eligible, even if you still have employer coverage. Your employer coverage can remain your primary coverage. Or, choose Medicare as your primary coverage. This will give you the broadest health coverage available.

▶ **What it costs you.** Assuming you've worked for the required period, you must pay a monthly premium for Medicare Part B ($93.50 per month in 2007). Those with high income (about 4% of Medicare beneficiaries who have adjusted gross income over $80,000 if single or $160,000 on a joint return) now pay a surtax on Part B premiums. The surtax for 2007 is based on adjusted gross income in 2005; the top premium in 2007 is $162.10 per month. There is no separate cost for Part A coverage, unless you don't otherwise qualify for Medicare and agree to buy into the system.

There is voluntary prescription drug coverage under Medicare Part D. Each Medicare drug plan has its own premiums and co-payments. In 2007, the annual premium ranges from zero to $265 and is withheld monthly from Social Security benefits. Those eligible to enroll in Part D who fail to do so become subject to a lifetime penalty unless they have other "creditable" coverage through an employer, union or other plan.

However, you may be responsible for certain deductibles and co-payments; these amounts are adjusted annually for inflation. For 2006, they are as follows:

Medicare deductibles and co-payments

Services	Your responsibility
Hospitalization	
First 60 days	$992
61–90 days	$248 per day
91–150 days	$476 per day
After 150 days	All costs
Skilled nursing facility	
First 20 days	Nothing
21–100 days	$124 per day
After 100 days	All costs

You can eliminate your obligation for deductibles and co-payments by opting for a managed care plan under Medicare (such as a Medicare-HMO); you'll still have to pay the monthly premium for Part B coverage.

Contesting claims

Medicare does not necessarily pay for all of your health-care costs. But you have a right to challenge any denial of benefits. The procedure you follow depends on what costs are involved. For Part A costs:

▶ **Find out why coverage has been denied.** It may not be covered by Medicare. Or it may be outside the range of average costs, but you may be able to fight for coverage. To learn your rights, click on **www.medicarerights.org**.

▶ **Bring your matter before a peer review organization (PRO),** a group of doctors under contract to Medicare. Ask it to consider your case on an individual basis. To find a peer review, go to helpful contacts at **www.medicare.gov**.

▶ **File a request for reconsideration of health insurance benefits** if the PRO does not act favorably. If you are contesting hospital-related benefits denials, use Form HCFA-2649, which must be filed within 60 days following the date of the notice of Medicare's claim determination.

▶ **Ask for a hearing before an administrative law judge** if the PRO does not act favorably in a redetermination.

▶ **Request an appeals council hearing** if the administrative law judge rules against you.

For Part B, the process is similar. However, first you request a review, then a hearing and last an administrative law judge hearing. There are special deadlines for each stage of the appeals process. And there are filing costs involved to pursue your case.

 Strategy: *If you are contesting a sizable claim, you may want to have an attorney represent you. Look for a knowledgeable elder-law attorney who routinely handles such matters. (See National Academy of Elder Law Attorneys at www.naela.org or call 520-881-4005).*

Medigap coverage

People 65 and older who are covered by Medicare may need additional medical insurance, called supplemental coverage or Medigap. This coverage picks up where Medicare leaves off to cover deductibles and other out-of-pocket costs. Consumers have a choice of policies in supplemental coverage. Obviously the more comprehensive the coverage, the higher the cost. By federal law, the types of policies have been standardized to help you compare coverage. Here are the key terms you need to evaluate Medigap coverage, and a chart that shows different kinds of coverage:

▶ **Basic benefits:** Part A coinsurance for 61–90 days of hospitalization, coinsurance for Part B services (generally 20% of approved charges), reasonable cost of the first three pints of blood.

▶ **Part A deductible:** $992 in 2007; *Part B deductible:* $93.50/month in 2007 for the basic premium; and *Skilled nursing coinsurance:* $124 per day in 2006.

▶ **Foreign travel emergency:** 80% of medically necessary emergency care in a foreign country (less a $250 annual deductible).

Medigap Plans for 2007

Medigap Benefits	A	B	C	D	E	F	G	H	I	J	K	L
Basic benefits	✓	✓	✓	✓	✓	✓	✓	✓	✓	✓	✓	✓
Hospital deductible		✓	✓	✓	✓	✓	✓	✓	✓	✓	✓	✓
Skilled nursing facility			✓	✓	✓	✓	✓	✓	✓	✓	✓	✓
Part B deductible			✓			✓				✓		
Part B excess charges						✓ 100%	✓ 80%		✓ 100%	✓ 100%		
Foreign travel emergency			✓	✓	✓	✓	✓	✓	✓	✓		
At-home recovery			✓				✓		✓	✓		
Part A hospice coinsurance (50% of covered benefits)											✓	
Part A hospice coinsurance (75% of covered benefits)												✓
Preventive services (up to $120 a year if ordered by doctor)				✓						✓		
Preventive services ($100 of Part B covered benefits)											✓	✓
Prescription drug costs (up to 50% of $2,500, after a yearly $250 deductible (up to $1,250)*								✓	✓			
Prescription drug costs (up to 50% of $6,000, after a yearly $250 deductible (up to $3,000)*										✓		
Out-of-pocket maximum: 100% of covered benefits after the beneficiary pays $4,000 out of pocket											✓	
Out-of-pocket maximum: 100% of covered benefits after the beneficiary pays $2,000 out of pocket												✓

*New plan H, I, and J policies sold do not include prescription drug coverage, but policies purchased prior to January 2006 (the date that the Medicare Part D started) may continue to provide drug benefits.

▶ **At-home recovery:** Up to $40 per visit ($1,600 per year total) for short-term assistance with daily living activities (bathing, dressing, etc.) for those recovering from surgery, illness or injury.

▶ **Hospice:** 50% or 75% of covered benefits.

▶ **Preventive care:** Up to $120 per year for physical examination, shots for flu, pneumonia or hepatitis B, serum cholesterol screening, hearing test and glaucoma screening, screening tests for prostate, breast and colorectal cancer, diabetes screening, thyroid function test and tetanus and diptheria boosters.

▶ **High deductibles:** Policies K and L, which cost less than other policies, pay less than 100% of out-of-pocket expenses until certain limits are reached (then the policy pays the full supplemental benefit for the remainder of the year).

> **Strategy:** If you have Medicare, don't automatically purchase a supplemental care policy; you may not need it. If you've chosen a managed care plan under Medicare (such as an HMO) or have employer medical insurance that is your primary coverage, no Medigap policy is necessary.

Medical coverage to avoid

Although health insurance is a critical part of any financial plan, certain types of coverage are superfluous. They're costly and rarely used. These include:

▶ **Automobile medical insurance.** Because your general medical insurance covers accident-related conditions, you don't need this separate coverage.

▶ **Cancer coverage,** which pays only if you have this specific condition.

Whether and when to get long-term care insurance

The average cost of nursing home care is now nearing $74,000 annually in 2005 (and more than $100,000 in some locations) and is projected to exceed $190,000 by 2030. Middle-income consumers who want to protect their life savings for their heirs need to consider long-term-care policies. Medicare and other medical insurance policies generally do not cover the cost of long-term care. You'll need a separate policy, called a long-term-care policy (also referred to as a nursing home policy). This policy provides a fixed dollar benefit per day (for example, $200 per day).

▶ **When to start.** The experts suggest taking out a long-term-care policy in your 50s, because the premiums for a long-term-care policy are fixed in the year you purchase it. The younger you are when you buy the coverage, the lower your premiums will be for the rest of your life. The total premiums paid over 25 to 30 years could be lower than the cost of one year's stay in a nursing home.

> **Strategy:** If you're under age 50, wait to buy a policy. It probably doesn't make sense to start before age 50, because you are likely to be paying premiums for 40 years or more.

▶ **What to look for in a long-term-care policy.** If you, like most people, want to stay in your home as long as possible, you'll want a policy that will cover in-home care as well as nursing home care. In shopping for a long-term-care policy, here are also some other things to look for:

Conditions for coverage. Some policies require a pre-hospitalization report before they will pay long-term care benefits. This type of policy isn't desirable.

Exclusions for certain conditions. Some policies don't cover mental conditions; their definition of mental condition may or may not include Alzheimer's disease. Don't buy a policy that excludes coverage for this condition.

Inflation rider. If you're under age 70 when you purchase your policy, include an inflation rider that increases the per-day benefits over time. Otherwise, you may find that your policy is inadequate to meet your needs.

Shopping for a long-term-care policy

Today, most major insurance carriers (CNA, GE Capital, John Hancock and Travelers) offer this coverage. You may also be able to purchase coverage through a trade association or other group. For example, AARP offers long-term-care coverage to its members. Or you may be able to pick up coverage through your employer. An increasing number of companies now include long-term-care policies as an option under their cafeteria plans.

Also check with Long-Term Care Quote (**www.ltcq.net**, 800-587-3279) and the American Association for Long-Term Care Insurance (**www.aaltci.org**, 818-597-3227).

Premiums for long-term care are based on several factors: The daily benefit provided under the policy (for example, $150 a day), the exclusion period (the time between the onset of nursing home care and the payment of benefits under the policy, such as 60 or 90 days), how long benefits will be paid (typically either three years or lifetime) and your age when you purchase the policy. The younger you are when you buy the policy, the lower your premiums will be. For example, a healthy 50-year-old would pay about $700 a year, while a healthy 70-year-old would pay about $3,000 a year for a three-year policy providing a daily benefit of $100.

 Strategy: *Obviously, a lifetime policy for long-term care is the best, but most expensive, coverage. Consider buying a policy with a set limit, such as a three-year policy. This period is long enough to allow for planning to qualify for Medicaid.*

Tax benefits for long-term-care insurance

You may be able to deduct a portion of your long-term-care premiums along with other medical expenses on your return. The portion depends on your age. The dollar limits for 2007 are:

Portion of long-term-care premiums treated as deductible medical expenses

Your age before the end of the year	Annual limit
40 or younger	$ 290
41 through 50	550
51 through 60	1,110
61 through 70	2,950
Over 70	3,680

About half of the states also offer tax incentives—deductions and/or credits—for long-term-care insurance premiums.

For general information about long-term-care insurance, visit the Long-Term Care Insurance National Advisory Council Web site (**www.longtermcareinsurance.org**).

Piggybacking long-term coverage

Instead of buying a separate policy, consider adding a long-term coverage rider to an existing or new annuity or life insurance policy. Under new law, these other insurance products can now offer long-term care coverage. But tax-favored treatment for the riders will not begin until 2010.

Medical coverage when traveling abroad

If you're injured or become ill and require medical attention while traveling overseas, your health coverage may reimburse you only for "customary and reasonable" medical claims *after* you've paid them. Medicare does not cover any overseas hospital or medical costs. Medigap policies C through J cover 80% of medically necessary foreign emergency care after a $250 deductible.

▶ **Short-term health coverage.** You can purchase medical coverage for the length of your trip (although minimum coverage may run for 30 days even if your trip is shorter). Find travel insurance carriers through your travel agent.

▶ **Medical evacuation coverage.** The expense of getting home when you have become injured or ill while traveling can run $10,000 or more. Even if your health coverage provides reimbursement for medical treatment abroad, few policies cover this special expense. However, you can buy separate "medical assistance insurance" to cover this contingency.

Medicaid

This type of medical coverage is provided under a joint federal-state program for those in need—that is, those with assets and income below set limits. It is not an insurance-type program like Medicare.

Portfolio planning

❝*Chiefly the mold of a man's fortune is in his own hands.*❞ —Francis Bacon

Your success with personal investing may mean the difference between achieving your financial goals—such as a comfortable retirement, paying for a child's education or purchasing a vacation home—or just getting by. In order to realize the returns you want, you need to understand more than how to pick a particular stock or mutual fund. You need to take a broad view of your portfolio so that it serves your overall financial goals. This is especially true in light of the abysmal stock market performance of the past several years.

The tools you use for your personal investments can be applied to your tax-advantaged retirement accounts—401(k) plans, IRAs, IRA rollovers and Roth IRAs. Understanding how to handle your portfolio will enable you to coordinate your personal investment accounts with your tax-advantaged accounts.

This chapter explains some basic investment concepts that will help you plan and monitor your portfolio. I emphasize the importance of savings so you have money to invest, show you how to avoid investment traps and offer ideas for making investment decisions. I explain the tax rules you need to know for effective portfolio planning. You'll find investment strategies unique to retirement plans and IRAs in Chapter 8.

LEARNING ABOUT INVESTMENTS

Investing isn't a course that's taught in high school. And most parents don't teach their children about investing, either. So you must learn about investment fundamentals on your own. You need to know the basics—investment terminology and strategies—to make wise investment decisions. Even if you work with financial professionals who advise you on investments, you need to understand basic concepts. Remember that the ultimate investment decision—for example, to buy or not to buy a particular security—and the consequences of that decision rest with you. While many people in the 1990s acted on stock picks of their friends and relatives, we now know you need to apply more rigorous standards when selecting investments.

Within this chapter you'll find explanations of investment terminology and strategies to consider. For example, the term "portfolio" refers technically to all of your assets—stocks, bonds, real estate, etc. But in more practical terms, it's used to mean the sum of your stocks, bonds, mutual fund shares and cash or cash equivalents—that is, your liquid assets. Expanding your investment vocabulary will help you understand and evaluate the wealth of investment information now available.

You need to know more than just the basics to make smart investment decisions. You must be informed about developments such as economic trends, new financial products and new trading methods, so that you can take advantage of opportunities and avoid pitfalls.

 Strategy: *Use the numerous resources available today—courses, books, online information—to broaden your knowledge of investment products and strategies. Be skeptical about information posted in online chat rooms and bulletin boards. Lots of it is just plain wrong.*

Resources

I encourage you to learn about investments and follow new developments in a variety of ways:

▶ **Adult education classes.** Check your town's adult education program for investment classes.

▶ **Investment seminars.** Brokerage firms and individuals offer half-day, full-day or multi-day seminars on investing. They may have proprietary products to sell, but the main content of these seminars is information about investing. Some seminars are free, while others charge sizable entry fees. *Caution:* Investment-related trips, such as investment cruises and seminars at resorts, are not tax deductible.

▶ **Newspapers** such as *The Wall Street Journal, Barron's* and *Investor's Business Daily.*

▶ **Magazines** such as *Money, Worth* and *Business Week.*

There are also television programs and channels that focus almost entirely on investment news, such as:

▶ **Bloomberg**

▶ **CNBC**

▶ *Jim Cramer's Mad Money* **on CNBC**

▶ *Lou Dobbs' Moneyline* **on CNN**

▶ *Nightly Business Report* **on PBS**

Online sites to explore for general information, breaking developments and other information include:

▶ CNBC (**http://moneycentral.msn.com/investor/home.asp**). Highlights of financial developments and stock prices.

▶ CNN Money (**http://money.cnn.com**). Breaking financial news and articles on investing.

- Investopedia.com (**www.investopedia.com**). Online dictionary of investment terminology.
- The Motley Fool (**www.fool.com** or AOL keyword: fool). Investment ideas and model portfolios.

If you're willing to pay for information (the rate varies with the information you subscribe to), you can use TheStreet.com (**www.thestreet.com**). While this site has some free information, you must pay to use portfolio tools and investment advice.

SAVINGS STRATEGIES

Unless you receive an inheritance, win the lottery or some other windfall, you need to save money (that is, not spend it) in order to have money to invest. Americans as a group are notoriously poor savers. We have one of the lowest savings rates among industrial countries. In 2006, the personal savings rate was–0.5% (the only other time that the savings rate had been in negative territory was in 1932 and 1933 during the Great Depression).

If you don't save, you won't have any capital to make investments. Find ways to direct a portion of your income toward regular savings.

 Strategy: Develop a savings plan to build capital to invest for your future. This may require sacrifices—eating at home instead of restaurants, keeping your old car another year or postponing the purchase of a home. But in the long run, you'll benefit. Rule of thumb: *Aim to save 10% of your after-tax income—a stretch for many but a good goal. If you're within 10 years of your projected retirement, you may need to increase this percentage considerably, depending on what you've saved.*

Automatic savings

Many people lack the discipline to save money on a regular basis. We say that "money burns a hole in their pockets." Fortunately, there are a number of automatic savings strategies that can be used to build up a savings fund that can then be used for investments:

- **Write yourself a check.** Consider yourself a creditor and write yourself a check each month *before* you pay your other bills. You'll limit your spending so you don't incur debt.
- **Payroll deductions.** An employer may offer a payroll savings plan that automatically directs a portion of each paycheck into savings. This savings may be held in a separate savings account or invested automatically in US savings bonds or other investments.
- **Systematic investments through account debiting.** You can direct that a set dollar amount be debited from your checking or savings account by a mutual fund company. You can set up a systematic investment program simply by providing the company with your bank account number and a signed authorization to make regular withdrawals. Systematic investing will help you set the funds aside for investment.
- **Plan ahead for tax refunds.** A tax refund generally represents a tax-free loan you're making to the government. In my opinion, tax refunds are not a shrewd money move. Some people regard them as a way to ensure the receipt of a lump sum of cash. If you plan for a tax refund or expect to receive one, decide in advance to apply at least some of the money to investments.

Strategy: Don't ignore your spare change as a source of extra funds. Simply empty the change from your pockets each day. At the end of each month, roll your coins and deposit into a savings vehicle that invests immediately or when a set amount is accumulated (such as $100). Ideas for small investments: US savings bonds starting at $25, additions to mutual funds (generally, minimum additions must be $100 or more) or additions to stock purchase plans (generally, minimum additions must be $100 or more, but some plans permit smaller additions). Remember that a mere $100 invested monthly means an additional annual investment of $1,200.

ASSET ALLOCATION

How much of your assets should be in stocks? Bonds? Cash? Real estate, collectibles or other assets? The answer depends on what is your desirable asset allocation. This concept involves splitting your asset pie among different types of investments. These types of investments include:

- ▶ **Equities** (stocks and stock mutual funds)
- ▶ **Fixed income** (bonds and bond mutual funds)
- ▶ **Cash** (cash, money market accounts, certificates of deposit)
- ▶ **Real estate** (direct ownership of investment property, REITs)
- ▶ **Collectibles** (stamps, coins, silver flatware, jewelry, rugs)
- ▶ **Other** (gold, commodities)

The reasoning behind asset allocation is simple—to cover all your bases, making sure you address your long-term goals and your short-term needs. Are you saving for the future? Do you need added income now? Are you concerned with the preservation of your capital? Will you need cash in the near future (for example, as a down payment on a home or for college expenses)? Whatever your goals, your asset allocation should reflect your needs.

Growth, income or both?

As a general rule, you need to grow your portfolio continually to maintain the buying power of your dollars. *Reason:* Inflation (a sustained rise in the cost of goods and services), no matter how modest, erodes your buying power over time.

Example: If inflation were 4% annually for a decade, at the end of that period, your dollar would buy just half of what it did at the start of the decade.

In the past decade, when inflation was low, some investors ignored its impact. But, like soil erosion that occurs almost imperceptibly with devastating effects over time, inflation erodes buying power with equally devastating effects. Just look at historic results over the past 30 years:

This overall (or core) rate of inflation, which is based on changes in the Consumer Price Index (CPI) compared to a historical reference point, may not reflect your personal rate of inflation. Certain expenses account for a greater portion of your budget, and these expense items may have a higher rate of inflation than others.

> **Example:** Medical care is just 5.8% of the CPI, but it may be 10% of your budget. Because medical care costs have tended to increase more rapidly than the core rate of inflation in recent years, your personal inflation rate may exceed the core CPI rate.

Inflation (increases in the Consumer Price Index)

Year	Rate	Year	Rate	Year	Rate
1974	12.3%	1985	3.8%	1996	3.3%
1975	6.9%	1986	1.1%	1997	1.7%
1976	4.9%	1987	4.4%	1998	1.6%
1977	6.7%	1988	4.4%	1999	2.7%
1978	9.0%	1989	4.6%	2000	3.4%
1979	13.3%	1990	6.1%	2001	1.6%
1980	12.5%	1991	3.1%	2002	2.4%
1981	8.9%	1992	2.9%	2003	1.9%
1982	3.8%	1993	2.7%	2004	3.3%
1983	3.8%	1994	2.7%	2005	3.4%
1984	3.9%	1995	2.5%	2006	2.5%

Source: US Bureau of Labor Statistics

To see how inflation erodes the buying power of a dollar, you can use a special inflation calculator at the US Department of Labor, Bureau of Labor Statistics' Web site **(www.bls.gov)**.

Which assets serve your goals?

In order to make an asset allocation that reflects your goals, you need to understand how different types of assets will serve specific goals:

▶ **Equities or stock investments.** These assets generally offer growth; you earn money because the prices rise. Equities may also provide some income from dividends and capital gains distributions.

▶ **Fixed income.** As the name implies, bonds and other fixed-income assets provide income, not growth. Although the price of bonds may fluctuate (creating the possibility that you could make money if you sell bonds before maturity when interest rates drop), they don't offer overall appreciation. A bond with a face amount at maturity of $5,000 will pay you only $5,000 on the maturity date.

▶ **Cash.** Like fixed income, money market accounts and other cash equivalent investments provide income. While there is complete preservation of your capital—except in rare circumstances, you can't lose any of your investment—there is no possibility for growth, other than the interest you may receive on your funds.

▶ **Real estate.** Like equities, real estate investments mainly provide growth opportunities. They may provide some income from rents and mortgages. However, real estate investments (other than publicly traded REITs) are not considered liquid assets like publicly traded stocks and bonds that can be sold at any time.

▶ **Collectibles.** These assets offer the possibility of growth. If the value of the collectibles increases, you may realize a profit when you sell them. *Caution:* Although collectibles can be sold through such public auction sites on the Internet as eBay **(www.ebay.com)**, they are not considered liquid. For most collectibles, there's no fixed exchange, like a stock market, where you can automatically find a market for these items.

▶ **Gold, commodities and other assets.** Each type of asset has different characteristics. For example, gold has been called an inflation hedge because it's believed to retain its value. Commodities are highly speculative, and while they provide the opportunity to make large profits, they also can cause an investor to sustain sizable losses. *Caution:* Gold values fluctuate like the value of other assets, and gold investments in recent years haven't proven to be a good inflation hedge.

Asset allocation formulas

Asset allocation formulas are expressed in percentages—for example, 60% equities and 40% fixed income. There's no single asset allocation formula to follow. Your formula depends on your age, goals, need for current income from investments and tolerance for risk. It also depends on market factors (for example, when markets are down for extended periods you may wish to shift money from equities into fixed income). And your asset allocation formula is certain to change from time to time. As a rule, no one should be 100% allocated to any single type of asset.

Determining your asset allocation formula isn't a one-time exercise. You'll need to adjust your formula as your circumstances change, such as retiring from work. *Caution:* Don't abandon equities completely in favor of fixed income in retirement. You also need to grow your portfolio to keep pace with inflation, and only equities can do this. Even when you're in your 80s it may be advisable to have at least 20% of your assets in equities to protect your buying power should you live past your century mark.

Fine-tuning asset allocation formulas

Asset allocation formulas may be fine-tuned to further allocate the equity and fixed-income portions among classes of investments. For example, your equities may be allocated among large-cap, mid-cap and small-cap stock (which may be further suballocated into growth, value and balanced objectives), and international and index-based investments. Your fixed income may be allocated between cash (money market funds and CDs) and bonds (tax-free, corporate, high-yield, etc.).

Sample asset allocation models

There are a number of asset allocation models in use today. These models include:

▶ **Conservative investment model:** Your age subtracted from 100 equals the percentage to invest in equities. *Example:* A 55-year-old would put 45% in stock and 55% in fixed income.

▶ **Less conservative investment model:** Your age subtracted from 110 is the percentage to invest in equities. *Example:* You're 55 years old so you would put 55% in equities and 45% in fixed income.

▶ **Bullish market model:** 80% in equities. *Caution:* The problem with allocating on the basis of market trends is that you may lag behind market changes.

▶ **80% rule:** With this conservative formula, multiply your age by 80% to find the percentage in fixed income and put the balance in equities. *Example:* If you're age 40, you'd put 32% in fixed income and 68% in equities. If you're 65, you'd want 52% in fixed income and 48% in equities.

▶ **Within five years of retiring:** 60% equities (40% large-cap; 10% small-cap; 10% international) and 40% fixed income.

▶ **20 years to retirement:** 70% equities (45% large-cap; 10% small-cap; 15% international) and 30% fixed income.

▶ **More than 20 years to retirement:** 80% equities (50% large-cap; 15% small-cap; 15% international) and 20% fixed income.

▶ **Aggressive:** 90% equities (40% large-cap; 30% small-cap; 20% international) and 10% fixed income.

You can get help in estimating your own asset allocation model by inputting certain information at Smart Money.com (**www.smartmoney.com**). This model helps you allocate your portfolio between stocks and bonds.

A number of mutual funds offer their own asset allocation among their holdings. A single fund may own stocks, bonds and cash, giving an investor asset allocation through the purchase of a single asset. There are two types of mutual funds that offer asset allocation:

▶ **Balanced funds** where asset allocations generally hold constant. *Examples:* Balanced Index (**www.summitfunds.com**, 888-259-7565); Old Mutual Asset Management (**www.oldmutualus.com**, 617-369-7300); Vanguard STAR (**www.vanguard.com**, 800-871-3879).

▶ **Asset allocation funds** that change their allocations according to the fund manager's perspective. *Example:* Country Asset Allocation (**www.countryfinancial.com**, 800-245-2100).

DIVERSIFYING YOUR PORTFOLIO

Asset allocation alone does not ensure that your portfolio meets your needs and provides a measure of protection against loss. You need to diversify your portfolio as well.

Diversification spreads your risk of loss by not putting all your eggs in one basket. Don't put all your money into just one stock or mutual fund. How does diversification differ from asset allocation? Asset allocation spreads your risk between different types of investments—stocks and bonds—whereas diversification spreads your risk among a class of investments.

> **Example:** Your asset allocation is 60% equities and 40% fixed income. Diversify by finding five equity funds with different asset classes (for example, small-cap, large-cap, international and an index fund). Also buy 10 different individual bonds. Now you're diversified.

How much diversification?

How many different stocks should an investor own? How many different mutual funds? As with asset allocation formulas, there's no fixed formula for diversification. Some suggest that your stock holdings (either in individual stocks or through mutual funds) should cover at least four segments of the equities market—aggressive growth, growth and income, small-cap and international.

Of course, different investment advisers suggest different diversification models.

 Strategy: *When buying individual stocks, try to acquire at least 100 shares at a time so you can monitor meaningful gains or losses in your holdings.*

EVALUATING ASSET ALLOCATION AND INVESTMENT HOLDINGS

Asset allocation and investment choices aren't something you make once and forget about. You need to monitor investment performance and make changes periodically. For example, assume a retired person wants to maintain a conservative asset allocation, but the stock portion value in his portfolio has increased from the target of 60% to well over 80% in a few years, the person must rebalance his holdings. At the end of 2000, when many stocks were down dramatically from their highs, causing a sharp decline in investor net worth, many investors rushed to reallocate their portfolios; despite the decline in some stock prices, these investors still wanted a greater allocation toward cash and bonds.

Strategy: *Rebalance your holdings in two ways—sell some holdings and use the proceeds to buy investments that put you back in balance...or put new money in investments that will bring you back into balance.*

Even if your overall portfolio continues to reflect your desired asset allocations, particular investments may require adjustments. For instance, if a particular stock underperforms the market (i.e., doesn't appreciate as quickly as increases in the S&P 500), you may want to sell and invest in a better performing stock. Or, if you believe stock appreciation will slow or has become too volatile for your risk tolerance, you may want to shift some holdings from equities to fixed income.

Strategy: *You can make these evaluations on your own. But you may wish to employ expert assistance. For example, a stockbroker or financial planner can help you assess the performance of your holdings and modify your portfolio.*

Investment checkups

How often should you review your holdings? This depends on your level of involvement. Some people check stock performance every day. Others simply review monthly statements from brokerage firms to monitor portfolio performance. Still others make less frequent checks on their holdings.

Strategy: *Review your portfolios on at least a quarterly or annual basis. Mutual fund shares held at the fund are reported on a quarterly statement, so you can readily check their performance and compare with prior quarters.*

What to look for

Most financial statements provide you with performance comparisons. For example, a monthly brokerage statement may compare the value of the account at the end of the month with the value of the account at the end of the previous month, quarter or year.

By making these comparisons, you'll be able to see whether the value of your account and the value of specific investments have gone up or down. To make fair comparisons, be sure to factor in any items you've removed from the account—for example, stock sold when you needed cash or cash you transferred from your personal investment account to your Roth IRA or a self-employed retirement plan.

Strategy: *If your checkup indicates that changes in your holdings are needed, factor in tax considerations when selecting or selling investments.*

TAX RULES FOR PORTFOLIOS

As an investor, you can't make wise investment decisions unless you keep in mind their tax consequences. Of course, you can't let tax considerations override economic considerations—for example, by holding onto an investment to achieve long-term capital gain while the price of the stock is on a downward trend. You need to look at your choices in terms of after-tax returns in order to make fair comparisons of investment choices.

Taxation of annual distributions from investments

Income from your investments can produce four types of tax results:

▶ **Tax-free income,** which is not subject to federal income tax. It includes interest on municipal bonds. Whether such interest is free from state income tax depends on your state's income tax rules (see Chapter 6 for an explanation of state income tax rules on municipal bond interest). *Caution:* Just because the interest on municipal bonds is tax free doesn't mean that gain from the sale of such bonds is tax free. The gain may be subject to capital gains rates, described below. And municipal bond interest is taken into account in figuring whether Social Security benefits are includable in income.

▶ **Tax-deferred income.** On this type of income, tax is postponed until some future time. It includes interest on US savings bonds (unless you opt to report the interest annually) and earnings on traditional IRAs, qualified retirement plan accounts and commercial annuities. For example, earnings from annuities aren't taxed until you start to receive annuity payments.

▶ **Capital gains.** This income is subject to lower rates than the rates on ordinary income. Capital gains relating to your portfolio result from distributions made by mutual funds and from the sale of investments. The tax rules for capital gains are discussed below under "taxation of proceeds from sales of investments." Dividends (with some exceptions) are taxed at the same favorable rate as long-term capital gains.

▶ **Ordinary income.** This income is subject to the highest income tax rates. The rate depends on the tax bracket resulting from your other income and deductions (federal income tax brackets for 2007 are 10%, 15%, 25%, 28%, 33% and 35%). Ordinary income includes interest on corporate bonds, certificates of deposit and savings accounts, and dividends from money market accounts. For example, earnings from money market mutual funds are distributed as ordinary dividends even though the underlying investment produced interest income, and are therefore taxed as ordinary income.

Taxation of proceeds from sales of investments

When you sell investments, you'll realize a capital gain if you have a profit (i.e., if the amount you receive on the sale exceeds your basis in the asset—typically, your cost) or a capital loss (the amount you receive on the sale is less than your basis in or cost of the asset). Capital gains and losses are either short term (assets held one year or less) or long term (assets held more than one year).

Short-term capital gains are taxed at the same rate as ordinary income. Long-term capital gains, generally are taxed at 15% (or 5% for those in the 10% or 15% tax bracket). Collectibles held long term are taxed at 28% for those in a tax bracket of 28% or higher. The portion of gain representing unrealized depreciation on real estate—the amount of straight-line depreciation claimed—is taxed at 25% for those in a tax bracket of 25% or higher.

Capital losses

Capital losses, which may be short term or long term, can be used to offset capital gains. Capital losses in excess of capital gains can also be used to offset ordinary income by up to $3,000 annually. If capital losses exceed capital gains and the amount allowed to offset ordinary income, the excess capital losses may be carried forward indefinitely and used to offset capital gains in the future.

Capital losses cannot be used in the current year if the wash-sale rule applies to a particular sale. This rule prevents reporting a capital loss from a sale if substantially identical securities are purchased within 30 days of the date of such sale.

 Strategy: *Watch for selling strategies that may trigger the wash-sale rule. For example, the wash-sale rule applies to a sale by one spouse if the other spouse acquires substantially identical securities within the wash-sale period. But it may be possible to sell from your personal account and buy for your IRA or other tax-deferred account (or vice versa) without triggering the wash-sale rule. This strategy has yet to be IRS-tested.*

Stepped-up basis rule

Currently, you can eliminate potential gain from investments for your heirs by holding onto your assets until your death. *Reason:* Inherited assets receive a stepped-up basis—the value of the property for federal estate tax purposes.

 Strategy: *Don't let the stepped-up basis rule prevent you from taking appropriate investment actions during your lifetime. If economic considerations support making a change in your investments, pay the tax now and make the change to protect your portfolio.*

HANDLING MARKET UPS AND DOWNS

The stock market isn't static—it moves up and down and provides considerable volatility. The swings in the market—whether up or down—shouldn't prevent you from making smart investments. Doing so depends on your understanding of how the market works and techniques for taking advantage of market movements.

Investing in up markets

The bull market that started in 1991 continued to move upward until early in 2000. This extended bull market created more millionaires than in any other time in history and, despite market setbacks, there were 8.9 million millionaire households by the end of 2005.

Millionaires 1990–1999

Number of households with a net worth of $1 million or more

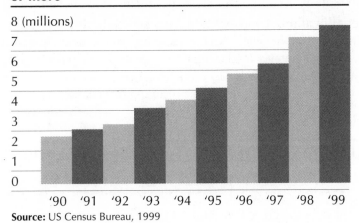

| | '90 | '91 | '92 | '93 | '94 | '95 | '96 | '97 | '98 | '99 |

Source: US Census Bureau, 1999

A bull market can, however, create problems for investors. For example, should you buy as prices rise? Careful stock selections can still be profitable in bull markets. But make sure you understand what you're buying—high price/earnings (PE) ratios may make certain purchases in bull markets too costly. Factors used in selecting stocks are discussed in Chapter 6.

Handling down markets

Bear markets—drops in market indices such as the S&P or Dow of at least 20%—occur from time to time. Bear markets may be temporary—a matter of months—or long term, lasting for years.

Fact: Since 1948 we have had a bear market about every six years, with the last completed one back in 1990. In 2000, the NASDAQ dropped by more than 40%, a bear market movement by any definition.

Bear markets can create problems for investors. The drop in portfolio value may mean postponing retirement because the portfolio won't produce the income that had been expected. And investors forced to sell stocks for cash needs or for other reasons will have to sell more shares to realize the same proceeds from their holdings. The challenge for investors in bear markets is to preserve capital and look for buying opportunities that buck the downward trend. The difficulty of this challenge is compounded by the fact that psychologically investors may be so beaten up and discouraged that they can't focus on improving their lot.

Fact: When the value of an asset decreases, a higher percentage increase is required to get back to square one.

> **Example:** A drop of 10% in the value of your portfolio will require a subsequent rise of 11.1% just to recover to your pre-drop value. So, if your stock worth $10,000 drops by 10% to $9,000, it would have to increase by 11.1% to get back to $9,999.

 Strategies: *Don't panic. Over time, bear markets subside and the bulls rage again, causing prices to recover. But you can try to minimize the effects of the down market.*

▶ **Sell losing stocks.** Even though you may have had substantial losses on a stock, you may need to face the fact that a stock may never fully recover. Holding onto faint hopes isn't a wise investment move. Bite the bullet and try to recover losses in a winning stock instead of holding onto a loser indefinitely. Remember that tax losses can be used to offset gains, producing some benefit to you.

▶ **Revisit your asset allocation.** If you expect the markets to head down, you may want to move money out of equities and into fixed income. This means selling stocks or stock mutual fund shares and buying bonds or parking money in money market funds. *Caution:* If you don't need the capital in the foreseeable future—perhaps you plan to retire 10 years from now—you may wish to ride out the downturn. This will avoid the need to pay commissions and taxes resulting from changes in your asset allocation.

COORDINATING HOLDINGS WITHIN AND WITHOUT TAX-ADVANTAGED VEHICLES

Today, many investors have both personal accounts and tax-advantaged investments—401(k) plans, self-employed retirement plans and IRAs. In portfolio planning, it's shrewd to coordinate holdings in both types of accounts. Here are some rules to consider:

▶ **Don't duplicate investments**. Look at all of your accounts as a whole and decide where to hold specific investments. Why hold the same mutual fund in your personal account that you hold in your IRA?

▶ **Generally, keep equities in taxable accounts.** This is because long-term capital gains on the sale of equities are subject to favorable tax rates. Equities held in tax-advantaged accounts don't benefit from favorable capital gains tax rates, as all distributions are taxed as ordinary income.

▶ **Generally, keep fixed-income assets** (bonds and money market accounts) in tax-advantaged accounts.

 Strategy: Modify these rules to suit your specific situation. For example, you may want to have the same investment in both your personal account and your IRA. You may want to hold equities in your 401(k) plan, because they may be the best investment option offered by the plan. Or, you may need to keep some personal investment funds in a money market account for use as an emergency fund.

See Chapter 8 for my discussion of retirement accounts, including 401(k) plans and IRAs.

WORKING WITH STOCKBROKERS

With stockbrokers, you get what you pay for. The higher the fees and commissions charged for transactions you make, the more investment advice you can expect to receive. The types of brokers—full-service, discount, deep discount and online—are discussed in Chapter 2.

Remember that *advice* is no guarantee of investment performance. A broker may offer suggestions that may not necessarily turn out to be wise. It's up to you to make the final decision on investments and to take responsibility for those decisions.

WORKING WITH MONEY MANAGERS

If you are overwhelmed by information and investment choices and don't want to handle decisions on your own, consider working with a money manager. Generally, for a flat fee (1% to 3% of your portfolio), the manager will handle your investments. This might include making asset allocations and selecting appropriate securities. It also includes transaction costs (commissions, etc.). Often, you'll see this arrangement promoted as a "wrap account."

In general, money managers limit their services to those with $500,000 or more in investments. However, through an online service, Envestnet Asset Management (**www.envestnet.com**, 312-827-2800), you can get the benefit of a money manager even if you have a $50,000 portfolio. This service lets you structure your portfolio after a number of model portfolios.

▶ **Use a money manager.** If you want your account actively traded but don't have the time or ability to do it yourself, then working with a money manager may make sense (provided you have sufficient capital to be of interest to one).

▶ **Don't use a money manager** if you typically buy and hold for the long term, particularly if you invest in mutual funds that already offer professional management. In this case, you probably don't need to use a money manager because the extra cost isn't justified, no matter how much money you have to invest.

INVESTMENT CLUBS

On the theory that two or more heads are better than one, some people approach investing with the help of an investment club. Today, more than 500,000 people participate in these investment clubs across the nation. These clubs allow you to exchange investment ideas, pool your funds to enable bigger investment positions and share expenses.

Getting organized

Most clubs are organized as general partnerships because they are easy and inexpensive to arrange; no lawyer is needed. (Although some are organized as limited liability companies [LLCs], the protection from personal liability afforded by this form of business organization is hardly necessary and much more costly than organizing general partnerships.) The partnership obtains an employer identification number from the IRS that enables it to open bank and brokerage accounts.

The club should designate one person to handle all investment transactions (talk to brokers, sell mutual fund shares, etc.). The club should also put fiscal safeguards in place to prevent a single member from misusing club funds (for example, require the signatures of two members on all club checks).

Each partner makes an initial contribution (typically a few hundred dollars) and agrees to contribute a set amount at regular intervals (for example, $100 per month). At monthly or other regular meetings, the club members agree on how to invest the funds—what to buy and when to sell.

 Strategy: *Make sure the club has a good general partnership agreement. For example, what happens if one member fails to make required contributions? What happens when another member needs to make withdrawals of his funds or wants to leave the club entirely? A model general partnership agreement is available to members of the National Association of Investors Corporation (NAIC)* **(www.better-investing.org)**.

Starting a club

Most clubs today are made up of family members, close friends or coworkers. If you want to start an investment club, you can obtain guidance through the NAIC. You can also find articles about investment clubs at **www.better-investing.org**.

If club members live far apart, consider online activities in lieu of monthly meetings. Investment clubs can use special Web sites geared for this purpose:

▶ Bivio's Investment Clubs **(www.bivio.com)**

▶ BuyAndHold's Investment Clubs **(www.buyandhold.com)**

Tax reporting

As a partner in the club, you report on your individual return your share of club income, deductions, gains, losses, etc., that are passed through to you. This information is provided to you on Schedule K-1 of Form 1065. You're *not* subject to self-employment tax on your share of partnership income from the investment club.

6

Stocks and bonds

❝*Ticker tape ain't spaghetti.*❞ —Fiorello LaGuardia

STOCKS AND BONDS, once considered investments only for the rich, are now the main investment vehicles for many individuals. Today, most US households own common stock directly or through mutual funds. Stocks and bonds are owned in personal investment accounts and in tax-sheltered retirement plans.

The reason for investing in stocks and bonds is to increase your wealth over time. You don't have to be an investment genius to do so. I believe that you only need to follow certain sound investment principles and pay careful attention to your investments to come out ahead.

In this chapter, I provide basic information about equity and debt investments—stocks and bonds—that will be useful to both the novice and the seasoned investor. It also contains strategies for maximizing gains and avoiding losses. Mutual fund investments are discussed in Chapter 7.

STOCKS VS. BONDS

Stocks are ownership interests in corporations represented by shares (stock certificates). There are two types of stocks—common stock and preferred stock:

▶ **Common stock** allows owners to share in the profits (or losses) of the company.

▶ **Preferred stock** pays a fixed dividend and gives preference on distributions if the company is liquidated.

Stock ownership gives you certain rights proportional to your ownership interests. Your rights include a share of the earnings of the company if they are distributed earnings, after the company has paid interest on its bonds and dividends on its preferred stock. You stand to gain or lose with the changing fortunes of the companies in which you hold stock. You make money from your stock investment in two ways—dividend payments made by the company as a distribution of its earnings, and capital gains resulting from a sale of the stock.

Bonds, by comparison, are debt instruments representing an investor's loan to the company. The principal of the loan is scheduled to be repaid at a fixed date (called the "maturity date") or earlier (called the "call date"). The lender is also paid interest for making the loan.

Over any significant time frame, stocks will outperform bonds, giving an investor a greater return on his or her investment. For example, since 1945, common stocks, measured by the S&P 500, have returned an average of 11.9% compared with just 4.7% for investments in Treasury bills.

Comparison of investment performance, 1926–2003

Small-company stock	Large-company stock	Long-term corporate bonds	US Treasury bills	Rate of inflation
12.1%	10.2%	5.9%	3.8%	3.03%

Source: Ibbotson Associates, 2003 Yearbook

 Strategy: Don't get discouraged by the performance of the stock market in recent years—it was down in 2000, 2001 and 2002, the first three consecutive down years since the 1940s and up only modestly in 2003 and 2004. The DJIA closed over 12,000 for the first time in 2006. Remember the historic performance rates, which are bound to repeat themselves at some time.

Assessing risk

Investments in stocks are not without risk. Stock prices can drop as readily as they rise. And the price of a particular company's stock may be down even when the market as a whole is up. But over any rolling 10-year period, stocks as a whole have been in the plus column. This means that if you can ride out the market's periodic swings, you'll probably make money in the long run. For example, even though October 19, 1987, saw the Dow Jones Industrial Average (DJIA) drop by more than 500 points in a single day, it was actually up 5% for the year. And the 1,500-point decline in the DJIA in the days following the September 11, 2001, terrorist attacks was recovered within a month.

Strategy: Be patient and remember that there are no guarantees in investing. Unlike bonds that pay the face amount upon maturity, there are no similar promises with common stocks. It's an old adage on Wall Street that past performance cannot guarantee future results.

In the case of stock in foreign corporations, there is an added risk to the rise and fall in the price of shares—fluctuations in the value of currency. Changes in the value of foreign currency in comparison with the dollar may make your returns greater (or less). When the foreign currency applicable to the foreign stock you own declines in relation to the dollar, the value of your investment also declines, diminishing your gain or increasing your loss.

Bonds are not completely risk free. There is the possibility that the borrower may default and fail to repay principal. Also, the borrower can stop making interest payments. Although not a frequent occurrence, this certainly happens from time to time with corporate and municipal borrowers. *Note:* Treasury bills have never defaulted and never will default because they are backed by the full faith and credit of the federal government. Bonds from US government agencies, although they are not backed by the full faith and credit of the federal government, have never defaulted and generally are considered as safe as Treasuries.

For bonds, there is also the risk that results from changes in interest rates. Bond prices move inversely to interest rates—when interest rates fall, the price of bonds rises, but when interest rates rise, the price of bonds falls. This isn't a problem if you plan to hold your bonds until maturity. But if you need to sell your bonds before their maturity date, you are subject to this market risk.

Other strategies for minimizing risk of loss from stocks or bonds are discussed later in this chapter.

STOCK PRICES

In choosing a stock, how do you know if a stock's price is high or low? The price of a share generally should reflect its value. This can be determined by various yardsticks.

Price/earnings (P/E) ratio

The current market price divided by the earnings per share gives you the stock's P/E ratio. There are no absolute norms for determining whether P/E ratios are high (prices are overvalued) or low (prices are undervalued). P/E ratios tend to run higher in bull markets.

Historically, the market as a whole had an average P/E ratio between 1953 and 1995 of 15. But acceptable P/E ratios change over time, so what was a high ratio a decade ago may be considered average today. And averages for P/E ratios vary according to industry. For example, the financial services industry—banks, brokerages and insurance companies—generally have lower P/E ratios than other industries.

 Strategy: Don't let a P/E ratio alone dictate an investment decision. Today, a high P/E ratio doesn't mean a stock is necessarily a bad buy. Although it's helpful to start a stock's evaluation by comparing its P/E ratio with historical standards and with current industry standards, you need to look beyond this factor in making an ultimate buy or sell decision. A low P/E ratio may simply be an indication of a less-than-average growth stock, while a high P/E ratio may still leave room for plenty of stock growth.

Price/book value

The relationship between a stock's current price and its book value (the corporation's assets less its liabilities) is a measure of value. It's expressed as a ratio that is figured by dividing the stock's price by the book value per share.

> **Example:** If a company's current price is $15 and its book value per share is $10, the price/book value ratio is 1.5. If the industry's average is 2 (two times book value), then this stock would be considered to be well priced, although other factors must also be factored in.

Dividend yield

Stocks that pay dividends give an immediate return on your investment; you don't have to sell your holding to realize a return on your investment. The dividend yield is a way of expressing return on investment. It's figured by dividing the stock's dividend per share by the stock's current price.

> **Example:** If a stock's dividend is $2 per share and its current price is $50, its dividend yield is 4% ($2 ÷ $50). If a 5% dividend yield is the current average for other stocks in the same industry, then the stock would be considered well priced, although other factors must be taken into account.

> **Strategy:** *Dividends can account for about a third of your return over the years you hold the stock, especially if you reinvest the dividends to compound returns. But there's a trade-off. You'll pay current tax on your dividends, typically at ordinary income rates. By comparison, if you opt for growth-oriented stock that doesn't generally pay dividends, you'll be able to report all of your gains over the years as capital gains when you sell the stock.*

Note: Most growth stocks do not pay a dividend. Instead, they reinvest the corporate cash flow back into the company to grow its value.

Dividends today can boost your *after-tax* yield more than ever. *The reason:* The tax rate on dividends is now the same as the rate on long-term capital gains. Instead of being taxed at ordinary income rates up to 35%, you pay just 15% on dividends (or 5% if you are in the 10% or 15% tax bracket). Ordinary dividends on stocks and stock mutual funds payable from a company's earnings and profits qualify for this tax-favored treatment. But certain payments, such as dividends from Real Estate Investment Trusts (REITs), do not qualify (they are taxed at ordinary income rates).

MAKING STOCK PICKS

You don't have to be a philosopher to have an investment philosophy—an approach to investing. You only need to understand different investment approaches and select the one you are most comfortable with. You don't have to limit yourself to one philosophy; you can buy stocks or stock funds that reflect different investment strategies.

Growth

Growth stocks aim to have earnings that grow at a rate greater than that of inflation and the economy. Generally, growth is measured against changes in the S&P 500 or another yardstick. Because growth stocks intend to give investors capital appreciation, they generally don't pay dividends but instead invest their earnings back into the business. But they can be risky, especially emerging growth stocks issued by start-up companies that may or may not succeed.

 Strategy: *Find growth stocks by looking for stocks with higher P/E ratios than those of the overall market.*

Value

Value stocks aim to return a combination of capital appreciation and dividends. Because value stocks combine dividends with appreciation, as opposed to growth stocks that rely on appreciation alone, value stocks generally are less risky than growth stocks. At times, especially in a market correction, growth stocks may have value or be considered value stocks.

 Strategy: *Find value stocks by looking for stocks that are currently out of favor. The prices of these stocks may even be lower than the book value per share.*

Balanced approach

Generally, the stock market tends to be dominated at any one time by either growth stocks or value stocks. Because it's impossible to know when their dominance will shift, it's generally a good idea to adopt both a growth and value philosophy to balance your portfolio.

Other factors

Within these general categories, you can fine-tune your selections. For example, you may prefer to hold mainly blue chips—certain large established companies. Or, you may want to take more risk on newer companies with the hope that you'll reap greater rewards.

 Strategy: *Consider your need for current income in making stock selections. If you require current income, look for companies that pay dividends. The following companies have consistently paid dividends for more than 30 years (including their stock symbols):*

- ▶ **Cincinnati Financial Corp. (CINF)**
- ▶ **Colgate Palmolive (CL)**
- ▶ **Heinz (HNZ)**
- ▶ **Illinois Tool Works, Ltd. (ITW)**
- ▶ **Johnson & Johnson (JNJ)**
- ▶ **Kellogg (K)**
- ▶ **Proctor and Gamble (PG)**
- ▶ **Questar (STR)**
- ▶ **The Coca-Cola Company (KO)**

DOLLAR COST AVERAGING

Conventional conservative wisdom says that individual investors shouldn't be market timers who attempt to find the highs and lows investing in stock or stock mutual funds. Instead, they are encouraged to consider adopting an investment strategy that generally works well over time. One such strategy is called dollar cost averaging. You do it by investing the same amount in a particular equity at the same time each month, quarter or other fixed period.

> **Example:** Instead of investing $1,200 all at once, you decide to invest $100 on the first day of each month. Your $100 will buy a different number of shares each month, depending on the price of the stock at that time.

Advantages of dollar cost averaging

This is a systematic investment approach that eliminates your need to track the market closely. It allows you to buy more shares when the price of the stock or mutual fund share is down, but fewer shares when the price rises.

Disadvantages of dollar cost averaging

You may miss some buying opportunities in a market that is in a rising mode. Also, the transaction costs of buying stock 12 times a year instead of less often (say, once a year) are greater.

> *Strategy: Set up your dollar cost averaging investment to buy on the most advantageous dates. Studies show that the last two trading days of each month and the first three of the next month are the days when prices rise. Thus, consider scheduling dollar cost averaging for the day before this five-day window—the third to last trading day of the month.*

WHEN TO SELL STOCK

Knowing when to sell a stock is as important as knowing when to buy a stock. Unfortunately, many investors overstay their welcome in a particular company, keeping it for reasons that aren't economically sound. For example, it makes sense to hold onto a stock that is down but that you expect to rebound. However, it doesn't make sense to hold it if all indications are that the stock may never recover or at least take a very long time to do so. In fact, the day you buy a stock should be the day you think of when you're going to sell it.

> *Strategy: Don't let emotional or other illogical reasons stand in the way of selling stock that no longer makes sense to own.*

Excuses for not selling

When your head says to sell but your heart says otherwise, ask yourself whether you're making excuses that prevent you from taking smart actions. Consider the following excuses:

▶ **Belief in recovery.** Some investors simply cling to the belief that in time the stock will recover. The stock may eventually recover, but this excuse ignores the time value of money. Even if the stock had been sold at a loss, the proceeds might have been invested in another stock that would have recouped the losses and provided better results.

▶ **Emotional attachments.** Some investors develop emotional ties to their holdings. For example, if they've inherited stock from a parent, they may be very reluctant to sell because it means cutting the attachment to that parent.

▶ **Tax costs.** Investors who have owned shares for a period of time and have a low cost basis may not want to sell even though the price has come down significantly from the stock's highs. Selling would entail a tax cost because of their low basis. But remember that the tax cost is modest—a maximum capital gains rate of 20% applies to stock held more than one year.

▶ **Big gamblers.** Some investors like the thrill of the ride for some stocks. For example, certain dot-com companies had explosive performance when they came on the market. Unfortunately, only some of these companies will be successful in the long run, and investors who fail to bail out when the stock tumbles may ride the price down to zero.

 Strategy: Consider taking your own money off the table once you've turned a profit in highly volatile stocks. For example, if you bought a stock that's doubled in value, sell half your holding so that you've recouped your initial investment. You can let your profit ride.

Minimizing gains (or maximizing losses)

Your gain or loss on the sale of stock is determined by your basis (typically, the amount you paid for the stock, including commissions). If you acquired shares in the same company at different times and at different prices and you sell only a portion of your holdings, you have the ability to control your gain (or loss) by selecting the basis you use for figuring such gain (or loss). There are two methods for determining the basis of stock you've sold under these circumstances (a third method applicable only to mutual fund shares is explained in Chapter 7):

▶ **FIFO (first in, first out) method.** If you don't use the specific identification method below, then you're treated as having sold the first shares you acquired.

Example: If you bought 100 shares in X Corp. at each of $5, $15 and $25, and sold 100 shares, you're treated as having sold the shares with a $5 cost basis. *Result:* Your gain is maximized (or your loss is minimized).

▶ **Specific identification method.** You can designate which shares to sell if you have the records to make the identification. You can direct your broker or mutual fund to sell the shares you want and receive a written confirmation of your instructions.

Example: Same as the example above except you instruct the mutual fund to sell. In this case, you've minimized your gain (or maximized your loss).

Benefiting from losses

Due to sharp market declines in the past few years, you may hold stock that's now worth less than you paid for it. When stock is sold at a loss, you have fewer dollars but also a tax benefit because you can utilize the loss to reduce your taxes.

Capital losses, which may be short term or long term, can be used to offset capital gains (including capital gain distributions from mutual funds). Capital losses can also be used to offset ordinary income—such as salary, dividends and interest—up to $3,000 annually (although Congress is considering an increase in this dollar limit). If capital losses exceed capital gains and the amount allowed to offset ordinary income, the excess may be carried forward indefinitely and used to offset capital gains in the future.

Strategy: *Don't get trapped by the wash-sale rule that prevents you from taking losses if you reacquire substantially identical securities within 30 days before or after the date of sale. Either wait out the wash-sale period or acquire securities that aren't substantially identical.*

DIVIDEND REINVESTMENT PLANS (DRIPS)

Dividend reinvestment plans, called DRIPs, provide for automatic dividend reinvestment. Depending on the dollars involved, this can result in the purchase of fractional shares. DRIPs afford a couple of benefits:

▶ **Compounding.** By adding shares through investment to your holding of a stock, you'll receive dividends on those reinvestments, producing compounding of your returns.

▶ **Transaction cost savings.** The fees charged for reinvestment generally are nominal, saving you on broker commissions. Of course, it's possible today to buy shares at very low commissions (for example, $8 per share through certain online brokers), so this benefit of DRIPs has been discounted, and DRIPs have fallen out of favor with some investors.

Finding DRIPs

Today, about 1,100 companies offer DRIPs. If the company has been paying a regular dividend, it probably has a DRIP. You can find out about DRIPs through:

▶ *DRIP Investor Newsletter* (**www.dripinvestor.com**) provides information on more than 1,000 DRIPs and their Web sites.

▶ *The Money Paper* (**www.moneypaper.com**) tracks about 1,300 DRIPs.

Starting DRIPs

You must sign up for DRIPs; enrollment isn't automatic. If you own these stocks through a brokerage account, notify your broker that you wish to have your dividends reinvested. *Caution:* If you transfer your brokerage account to a different firm, your fractional shares typically will be liquidated, resulting in a transfer of your whole shares plus cash for the liquidation of your fractional shares.

Traps in DRIPs

Dividends reinvested in DRIPs are still taxable even though they are not cash. This means you'll need to use other cash to pay the tax on these dividends.

Also, since reinvestment becomes automatic, you may fail to keep track of what you've reinvested. This can cause you to pay a double tax—once when you receive the dividend, and again when you sell the shares and fail to include these reinvestments in your basis for determining gain or loss.

 Strategy: *Keep careful records of DRIPs. Most mutual funds keep records of your reinvestments for you. Include the cost for shares acquired through DRIPs in your stock basis if you make an annual entry in your records. Simply add to your stock basis records the amount of the dividends reported for the year.*

DIRECT INVESTMENT PLANS (DIPS)

Instead of going through a broker who acts as a middleman for the transaction, you can make certain investments directly. For example, you can purchase Treasury securities directly from the federal government through the Federal Reserve. You can purchase mutual fund shares directly from the fund family, but the transaction costs are the same as if you bought them through a full-service broker or any other broker.

You can even purchase certain stock directly from the company issuing it. More than 600 companies now have direct stock purchase plans that allow you to buy a small number of shares directly from the company with little or no sales charges. Examples:

- ▶ Home Depot **(www.homedepot.com)**.
- ▶ McDonalds **(www.mcdonalds.com/corp/invest.html)**.
- ▶ The Walt Disney Company **(http://disney.go.com)**; click on the link for investor relations and you'll find out how to invest in Disney.

For a list of companies offering direct stock purchase plans, contact the Direct Purchase Plan Clearinghouse at **www.enrolldirect.com**, 800-774-4117.

Advantages of direct stock purchase plans: Low or no transaction costs, although there is generally an initial setup fee (for example, $10).

Another advantage for small investors is the modest minimum investment requirements, which can be as small as $100. This can enable you to purchase odd lots and even fractional shares through direct stock purchase plans.

Disadvantage of direct stock purchase plans: Record-keeping difficulties because direct purchases result in separate statements instead of the consolidated statement provided by brokers.

TRADING STRATEGIES

Because you probably don't want to track your investments on a minute-by-minute basis, you can employ certain trading strategies to protect your gains and minimize possible losses.

Short selling

Generally, when you buy a stock, you're hoping that its price will rise. But when you sell short, you're looking for the opposite result. Profit on short selling results when the price of a stock goes down.

A short sale occurs when you sell shares you don't own. You "borrow" the shares from your broker and hope that the price of the shares will drop so you can buy at a low price to redeliver the borrowed shares back to the broker.

Caution: The risk involved in short selling is great. With a typical stock purchase, the most you can lose is the amount of your investment. But with short selling, your potential loss is unlimited.

 Strategy: *Don't engage in short selling unless you fully understand the risk and are willing to take it. You need sufficient resources to withstand a rise in the stock's price or risk being squeezed out and losing your money. Short selling usually isn't shrewd for long-term investors.*

Selling short against the box

An investor can make a particular type of short sale to lock in gain already realized in a year but defer recognition of that gain to the next year.

Example: You own 100 shares of X Corp. that you want to sell in 2003, but would prefer to recognize the gain in 2004. Hold these shares while selling short the same number of shares you borrow from a broker. In 2004, you can close out your short sale by replacing the shares borrowed from the broker with your original shares and you can recognize the gain at that time.

Caution: Tax law requires you to have some risk exposure to achieve the desired tax deferral. If you don't, then the short sale is treated as a constructive sale of the long-term holding in the year you sold short. But the constructive sale doesn't apply if the short sale against the box is closed within 30 days after the close of the year, and for 60 days after closing the transaction the investor holds the appreciated position without any protection against risk of loss. Consult with a tax adviser before using this strategy to lock in your gain.

Puts and calls (options)

You can leverage a position in a stock by using puts and calls—options to buy or sell stock. Options can also be used in tandem with stock you already own. Options are standardized contracts representing 100 shares of a particular stock.

Caution: Option trading is a sophisticated trading strategy that you should not undertake without a complete understanding of how it works.

Stop orders

These are orders to sell your stock at a certain point so that you don't lose your entire investment. There are two types of stop orders:

▶ **Stop order.** You set a price and when the stock price reaches your target, your sell order is converted to a market order. This means you'll be sold out at the next market trading price.

Example: You bought stock at $50 and put in a stop order for $25. If the stock price reaches $25, you are deemed to have made a market order at that time. If the next trade of the stock is $24 or $25, that's the price at which you'll be sold out.

▶ **Stop limit order.** Like an ordinary stop order, you set a target price. But when that price is reached, instead of being converted to a market order, your "limit"—the price you specify—is applied.

Example: You bought stock at $50 and put in a stop limit order for $25. Your stock can only be sold when the stock price reaches $25. The stop limit order does not convert to a market order.

Downside: A temporary swing in price can trigger your sell order. While the stock's closing price may be well above your targeted sell price, you will have been automatically sold out earlier in the day. You can, of course, buy back your stock to retain your position, but you will incur commissions for your efforts. And, if you are subject to the wash-sale rules, you won't be able to recognize your loss. *Note:* You can't use a stop limit order for shares trading on the American Exchange. You may not be able to use a stop limit order for online trades.

USING STOCK SALES TO RETURN MORE AFTER-TAX INCOME

In the past, investors who wanted income shunned stocks in favor of bonds to obtain the income stream from bond interest. Today, it's possible to use stock to generate steady income and at more favorable tax rates. The income tax laws currently favor long-term capital gains over ordinary income. Gain resulting from stock held more than one year is taxed at no more than 15%, while interest on a bond is taxed at up to 35% in 2005.

 Strategy: Sell stock to generate a specific income target. For example, assume you need $2,500 a month in after-tax income from your investments. If you are in the 28% bracket, you would need $43,500 in stocks that pay 8% in dividends. By contrast, you would have to sell only $3,100 in stock held long term (assuming a zero basis) to give you the same after-tax income. (The higher your basis in the stock, the less you would have to sell to yield the same after-tax proceeds.) The value of the stock would have to appreciate only by about 6% annually to maintain your $45,000 in capital.

ONLINE TRADING

Investors are using online brokers increasingly to trade stocks and other securities. The attractions of online trading are greatly reduced transaction costs—as low as $4.95 per trade—and making transactions is quick and easy. You can set up online trading accounts through a number of brokerage firms (see page 17).

▶ Banc of America Investment Services (**www.baisi direct.com**)

▶ Charles Schwab (**www.schwab.com**)

▶ E*Trade (**www.etrade.com**)

▶ Fidelity (**www.fidelity.com**)

▶ Merrill Lynch (**www.ml.com**)

Dangers of online trading

Although online trading offers convenience and cost savings, these very features can prove to be an investor's undoing. They make it too easy to trade frequently rather than taking a long-term investment approach.

Other problems of online trading include:

▶ **Trades that are unfilled.** If there's heavy traffic at a site or if your computer connection is slow, your order may not be acted upon.

▶ **Duplicate trades.** If you think your trade hasn't been processed, you might place a second one, only to find that you've doubled your trade—and your costs.

▶ **Cancellations may not be respected.** If you cancel an order online, make sure you follow up to see that the transaction has not been executed.

▶ **Trades placed online can't be canceled offline.**

Strategy: Review your monthly statement carefully to confirm all online transactions. Check the number of shares and the prices of the transactions against your confirmation slips.

▶ **Frozen accounts.** If you sell stock before you've paid for it (an illegal practice called free-riding), your account can be frozen for 90 days. This means that you can trade during the freeze period but you'll have to fully pay for any purchase prior to the date the trade is made.

 Strategy: Use limit orders to purchase stock at your targeted price and to protect against losses. But make sure you understand how limit orders operate. For example, if you want to buy a stock at $10 that is currently trading at $12, you put in a limit order at $10. You may never buy the stock, because the stock price may pass your limit before it can be filled. About 40% of limit orders are never filled.

Do your research

If you're trading online, make sure to stay on top of developments affecting your holdings. Take advantage of free research from the following Web site:

▶ **www.etrade.com**

DAY TRADING

When the stock market flourished, many individuals thought that day trading—a practice of rapidly buying and selling stock online—was a quick road to riches. Unfortunately, many of these people failed to appreciate fully the perils of day trading. With quick in-and-out moves in stock positions, there is a substantial risk of loss. This is especially true as the market declines.

Caution: Those who day trade should understand that gains—which are short-term capital gains—are taxed at the same rates as ordinary income. And the time—and investment risk—necessary to be successful in day trading may not be justified by the returns.

Although a few professionals make their living by day trading, for many individuals, this practice becomes a form of gambling, not investing. Those who have become addicted to day trading may need help from Gamblers Anonymous (**www.gamblersanonymous.org**, 213-386-8789).

BONDS

Bonds are debt instruments in which the investor acts as lender to the company or other borrower. As a bondholder, you make money from your investment as follows:

▶ **Interest.** You collect interest on the money you've loaned to the borrower—corporation, government body or other borrower. Generally, interest is paid semiannually at fixed dates. However, there are zero coupon bonds, including US government savings bonds that accrue interest over time but don't pay the interest until the bonds mature. And, if held in taxable accounts, accrued interest is taxable currently even though no cash is paid out.

▶ **Principal.** At the bond's maturity date, you expect to recoup the face amount. This may be more or less than what you paid for the bond. If you bought the bond at a discount (less than the face amount), you'll receive more than you paid for it. Conversely, if you bought the bond at a premium, you'll receive less than you paid for it. The gain or loss is taxable.

▶ **Gain.** If you sell the bond before maturity for more than you paid for it, you may have a capital gain. This gain is taxable, even if the bond itself is a tax-free municipal bond, as only the interest on the bond is tax free.

Bonds are considered more conservative investments than stocks because there is less risk. Check on a bond's potential risk by looking at its rating from a bond rating service, such as Moody's Investor Service, Standard and Poor's and Filch Investor Services.

The following chart illustrates a couple of these services' ratings systems, from the least risky to the most. Although bonds are considered less risky than stocks, even bonds aren't risk free:

▶ **Default.** The borrower can default. You can lose your principal and interest if the borrower goes into bankruptcy. This can even happen (although it is rare) when the borrower is a municipality or state agency.

 Strategy: *Buy bonds backed by insurance for added security. Major insurers include MBIA, AMBAC, FGIC and TFSA. Insured bonds are triple-A rated.*

Ratings from Moody's and Standard & Poor's

Meaning of the rating	Moody's	Standard & Poor's
Top rated	Aaa	AAA
	Aa1	AA+
	Aa2	AA
	Aa3	AA–
	A1	A+
	A2	A
	A3	A–
	Baa1	BBB+
	Baa2	BBB
	Baa3	BBB–
Not investment grade ("junk" bond)	Ba1	BB+
	Ba2	BB
	Ba3	BB–
	B1	B+
	B2	B
	B3	B–
	Caa1	CCC+
	Caa2	CCC
	Caa3	CCC–
	Ca	–
May be in default	C	–
In default	-	D

Strategy: *For absolute safety, buy US government bonds with no risk of default. These are backed by the full faith and credit of the federal government, so there can never be any default. Bonds issued by most federal agencies—for example, Fannie Maes and Freddie Macs—are not backed by the government's full faith and credit but are still considered completely safe. There's never been a default in any agency bond.*

▶ **Market risk.** If you need to sell a bond before maturity, you are subject to market fluctuations in the price of the bond. When interest rates rise, the value of your bond typically drops (and vice versa).

▶ **Callability.** Bonds, other than US Treasury bonds, can usually be called before maturity. This means that the issuer can redeem the bonds early if it chooses to. The downside or "risk" from this feature is that as an investor you can't lock into a high rate of interest. If rates come down, the issuer may call the bond. Bonds often note a "call date"—one year, five years or 10 years—after the date of issuance when the issuer may redeem the bonds at a specified price. Once the call date has passed, the issuer can call the bond just about any time thereafter. But most bonds have 10-year call protection—they can't be called during this period. And some corporate bonds are not callable.

Buying and selling bonds

Most bonds aren't traded on an exchange. Instead, brokers and other sellers create the bond market, charging essentially what the market will bear (within statutory limits) and burying commissions in the price of the bonds. In effect, bonds are sold at a "net" price—the commissions are already factored in.

Bonds are usually sold in $5,000 increments (that is, $5,000 equals one bond).

Most brokers typically build their commission into the cost of the bond so you don't really know how much you're paying for the bond and how much of the price represents commission. E*Trade, which trades corporate and municipal bonds, charges a flat $25 per bond fee **(www.etrade.com)**. You can also buy municipal bonds online (minimum transaction is $25,000) and have your bonds delivered to a brokerage account of your choice.

Brokerage firms list a bond value on your monthly statement, but since bonds aren't traded on an exchange in the way that stocks are traded, these values may or may not be accurate. You can, however, check on value at CNN Money, a Web site from the editors of CNN and *Money* magazine **(http://money.cnn.com/markets/bondcenter)**.

For a one-stop bond shop—for information or to trade any type of bond—click on BondsOnLine at **www.bondsonline.com**.

Yield

What you earn on a bond depends on its purchase price and interest rate. But yield can vary, depending upon the perspective you use to measure it.

▶ **Yield to call.** If the bond has a call date, yield is figured as if the call will be exercised, so earnings are figured based on interest to that date, using the call price.

▶ **Yield to maturity.** This yield assumes that the bond, even if callable, won't be called. It measures yield until maturity, using the bond's interest and the price you paid for the bond to determine your gain or loss at maturity.

Laddering maturities

Reduce your risk that the price of bonds will fall as interest rates rise by laddering your bond holdings, that is, buying bonds with staggered maturities. By holding short-term, mid-term and long-term bonds, you'll always have some bond coming due so you can reinvest at current market rates.

Example: If you have $50,000 to invest, ladder the maturities by investing $10,000 each in bonds that will mature in one year, three years, five years, eight years and 10 years. If the rates rise, the maturing bonds can be reinvested at the new higher rates. But if the rates fall, reinvest at the new lower rates.

Another advantage of laddering can be the staggered receipt of interest. It's possible to devise a portfolio that will pay you some interest each month.

 Strategy: If you can't afford to invest to ladder maturities, invest through bond mutual funds that offer different maturities. The funds typically pay interest to investors monthly, unless they opt to reinvest.

Yield curves and interest rates

The longer the period until the bond's maturity, the higher the interest rate you'll receive. But there may be a point at which interest does not increase appreciably by lengthening the period until maturity. This is called a yield curve. Historically, 10 to 12 years may be the optimum maturity period for obtaining the highest interest rate possible. A longer maturity period will produce only a slightly higher interest rate.

 Strategy: Look at the yield curve and select a bond with a maturity period that's just long enough to justify the highest interest rate available.

For more information about bonds, visit **www.bondsonline.com**.

TREASURIES

US government instruments, such as Treasury bonds, notes and T-bills, are the safest investments available. *Reason:* They're backed by the full faith and credit of the federal government. What's the difference among these government instruments?

▶ **Treasury bonds.** Ten-year to 30-year bonds, with minimum investments in $1,000 increments. Interest is paid semiannually. *Note:* Issuance of new 30-year bonds is possibly being phased out.

▶ **Treasury notes.** Two-year to less than 10-year notes, with minimum investments of $1,000 to $5,000. Interest is paid semiannually. *Note:* These are going to be phased out as well.

▶ **T-bills.** Three-month and six-month, with a minimum investment of $10,000, plus $1,000 multiples in excess of the minimum. They are purchased at a discount and redeemed at face value (for example, $9,500 cost, redeemable at $10,000 upon maturity).

Strips

Brokerage firms may strip the interest coupons from the bonds, selling the instruments as zero coupon bonds. Firms have their own proprietary names for the instruments (e.g., Merrill Lynch has TIGRs; there are also CATS, COUGARS and LIONS). Although no interest is paid annually—you buy the stripped instruments at a discount and receive the face amount at maturity—you're still subject to tax on the phantom interest. This interest is reported to you annually as original issue discount on Form 1099-OID.

The Treasury also has its own strips, which are sold through banks and brokerage firms in denominations of $1,000.

Treasury inflation-indexed securities (TIIS or TIPS)

Issued in five-year, 10-year and 30-year maturities, these relatively new Treasury bonds have a fixed rate of interest and adjust the principal of the bond for inflation protection. Some experts suggest that TIPS are really a separate asset class—not an equity and not a bond—because they react uniquely to market forces. While a bond's price changes inversely to interest rates (when rates rise, the price of bonds falls), this isn't so with TIPS. They tend to hold their value when rates rise because it means that they'll be adjusted for inflation as well as benefit from the higher rates.

Both the interest and the inflation adjustment to principal are currently taxable for federal income tax purposes.

 Strategy: Own TIPS in tax-deferred accounts (such as IRAs). Investors in TIPS must report both the interest and adjustment to principal as income each year (even though the principal adjustment is merely accrued and won't be payable until maturity).

 Strategy: Buy TIPS through a handful of mutual funds if you want to own TIPS outside of tax-deferred accounts. The advantage to mutual funds is that the funds actually distribute amounts related to the inflation-adjustment to principal, thereby offsetting what must be included in income. Examples:

▶ **American Century Inflation Adjusted Treasury Fund** (**www.americancentury.com**, 800-826-8323)
▶ **Pimco Real Return** (**www.pimco.com**, 800-426-0107)
▶ **Vanguard Inflation-Protected Securities** (**www.vanguard.com**, 800-662-7447)

Features

Interest on Treasuries is subject to federal income tax but is exempt from all state and local income tax.

Treasuries offer one key feature that is unique for bonds: They can't be called. This means you're guaranteed to receive the interest until the bonds' maturity.

Comparing Treasuries with CDs

You can buy Treasury instruments that offer terms comparable to bank CDs. Rates may be similar although not necessarily identical. But there are important differences to consider:

Treasuries vs. CDs

Aspect	Treasuries	CDs
Safety	Fully protected (no limits)	FDIC insured up to $100,000
Taxes on interest	Free from state income taxes	Subject to state income taxes
Early disposition before maturity	Market risk	Bank penalties

 Strategy: *Use T-bills with maturities under one year for tax deferral. If you buy six-month T-bills after June 30, your interest isn't taxable until the following year.*

Buying Treasuries

When you buy Treasuries, you don't receive a bond certificate for your purchase. Instead, purchases are noted by book entry (that is, you get a receipt or confirmation statement for your purchase). You have several options on where to buy Treasuries:

▶ **Banks.** You can buy T-bills from commercial banks. Typically, there's a flat charge for the transaction (*Range:* $55 to $75).

▶ **Brokerage firms.** You can buy Treasury instruments from brokerage firms. Typically, there's a flat charge for the transaction (*Range:* $55 to $75), no matter how many bonds you buy.

▶ **US Treasury Department.** You can buy T-bills directly from the US Treasury Department. Complete an application form by mail to register for online buying (call 800-722-2678). Then place your order online (**www.treasurydirect.gov**). Generally, you place a noncompetitive tender to buy the bond at the going rate. But you can make a competitive tender offer to specify what you're willing to pay for the bond; you may or may not get it for this price. The advantage of direct purchases is there are no fees for the transaction.

 Strategy: *Direct that interest (and principal upon maturity) be deposited into your bank account if you buy directly from the government.*

Selling Treasuries

Regardless of where you purchased your Treasuries, you can sell them through banks or brokerage firms. However, you can't sell them through the government even if you bought them directly from the government. What you receive on the sale depends on the direction interest rates are going. If rates are higher than when you purchased the bonds, you'll receive less than you might expect. But if rates are lower than when you purchased the bonds, you'll receive more.

When you sell before maturity, you may have two types of income:

▶ **Interest income** for the interest earned up to the date of sale.

▶ **Capital gain** (i.e., the amount in excess of interest). If, however, you suffered a loss on the sale, your entire loss is a capital loss, and there's no interest income to report.

AGENCY BONDS

The US Treasury isn't the only arm of the federal government that issues bonds. Several federal agencies also sell bonds. Examples:

▶ **Federal Home Loan Mortgage Corporation** (Freddie Macs)

▶ **Federal National Mortgage Association** (Fannie Maes)

▶ **Government National Mortgage Association** (Ginnie Maes)

These bonds represent pools of government-backed mortgages and are sold in denominations of $25,000 but can be purchased in increments of as little as $1,000. However, there are a number of mutual funds investing in particular types of agency bonds. For example, Fidelity, Vanguard, T. Rowe Price and American Century each have Ginnie Mae funds.

Don't confuse agency bonds with Treasuries. There are important differences. For example, callable agency bonds typically pay about 1% to 1.5% or more than Treasuries of comparable maturities. Other differences are shown in the following chart:

Comparison of agency bonds to Treasuries

Feature	Agency bonds	Treasuries
Callable before maturity	Sometimes	No
Backed by full faith and credit of US government	No* (although they are considered completely safe)	Yes
Payments	Interest only	Interest only

*Ginnie Maes are an exception to the general rule and are backed by the full faith and credit of the US government.

Keep in mind that as a fixed-income investment, agency bonds aren't all that fixed. Because they are mortgage-based, when interest rates fall, homeowners tend to refinance, paying off existing mortgages that, in turn, result in early repayment on these bonds. For example, a 15-year agency bond may, in fact, have a life of less than half that period.

COLLATERALIZED MORTGAGE OBLIGATIONS (CMOS)

A collateralized mortgage obligation is a fixed-income security that is backed by a pool of mortgage-backed securities or mortgage loans (including mortgages backed by certain federal agencies). CMOs have a stated maturity date, which may run 25 or 30 years, but in actuality, CMOs mature on an average life basis—the time it takes for mortgages within the pool to be paid off.

CMOs may be suitable investments for those seeking a steady flow of income, a high degree of safety (because of the US agencies that back the underlying mortgages), a higher rate of return than on other types of fixed-income investments and the opportunity to sell before maturity (CMOs are actively traded). Minimum investments can be as low as $1,000.

 Strategy: *If you live off your interest, don't spend all of the money you receive from your investment in CMOs. Each payment can include not only interest but also a return of principal. Segregate the principal amounts for reinvestment so you don't deplete your capital.*

TAX-FREE BONDS

State and local governments and agencies sell bonds to the public to raise money for public works and governmental needs. Interest on these bonds—whether owned individually or through a bond mutual fund—is free from federal income tax. State and local government bonds are referred to as municipal or muni bonds.

Whether interest is free from state and local income tax varies. Most states with income tax exempt the interest on their own bonds. For example, if you reside in New York and own NYS bonds, the interest is free from both federal and state income taxes. But the rules differ from state to state, as the chart shows:

State income tax on municipal bonds

Tax treatment	States
No state income tax	Alaska, Florida, Nevada, South Dakota, Texas, Washington and Wyoming
Interest exempt from state income tax if the bond is issued by the state (or Puerto Rico, US Virgin Islands and American Samoa)	Alabama, Arizona, Arkansas, California, Colorado, Connecticut, Delaware, Georgia, Hawaii, Idaho, Kentucky, Louisiana, Maine, Maryland, Massachusetts, Michigan, Minnesota, Mississippi, Missouri, Montana, Nebraska, New Hampshire, New Jersey, New Mexico, New York, North Carolina, Ohio, Oregon, Pennsylvania, Rhode Island, South Carolina, Tennessee, Vermont, Virginia and West Virginia
Interest is tax free (even if issued by another state)	District of Columbia, Indiana, North Dakota (if long form not used) and Utah
Interest is fully taxable for state income tax purposes regardless of the state of issuance	Colorado, Illinois, Iowa, Kansas, Oklahoma and Wisconsin

Comparing the after-tax yield

If you want to determine which bond offers the more attractive interest rate, then you must compare the after-tax yields. In the case of a tax-free bond vs. a taxable corporate or Treasury bond, be sure to do the evaluation.

You can figure the yield of a municipal bond to compare with a taxable instrument using the following formula:

Interest rate on tax-exempt bond

1 minus your tax bracket

Example: In 2007, someone in the 33% tax bracket is considering the purchase of a municipal bond paying 4.5% interest. He would have to earn about 6.7% on a taxable instrument to receive the same after-tax income (4.5% ÷ [1 − 33%]).

You can compare the after-tax yield of a taxable bond with a muni at **www.investinginbonds.com.** Or use the following chart to compare the after-tax yield of a taxable bond with a muni bond, assuming only a federal income tax bracket.

Comparison of after-tax yield for 2007

Your tax bracket*	Tax-exempt interest rate							
	2.5%	**3%**	**3.5%**	**4%**	**4.5%**	**5%**	**5.5%**	**6%**
25%	3.3%	4.0%	4.7%	5.3%	6.0%	6.7%	7.3%	8.0%
28%	3.5%	4.2%	4.9%	5.6%	6.3%	6.9%	7.6%	8.3%
33%	3.7%	4.5%	5.2%	6.0%	6.7%	7.5%	8.2%	9.0%
35%	3.8%	4.6%	5.4%	6.2%	6.9%	7.7%	8.5%	9.2%

*It usually isn't advisable to buy tax-free bonds for those in the 10% or 15% tax bracket or for those whose income is below the tax-filing threshold.

Strategy: *Be sure to factor in state income tax treatment in your decisions. For example, if you live in New York City and buy a NYS instrument, the interest is triple tax free (free from federal, state and city income tax).*

SAVINGS BONDS

Originally sold by the federal government to raise money for the war effort (initially, the First World War and again for World War II), savings bonds have become a permanent debt instrument of the federal government. EE and I bonds offer some solid investment advantages. They are available in small denominations, so even people of modest income can afford to buy them. They are completely safe. As instruments of the federal government, they are backed by the full faith and credit of the US.

Strategy: *Buy savings bonds only if you plan to hold them long term. They can't be redeemed within six months of the date of purchase. And there's a three-month interest penalty for redemption of EE and I bonds within five years of purchase.*

Note: Eventually, the Treasury hopes to discontinue the issuance of paper savings bonds and will only sell them in electronic form.

EE bonds

These are discount bonds sold at half their face value (for example, a $100 bond costs $50). Over time, the incremental increase in the value of the bond represents interest. EE bonds purchased May 2005 and later pay a fixed rate. EE bonds purchased earlier pay current market rates for 30 years.

I bonds

These are sold in the same denominations as EE bonds but at face value (for example, a $100 bond costs $100).

EE vs. I bonds

EE bonds are similar to I bonds in several respects. They both offer tax deferral and the opportunity for tax-free interest if the bonds are used for higher education purposes. But there are also important differences in the bonds:

▶ **The interest rate payable on the I bonds** differs from the rate on the EE bonds. For example, in the period from November 1, 2006, through April 30, 2007, the composite interest rate on I bonds was 4.52% compared with 3.60% on EE bonds.

Interest

The rate of interest on EE bonds depends on when the bonds were issued. Bonds bought on or after May 1, 1997, earn interest of 90% of the five-year Treasury security yield for the prior six months.

Fixed rates in I bonds

Date of issuance	Fixed rates (annual rates compounded semiannually)
September 1, 1998 (first issue of I bonds)	3.4%
November 1, 1998	3.3%
May 1, 1999	3.3%
November 1, 1999	3.4%
May 1, 2000	3.6%
November 1, 2000	3.4%
May 1, 2001	3.0%
November 1, 2001	2.0%
May 1, 2002	2.0%
November 1, 2002	1.6%
May 1, 2003	1.1%
November 1, 2003	1.1%
May 1, 2004	1.0%
November 1, 2004	1.0%
May 1, 2005	1.2%
November 1, 2005	1.0%
May 1, 2006	1.4%
November 1, 2006	1.4%

Inflation-adjusted rates

Date of rate change	Inflation-adjusted rates
September 1, 1998	0.62%
November 1, 1998	0.86%
May 1, 1999	0.86%
November 1, 1999	1.76%
May 1, 2000	1.91%
November 1, 2000	1.52%
May 1, 2001	1.44%
November 1, 2001	1.19%
May 1, 2002	0.28%
November 1, 2002	1.23%
May 1, 2003	1.77%
November 1, 2003	0.54%
May 1, 2004	1.19%
November 1, 2004	1.33%
May 1, 2005	1.79%
November 1, 2005	2.85%
May 1, 2006	0.50%
November 1, 2006	1.55%

The rate of interest on I bonds is actually composed of two separate rates: A fixed rate and a rate that adjusts every six months on November 1 and May 1. The fixed rate portion remains constant for bonds issued when that rate was effective. The adjustable rate changes every six months regardless of when the bond was purchased.

Example: You bought a bond on November 1, 2006. Your total interest rate through May 1, 2007, is 4.52% (based on the assumption that rates remain constant for the year). This is a composite rate figured using the following formula:

Composite rate = 2 x [fixed rate ÷ 2 + inflation rate + (inflation rate x fixed rate ÷ 2)] x 100

▶ **Too complicated?** You can check on the interest that has already accrued on bonds you own using a special calculator at **www.treasurydirect.gov/indiv/indiv. htm**, then click on "Tools."

Maturities

EE bonds and I bonds have 30-year final maturity dates. This means that when the bonds reach their final maturity, they cease to pay interest. All E bonds have reached their final maturity.

Strategy: Don't forget to cash in bonds that have matured. More than $12.5 billion in bonds outstanding in 2005 had ceased to accrue interest because the bonds have reached their final maturity date. To determine whether your bonds have stopped earning interest, use Treasury Hunt at **www.treasurydirect.gov/indiv/tools/tools_trea suryhunt.htm**.

Buying bonds

EE bonds are sold in denominations of $50 to $10,000 and cost one-half of this amount. I bonds are sold at face value in denominations of $50, $75, $100, $200, $500, $1,000, $5,000 and $10,000. The annual limit on EE bond purchases is $15,000 (which would buy $30,000 of bonds). For I bonds, the limit is $30,000.

You can buy bonds directly from the government at **www.savingsbonds.gov**, 800-722-2678; click on "Savings Bonds Direct." The limit for online purchases is $1,000 per transaction. Purchases can be charged to American Express, MasterCard, Visa or Discover.

Redeeming bonds

After the first six months of bond ownership, you can redeem bonds at any bank that sells them; you don't have to redeem them at the bank where you bought them. *Caution:* The federal government generates an information-type return informing you of the accrued interest on the redeemed bond, which presumably the IRS uses to match against the interest reported on your tax return.

 Strategy: Watch the timing of bond redemptions to maximize your interest. Because bonds are issued on different dates, they may have different accrual dates for interest. Redemption before the accrual date can cost you interest.

Example: You own an EE bond purchased in January 1997. EE bonds purchased between May 1995 and April 1997 accrue interest six months from the month of issue and each six months thereafter. So interest on your bond would have first accrued in July 1997, then in January 1998, etc. If you cash in your bond in June 2007, you lose interest from January 2007 through June 2007.

Record keeping for bonds

Keep track of your bonds, noting each bond's serial number and issue date. This information is essential for replacing your bonds if they are lost, stolen or destroyed. See page 94 for a handy record keeper for your savings bonds.

You can also keep track of your holdings and the interest accruing on them using a savings bond wizard that can be downloaded from the government's savings bond Web site **(www.treasurydirect.gov/indiv/tools/tools_sav ingsbondwizard.htm)**.

Tax deferral

You do not have to pay tax on interest each year. Instead, you can opt to defer the reporting of interest until the earlier of the bond's redemption (sale) or maturity. You don't have to take any affirmative action to defer the interest. You simply don't report it.

 Strategy: Report interest annually rather than defer it if such a choice produces tax-free income. For example, if you elect to report the interest annually, file a tax return showing the interest even if a return is not otherwise required. For example, you buy $2,500 worth of EE bonds for your child who has no other income. By electing to report the interest annually, your child will avoid tax on the interest. This tax-free treatment continues until the child's overall income reaches taxable amounts. However, if the election was not made and the child cashed in the bonds in adulthood, the accrued interest could be taxable at rates up to 35% or more (depending on the year they're redeemed).

Tax-free interest

If you redeem savings bonds to pay qualified higher education costs, the interest may be fully or partially tax free. This exclusion applies to interest on Series EE bonds purchased after 1989 and Series I bonds. *Caution:* Income limits, which are adjusted annually for inflation, apply, so high-income taxpayers may not be eligible for the exclusion. Also, only bonds purchased by an individual age 24 or older who uses the proceeds for higher education costs for himself or herself, his spouse or dependents is eligible for this exclusion.

JUNK BONDS

Junk bonds aren't necessarily that junky. High-yield corporate bonds are called junk bonds because their investment rating is below the investment grade that fiduciaries are permitted to own. Junk bonds are rated BB+ or lower by Standard & Poor's or Ba1 or lower by Moody's. Such bonds account for more than 20% of all outstanding corporate debt today.

Junk bonds illustrate the risk-vs.-reward concept of investing. Because they are considered risky, they must offer a higher interest rate to attract investors. And they sell at deep discounts from their face amount, allowing your investment dollars to purchase more bonds.

Of course, junk bonds aren't all the same. There's good junk and bad junk. You should believe that the company will stay in business and be able to make good on its obligation to pay interest as well as pay back its debts. Historically, junk bonds have had just a 1% to 2% default rate, so most do repay investors. But there have been periods when default rates have approached 8%.

Owning some junk bonds (or a junk bond fund) may have a place in your investment portfolio. If you're willing and able to take the risk, you can receive a greater return on your investment.

Junk bonds can also be owned through mutual funds (explained in Chapter 7).

CONVERTIBLE BONDS

Investors can achieve the best of both worlds—income from bonds with the appreciation potential of stocks—through convertible bonds. Convertible bonds give holders the option of changing from bondholder to shareholder. They can convert the bond to a specified number of common shares.

Advantages: As debt instruments, they have a fixed rate of interest and a fixed maturity date. However, if the stock price of the company rises, bondholders can take advantage of the upswing by converting the bond to shares of common stock.

Disadvantages: As a debt instrument, they are subordinated to other debt; if there's a company default, convertible bondholders are paid off after certain other creditors. And there's a cost for the conversion feature. You're accepting a lower interest rate than a comparable bond that isn't convertible.

INVESTING IN A WORLD ECONOMY

The global economy is a factor to consider in making investments. US stock prices and interest rates on bonds are affected by such foreign factors as the performance of the euro, the Japanese economy and the potential of the China market.

Should you invest in international companies? Many investment advisers suggest that international stocks should play a role in an investor's portfolio; the portion of that role—5%, 10% or otherwise—depends on the adviser. If you decide to include some international flavor in your holdings, consider these alternatives:

▶ **Buy US companies with substantial foreign sales.** Worldwide sales account for a significant portion of revenue at companies such as Coca Cola, McDonalds and John Deere.

▶ **Buy foreign stocks.** You can acquire foreign stocks by buying America Depository Receipts (ADRs) that trade on US exchanges like US companies. ADRs represent custodial ownership of shares that actually trade on foreign exchanges and are held by US custodians. ADRs have lower commissions than you would pay for buying the actual stock on foreign exchanges.

▶ **Buy shares in mutual funds that invest in international companies.** Mutual fund investments are discussed in Chapter 7.

When you invest in foreign companies, you face a double risk: A stock price risk (that the price of the stock will fall) and a currency risk (that the value of the foreign currency will drop relative to the dollar).

UNDERSTANDING NEW OR CHANGING SECTORS

The pace of new technology advances is relentless. New technology developments usually generate investor interest, publicity, and frequently, a boom in new stock issues by these companies. Within the past five years, for example, there have been many newly public companies in such areas as the Internet, broadband communications and genome-related research.

Although many new technology stocks hold the promise of great rewards—soaring stock prices and overnight millionaires—they also involve substantial risk. As quickly as stock prices rise, they can easily, and often do, plummet and cost investors dearly. In 2000, more than 200 Internet companies went out of business.

▶ **Before you invest in new technology companies,** use some common sense. Don't invest in technologies you don't understand; chances are that other investors will also be confused and steer clear of these companies.

▶ **Don't invest heavily in any one stock involving new technology.** Although the upside potential is great, the downside potential can be devastating.

▶ **Don't invest on the word of company insiders.** Just because your neighbor's nephew's best friend is a computer expert at a company going public doesn't make it a sound investment. Insider trading is illegal and foolhardy because of misinformation. Do your research and check out the fundamentals of the industry that the company is in.

Record keeper for savings bonds

Serial number	Issue date (month/year)	Face value

7

Mutual funds

"*We must cultivate our garden.*" —Voltaire

THERE ARE CURRENTLY more than 8,600 mutual funds available. Nearly half of all US households own mutual funds, totaling more than $6 trillion in investments. There are good reasons for the widespread investment in this type of vehicle. First, mutual funds offer professional management—a team of experts making decisions on when to buy and sell particular securities. Second, mutual funds offer more diversity than most individual investors can otherwise afford. For instance, with $1,000, you can buy shares in a stock mutual fund that effectively gives you interests in hundreds of companies, whereas that same $1,000 could not buy shares directly to replicate the diversity of that fund's portfolio. And, like individually-owned stocks and bonds, mutual funds are completely liquid, allowing you to cash out your holdings on any day the stock market is open.

Of course, owning shares in mutual funds differs from direct investments in stocks and bonds. For instance, mutual fund shares can only be sold at the close of the day, whereas stocks and bonds can be sold at any time during the trading day.

There are many different types of mutual funds—stock, bond and money market funds. There are also many factors to consider when making mutual fund investments: Fees and other costs involved, how to make transactions and what tax effect these decisions will have.

This chapter provides practical information about the fundamentals of mutual funds in order to be a savvy investor. It also explains tax issues involved in owning and selling mutual fund shares and strategies for making good investment decisions. And it provides you with ideas for record keeping, socially responsible investing and other special aspects of mutual funds.

THE FUNDS

Mutual funds are regulated investment companies that pool investor dollars to provide diversity of investments and professional management. There are many different types of mutual funds, which fall within three general categories:

▶ **Stock funds**—equities

▶ **Bond funds**—bonds and other debt instruments

▶ **Money market funds**—cash equivalents

Within the category of stock funds, there are numerous varieties. These include:

▶ **Growth funds,** which generally focus on companies with growth potential (companies expected to have high earnings).

▶ **Value funds,** which generally focus on solid companies that offer value in comparison with other companies based on P/Es, price to book and other measurements.

Growth funds vs. value funds

	Growth averaged	Value averaged
Late 1920s to 2000	10.2%	13.4%
1995 to 1997	32.88%	29.66%
1997 to 2002	9.5%	10.2%
2003	25.66%	31.79%
2004	6.13%	15.71%
2005	3.46%	6.37%
2006	6.83%	24.1%

 Strategy: *Include both growth and income funds in your portfolio. Since they will each outperform each other at different times, you can hedge your bets and profit from whichever type has the advantage at a particular time.*

▶ Index funds, which own stocks that mirror a particular index, such as the S&P 500, the Dow Jones Industrial Average (consisting of the 30 stocks that make up the DJIA), the Russell 2000 Index, the Wilshire Total Market Index or the NASDAQ Composite Index.

▶ **Sector funds,** which own stocks within a particular sector of the economy (e.g., biotechnology, technology, telecommunications or transportation). *Caution:* Risk in sector funds is higher than overall market risk. When a sector is hot, the funds tend to outperform the market in general, but when the sector is out of favor, the funds usually do much worse than the market in general. What's more, sector funds tend to have higher sales loads and operating expenses.

▶ **International funds,** which own stocks in foreign countries. Regional funds own stocks in a particular area of the world: Europe, Latin America or Asia. *Caution:* When the dollar is strong, the value of international funds may decline because the investment is simply worth less in US dollars.

Strategy: *To avoid extreme currency risk, buy global funds—which own both international and US stocks—instead of international funds. The US portion of the fund's portfolio will balance out the currency risk, if any, in the foreign portion.*

Open-end funds vs. closed-end funds

Most funds are open-end funds, although you usually don't see this label attached to them. Open-end simply means that as new investment dollars flow into the fund, new shares are added. Open-end funds trade at net asset value (NAV)—the value of the fund's assets divided by the number of shares in the fund.

In contrast to open-end funds, closed-end funds have a finite number of shares to be traded among investors. Closed-end funds may trade at a price that's lower (a discount) or higher (a premium) than the fund's NAV. There are both benefits and problems with closed-end funds:

Advantages: Closed-end funds trade like stocks. They're listed on an exchange and can be bought or sold at any time during the day (in contrast to open-end funds that can only be bought or sold at the fund's price at the close of the day). Also, it's possible to buy shares in closed-end funds at a discount from NAV.

Disadvantage: Because closed-end funds don't trade at NAV, you may pay a premium on NAV when acquiring shares.

EXCHANGE-TRADED FUNDS (ETFs)

Exchange-traded funds (ETFs) are merely a bundle of securities traded like stocks on the American Stock Exchange (AMEX). They carry such exotic names as Diamonds, Qubes (QQQs), Spiders (SPDRs), HOLDRs, VIPERs, iShares and WEBs, although only the QQQ and SPDRs are traded regularly. There are only a few bond ETFs.

Advantages: They can be bought or sold at any time during the trading day just like individual stocks. And, just like individual stocks, they can be sold short or bought on margin. They typically have lower annual expenses than even index mutual funds. And they usually are more tax efficient than many mutual funds because they don't redeem shares for cash (explained below) and so don't have to sell holdings to raise this cash.

Disadvantages: The purchase or sale of ETFs carries commission charges. ETFs may have 100-share increment requirements (e.g., you must buy or sell 100, 200, etc., shares at a time).

UNIT INVESTMENT TRUSTS (UITS)

Unit investment trusts (UITs) are similar to mutual funds because they hold a bundle of securities, which offer diversity to investors. But that's where the similarity ends. UITs aren't traded like mutual fund shares but instead are sold through brokerage firms. Although the firms can buy back UITs, these are investments designed for buy-and-hold investors, not for those who prefer to trade securities. There's a fixed maturity for UITs—one to six years or as much as 20 years.

At maturity, investors generally realize long-term capital gains. But investors can defer recognition of gain by rolling over the proceeds into a new UIT.

 Strategy: *Buy UITs if you're looking for tax efficiency. Because UITs buy and hold their securities, there are generally no gains to pass through to investors. But a bond UIT can have redemptions of bonds and thus lower monthly interest payments to investors.*

HOLDRs

A relatively new investment product (introduced by Merrill Lynch in 1998) is Holding Company Depository Receipts (HOLDRs). They are similar to UITs except that they trade on the American Stock Exchange.

Like equity UITs, HOLDRs bundle stocks to offer investors both diversity and professional stock selection. And they have a fixed maturity of 40 years, so there are few, if any, gains annually passed through to investors.

Key difference between HOLDRs and UITs: Investors can exchange HOLDRs for the underlying stock, allowing them to sell for tax gains or losses as individual tax considerations dictate.

BOND FUNDS

Bond funds are mutual funds that hold debt instruments. They pay the interest they collect on these debts as dividends to investors, providing an income stream. For even small investments, you can own fund shares that essentially give you a piece of many debt instruments, which you probably couldn't afford to buy on your own. This provides you not only with diversity but with the opportunity to receive income in fixed monthly amounts.

Like stock funds, the value of shares in bond funds can increase or decrease. Generally, as interest rates rise, the value of shares in a bond fund may fall. *Caution:* Bond funds can be quite risky as investments. Unlike individually-owned bonds that promise to pay the face amount of the instrument upon maturity, there's no guarantee that you'll get back your initial investment.

Types of bond funds

Like stock funds, there are a variety of bond funds that you can invest in:

▶ **Short-term, intermediate or mid-term and long-term bond funds.** In short-term funds, most of the bonds mature in two to three years. In intermediate funds, maturities are primarily seven to 10 years. Long-term funds hold bonds maturing in 20 years.

▶ **Municipal bond funds.** Like interest on individually owned municipal bonds, dividends on these funds are free from federal income taxes. Some or all of the interest may also be state tax free. State income tax exemptions on municipal bond interest are discussed in Chapter 6.

 Strategy: If you live in a state with high income taxes, look for a single-state municipal bond fund to achieve completely tax-free returns. Example: *New York residents can buy NYS muni-bond funds so that dividends are free from federal and state income taxes. If you buy a fund of mixed bonds from various states, the fund will tell you which portion relates to which state.*

▶ **High-yield funds.** These funds hold corporate bonds with ratings below investment grade (explained in Chapter 6). The riskier the holdings in the fund, the higher the yield being paid.

▶ **Government bond funds.** These funds hold Treasury bonds and agency bonds, providing the safest investment possible.

MONEY MARKET FUNDS

Money market mutual funds hold short-term, high quality debt instruments. These funds collect interest and pay dividend income. They are designed primarily as vehicles in which to park cash for a short term. Of course, investors may leave some of their money in money market funds at all times to ensure they have ready access to cash.

Advantages: The value of money market accounts remains constant even if interest rates change, the stock market swings or the economy changes. *Reason:* They have a constant $1 NAV. Thus, they are safe and contain little, if any, risk to principal (in contrast to bond fund shares that may lose value as interest rates rise). They generally offer check-writing privileges for easy access to money held in the fund. There are usually low minimum investment requirements that differ from fund to fund.

Disadvantages: There is no appreciation in the value of the shares in a money market mutual fund. Account values increase only because of earnings on shares. And there's generally no FDIC guarantee on investments as there is with bank CDs. However, the risk of loss is small because money market accounts are regulated by the SEC and, to date, only rarely have funds lost money for investors.

 Strategy: Don't assume you're getting the best rate from the money market fund associated with your brokerage account. The firm may have several money market funds and may not be sweeping your earnings into the highest-yielding one—unless you ask for it.

Types of money market funds

Money market funds are not all the same. Some offer taxable income while others concentrate on tax-free returns for investors:

▶ **Regular money market funds.** Dividends from these funds are not exempt from federal or state income taxes. However, they may offer higher yields than partially or fully exempt funds.

▶ **Federal government money market funds.** These funds, which invest in Treasuries and securities issued by US government agencies, offer taxable dividends for federal income tax purposes, but these dividends may be exempt from state income taxes.

▶ **Tax-exempt money market funds.** Like municipal bonds, dividends from these money market funds are exempt from federal income taxes and may be exempt from state income taxes as well. Single-state tax-exempt money market funds—for example, the Vanguard New York Tax-Exempt Money Market Fund—offer complete exemption from federal and state income taxes to New York State residents.

 Strategy: *Don't buy tax-exempt funds unless your tax bracket is higher than the 25% tax bracket. You'll probably receive lower yields from tax-exempt funds, but if your tax bracket is high enough, this may translate into higher after-tax returns than you could achieve with taxable money market funds. Comparing the tax-free return with the after-tax return on a taxable investment is explained in Chapter 6.*

To compare money market mutual funds:

▶ iMoneyNet (**www.imoneynet.com**)

▶ Bankrate.com (**www.bankrate.com**)

BUYING MUTUAL FUNDS

When you purchase shares in a mutual fund, decide on the amount of money you want to invest. Your dollars determine the number of shares purchased. Share purchases may be reported to four decimal places—for example, 6.2384 shares.

You have several options for buying mutual funds. These include:

▶ **Brokerage firms.** You can buy shares through brokerage firms. Merrill Lynch, Salomon Smith Barney, Morgan Stanley Dean Witter and other firms primarily sell load funds. Brokerage firms also sell proprietary funds—their own funds, which they sell exclusively. Shares purchased through brokerage firms are held in your account at the firm.

▶ **Fund companies.** You can buy shares directly from the fund's family—Fidelity, Vanguard, Janus, etc. Shares are then held by the fund.

▶ **Mutual fund supermarkets.** Certain brokerages and fund families provide a wide selection of mutual fund purchases. Charles Schwab and the brokerage arms of Fidelity and Vanguard, for example, sell thousands of different funds (not just their own), but they don't sell other companies' proprietary funds.

You generally don't pay any more to buy funds through brokerage firms or fund supermarkets than you do buying directly from the fund. Some brokerage firms charge a fee to buy a no-load fund that wouldn't be incurred with direct purchase from the mutual fund company. The advantage of using firms or fund supermarkets is having all your holdings in one place—a great convenience for record-keeping purposes.

Learning about mutual funds

Before you invest in mutual funds, understand what you're buying. Learn about their fees and charges. Understand how different funds are designed to meet different investment objectives.

You can learn about mutual funds through:

▶ American Association of Individual Investors **(www.aaii.com)**

▶ Mutual fund link at the Investment Company Institute **(www.ici.org)**

▶ Mutual Fund Investor's Center **(www.mfea.com)**

Stay current on mutual fund developments and check on fund performance at:

▶ MAX Funds.com **(www.maxfunds.com)**

▶ Morningstar **(www.morningstar.com)**

▶ Fund Alarm **(www.fundalarm.com/lists.htm)**

▶ Brill's Mutual Funds Interactive **(www.brill.com)**

Read the fund's prospectus before you buy

The prospectus discloses the funds' investment objectives, its largest holdings and its fees and charges. It will show the fund's performance over time, unless this is the initial offering of the fund.

Obtain a prospectus simply by asking the fund to send one to you. You don't have to get lost in the fine print to find the key information you're looking for, such as the fund's management fees. You may find some funds' prospectuses online.

Fund rankings

What's a five-star fund and what does that mean to you? Certain independent companies rate mutual funds to enable investors to compare them carefully. For example, each month Morningstar **(www.morningstar.com)** rates funds from zero to five stars, with five stars being the top rank.

 Strategy: Continue to check the ratings of the funds you own, because ratings change. According to one source, less than 50% of four-star and five-star rated funds keep those ratings more than three years.

In addition to Morningstar, other ratings services include Lipper Analytic Services **(www.lipperweb. com)**, which gives grades A, B, etc., to funds, and Value Line **(www.valueline.com)**, which gives a grading of one to five.

Fund rankings are based on both fund risk and fund performance (i.e., return). Funds are compared with like funds within four basic fund groups—domestic stock, international stock, taxable bond and municipal bond funds. The rating demonstrates how risky a particular fund is when compared with its group. A similar analysis applies for fund return. Morningstar's star rating essentially produces a risk-adjusted performance rating—comparing the fund's performance with the level of its risk. The top-performing 10% each month earn five stars, 22.5% earn four stars, 35% earn three stars, 22.5% earn two stars and the bottom 10% earn one star.

Once you have the general rating for a fund, compare it with other funds of similar investments. For example, you need to compare the star ratings of an aggressive growth fund from one company with an aggressive growth fund from another company.

LOAD VS. NO-LOAD FUNDS

Funds fall into three main categories—load funds, low-load funds and no-load funds. No-load funds are sold without commission but they have "12b-1 fees" or expenses that are low. Load funds contain sales charges. But sales charges aren't the only fees involved. No-load funds, for example, may charge redemption fees of 1% or so if shares are sold within six months of purchase.

*Strategy: Use the SEC's mutual fund cost calculator to compare the costs of owning mutual funds over the long term (**www.sec.gov/index.htm**; then go under "Investor Information" and click on "Interactive Tools"). This tool allows you to compare the costs of a no-load fund with yearly 12b-1 expenses of 1.5% to a fund with a front-end load sales charge of 3.2% and yearly expenses of 0.95%.*

Fund classes

The types of fees and charges depend on the class of shares you buy:

▶ **Class A shares:** Front-end load charges, which are sales commissions ranging from 2% to 6% of the amount invested. If you invest $10,000 and there's a 5% front-end load ($500), you'll have $9,500 to buy shares. In addition, there are annual 12b-1 fees (although these fees are lower for A shares than for B shares).

▶ **Class B shares:** Back-end charges (contingent deferred sales charges or CDSC) when shares are sold. Back-end charges generally are waived if shares are held more than a set number of years, typically six years, declining one percentage each year. In addition, there are annual 12b-1 fees of about 0.5% of the account. B shares are usually converted to A shares after the deferred sales charge period ends, usually in the seventh year. Most investors buy B shares because they like to put all their money to work immediately (a $10,000 investment buys $10,000 worth of shares).

▶ **Class C shares:** Level-load charges (usually 1%) each year.

▶ **Other classes (e.g., D, M):** Various charges spelled out in fund prospectuses.

Strategy: Compare fund performance, not merely sales charges, when making investment picks of load versus no-load, A shares vs. B shares, etc. High-cost funds with strong performance can outperform low-cost funds.

Some no-load fund families now issue load funds, as they have decided to charge sales commissions.

Strategy: To avoid sales charges on load funds when switching investments, stay within a fund family—for example, American Century, Fidelity or Vanguard. If you sell shares in a load fund within the family, you can switch into another fund in that family without additional sales charges.

Transaction expenses vs. operating expenses

67%   205%

28,501.00   185,320—

80%

149,013.00   603.94   197.31

45%   372.05

715   426.00

Fees and charges fall into two categories. Transaction expenses, which include load charges and redemption fees, are amounts investors pay. Operating expenses, which include management fees and 12b-1 fees, are amounts subtracted from the fund's return. These reduce the distributions that may be made to investors.

> **Strategy:** *An expense ratio is the relationship between the fund's expenses (management fees and administrative costs) and its assets. Look for stock funds that have an expense ratio of 1.25% or less (0.5% for bond funds, money market funds and stock index funds).*

Find information about money market funds at **www.imoneynet.com**.

HOW MANY FUNDS DO YOU NEED?

With more than 12,000 funds on the market and new funds introduced almost daily, the choices among mutual funds can be overwhelming. The number of funds you should own depends on your investment objectives and money you have to invest. To determine which type of funds to own, review your asset allocation models (Chapter 5).

Don't buy two different types of funds that have the same investment objectives. For example, if your investment objective is growth and income, you may want a hybrid fund that invests in both stocks and bonds, offering you both growth (from stocks) and income (from bonds). If you want a growth fund and buy a second fund with the same objective, you'll pay additional fees, and you may still own, through the two funds, virtually the same companies.

> **Strategy:** *Coordinate your personal fund holdings with fund investments made through your 401(k) plan and your IRA. For example, if you own an S&P 500 index fund through your employer's 401(k) plan, you may not want to duplicate this investment in a personal fund.*

TIMING PURCHASES OF MUTUAL FUND SHARES

Like stock or bond purchases, you can buy when you believe the price is right. However, it's very difficult to time the market, selecting the best time to purchase your shares. Consider dollar cost averaging (explained in Chapter 6) to make regular and systematic purchases within a fund.

When you buy shares in open-end mutual funds, your order is executed at the fund's closing price for the day. For example, if you place a buy order at 10 am EST and the market zooms for the rest of the day, your order will go off at the fund's closing price at 4 pm EST, which will reflect the market's activities for the day. In contrast, closed-end mutual funds trade like stocks and can be purchased throughout the trading day.

Strategy: *Late in the year don't buy shares in non-tax-deferred accounts if they cause you to report a year's worth of earnings on stock held for only a short time. Distributions are payable to shareholders of record. Check with the fund manager to learn the record date (typically in November but sometimes in October or even December). Buy after the record date.*

SELLING MUTUAL FUND SHARES

Buying and holding mutual funds may be sound investing. But there may come a time when you want or need to liquidate the fund. The fund may not be performing as well as you expected or you may need use of the cash. Knowing *when* to sell your shares can help you optimize tax consequences and avoid investment losses. Knowing *how* to sell your shares will allow you to make necessary arrangements before you decide to sell.

Understanding limitations

When you sell shares in open-end mutual funds—most mutual funds—your sale price is the fund's price at the close of the day (or the following day if you place the order too late). Generally you have to place your order by a certain time of the day. For example, some brokerage firms may have a 2 pm EST deadline for sales of mutual fund shares. Sales made directly through the fund may be permitted until the close of the market (4 pm EST).

The fact that a fund's price may be up or down for the day may not translate into profits unless the higher price is the fund's closing price. This makes it impossible to time precisely when to sell your shares—you can never be a market timer with open-end mutual fund shares.

Selling to minimize gain/maximize loss with smart basis choices

When you sell some, but not all, of your shares in a mutual fund you have acquired at different times (for different prices), you can control the amount of your gain or loss. If you don't take action, you're deemed to have sold the earliest shares you acquired.

▶ **FIFO (first in, first out)** method. Normally, you're considered to have sold the first shares you acquired, unless you opt for the methods described below.

> **Example:** If you bought 100 shares each in the XYZ Fund at $5, then $15 and then $25, and sold 100 shares, you're treated as having sold the shares with a $5 cost basis. *The result:* Your gain is maximized (or your loss is minimized).

▶ **Specific identification method.** If you have the records to identify them, you can designate which shares you are selling. Direct your broker or mutual fund company to sell the specific shares you want and receive written confirmation of your instructions. Your confirmation of the trade, including the shares you identified, meets this requirement.

Example: In the same example used above, you would instruct the mutual fund company to sell 100 shares with a cost basis of $25. In this case you've minimized your gain (or maximized your loss).

 Strategy: Place standing instructions to your broker to always sell the latest shares acquired or highest basis shares first. As long as your broker confirms your specifications in writing, this standing instruction can be viewed as a specific identification.

▶ **Average cost method.** You can average the cost of your shares to obtain a basis for determining your gain or loss.

Example: Same as above. Here your average cost for the three lots of shares is $15 ([$5 x 100] + [$15 x 100] + [$25 x 100] ÷ 300).

You can even fine-tune the average cost method by using a single category of all your shares; as illustrated in the example above, or a double category method by segregating shares into those held short term and those held long term. You then find the average cost within each category.

 Strategy: Think carefully before choosing the average cost method. You must continue to use it for all subsequent sales from the same fund. You can't change your method for figuring basis without IRS approval.

Year-end tax planning for investments, including mutual fund shares, is explained in Chapter 24.

When to get out

Many investors have a buy-and-hold policy regarding their mutual funds and are reluctant to change their holdings. But a fund may be underperforming or you may need to raise some cash. It's always shrewd to know when to get out of a fund.

▶ **Watch for early sales charges.** In an effort to discourage active trading and encourage long-term investments, some funds charge fees for early redemptions. These charges may be for sales within 30 days of purchase or within a six-month period.

▶ **Watch for deferred sales charges.** If you sell the shares before a set time (generally six years), you may incur back-end charges. By holding the shares for an additional period of time (it may be only a matter of days or months before these charges are waived), you can avoid these unnecessary costs.

 Strategy: Only sell shares that are no longer subject to deferred sales charges. A number of shares in a fund may be freed from these charges. Ask your broker or the mutual fund company to tell you how many shares are free from sales charges.

▶ **Watch for distributions.** Selling shares before income distributions does not necessarily avoid tax on the distributions. Check for the record dates to determine when these distributions will be credited for tax purposes.

> *Strategy: Sell shares no later than November to avoid year-end distributions and their tax costs. Check with the fund manager to determine the exact date on which the tax consequences of distributions hinge.*

Generally, a change in fund management isn't an event that triggers a sale. If the new management team continues the fund's investment philosophy, a sale may not be warranted.

Redeeming your shares

Selling your shares to receive cash (or to use the money for other investments) can be accomplished in several ways:

▶ **Written instructions to sell.** You can instruct the fund company by letter to sell a number of shares (or your entire holding) in a particular fund. Some funds may accept a faxed letter, although they may require you to mail the original.

▶ **Telephone redemptions.** If you have authorized that telephone redemptions be allowed, you can instruct the fund company by telephone to redeem your shares.

▶ **Wire transfers.** You can direct that your redemptions be deposited directly in your checking account via a wire transfer. You must provide a signature guarantee when requesting a wire transfer or when you open the account and include wire transfers as a redemption option.

▶ **Check writing.** Money market mutual funds (and even some non-money market mutual funds) may allow you to write a check that effectively serves as a sale of shares. If you own both a stock or bond fund and a money market fund within the same fund family, you can direct that the proceeds from the sale of shares in the stock and/or bond fund be directed into your money market fund, allowing you access to the money via your checking account.

> *Strategy: When you buy a fund, consider your redemption options. If you fail to indicate a redemption option, you'll have to advise the fund in writing when you want to make a change.*

TAX TREATMENT OF MUTUAL FUND DISTRIBUTIONS

You may receive yearly distributions from your mutual funds. What these distributions mean for tax purposes is reported on Form 1099-DIV (and possibly Form 2439, "Notice to Shareholders of Undistributed Long-Term Capital Gains"). Even if you automatically reinvest these distributions, for tax purposes you must treat them as if you had taken them out in cash. If you receive distributions in January on shares you held on the record date in the prior year (typically November or December), report them as if they had been received by December 31 of the year of the record date—that's how they'll be reported to you on the information returns you receive. There are four basic types of distributions you may receive from a fund:

▶ **Ordinary dividends.** These are distributions from the funds earnings and profits which are taxable at capital gain rates (at rates up to 15%).

▶ **Capital gains distributions.** These are your share of a fund's long-term capital gains. You report them as long-term capital gains (taxed at rates up to 15%). They are long-term gains to you regardless of how long you've owned the shares.

 Strategy: Report capital gains distributions and pay tax on them if the fund reports them as taxable, even if it doesn't distribute them to you. Two offsetting moves can lessen the effects of this tax rule. You can claim a tax credit for your share of the taxes that the fund paid. And you can increase the basis in your shares by the amount of the undistributed capital gains.

▶ **Exempt-interest dividends.** If the mutual fund earns tax-exempt interest (for example, it owns municipal bonds), you aren't subject to regular tax on the share of this exempt interest paid as dividends. However, this income may be subject to the alternative minimum tax (AMT). The AMT is discussed in Chapter 15.

▶ **Return of capital distributions.** A distribution that is not out of the fund's earnings and profits is simply a return of your own investment and is therefore not taxed. These nontaxable distributions are sometimes referred to as tax-free dividends. You're required to reduce the basis of your shares by the amount of these nontaxable distributions. Basis cannot be reduced below zero, so if you continue to receive these distributions after you no longer have any basis in your shares, any excess is treated as capital gain.

TAX TRAPS

Mutual funds are great investment vehicles. But even with reduced tax rates, tax costs can erode your after-tax returns from these funds. Be aware of certain tax traps relating to mutual fund investments.

Tax efficiency

In obtaining professional management, you surrender control over your investments and, to a degree, over their tax consequences. The fund may make distributions on which you're taxed whether or not you want them. When the fund is held in a tax-deferred account, such as an IRA, this may not matter. But when the fund is in your personal account, distributions can be costly.

 Strategy: Look for funds advertised as tax efficient. Generally, the less turnover there is within the fund's holdings, the more tax efficient the fund. For the most tax-efficient fund, consider an index fund; the only change in holdings is made when a company is added or dropped from the index.

You can check on a particular fund's tax efficiency at **www.morningstar.com** or at **www.personalfund. com/index.html**.

Strategy: *Hold tax-inefficient funds in tax-deferred accounts and tax-efficient funds in personal accounts.*

Note: Morningstar now rates funds according to tax efficiency in addition to their risk and return. In figuring tax efficiency, it calculates the effect on the highest income tax bracket to determine the fund's after-tax return. Whether this tax efficiency rating is correct for you depends on your federal income tax bracket and whether you are subject to state and local income taxes.

 Strategy: *Opt for fund alternatives (EFTs, UITs or HOLDRs), bundles of securities that offer tax efficiency by their nature.*

Taxable events

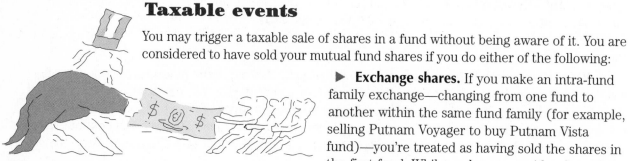

You may trigger a taxable sale of shares in a fund without being aware of it. You are considered to have sold your mutual fund shares if you do either of the following:

▶ **Exchange shares.** If you make an intra-fund family exchange—changing from one fund to another within the same fund family (for example, selling Putnam Voyager to buy Putnam Vista fund)—you're treated as having sold the shares in the first fund. While exchanges avoid redemption charges instituted by the fund, tax consequences may nonetheless result.

▶ **Write checks.** If you have check-writing privileges, then drawing a check on the fund causes the sale of shares required to meet the amount of the check.

Double taxation

If you use fund distributions to reinvest in additional shares in the same fund, be sure to include these distributions in your cost basis for the shares. If you don't make this record-keeping entry, you may pay tax twice on the same money—once when the distributions are made and again when you sell the shares if you fail to include the distributions in your basis (thereby increasing your gain or minimizing your loss). Record-keeping tips for mutual fund shares are explained later in this chapter.

You may also incur unnecessary tax if you fail to increase your basis by undistributed capital gains. Check IRS Form 2439 (sent to you by the fund) to find the amount you should add to your basis.

Wash-sale rules

If you sell shares at a loss and reacquire shares in the same fund within 30 days before or after the date of sale, you can't take your loss for the year. If you're in a dividend reinvestment plan, you may be reacquiring shares automatically. Still, this reacquisition triggers wash-sale rules and prevents you from recognizing your loss.

SOCIALLY RESPONSIBLE INVESTING

Do you want your investments to make a difference to others? Do you want to avoid certain companies with whose policies or products you disagree? Consider socially responsible or socially conscious investing. Today, there are more than 200 mutual funds designed for this purpose. For example, there are "green funds" that invest only in environmentally sensitive companies. Other funds avoid investments in companies that do animal testing, employ workers overseas in conditions that violate human rights or produce weapons, alcohol, pornography or tobacco.

You can choose stock funds that limit their portfolios to select companies. Examples:

▶ Amana Funds (**www.saturna.com**) follow the Muslim bans on usury, alcohol, pornography and gambling to limit investments to companies that are not involved in these practices or products.

▶ Citizens Funds (**www.citizensfunds.com**) look for companies with a positive record on the environment and human rights and avoid those involved in weapons and animal testing.

▶ LKCM Aquinas Funds (**www.lkcm.com**) follow Catholic family values, avoiding companies supporting abortions.

▶ The Women's Equity Mutual Fund (**www.womens-equity.com**) invests in companies that provide leadership opportunities for women.

▶ Vanguard Calvert Social Index (**www.vanguard.com**) does not own stock in companies involved in alcohol, tobacco, gambling and nuclear power.

As a general rule, socially responsible funds may have higher fees because the funds are forced to do added screening of potential investments. To learn about socially responsible investing in general, visit the SocialFunds Web site (**www.socialfunds.com**).

 Strategy: Don't abandon basic investment concepts when evaluating socially conscious funds. Consider risk and return. Select a fund that satisfies your social conscience and your investment objectives.

DESIGNING YOUR OWN MUTUAL FUND

Some investors may still want to customize their holdings. You can effectively create your own mutual fund (also called a synthetic fund) by diversifying your stock portfolio in a variety of ways. For example, you might want to create your own index fund by purchasing shares included in a specific index, such as the DJIA, which has 30 companies. But you can eliminate from your fund any companies you don't want to include, such as tobacco or alcohol companies.

▶ BuyandHold (**www.buyandhold.com**, 800-646-8212) offers incremental investing (fractional shares) by bundling customer orders and placing block trades twice a day. *Cost:* $6.99 per month, two trades included.

▶ Folio[fn] (**www.foliofn.com**, 888-973-7890) provides model funds that you can customize as you wish. You can buy fractional shares to obtain your desired portfolio without incurring substantial costs. *Cost:* $295 per year for the Premium Diversification Package; $149 per year for the Basic Diversification Package.

► ShareBuilder (**www.sharebuilder.com**, 800-747-2537) lets you buy fractional shares to build your own mutual funds. *Cost:* $4 per investment.

► USA Account (**www.usa-account.com**) lets you buy shares at prices comparable to dividend reinvestment plans (DRIPs).

Should you consider building your own mutual fund? It depends on your goals and resources:

Advantages: You eliminate the costs involved in obtaining professional management. Your only costs are commissions to buy the stocks. And you obtain control over tax efficiency. If you are a long-term investor, you can thereby minimize your capital gains.

Disadvantages: You lose the very advantages associated with mutual funds—professional management and diversification (unless you can afford to acquire enough shares in different companies to obtain such diversification).

RECORD KEEPING FOR MUTUAL FUND REINVESTMENTS

Record keeping is a tedious task for most people. But it's the only way for you as a mutual fund investor to know how your funds are performing. Record keeping also allows you to optimize your gains and losses and avoid double taxation. You need to keep track of your basis in the shares, when you acquired or sold shares (including shares acquired by reinvestment) and other pertinent information.

Basis

Generally, your basis in your shares is your cost, including any commissions and load charges paid to acquire the shares.

► **Shares acquired by gift.** Your basis in these shares is your donor's basis (and any gift tax paid by the donor on the shares). But if the value of your shares is less than your donor's basis, you must use the lower amount—value—to determine loss.

► **Shares acquired by inheritance.** Your basis in such shares is the value of the shares used for estate tax purposes. This is generally the value—the last quoted redemption price—on the date of the decedent's death or the alternate valuation date six months later.

► **Increases or reductions in basis**. If you reported undistributed capital gains, you increase your basis by the difference between these gains and the amount of tax you claimed as a credit on the distribution.

Decrease your basis by any nontaxable distributions (i.e., return of your capital). No adjustment to basis is required for exempt-interest dividends.

Paper records

You can, of course, keep your own paper records on your mutual fund purchases and sales. The IRS worksheet on page 112 can guide you on the type of information you need to track for effective tax planning of your mutual fund investments.

 Strategy: *Update your records at least once a year, at the end of January after you've received Form 1099-DIV from each mutual fund. This will let you add to your records any dividends you've reinvested in new shares.*

Fund records

Mutual funds are now doing record keeping for investors by tracking basis and other necessary information. *Caution:* Records for fund shares owned before this record keeping began may be incomplete and should not automatically be relied upon.

Online records

You can keep your records on certain Web sites. For example, AOL (Time Warner) allows you to set up your own portfolio records. It's up to you to update them when necessary. *Caution:* These records can be lost when you update software (for example, if you change your version of AOL).

Computer records

You can keep your records on personal software (e.g., Quicken®). As a precaution, be sure to back up your information on disk or otherwise and store your backup in a fireproof safe or off-premises (for example, in a safe-deposit box).

Mutual fund record

| Mutual fund | Acquired[1] | | | Adjustments to basis per share | Adjusted[2] basis per share | Sold or redeemed | |
	Date	Number of shares	Cost per share			Date	Number of shares

[1]Include shares received from reinvestment of distributions.   [2]Cost plus or minus adjustments.

8

Putting money into retirement plans

"Who is not ready today will not be ready tomorrow." —PROVERB

QUALIFIED RETIREMENT PLANS and IRAs offer a tax-advantaged way to save for your retirement and provide substantial wealth for subsequent generations. Today, if you work, you probably have some type of retirement plan—company sponsored or your own IRA, or both. You can even provide an IRA for a nonworking spouse. And the tax law allows those age 50 and older to save additional amounts.

How you invest in retirement plans will affect the amount of money you have for your retirement. So make sure you understand your options and take advantage of strategies now and in coming years to maximize your savings.

This chapter explains how to make the most of savings opportunities through retirement plans and IRAs. It explains contribution limits, investment options and strategies for optimizing your accumulations as well as plan options for self-employed individuals. In chapter 9, you'll find strategies for taking money out of retirement plans.

BUILDING UP FUNDS IN RETIREMENT PLANS

Retirement plans are tax-deferred savings vehicles where funds compound without any reduction for taxes. This means that funds build up faster than in taxable vehicles. Over time, the difference can be quite dramatic (depending, of course, on the rate of return).

 Strategy: *Shift money into tax-deferred savings early in the year as to optimize the effect of compounding. Example: Although you are permitted to make a deductible IRA contribution for 2007 at any time between January 1, 2007, and April 15, 2008, a contribution at the start of 2007 means 15½ months of additional compounding. Over time, this can add considerably to your savings.*

Roth IRAs

The Roth IRA is the best of all possible worlds because it offers the opportunity for tax-free buildup of income. As long as certain holding requirements are satisfied—funds aren't withdrawn until the account has been open for five years and distributions are started at attaining age 59½, paying first-time home buying expenses (up to $10,000 in a lifetime) or becoming disabled or dying—there's never any tax on the earnings.

Catch: You must fund the Roth IRA with after-tax dollars, so you don't get any immediate tax benefit by making the contributors. And there are limits on eligibility to contribute to a Roth IRA. High-income tax-payers—modified adjusted gross income in 2007 of more than $166,000 on a joint return or $114,000 for singles—are barred from doing so.

Roth 401(k)s

Like Roth IRAs, those participating in 401(k) plans offering a Roth 401(k) contribution option can contribute funds on an after-tax basis in order to build up a tax-free retirement pot. Unlike the Roth IRA, there are no income limits barring contributors from putting money in a Roth 401(k). However, total annual contributions in a regular and/or Roth 401(k) cannot exceed dollar limits listed below.

401(K) CONTRIBUTIONS

401(k) plans are widespread because they allow companies to shift the cost of retirement contributions largely to employees. Employees can contribute limited amounts to company-sponsored 401(k) plans to build up their retirement savings. Contributions are made on a pretax basis through salary reduction agreements.

Example: If your salary is $50,000 and you agree to contribute $5,000 to your 401(k) plan, your taxable salary is only $45,000 ($50,000 less $5,000 salary reduction contributed to the plan).

There's an annual limit on salary reduction amounts. The limit is $15,500 in 2007. The dollar limit is adjusted annually for inflation.

Those age 50 or older are permitted to make additional "catch-up" contributions—regardless of whether they under-contributed in prior years. The dollar limit on these contributions is $5,000 in 2007. Thereafter the catch-up contribution limit is also adjusted annually for inflation.

Despite the obvious benefits of participating in the plans, it's been estimated that about 30% of eligible employees don't participate. Whether you're a new or current employee, you may be automatically enrolled in your company's 401(k) plan. The company can set a limit on your salary reduction amount, but only you can choose whether to participate. Don't opt out! It's shrewd to contribute.

Your contributions may yield more than you think. Many employers provide matching contributions as a means of encouraging employees to participate in these plans.

> **Example:** Your employer matches 50% of all employee contributions, so making your own $5,000 contribution would entitle you to a $2,500 employer contribution on your behalf. The $2,500 is like "free" money—you get it simply by making your own contribution.

Caution: Although your contributions through salary reductions are fully vested (you can't lose them even if you leave employment), you may have to complete a fixed number of years of employment to be fully vested in employer contributions. If you leave a job before you're fully vested in the plan, you will lose the employer contributions.

Timing contributions

Salary reductions are usually made ratably with each pay period or once a month. If you have employer-matching contributions and you plan to make the largest permissible contributions, time your contributions to obtain the highest matching contributions possible. Generally it's advisable to make your annual contribution ratably over 12 months. So if you plan to contribute the maximum allowable amount of $15,500 in 2006, you would contribute $1,000 via salary reduction each month.

> **Example:** If you earn $100,000 per year and participate in a company 401(k) plan that matches 50% of your contribution of up to 6% of your income, you may receive an employer contribution of up to $6,000. You're permitted to contribute $15,500 in 2007. If you make your $15,500 contribution in $1,600 monthly payments, you'll complete your contributions in October and lose out on some employer matching. The employer contribution in this situation would be only $2,500 ($83,333 x 6% x 50%), or $500 less than if you made your $15,500 contribution ratably over 12 months.

On the other hand, if you anticipate retirement or otherwise leaving employment during the year, accelerate your contributions to put as much into your account as possible.

Coordinating contributions for married couples

If you and your spouse both work for employers with 401(k) plans but as a couple can't afford the maximum contributions to both plans, consider coordinating the contributions that each of you makes. Decide how much you can afford to contribute in total as a couple. Contribute the maximum (up to the salary reduction limit) to the plan with the better investment options.

> **Example:** Your budget permits total contributions for the year of $20,000 (when the salary reduction limit per participant is $15,500). Each person may contribute $10,000. Or you may contribute $15,500 to the plan that offers the better investment options and $4,500 to the other person's plan.

If both spouses' plans offer similar investment options, consider putting the greater share into the 401(k) of the younger spouse. This will allow for longer deferral, as funds won't have to be tapped until the younger spouse attains age 70½ (or even later, if the younger spouse continues to work).

In deciding how to split your 401(k) contributions, consider the psychological benefit for each spouse having independent retirement savings. This may be especially important if you experience marital difficulties in the future. *Note:* Qualified retirement benefits may be divided in a divorce settlement on a tax-free basis. Thus, if a couple decides that one spouse will make the full contribution and the other spouse makes no contribution, the noncontributing spouse could still receive a share of the other spouse's 401(k) plan if the couple splits up.

Selecting your investments

By law, your employer must offer a menu of investment options—at least three, but many companies' 401(k) plans typically offer 10 to 15 choices. Your employer does not give you investment advice and, in fact, is not permitted to do so by law.

However, your employer may provide you with information—booklets or seminars—and suggest Web sites that provide 401(k) investment advice. Research your investment choices through the Web sites of brokerage firms. Other useful sites include:

▶ InvestorLinks.com **(www.investorlinks.com)**

▶ Investopedia.com **(www.investopedia.com)**

▶ CNN Money **(http://money.cnn.com)**

▶ Morningstar **(www.morningstar.com)**

To make the most of your investment choices, use the same approaches and strategies you would adopt for personal investments made outside of the 401(k) arena. Most importantly, coordinate the holdings in your 401(k) with those in your personal investment accounts.

▶ **Employer stock.** You may be permitted to invest in company stock, an advantage because you usually obtain employer stock at attractive prices. The downside to this is that it concentrates too much of your financial interests in one company. Not only does your job depend on the fiscal health of the business, but your future retirement income is also dependent on the company's financial success if you invest your retirement funds heavily in company stock.

Asset allocations and investments (stocks, bonds, mutual funds, etc.) are discussed in Chapters 5 through 7.

IRAS

Individual retirement accounts (IRAs) are personal retirement plans that you may hold in addition to employer-sponsored plans. There are several types of IRAs:

▶ **Deductible IRAs.** In 2007, you can contribute and deduct up to $4,000 provided that you don't participate in a qualified (employer-offered) plan. If you do participate in a qualified plan, and your modified adjusted gross income (MAGI) is below threshold amounts (depending on filing status), you may also be able to contribute to an IRA. The dollar limit on IRA contributions will rise to $5,000 in 2008. After 2008, this dollar limit will be readjusted for inflation. Those age 50 and older by year end can make an additional IRA contribution of $1,000.

▶ **Nondeductible IRAs.** If you are an active participant in a qualified plan and your MAGI exceeds threshold amounts, you can contribute to a nondeductible IRA if your MAGI prevents a contribution to a Roth IRA. The same dollar limits for deductible IRAs apply to nondeductible IRAs.

▶ **Roth IRAs.** You can contribute up to $4,000 to a Roth IRA in 2007 ($5,000 if age 50 and older by year end), but you can't deduct your contributions from income taxes. The same dollar limits for deductible IRAs apply to Roth IRAs. Your eligibility to make Roth IRA contributions depends on your MAGI.

To make contributions to the above IRAs, you must have earned income (or receive taxable alimony). This can be from a job or from self-employment. However, your total annual contributions cannot exceed $4,000 (or $4,500 if applicable).

▶ **Conversions to Roth IRAs.** If you have a traditional IRA (whether deductible or nondeductible), you can convert to a Roth IRA but you must treat any income resulting from the conversion as a distribution. Future earnings can start to accrue on a tax-free basis. You may convert if your MAGI—without regard to the converted amount—does not exceed $100,000 (regardless of filing status) and, if married, you file a joint return.

▶ **Rollover IRAs.** If you receive a distribution from an employer plan, you can roll it over to your own IRA. A rollover IRA preserves the identity of funds from a qualified plan, allowing you to later roll over those funds and earnings on those funds—to the qualified plan of a new employer. Check whether the new employer's plan accepts rollovers.

Before 2002, you were not permitted to make any IRA contributions to rollover IRAs. Now you don't have to maintain a segregated (or "conduit") IRA to hold rollovers. Keep good records of what's in the IRA. *Reason:* Only amounts that will be includable in income can later be rolled over to a qualified plan. Thus, if you make nondeductible IRA contributions (not includable in income) to an account that includes a rollover of benefits from a qualified plan (includable in income), the nondeductible IRA contributions cannot be rolled back to another qualified retirement plan.

There are also other types of IRAs. Employers may sponsor SIMPLE-IRAs and SEP-IRAs. These IRAs are treated as qualified retirement plans. There are also education IRAs, which are savings accounts for higher education purposes and not for retirement.

Making contributions

You can make contributions for the current year at any time from January 1 through April 15 of the following year. That is, a 2007 contribution can be made from January 1, 2007, through April 15, 2008.

 Strategy: Make contributions as early in the contribution period as possible to gain additional compounding of investment return. You need not make the entire contribution at once. For example, consider making a $1,000 contribution at the start of the year and another $1,000 as soon as possible thereafter.

 Strategy: Use a payroll deduction arrangement with your employer if this option is available. If you have a deductible IRA, you can take this into account in figuring your income tax withholding, in effect receiving the benefit from your deduction up front.

*Strategy: Make IRA contributions using rebates on purchases you make. Through Ne$tEggz Loyalty Reward Program, you can receive rebates on purchases at participating merchants (e.g., 5% back from Macy's) that are automatically contributed to the IRA you designate. Go to **www.nesteggz.com.***

IRA investments

The type of IRA account you select dictates the range of investments you can make. For example, with a self-directed IRA with a brokerage firm, you can buy stocks, bonds, mutual funds and more. If you open an IRA annuity through a bank or insurance company, you're limited to buying an annuity.

Companies that act as custodians for self-directed IRAs offering the widest range of investment options include:

▶ Entrust Administration, Inc. (**www.entrustadmin.com**, 800-392-9653)

▶ Mercantile Bankshares Corporation (**www.fmbancorp.com**, 410-237-5900)

▶ Security Bank Corporation (**www.securitybank.com**, 632-867-6788)

▶ Equity Trust Company (**www.trustetc.com**, 440-323-5491)

▶ Northfield Savings Bank (**www.nsbvt.com**, 800-NSB-CASH)

▶ Fiserv (**www.fiserviss.com**, 800-521-6974)

▶ Sterling Trust Co. (**www.sterling-trust.com**, 800-955-3434)

▶ Trusource (**www.cnatrust.com**, 800-274-8798)

Although IRA annuities are often touted as good investments because they offer a guaranteed death benefit, you pay dearly for it. True, when you die, your heirs are guaranteed to at least recoup your investment—that's the guarantee. But this won't help you with your retirement. And, over time, you expect an IRA account to increase in value over your investment, not stay the same. What's more, you pay substantial commissions to buy an annuity. *Net results:* Annuities are a bad investment choice for IRAs.

 Strategy: Don't buy an annuity in your IRA. Because the IRA is already tax deferred, you don't gain anything extra from the tax-deferred annuity investment.

 Strategy: Don't buy municipal bonds for your IRA. You'll merely convert what would have been tax-free interest into income that is fully taxable when you take distributions from a traditional IRA. And for a Roth IRA, all earnings would be tax free. You can earn more income from other investments, such as taxable bonds.

You can even put IRA funds into certain specialized investments, such as gold, silver, platinum or palladium bullion held by the trustee. By law, you can't put IRA funds into certain other investments:

▶ **Collectibles** (artworks, gems, stamps, antiques, rugs, metals)

▶ **Coins** other than state-issued coins, certain US government–minted gold, or silver coins, or platinum coins.

If you want to include real estate in your IRA, you must follow certain strict rules to avoid self-dealing and find a company willing to act as custodian, such as Entrust Group (**http://theentrustgroup.com/self-direct ed/real-estate-tour.aspx**), Equity Trust (**www.trustetc.com**) and Guidant Financial Group (**www.guidant financial.com**). Alternatively, consider investing in mortgages—first mortgage loans, second mortgage loans and participating mortgages. *Caution:* These investments require greater vigilance on your part to ensure against borrower defaults. Such defaults can wipe out your IRA. Make sure you know what you're doing.

Coordinating retirement plan investments with personal investments

In deciding which type of investments to make with IRA funds, you need to look at your big financial picture. Your retirement investments for IRAs and 401(k) plans—sometimes referred to as "inside investments" because they're inside a tax-deferred account—should not duplicate your personal investments ("outside investments").

Generally, it's advisable to use investments yielding ordinary income—interest, dividends and short-term capital gains—in your inside accounts. *Reason:* Distributions are taxed as ordinary income regardless of the type of investment that produced the funds. Conversely, it's generally wise to use investments yielding long-term capital gains, such as stocks and stock mutual funds, for outside investments. In this way, you'll be able to use favorable capital gains tax rates when you report gains from these investments.

Multiple IRAs

You are not limited to having a single IRA account. You can have as many IRA accounts as you desire.

Advantages: You can name different beneficiaries for each separate account, providing more flexibility in distribution planning as well as estate planning. You can also use different accounts for different purposes.

> **Example:** You may wish to maintain a "safe" account invested in CDs with a local bank, while using other accounts for investments in stocks or mutual funds.

Disadvantages: Having multiple accounts means added record keeping to follow the investments in each account. It also means added custodial fees.

DEDUCTIBLE IRAS

If you have earned income, you *may* be able to fund your IRA on a tax-deductible basis. It depends on whether you participate in a qualified retirement plan and, if so, what your income is:

▶ **If you don't participate in a qualified plan,** you can make deductible IRA contributions, regardless of the amount of your income.

▶ **If you do participate in a qualified plan,** you can make a *full* deductible IRA contribution if your modified adjusted gross income (MAGI) is below the following limits.

For 2007, a fully deductible IRA can be made only by singles with MAGI of no more than $52,000, or $83,000 on a joint return.

If one spouse is an active participant, the nonparticipant spouse can make a fully deductible contribution in 2007 only if the couple's MAGI does not exceed $156,000.

▶ **Partially deductible contributions.** For those with MAGI above these limits, a partial deductible contribution is permissible. The phase-out range for singles is $52,000 to $62,000 ($83,000 to $103,000 on a joint return). In the case of a nonparticipant spouse, the phase-out range is $156,000 to $166,000.

▶ **Nondeductible contributions.** If active participants are barred from making deductible IRA contributions and do not fund Roth IRAs, they can opt to contribute on a nondeductible basis. *Benefits:* Income grows tax-deferred and funds can be converted to a Roth IRA for tax-free income (see page 121).

▶ **Qualified retirement plans include:** Company pension or profit-sharing plans, 401(k) plans, SEPs, SIMPLE plans, 403(b) annuities and 457 government plans. These MAGI limits do not change even though the dollar limit on contributions increases.

ROTH IRAS

Whether or not you participate in a qualified retirement plan, you can fully fund a Roth IRA if you have earned income and your modified adjusted gross income in 2007 is no more than $99,000 if single or $156,000 on a joint return.

▶ **Partial contribution.** The contribution limit phases out for singles with MAGI between $99,000 and $114,000 and for those married and filing jointly with MAGI between $156,000 and $166,000.

Eligibility

There's no age limit for making a Roth IRA contribution. As long as you continue to work—at a job or self-employment—you'll be able to contribute to a Roth IRA (assuming your income level allows it).

Although contributions to a Roth IRA are not tax deductible, there's an even bigger tax incentive for making contributions. Income earned in the Roth IRA can be transformed into tax-free income under certain conditions: If the account has been open for at least five years and distributions are taken after age 59½, to pay first-time home-buying expenses (up to $10,000 in a lifetime) or on account of disability or death. The five years starts on the first day of the year to which the contributions relate.

 Strategy: Contribute by April 15 to start the five-year clock on January 1 of the preceding year. For example, if you make your Roth IRA contribution for 2007 on April 15, 2008, the five years starts to run from January 1, 2007.

Continued tax-free buildup

There are no required lifetime minimum distributions for Roth IRAs. If you don't need the funds, leave them in the account to build up on a tax-free basis for your heirs.

Deductible IRAs vs. Roth IRAs

Assuming you may have the choice between deductible IRAs and Roth IRAs, which should you choose? Consider the advantages to each option.

Comparison of deductible IRAs and Roth IRAs

Attribute	Deductible IRA	Roth IRA
Annual contribution limit	$4,000 ($5,000 in 2008)	$4,000 ($5,000 in 2008)
Catch-up contributions	$1,000	$1,000
Minimum age requirement	None	None
Maximum age limit for making contributions	70½	None
Lifetime distributions	Must commence at age 70½	Not required
Tax treatment of distributions	Fully taxable as ordinary income	Contributions can be withdrawn tax free at any time; earnings on contributions tax free after five years if taken after age 59½, for first-time home-buying expenses or on account of disability or death.

Converting to Roth IRAs

If your modified adjusted gross income does not exceed $100,000 (excluding income resulting from a conversion), you can convert a traditional IRA to a Roth IRA. *Caution:* If you're over age 70½, your required minimum distribution for the year must be included in your MAGI. Required minimum distributions will not count in figuring MAGI. *Note:* Starting in 2010, the MAGI limit on conversions is removed so anyone can make them at that time. For conversions made in 2010 only, resulting income is reported 50% in 2011 and 50% in 2012, unless you opt to report all of the income in 2010.

Advantages: You can create tax-free income. Earnings on converted amounts are tax free if distributions are not taken before the funds have been in the account for at least five years and you are at least age 59½, disabled or use the funds to pay first-time home-buying expenses (up to $10,000 per lifetime) or medical expenses. As explained earlier, the five-year period starts on the first day of the year to which the contribution (the conversion amount) relates.

Disadvantages: You pay tax on the converted amount as you would on a distribution. You would need money in addition to the funds in the IRA with which to pay the tax. If you use the IRA funds, you lose the conversion benefit to that extent.

 Strategy: Convert from a traditional to a Roth IRA provided that:
- ▶ *You are eligible to do so.*
- ▶ *You have the funds (outside of the IRA) to pay the resulting income tax.*
- ▶ *You have a long time horizon for savings.*

Generally, conversion works best for younger individuals with modest incomes, minimal IRA accounts and a long time frame for saving for retirement.

If you want to convert, do so before the end of the year to which the conversion would apply. Unlike making contributions, conversions must be made by year-end.

Strategy: Maximize above-the-line deductions (e.g., job-related moving expenses, student loan interest deduction and the deduction for early withdrawals from CDs) to bring down MAGI to be eligible for a conversion. Keep income down by agreeing to salary reductions (e.g., Flexible Spending Account contributions or 401(k) plan contributions).

▶ **Undoing conversions.** If you decide that converting your IRA was a wrong move because you weren't eligible or the value of the account dropped since the conversion—you are permitted to undo the conversion by recharacterizing the account as a traditional IRA. You may undo the conversion until October 15 of the year following the year of conversion. You'll have to file an amended return, if you've already filed, to delete the income resulting from the conversion and claim a refund.

 *Strategy: If the value of your IRA dropped since the conversion, you may wish to undo it so that you don't pay tax on the value that's disappeared. For example, if your IRA was worth $50,000 on September 1, 2006, when you converted it to a Roth IRA, but it's only worth $30,000 on February 1, 2007. Undoing your conversion will prevent you from having to report the $50,000 income when the account is now worth just $30,000. **Caution:** You can't reconvert in the same year. You must wait until the following year to convert to a Roth IRA.*

QUALIFIED RETIREMENT PLANS

 If you participate in a company-sponsored qualified retirement plan—profit-sharing, money purchase or pension plan—you have an excellent opportunity to build up retirement savings without any outlay. But make sure you understand your rights in the plan so you don't miss out on anything.

▶ **Vesting.** Although you may be allowed to participate in a plan, you may not automatically have an unconditional right to any benefits. In most plans, benefits "vest" over time—that is, become yours even if you leave employment.

Ask your plan administrator about the plan's vesting schedules...and how vested you are. If the new job won't wait, be sure to negotiate some compensation from your new employer for your lost retirement benefits. Some employers may offer nonqualified retirement plans to make up for your lost qualified plan benefits.

Strategy: Know vesting deadlines if you're thinking of changing jobs. You may benefit from additional vesting of significant retirement dollars by remaining in your current job a little longer.

▶ **Summary annual report (SAR).** Each year, the plan is required to give you at minimum a one-page report about the plan—how much money is in it, its investment performance, what plan trustees are paid and other administrative costs. If you suspect problems or have any questions that the plan administrator doesn't answer to your satisfaction, contact the US Department of Labor's Employee Benefits Security Administration (EBSA) (**www.dol.gov/ebsa**).

▶ **Naming beneficiaries.** Make sure to provide the plan administrator with the name or names of your beneficiaries. Your choice is important for two key reasons. First, it can affect how benefits are paid to you in retirement. For example, by naming a younger beneficiary you may be able to spread out your required minimum distributions. Second, when you die, benefits will be payable to the parties you name. In some cases, the law protects spouses by requiring that certain benefits be paid to them unless they waive this right in writing.

 Strategy: Place copies of all beneficiary designations with your other important papers. The plan administrator should have up-to-date designations in order to pay benefits to the correct beneficiaries.

EMPLOYEE STOCK OWNERSHIP PLANS (ESOPS)

You may own a part of the company where you work. You're an owner if you participate in a company employee stock ownership plan (ESOP). As with other qualified retirement plans, you're not taxed on what the company contributes to the plan on your behalf.

Participating in an ESOP means that the investment used to build your retirement savings is primarily employer stock. But whether you actually receive the stock or a cash equivalent, when to take a distribution depends on the plan. For example, if your employer is a closely held S corporation, the terms of the ESOP probably restrict distributions to cash so that the 100-shareholder limit on S corporations won't be violated.

Employee stock purchase plans

Note: These are not qualified retirement plans that defer taxes until some future date. But they can be an important way to save for retirement. These plans let you buy company stock at a discount—typically $10,000 worth. For example, you may be able to purchase the stock at a 10% or 15% discount from its market value.

Example: Under an employee stock purchase plan with a 10% discount, you invest $10,000 in employer stock in 2007. You have an immediate $1,000 gain (the difference between the value of the stock and its cost).

If you sell the stock immediately, your gain is short-term capital gain taxable at ordinary income rates. But, if you hold the stock for more than one year, your gain is long-term capital gain which will be taxed at no more than 15%.

SELF-EMPLOYED QUALIFIED RETIREMENT PLANS

Self-employed individuals can save for retirement through specially designed qualified plans. In the past, they were referred to as Keogh plans or HR-10 plans, but these designations are no longer used. Instead, self-employed individuals can use the same types of qualified plans open to corporations. These include:

▶ **Profit-sharing plans.** These are defined-contribution plans that do not require a definite formula for figuring the profits to be shared as long as there are systematic, substantial and nondiscriminatory contributions. Your retirement benefits depend on the plan's investment performance.

▶ **Money purchase plans.** These are defined-contribution plans that provide a definite formula for allocating contributions among participants (even if you're the only participant). Like profit-sharing plans, your retirement benefits depend on the plan's investment performance. Now that the increased deduction for profit-sharing plans equals the deduction for money purchase plans, the use of money purchase plans will decrease.

▶ **Defined benefit plans.** These are pension plans that provide promised benefits at retirement and actuarially determine the contributions required to fund these benefits. Investment risk is borne by the plan; you receive your promised benefit regardless of how well or how poorly the plan performs.

Comparison of plan options

Features	Profit-sharing or money purchase	Defined-benefit
Deduction limit	25% of compensation, but no more than $45,000*	Based on promised benefit
Guaranteed retirement benefit	No (whatever has accumulated in the plan)	Annual payments up to $180,000*
Annual reporting to the Department of Labor's Pension and Welfare Benefits Agency	Yes	Yes
Administrative costs	Plan adoption costs; annual accounting fees; fiduciary costs	Actuarial fees to determine contribution requirement; plan adoption costs; annual accounting fees; fiduciary costs

*These may be adjusted for inflation after 2007.

Choosing among plan options

The plan you select depends on several factors—the amount of money you want or can afford to contribute, the number of employees you must cover, if any, and your age.

You are permitted to adopt more than one plan. For example, you may combine a profit-sharing plan with a defined-benefit plan.

When defined-benefit plans make sense

If you, the owner, are more than 20 years older than your employees, you can garner the lion's share of company contributions. This is because there are fewer years for the plan to meet its pension obligations to you, so, to fund the obligation, the business must allocate the bulk of its contributions for your benefit.

Contribution limits for defined-contribution plans

Contributions for self-employed individuals are based on net earnings from self-employment—the same number used for figuring self-employment tax. To figure the deduction for contributions, net earnings from self-employment must be reduced by one-half of the self-employment tax payable.

You can deduct up to 25% of compensation to a defined-contribution plan (but no more than $45,000 in 2007). Your plan need not require the maximum percentage—you can, for example, opt for more modest amounts. As mentioned earlier, for self-employed individuals, the deduction percentage applied to net earnings from self-employment must be reduced by the contribution itself. The following chart shows the actual rate (the percentage specified in the plan minus the contribution under that percentage). For example, if your plan provides for a 20% limit, the actual rate of your deductible contribution is 16.6667%.

Tax-deductible contribution percentages for defined-contribution plans

Plan contribution rate	Your actual contribution rate
1%	0.9901%
2	1.9608
3	2.9126
4	3.8462
5	4.7619
6	5.6604
7	6.5421
8	7.4074
9	8.2569
10	9.0909
11	9.9099
12	10.7143
13	11.5044
14	12.2807
15	13.0435
16	13.7931
17	14.5299
18	15.2542
19	15.9664
20	16.6667
21	17.3554
22	18.0328
23	18.6992
24	19.3548
25	20.0000

Source: IRS Publication 560

Use the following worksheet to figure your maximum deductible contribution:

Worksheet for figuring your maximum deductible contribution for 2007

Step 1: Enter your rate from the rate table on page 125. _____

Step 2: Enter your net earnings (net profit) reported on Schedule C, C-EZ, F or K-1. _____

Step 3: Enter one-half of self-employment tax. _____

Step 4: Subtract Step 3 from Step 2 and enter the result. _____

Step 5: Multiply Step 4 by Step 1 and enter the result. _____

Step 6: Multiply $225,000 by your plan contribution rate. Enter the result, but not more than $45,000. _____

Step 7: Enter the smaller of Step 5 or Step 6. _____

Source: Based on worksheet in IRS Publication 560

SIMPLIFIED EMPLOYEE PENSIONS (SEPs)

Small businesses and self-employed individuals may want to provide retirement savings but don't want the complications and costs associated with qualified plans. The tax law allows them to set up Simplified Employee Pensions (SEPs). SEPs are a type of IRA. The employer (or self-employed person) contributes to a participant's separate IRA. Thus, funds for each participant are segregated from contributions made on behalf of other participants.

 Strategy: *Use a SEP to receive contributions even if you're over age 70½. There's no age limit on a SEP. However, you must take required minimum distributions if you have attained this age. Still, the account may grow—through new contributions and earnings on the account—even though distributions are being taken.*

Deductible contribution limits

SEPs have a deduction limit that's the same as profit-sharing plans: 25% of compensation up to a maximum contribution of $45,000 in 2007. But only a limited amount of compensation can be taken into account for purposes of figuring the deduction. For 2007, the limit is $225,000.

Comparison of self-employed SEPs to qualified plans

Feature	SEP	Qualified plan
Deductible contribution limit for self-employed individual	25% of net earnings from self-employment (reduced by one-half of self-employment tax and own contribution) up to $45,000*	*Profit-sharing or money purchase plan:* 25% of net earnings from self-employment (reduced by one-half of self-employment tax and own employment tax and own contribution) up to $45,000.* *Defined-benefit plan:* Actuarial amount necessary to fund benefit (generally higher than above limits for older self-employed individual).
Deadline for setting up plan	Extended due date of return	December 31
Deadline for making contributions	Extended due date of return	Extended due date of return (except plans subject to minimum funding requirement must do so by 7½ months after close of year).
Administration costs	Minimal	Fees to set up plan and keep it up to date. Also, for defined-benefit plan, annual actuarial fee to determine contribution.
Filing requirements	None	Annual reporting to the Pension and Welfare Benefits Administration (except for plans in 2007 and later years with total assets under $250,000 and no participants other than self-employed and spouse or partners and spouse).

*May be adjusted for inflation after 2007.

Self-employed SEP or other qualified plan?

Self-employed individuals can choose a variety of plans to save for their retirement on a tax-advantaged basis. However, as the name implies, SEPs may offer a significant savings opportunity with minimum trouble and cost.

SAR-SEPs

Before 1997, SEPs could be structured as salary reduction arrangements (SARs) under which employees agreed to make contributions with their pretax dollars. Although the opportunity to set up SAR-SEPs no longer exists, companies that had such plans in place before 1998 can continue to permit salary reduction contributions. The maximum salary reduction contribution is the same as the annual limit for 401(k) plans (for example, $15,500 in 2007). Catch-up contributions are also permitted.

SAVINGS INCENTIVE MATCH PLANS FOR EMPLOYEES (SIMPLEs)

SIMPLEs are a type of retirement plan limited to small businesses. So, if your employer has this plan or you're self-employed and set one up, you have the opportunity to squirrel away retirement dollars on a tax-advantaged basis.

SIMPLE plans can be set up either as SIMPLE IRAs or SIMPLE 401(k) plans. You can participate in the plan as long as you earned at least $5,000 in either of the two preceding years and reasonably expect to earn at least $5,000 this year. *Note:* For SIMPLE 401(k)s, you may be required to complete one year of employment before participating.

Contribution limits

You can contribute up to $10,500 in 2007 to a SIMPLE plan through a salary reduction plan. If you're self-employed, you can also contribute up to this amount based on your net earnings from self-employment without regard to any SIMPLE plan contributions you make on your own behalf. *Note:* For SIMPLE 401(k)s, contributions are limited to 25% of compensation, with an annual dollar limit ($10,500 in 2007).

The limit is adjusted for inflation. Also, those age 50 and older by the end of the year can make catch-up contributions of $2,500 in 2007. The catch-up contribution limit will be adjusted for inflation thereafter.

As an employee, if you agree to make salary reduction contributions to a SIMPLE plan, you aren't taxed on this amount. Your contributions are excluded from your income for federal income tax purposes. However, the salary reduction amounts are still considered wages for FICA tax, so Social Security and Medicare taxes on these amounts will be withheld from your paycheck.

Your employer must give you 60 days' notice about eligibility to participate in the plan. Within that time frame, you can sign a salary reduction agreement specifying the amount you wish to contribute. You retain the right to stop contributions at any time and for any reason. *Caution:* If you stop your contributions, you may not be able to resume them until the following year. The plan may allow you to resume contributions at the start of the next quarter but is not required to give you this option.

Employer contributions

In order to make SIMPLE plans nondiscriminatory (so that they don't favor owners and other highly compensated employees), an employer is required to make certain contributions on behalf of participants. Depending upon the contribution method selected by your employer, you may be able to optimize their contributions on your behalf by making the largest salary reduction contribution permitted.

▶ **Matching contribution formula.** Your employer may agree to match employee contributions, dollar for dollar, up to 3% of compensation. There's no limit on the amount of compensation taken into account for this purpose if the plan is a SIMPLE IRA; the compensation limit for qualified plans ($225,000 in 2007) applies to SIMPLE 401(k)s.

Example: Your compensation for 2007 is $100,000, and you agree to contribute $10,500 to your employer's SIMPLE IRA. If your employer is using the matching contribution formula, your employer will contribute $3,000 on your behalf ($100,000 x 3%). If you contributed only $2,500, the employer contribution would have been limited to $2,500 (3% of compensation up to a match of your own contributions).

 Strategy: *With SIMPLE IRAs, an employer is permitted to reduce matching contributions as low as 1% for any two years in a five-year period. If you participate in the plan solely to gain the matching funds, and your employer lowers the contribution, cut back on your salary contributions. In the example above, if the employer reduces its matching contribution to 1%, the employee maximizes by contributing just $1,000.*

▶ **Nonelective contribution formula.** Employers may opt to contribute 2% of employee compensation without regard to the employee's salary reduction amounts, instead of tying employer contributions to employee salary reduction amounts. Compensation for this purpose is limited to the compensation limit for qualified plans—$225,000 in 2007.

Example: Your compensation for 2007 is $100,000. If your employer has a nonelective contribution formula, he would contribute $2,000 to your account, whether you contribute the maximum of $10,000 or zero.

Self-employed individuals

You're treated as both the employer and employee under SIMPLE plan rules, even though you're self-employed. This means you can make *both* employer contributions and employee salary reduction contributions based on net earnings from self-employment.

Comparing retirement plan options for 2007: Maximum deductible contributions for self-employed individuals

Compensation*	SIMPLE IRA (combined salary reduction plus 3% employer matching)	SEP, profit-sharing plan or money purchase plan
$ 25,000	$11,250	$ 5,000
50,000	12,000	10,000
100,000	13,500	20,000
200,000	16,500	40,000
250,000	18,000	45,000

*Illustrations do not reflect any reduction in self-employment income for one-half of the self-employment tax.

Strategy: Optimize your retirement savings with a SIMPLE plan if your self-employment income is about $40,000. You may be able to save more through a SIMPLE plan than with a SEP or other qualified retirement plan. If you have self-employment income of $30,000 from a sideline business, consider the SIMPLE IRA to save for retirement on a tax-advantaged basis.

Converting SIMPLE IRAs to Roth IRAs

You are allowed to convert your SIMPLE IRA to a Roth IRA. Doing so means reporting all of the funds in the account—your own contributions, employer contributions and earnings on contributions—as income in the year of the conversion. Although rollovers to regular IRAs are subject to a 25% penalty if made within the first two years of plan participation, this penalty does not apply to conversions to Roth IRAs.

 Strategy: Convert from a SIMPLE IRA to a Roth IRA to create future tax-free income only if you have the cash to pay the tax on the conversion. Using SIMPLE IRA funds for this purpose limits your future tax-free income and triggers a penalty on the funds not converted if you're under age 59½ and/or you haven't participated in the plan for at least two years.

IRA RECORD KEEPER

In order to coordinate your investments, you need to maintain good records for each of your IRAs. You can do this with paper records, with computer software or even online. Record keeping for investments in general, which would include IRAs, is discussed in Chapters 7 and 22.

Also keep track of beneficiary designations. Don't rely on your IRA custodian to maintain beneficiary designation forms. Financial institutions merge, relocate or simply lose records over time.

 Strategy: Make new beneficiary designations if you no longer have copies of former designations. Ask each IRA custodian for a beneficiary designation form. Retain a copy of each new form for your records.

SPECIAL CONSIDERATIONS FOR MARRIED COUPLES

Married couples have a unique opportunity to save for their retirement. The tax laws permit contributions to an IRA for a nonworking spouse. And they create special protections for certain qualified retirement plan benefits for the nonparticipant spouse. But the law also adds restrictions on the ability of one spouse to contribute to an IRA when another spouse participates in a qualified retirement plan.

IRA benefits for a nonparticipant spouse

What happens if your spouse is covered by a qualified retirement plan but you're not? If you're working, you may be eligible to make deductible contributions to your own IRA. (Different MAGI limits apply in the case where both spouses are active participants.) You can make a fully deductible contribution if your combined MAGI is no more than $156,000. The deduction phases out for MAGI between $156,000 and $166,000. No deduction can be claimed if MAGI exceeds $166,000.

Example: In 2007, you and your spouse both work but only one is covered by a qualified retirement plan. If your combined MAGI in 2007 is $60,000, you can each make a fully deductible IRA contribution because you don't exceed the $83,000 MAGI limit. If your combined MAGI is $125,000, only you can make a fully deductible IRA contribution. In this event, you've exceeded the $103,000 limit but are below $156,000. But if your combined MAGI is $175,000, neither you nor your spouse can make a fully deductible IRA contribution because you've exceeded the $166,000 limit.

IRA benefits for a nonworking spouse

If only one spouse works, you can fund an IRA for the nonworking spouse based on your income. Your contribution limit for your spouse is $5,000 in 2007. Of course, if you're an active participant in a qualified retirement plan, your MAGI must permit you to make a contribution. The same is true if you opt for a Roth IRA.

 Strategy: *Contribute to a deductible IRA on your spouse's behalf even if you can't contribute to your own account because of the age limit. If you're over age 70½ but your nonworking spouse is under age 70½, you can contribute to a deductible IRA for your spouse. Age is no barrier to making Roth IRA contributions—for yourself or a nonworking spouse.*

Coordinating contributions

Married couples should consider dividing available funds between both spouses' IRAs if they lack the funds to make maximum IRA contributions to each account. This will enable each spouse to build up a personal retirement fund.

 Strategy: *Contribute more heavily to the younger spouse's IRA for a longer period of tax-free buildup. But if the couple expects to tap into IRA funds for retirement income, contribute more heavily to the older spouse's IRA.*

Tax Credit to Encourage Savings

If you are over age 18 and have modest adjusted gross income, you may be entitled to double-dip: Defer income for a 401(k) plan contribution or deduct an IRA contribution *and* claim a credit for doing so. There is a federal income tax credit of up to $1,000 for eligible individuals (details can be found on IRS Form 8880).

ABOVE AND BEYOND RETIREMENT PLANS AND IRAS

When you've contributed the maximum allowed to your 401(k) plan, IRA or other plan, you may still have available funds that you wish to save on a tax-advantaged basis. Consider the following approaches to supplement your retirement savings and improve your retirement income:

▶ **Annuities.** Annuities allow you to defer tax on earnings until you take distributions (i.e., begin to annuitize). Depending on state law and the terms of your policy, you may not have to take any distributions before age 90, allowing for years of tax-deferred buildup. If you die before starting distributions, the funds generally are payable to your named beneficiary.

▶ **Pay down debt.** A shrewd way to position yourself financially for retirement is to reduce debt and lower your monthly obligations. If you've maximized contributions to qualified plans and IRAs, use extra cash to pay down outstanding debt. *Caution:* Carefully weigh the advantages of paying off a home mortgage. You lose a tax deduction for the interest portion of payments. And, if the mortgage interest rate is low, you may profit by investing the extra cash.

Personal investments in stocks, bonds and mutual funds are discussed in Chapters 5 through 7.

9

Using your retirement savings

❝...*that happy age when a man can be idle with impunity.*❞ —Washington Irving

QUALIFIED PLANS AND IRAs offer the distinct advantage of tax deferral (and even tax-free income in the case of Roth IRAs). But there usually comes a day of reckoning when distributions must be taken. How you approach withdrawals is the key to minimizing taxes and making sure that the money lasts as long in your accounts as you do.

You can use your retirement savings for other than retirement purposes, such as making withdrawals or, in some cases, taking loans before you stop working. But most individuals want to keep retirement plans in reserve for the purpose they were intended—providing retirement income. And many want to use their retirement plans to provide an inheritance for their family.

This chapter explains how to tap into retirement plans *before* retirement should you want or need to do so. It covers the minimum distributions required to be taken from both qualified plans and IRAs in order to avoid penalties. It suggests strategies for minimizing distributions and avoiding problems. Throughout the chapter, "IRA" refers to the traditional, deductible IRA unless otherwise noted.

Building up retirement plans is discussed in Chapter 8.

BORROWING FROM RETIREMENT PLANS

Retirement plans may offer the flexibility of using money before retirement—tax free—by taking loans. This allows you to use the money without having to pay tax on it—if you do it right. If this option is open to you, you'll have to decide whether it's a good idea to borrow from your retirement plan or whether you should borrow elsewhere.

Advantages: The loan is easy to arrange. You simply ask the plan administrator, complete a short loan request and receive your check, usually in a few days. Also, the interest rate you pay on plan loans is usually low (about 1%–2% over the prime rate). And, best of all, you're actually paying the interest to yourself, because it's credited to your 401(k) account.

Disadvantages: You lose the opportunity to accumulate funds for retirement on a tax-deferred basis. Although repayments you make go back into your account, you don't earn anything on those funds until they're replaced. *Caution:* If you leave employment before you have fully repaid the loan and can't immediately pay back the remaining balance, the outstanding balance is treated as a distribution and becomes taxable at that time.

Qualified plans (including 401(k) plans)

A qualified plan may, but is not required to, allow participants to borrow against their benefits in the plan. If borrowing is permitted, the terms are governed by tax law:

▶ **Limit on borrowing.** You can borrow up to 50% of the amount in your 401(k) plan or your other plan benefits up to a maximum loan of $50,000.

▶ **Repayment terms.** The plan must require level payments that extend no more than five years (except in the case of borrowing for the purchase of a principal residence, where any reasonable repayment period is allowed).

▶ **Interest.** The plan must charge a fair rate of interest on the loan. Generally, this runs about 1%–2% above the prime rate.

 Strategy: Deduct the interest on the loan if the proceeds are used to buy a primary residence. The interest is treated as home mortgage acquisition debt and interest on up to $1 million is deductible. Caution: *You can't deduct interest if you're considered a "key employee"—an owner or highly paid employee (e.g., an officer earning more than an annual limit—$145,000 in 2007).*

IRAs

You can't borrow from your IRA or use it as collateral for a loan. Any amounts borrowed or pledged as collateral are treated as distributions.

Strategy: Use your IRA for a short-term loan. You can avoid taxation by replacing the borrowed funds within 60 days. You can only make one such withdrawal and repayment within a 12-month period ("one-year rule") for each IRA account you own. So you can tap into each separate IRA as long as each does not violate the one-year rule.

GETTING AT MONEY IN QUALIFIED RETIREMENT PLANS

Generally, distributions are not permitted before the normal retirement age fixed in the plan (such as 65), separation from service (leaving employment), disability or death. Plans are not *required* to distribute benefits when you leave the company, but they may (and generally do) offer this option.

Hardship distributions from 401(k) plans

These plans can permit distributions to participants, even those under age 59½, if there's a hardship—an immediate and heavy financial need for which no other funds are available. There's no dollar limit on the amount of distribution—the limit is the extent of your financial hardship. You have to demonstrate to the plan administrator that you have attempted unsuccessfully to raise the money through other means. *Caution:* If you receive a hardship distribution, you're barred from making any salary reduction contributions to the plan for the following 12 months.

What qualifies as a hardship?

▶ **Down payment** on the purchase of a principal residence for the participant or funds needed to keep the participant from being evicted from his/her home or suffering foreclosure on the home.

▶ **Medical expenses** for the participant and dependents.

▶ **Higher education costs** (e.g., tuition) for the participant and dependents.

▶ **Funeral costs** for a member of the participant's family.

Strategy: Factor into the hardship distribution proceeds any penalty tax you may owe if you're under age 59½. Eligibility for the hardship distribution doesn't negate the penalty. But the reasons for taking the distribution (for example, to pay heavy medical expenses) may qualify as an exception to the 10% early distribution penalty. Other exceptions to the 10% are summarized on page 139.

WHEN YOU LEAVE EMPLOYMENT

When you leave the company—voluntarily or otherwise—do your benefits come with you? It depends on the terms of the plan. Increasingly, benefits in qualified plans are "portable"—you can take them with you. If you have a choice of whether to leave benefits in the company plan or take them with you, consider the advantages and disadvantages of each alternative:

Advantages of taking benefits with you

▶ **Greater investment options.** If you transfer the funds to a separate IRA, you may gain access to a greater number of investment options. This may be advantageous when the company plan's performance has been mediocre or if your investment options in a 401(k) plan are limited.

▶ **You avoid spousal rights.** Although benefits in a 401(k) plan generally must be paid out in the form of a joint and survivor annuity (unless the spouse who isn't in the plan waives the joint and survivor right), benefits can be rolled over to an IRA where the spouse need not be a beneficiary on the account. No spousal consent is required to make a transfer from a 401(k) plan to an IRA.

▶ **Ease of tapping into the funds.** If you anticipate needing to take money from your benefits, transferring the benefits to an IRA will make things easier.

▶ **Ease of estate planning.** You generally gain greater flexibility in beneficiary planning if you roll over funds to an IRA. You can use multiple IRAs to provide for different beneficiaries. For instance, you can create one IRA to pass to charity if this is your wish, while having other IRAs for your children or grandchildren.

Disadvantages of taking benefits with you

▶ **Increased investment responsibility.** You may not want to take on investment responsibility, especially when the company plan's performance has been outstanding or at least respectable.

▶ **Loss of borrowing power.** You lose the opportunity to use the money as a source of borrowing; you can't borrow from an IRA other than the 60-day option discussed earlier.

▶ **Loss of benefits.** Retirement plans are supposed to be separate entities from the company. But a company's rocky finances can translate into a shaky plan, because the company can't make the contributions required to meet the plan's pension liabilities, which are your benefits. Defined-benefit and other plans subject to minimum funding requirements are "insured" by the Pension Benefit Guaranty Corporation (**www.pbgc.gov**), a federal agency that promises to pay a minimum benefit to participants of plans that can't meet their liabilities; the maximum pension guarantee for 2006 is $3,971.59 per month. But 401(k) and other defined-contribution plans, such as IRAs, don't have this government protection.

Taking employer securities

When you leave employment, you may be eligible to take employer securities with you. Taking the shares rather than cash can provide you with a significant tax-saving opportunity. Ask the plan administrator whether the plan allows for in-kind distributions.

Instead of rolling over the shares to your IRA, if you have the funds, pay the required taxes to reap a benefit in the long run. You will owe ordinary income tax on your basis in the shares (the value of the shares when they were contributed to the plan). All appreciation above that value—called net unrealized appreciation (NUA)—plus any future appreciation on the shares, will be converted to capital gains.

Example: You receive shares worth $200,000 that were valued at $50,000 when they went into the plan. You only owe income tax on $50,000.

 Strategy: *If you sell the shares immediately, the NUA qualifies for long-term capital gains tax rates. For example, you can sell enough shares to raise the cash needed to pay income tax both on the ordinary income plus the capital gains on the NUA.*

For future appreciation to qualify for long-term capital gains tax rates, you must hold the shares for more than 12 months following their distribution to you.

 Strategy: *Keep asset allocations in mind when holding onto employer securities. Your portfolio may become overloaded and risk having too many of your eggs in one investment basket. Weigh the tax cost of selling some shares in order to diversify and to protect yourself against the potential risk of a severe market decline in these shares.*

Cashing out

If you only have a small amount of benefits in the plan—$5,000 or less—your employer can (but is not required to) distribute the funds to you, whether you want to take a distribution or not.

 Strategy: *Direct funds to be transferred directly into an IRA of your choice to avoid immediate income tax on the funds (and a 20% withholding tax on the distribution). You can do this no matter how small the amount of your benefits.*

TAX DECISIONS FOR TAKING DISTRIBUTIONS FROM EMPLOYER PLANS

When you're entitled to take a distribution from a company retirement plan, you have certain choices—direct that the distribution be transferred directly to your own IRA (or to a qualified plan of a new employer if that plan accepts such distributions), keep the distribution and pay tax now or roll the distribution over to defer tax.

Direct transfers

You can instruct the plan administrator to transfer your benefits to an IRA. Because the benefits are not distributed to you directly, there's no 20% withholding tax.

In the past, to preserve the right to later roll over funds that were transferred to the IRA back into a qualified retirement plan, the IRA must have been a "rollover account" called a "conduit IRA." However, qualified retirement plans can now accept rollovers even if they don't come from conduit IRAs. Plans can accept all IRA rollovers except after-tax contributions, required minimum distributions and distributions to beneficiaries from inherited IRAs (unless the beneficiary is the participant's spouse).

Lump-sum distributions

If you keep the distribution—you need the cash for some immediate purpose such as starting a business—you must pay tax on the distribution. If you haven't made any after-tax contributions to the plan, the entire distribution is taxed as ordinary income.

▶ **10-year averaging.** If you were born before 1936, use special averaging to figure the tax on the distribution. The distribution must be a lump-sum distribution—that is, your entire account balance must be distributed to you within one year and you must have participated in the plan for at least five years. You're treated as having received it in equal amounts over 10 years. The tax is figured using the income tax rates in effect in 1986 for a single individual, regardless of your actual filing status in 1986 or now.

▶ **Withholding.** When a distribution is made to you, the plan is required to withhold 20% income tax from it. You report the withholding as a federal tax payment on your return to offset any tax liability on the distribution.

▶ **Subsequent rollover.** Taking a distribution does not prevent you from transferring the funds to an IRA to defer income tax. You have 60 days in which to complete the rollover to an IRA. *Caution:* In order to defer income tax on the entire distribution, you must put into the IRA not only the funds you received from the plan but also the 20% withheld from the distribution.

> **Example:** You opt to take a $100,000 distribution. The plan withholds $20,000, and you receive $80,000. Should you decide to make a rollover to avoid *all* income tax from the distribution, you'll have to add $20,000 from your pocket to the $80,000 from the plan to roll over the full $100,000. Then the $20,000 can be claimed as a credit on your return for the year of the distribution.

PENALTY-FREE MONEY BEFORE AGE 59½

Generally, withdrawals before age 59½ are subject not only to regular income tax but also to a 10% penalty. However, with some care, you can use the money in your qualified plan or IRA before age 59½ without penalty.

Caution: Consider tapping into these funds only as a last resort because of the disadvantages. You'll still owe regular income tax on the distribution. More importantly, you'll miss out on the opportunity to continue tax-deferred buildup of your retirement savings.

If you decide to tap into your retirement accounts, be sure that the exception to the penalty in question applies to your situation. Different exceptions may apply to qualified plans and IRAs.

Death

Benefits payable to a beneficiary on account of the death of an IRA owner or plan participant are free from the 10% penalty, regardless of the deceased person's age and regardless of the beneficiary's age. *Caution:* If a spouse inherits an IRA and elects to treat it as his or her own IRA, any distributions from this IRA before the surviving spouse's attainment of age 59½ would be subject to penalty.

Exceptions to the 10% penalty

Exception	Qualified plan	IRA
Death	Yes	Yes
Disability	Yes	Yes
Divorce (payments to spouse or ex-spouse)	Yes, if payable under a qualified domestic relations order (QDRO)	Yes, if made incident to divorce
First-time home-buying expenses	No	Yes
Health insurance premiums for unemployed individuals	No	Yes
Higher education costs	No	Yes
IRS levy	Yes	Yes
Medical expenses	Yes	Yes
Military on active duty at least six months since September 11, 2001, through December 31, 2007	Yes	Yes
Separation from service after attainment of age 55	Yes	No
Series of substantially equal periodic payments	Yes	Yes

Disability

If you become disabled and choose to take distributions, you will not be charged the 10% penalty. For this purpose, disability is very strictly defined, similar to the definition used for Social Security disability benefit purposes. A doctor must certify you are unable to engage in any substantial gainful employment because of a physical or mental condition expected to result in death or last at least 12 consecutive months. Gainful employment means the same type of work you performed before the disability. Partial disability isn't good enough. Having a mental condition, such as depression, won't be considered a disability unless it prevents you from working.

Divorce

If you're required to give all or a portion of your IRA or qualified plan benefits to your spouse or former spouse because of a marital split, you won't be taxed on those amounts as long as the distributions conform to special requirements:

▶ **Qualified domestic relations order (QDRO).** For qualified retirement plans, benefits must be directed to a spouse or former spouse as "alternate payee" by means of a QDRO. This is a court order specifying the alternate payee and the amount of the benefits (as a dollar amount or percentage of the participant's benefits).

▶ **IRA benefits.** You don't need a court order to split IRAs and avoid penalty. As long as distributions are made, incident to divorce, directly to the spouse or former spouse (or directly to the spouse's IRA custodian or trustee), the penalty is avoided. However, if distributions are made to you and you turn them over to your spouse, you'll be taxed on the distribution even if you're required by a divorce decree or separation agreement to make a certain payment to your spouse.

First-time home-buying expenses

You can use IRA money for a down payment, purchase price or other home acquisition costs for several people: You, your spouse or any child, grandchild, parent or grandparent of you or your spouse. The home must be a "first home," which means there was no home ownership within the past two years. And the expenses must be paid within 120 days of withdrawal from the IRA. This is a limited exception to the 10% penalty, because there's a lifetime cap of $10,000 that can be used for this purpose.

 Strategy: Roll the funds back into an IRA if the home purchase is delayed or falls through. If you take a withdrawal from an IRA for first-time home-buying expenses, you can replace the funds in your IRA within 120 days of the initial withdrawal. Replacement avoids not only the penalty but also income taxes on the distribution. And you preserve the right to take distributions for first-time home-buying expenses in the future.

Health insurance premiums for unemployed individuals

If you're unemployed and receiving unemployment benefits for at least 12 consecutive weeks, you can tap into your IRA to pay health insurance premiums without penalty. This exception also applies to self-employed individuals who aren't eligible for unemployment benefits because they are self-employed. This exception ceases to apply to distributions made more than 60 days after you've returned to work.

Higher education costs

You can withdraw funds to pay qualified higher education costs for yourself, your spouse or a child or grandchild of either you or your spouse. Qualified higher education costs include tuition, books, supplies and equipment paid during the year of the distribution. It also includes room and board for a student enrolled at least half time.

IRS levy

If the IRS levies upon your benefits to satisfy an outstanding tax liability, you aren't subject to penalty. But you still have to pay tax on the distribution even though it isn't a voluntary distribution.

Medical expenses

Distributions aren't taxable if used to pay substantial medical expenses, defined as those in excess of 7.5% of your adjusted gross income. This exception applies whether or not you itemize your deductions.

Military personnel on active duty

For a limited time—September 11, 2001, through December 31, 2007—those on active duty for more than six months can take penalty-free withdrawals from IRAs and/or qualified retirement plans. *Bonus:* Funds can be replaced in accounts within two years of returning from active duty. However, if a reservist's active duty ended before August 17, 2006, these re-contributions must be completed by August 17, 2008.

Separation from service after age 55

If you take early retirement after you turn 55, you can take a distribution from your company retirement plan penalty free. This exception to the 10% penalty doesn't apply to distributions from IRAs, which continue to be subject to penalty until you attain age 59½ unless another exception to the penalty applies.

Substantially equal periodic payments

Avoid the penalty by taking distributions in equal payments similar to an annuity. The payments must run at least five years or until you attain age 59½, whichever comes later. For example, if you start distributions at age 52, they'll have to continue until age 59½. If you start at age 57, they'll have to continue until age 62 (five years).

There are certain IRS-approved ways to figure these periodic payments. Select the method that gives you the payments you want:

▶ **Amortization method.** Divide your account balance by your life expectancy (see the IRS life expectancy table in IRS Publication 939, *General Rules for Pensions and Annuities*) but include a reasonable interest factor. The interest rate factor ranges from 80% to 120% of the long-term applicable federal interest rate (AFR) in effect at the time you start distributions. For example, in November 2006, the long-term rate was 4.9%, so any rate from 3.92% to 5.88% would be considered reasonable. *Note:* Generally, this method results in the largest annual payments.

▶ **Annuity factor method.** Same as above, but instead of using the IRS life expectancy table, use insurance mortality tables (such as UP-1984 Mortality Table).

▶ **Life expectancy method.** Divide your account balance by your life expectancy (a factor that's stated in the IRS life expectancy table). Generally, this method results in the smallest annual payments.

 Strategy: Break your IRA into two or more separate IRAs and tap into just one if you only need a small monthly income. Substantially equal periodic payments are figured on a per-IRA basis.

 Strategy: Work with an accountant or tax professional to make sure payments conform to IRS requirements. If the payments don't conform, the penalty relates back to all distributions. For example, if you start taking distributions at age 52 and stop after five years at age 57, you'll owe the penalty tax on all distributions taken during those five years. Fees for professional advice will be less than penalties that you might otherwise owe.

Using the periodic payments exception requires special care. Little mistakes can cause big tax consequences, triggering the penalty on *all* distributions as explained above. Here are some things to avoid:

▶ **Don't take any distributions other than those required** under the substantially equal exception in the same year as the required fifth year. The additional distribution will be viewed as part of the required distribution and the total will not be equal to the distributions in the four prior years.

▶ **Don't change the required payments in any way**—increasing or decreasing them—because they'll no longer be considered equal.

Special rules for Roth IRAs

You can withdraw your own contributions to a Roth IRA at any time without penalty. But if you want to withdraw earnings on your contributions, only certain withdrawals are permitted penalty free and income tax free. Distributions are treated as being taken in the following order:

► First, your own contributions.

► Then, earnings on your contributions.

Distributions of earnings can be taken income tax free *if* the funds have been in the account for five years *and* at least one of the following conditions is satisfied:

► You attain age 59½.

► You die or become disabled.

► You use the funds to pay first-time home-buying expenses up to $10,000 (the lifetime limit), medical expenses or health insurance premiums.

The five-year period starts on the first day of the year to which the contribution relates.

Example: If you contributed $4,000 on April 15, 2007, for the 2006 tax year, the five-year period commenced on January 1, 2006.

Special rules for converted IRAs

The distribution may be income tax free, yet still subject to the 10% penalty if you tap into your funds within five years of converting your traditional IRA to a Roth IRA. If separate conversions are made, the five-year period applies to each conversion. For example, you converted to a Roth IRA in 2006 and, in 2007, you take a distribution of the initial conversion amount, leaving the earnings in place. If you're not at least 59½, disabled or using the money to pay first-time home-buying expenses, you're subject to the 10% penalty.

AVOIDING MINIMUM DISTRIBUTION PENALTIES

When the day of reckoning comes and you start to take distributions from qualified plans or IRAs, withdrawals generally are taxed as ordinary income. Special rules on the tax treatment of lump-sum distributions were discussed earlier in this chapter.

Strategy: Check for state income tax exemptions or special tax rules on pensions and other distributions. Part or all of the distributions may be free from state income tax. Remember that the tax on retirement benefits is determined by the state in which you live when you receive distributions, not the state in which you lived when you earned them.

The law imposes a hefty penalty of 50% on insufficient distributions after age 70½. To avoid this penalty, make sure you know when distributions must commence and how much they must be. You can, of course, take all of your funds at any one time without penalty after age 59½ (or, if under age 59½, you meet another exception to the 10% penalty).

When distributions must begin

Distributions must begin for the year in which you attain age 70½. So if you turn 70½ on August 1, 2007, you generally must take your first distribution by the end of 2007.

For the first year, instead of taking the first distribution by December 31, you can postpone it until as late as April 1 of the year following the year in which you attain age 70½.

 Strategy: *Take your first distribution by December 31 of the year in which you turn age 70½. Although you're allowed to postpone your first required distribution until April 1 of the following year, it's generally not a good idea. This will result in receiving two distributions in the same year—the first distribution by April 1 and the second distribution by December 31. Delay the first distribution to April 1 of the following year only when you project that your overall income will drop in that year, putting you in a lower tax bracket.*

Exception from commencing distributions at age 70½: Distributions from qualified retirement plans—but not from IRAs—can be postponed until you retire if the plan includes this postponement option. For example, if you turn age 70½ in 2007 but continue to work at your job, you can delay taking distributions from the company's qualified retirement plan until you retire, if the plan gives you this option.

This exception does not apply to individuals who own more than 5% of the company. For example, sole proprietors cannot postpone required minimum distributions even though they continue to work in their self-employment business.

It's not clear whether this rule applies to distributions from plans at former employers. For example, if you worked at Company A for 20 years and amassed a pension there, can you delay distributions if you're age 70½ but currently working at Company B? The IRS hasn't ruled on the question, and the courts haven't considered it yet.

Multiple IRAs

If you have more than one IRA, you add up the account balances to figure a single required minimum distribution for the year. Take that required amount from any one or more of your IRA accounts.

 Strategy: *If you have multiple IRAs, take distributions from the lowest-performing IRA account first. But if you've set up multiple IRAs to provide separately for beneficiaries, consider the impact of distributions on the beneficiaries and their eventual inheritance. In this case, you may want to take equal amounts from each IRA to maintain the relative size of each beneficiary's account.*

If you have multiple self-employed retirement plans—for example, one for a profit-sharing plan and another for a money purchase plan—you must take required minimum distributions from each plan. You cannot opt to take distributions from just one plan as you can with IRAs.

FIGURING REQUIRED MINIMUM DISTRIBUTIONS

Tax deferral can go on for only so long. At some point you must start taking money out of your retirement accounts and paying taxes on your distributions. Required minimum distributions (RMDs) are amounts that must be taken in order to avoid a 50% penalty. RMDs are figured according to a simplified method using a Uniform Lifetime Table that treats the individual as if he or she has a beneficiary who's 10 years younger, regardless of whether there's any named beneficiary or whether any named beneficiary is younger or older.

The required minimum distribution is based on the account balance on December 31 of the previous year. If you're figuring your required minimum distribution for 2007, look at the account balance as of December 31, 2006.

 Strategy: *Check your year-end statement for the account to find the IRA's value on December 31. Or look at IRS Form 5498,* IRA Contribution Information, *that custodians give to IRA owners in May to report year-end account balances for the prior year.*

Uniform Lifetime Table

Age	Distribution period	Age	Distribution period
70	27.4	93	9.6
71	26.5	94	9.1
72	25.6	95	8.6
73	24.7	96	8.1
74	23.8	97	7.6
75	22.9	98	7.1
76	22.0	99	6.7
77	21.2	100	6.3
78	20.3	101	5.9
79	19.5	102	5.5
80	18.7	103	5.2
81	17.9	104	4.9
82	17.1	105	4.5
83	16.3	106	4.2
84	15.5	107	3.9
85	14.8	108	3.7
86	14.1	109	3.4
87	13.4	110	3.1
88	12.7	111	2.9
89	12.0	112	2.6
90	11.4	113	2.4
91	10.8	114	2.1
92	10.2	115 and thereafter	1.9

Source: IRS Publication 590

To figure your RMD, each year simply look at your age in the table to find the distribution period—that is, the number you use to divide your account balance to arrive at your RMD.

> **Example:** Someone age 72 with an account balance of $100,000 as of December 31 of the prior year would have an RMD of $3,906 ($100,000 ÷ 25.6).

IRA custodians must inform IRA owners and beneficiaries of the need to take RMDs and report this information to the IRS.

Spouse more than 10 years younger

If your beneficiary is your spouse and he or she is more than 10 years your junior, you can figure your RMD using a joint and last survivor table based on your joint life expectancies. This will produce an even smaller RMD than if the Uniform Lifetime Table is used.

Naming beneficiaries

You can name someone as the beneficiary of your account. This beneficiary inherits whatever remains in the account upon your death. The beneficiary need not be your spouse, child, relative or even a friend. You can name a trust as beneficiary. Or you can name your estate as beneficiary, distributing your retirement benefits or IRA to beneficiaries according to the terms of your will. You can even name a charity as beneficiary. *Note:* In the past, naming an estate or charity as beneficiary would result in larger lifetime RMDs, but this is no longer the case. The only beneficiary designation that affects lifetime RMDs is a spouse who is more than 10 years younger than you.

Your choice of beneficiary will, however, affect RMDs after your death. This is because distributions after your death can be based on the life expectancy of the beneficiary who inherits the plan benefits or IRA account. In order to use life expectancy for figuring post-death RMDs, there must be a "designated beneficiary"—an individual (or in some cases a trust) specified in a beneficiary designation form who is alive on September 30 of the year following the year of your death. If there is no specified beneficiary on September 30, then there is no "designated beneficiary." If the original beneficiary disclaims an interest or takes his full portion of an interest before this date, then the successor or remaining beneficiary is considered the designated beneficiary.

Note: An estate or charity can *never* be considered a designated beneficiary. If a trust is named to inherit benefits, the trust beneficiary is treated as the designated beneficiary (as long as certain documents are provided to the IRA custodian or trustee).

 Strategy: You can change beneficiary designations, including contingent (or successor) beneficiary designations, at any time until your death.

The amount of the RMD for a beneficiary depends on whether you die before your required beginning date or on or after it and who the beneficiary is:

▶ **If you die on or after the required beginning date.** If there is a designated beneficiary, he generally must take required minimum distributions over his life expectancy (based on the distribution period found in the Single Life Expectancy Table, a different table from the Lifetime Distribution Table). Each year thereafter, the beneficiary simply reduces the initial distribution period by one.

If there is *no* designated beneficiary, then required minimum distributions are figured using your age on your birthday during the year of your death. Each year thereafter, the beneficiary simply reduces the initial distribution period by one.

▶ **If you die before the required beginning date.** If there is a designated beneficiary, the beneficiary must take distributions over his life expectancy based on the Single Life Table, *unless* the IRA trustee requires or allows the beneficiary to elect to the use of the five-year rule. Under the five-year rule, no distributions need be taken until the end of the fifth year following the year of death—but there must be a complete distribution by this date.

If there is no designated beneficiary, the five-year rule automatically applies and the account must be distributed in full by the end of the fifth year following the year of death.

If you name your spouse as the designated beneficiary, she may roll over the funds into her own IRA. This will allow her to postpone starting RMDs until her required beginning date and then figuring RMDs based on her own life expectancy.

Strategy: *Retain all of your beneficiary designation forms. Banks and other plan administrators can easily lose these documents. If you don't have the forms now, request new forms so you can complete them and retain copies.*

Multiple beneficiaries

You can opt to have more than one beneficiary for a retirement plan or IRA (for example, your two siblings or your three children). Alternately, you can divide your IRA accounts to name separate beneficiaries for each account.

Be sure to provide for successor beneficiaries in case any of your designated beneficiaries dies before you. For example, if you name your three children as beneficiaries and one child predeceases you, provide that your deceased child's children (your grandchildren) will inherit their parent's share.

Strategy: *Amend the beneficiary designation form to allow for successor beneficiaries if the plan administrator or custodian permits it. If not, you may wish to change to a financial institution that allows successor beneficiary designation.*

Beneficiaries may be changed at any time—even *after* death. For example, a beneficiary might opt to decline an IRA bequest by disclaiming an interest in the account; payment would then be made to the successor beneficiary.

Additional thoughts for your beneficiaries

To enable your beneficiaries to optimize tax deferral from your IRA, do one important thing in addition to naming your beneficiaries: Plan for the payment of estate taxes if your estate is substantial. If you don't plan who will be responsible for the payment of estate tax on the inherited IRA—the designated beneficiary or the executor of your estate—it may fall on your beneficiary. Unless your beneficiary has outside funds to pay the estate tax, he'll have to invade the IRA for this purpose. This, in turn, will trigger a tax cost in addition to the estate tax. Withdrawing funds from the IRA will also result in income tax to the beneficiary.

Strategy: *Consider leaving your IRA to a trust for the benefit of your named beneficiary. Instruct the trust to pay its share of estate tax before any distributions are made to the beneficiary.*

PLAN DISTRIBUTION ROLLOVERS

Rollovers are transfers of retirement plan funds that postpone immediate income recognition. They can be used to move money from qualified plans into IRAs or between IRAs or even from IRAs back into qualified plans (if the plans accept such rollovers).

Rollover of distributions from qualified plans

When you retire or otherwise leave employment, you may have the option of receiving your benefits in the company's qualified plan. If you decide to take a distribution, payment can be made in two ways:

▶ **Direct transfer.** The plan transfers the assets or cash directly to an IRA of your choosing. Because no funds are disbursed to you, there's no 20% withholding.

▶ **Rollover.** The plan can transfer assets or cut a check payable to you. *Catch:* The plan is required to withhold 20% of the distribution. If you later move the money into an IRA, you'll have to deposit not only the funds you received but also the 20% withheld in order to avoid having any portion of the distribution treated as taxable. If you make up the 20% out of pocket to complete the rollover, you can effectively claim the 20% as a credit on your tax return and receive a refund at that time.

Rollovers can be made for distributions from qualified retirement plans, including 401(k) plans, SEP-IRAs and SIMPLE IRAs (although a rollover from a SIMPLE IRA is penalty free only after the account has been open for two years).

Rollovers can include after-tax contributions. However, this rollover rule does not apply to IRAs.

IRA rollovers

You can roll over funds from one IRA to another once within a 12-month period. This one-year limit applies on a per-IRA basis.

A rollover is made by taking a distribution from one IRA and then placing the funds back into the same IRA or into a new IRA. The replacement of funds or the transfer to a new IRA must be completed within 60 days of taking the distribution.

The IRS now has the authority to extend the 60-day rollover period if the inability to complete the rollover was out of your control (for example, your hospitalization, error by the financial institution or the post office, or restrictions imposed by a foreign country).

> **Strategy:** *Avoid the one-year rule by making a direct trustee-to-trustee transfer of IRA funds. Instruct funds to be shifted directly from one IRA to another and not to you. The trustee or custodian of one IRA can be instructed to transfer the funds directly to the trustee or custodian of another IRA. There is no limit under the tax law on the number of direct transfers you can make each year. But, as a practical matter, the trustee or custodian may put its own restrictions on direct transfers by charging commissions or transfer fees or not allowing them.*

Note: You may be forced to use the rollover method to make a transfer if a current trustee or custodian is reluctant to move the money and delaying would foul your investment opportunities. Weigh the inconvenience of a direct transfer against any lost investment opportunity.

When not to make a rollover

Rollovers are encouraged as a means of deferring recognition of income on receipt of company retirement plan benefits. But sometimes it may make sense *not* to make a rollover. If you receive company stock as part of the distribution, it is advisable *not* to roll over the shares but rather to pay tax currently.

WHEN YOU INHERIT AN IRA

Inheriting an IRA

Even if you saved nothing yourself, you might inherit an IRA that could become one of your largest assets. Make sure you act promptly to preserve your rights in the account:

▶ **If you're a surviving spouse,** decide whether to roll over an inherited IRA. You must act no later than December 31 of the year following your spouse's death. You don't have to make a rollover; you can simply commence RMDs over your life expectancy. But if you don't make the rollover or commence RMDs by this date, you'll have to take all of the funds from the account no later than the end of the fifth year following the year of your spouse's death.

▶ **If you're a beneficiary other than a surviving spouse,** you must decide no later than September 30 of the year following the year of the IRA owner's death how you'll take distributions from the IRA: Over your life expectancy or in full by the end of five years (if the owner died before his required beginning date and the IRA custodian allows you to use the five-year rule).

 Strategy: If the funds in an inherited IRA won't raise your standard of living, consider disclaiming it so that the funds will pass to a younger person. This will allow the inherited IRA to be distributed over the new beneficiary's life expectancy. For example, if a grandparent leaves an IRA to his child, the child might disclaim, passing the IRA to the grandchild if the grandchild was designated as the successor beneficiary. Funds would thus be distributed over the grandchild's longer life expectancy. Caution: This disclaimer must be made within nine months following the IRA owner's death.

Splitting IRAs

If one IRA has been left to multiple beneficiaries, required minimum distributions are based on the life expectancy of only the oldest beneficiary. However, the account can be split among the beneficiaries. As long as this is done no later than September 30 of the year following the year of death, then this will allow each beneficiary to decide whether to take the money immediately, whether to let it continue to build up on a tax-deferred basis and which investments to make with the account funds.

Multiple IRAs

Using more than one IRA account makes sense for a number of reasons. You may want to have different types of investments—for example, just mutual funds in one IRA but a variety of investments through a self-directed IRA at a brokerage firm.

But a more important reason to consider multiple IRAs is for beneficiary planning. Having multiple IRAs allows you to name a single beneficiary for each account. This, in turn, gives your beneficiaries greater flexibility. For example, after your death, one beneficiary may want to spread out required distributions while another may want immediate cash. If each is the beneficiary of a separate IRA, the choice of each can easily be accommodated. Although IRA accounts can be divided among multiple beneficiaries after your death, this is an added administrative step that can be avoided by establishing multiple IRAs.

For required minimum distribution purposes, annual distributions can be taken from any one or more of your multiple IRA accounts. You can consequently tailor your beneficiaries' inheritances by choosing to tap into one or more accounts while leaving others untouched.

DONATING IRAs TO CHARITY

For 2006 and 2007 only, those age 70½ and older can opt to transfer funds directly from their IRA to a public charity. While no charitable contribution deduction can be claimed, the transfer is tax free. The limit on these transfers is $100,000 per year. You can name a charity as a beneficiary of your IRA. Because charities aren't subject to income or estate taxes, a charitable beneficiary will inherit the IRA completely tax free. If you planned to leave something to charity, then using an IRA for this purpose is wise, because you can then use other assets—free from income tax—to benefit your other heirs. Thus, more of your assets will pass to beneficiaries and less to the US Treasury.

TAPPING INTO SIMPLE PLANS

You are fully vested in all contributions made to a Simplified Savings Incentive Match Plan for Employees (SIMPLE) plan—your own salary reduction contributions as well as employer matching contributions. However, if you make withdrawals before age 59½, you're subject to a 10% early distribution penalty unless one of the exceptions explained earlier in this chapter applies. *Caution:* If you take distributions within the first two years of plan participation, the penalty increases to 25% unless another exception to the early distribution penalty applies.

Distributions

As with IRAs and other qualified plans, you must commence taking required minimum distributions from SIMPLE plans at age 70½.

Rollovers

You can roll over your SIMPLE IRA to another SIMPLE IRA or to a regular IRA. *Caution:* A rollover from a SIMPLE IRA to a regular IRA within the first two years of plan participation is treated as a taxable distribution and may also be subject to penalty.

SPOUSAL BENEFITS UNDER QUALIFIED RETIREMENT PLANS

Certain qualified retirement plans are required to protect a spouse's interest in the participant's plan benefits by mandating that distributions be made in the form of a joint and survivor annuity.

Waiving spousal benefits

A spouse can waive this benefit, allowing the participant to take a lump-sum distribution (that can be rolled over to an IRA) or a single life annuity. Why make the waiver? The couple may prefer *not* to take benefits in the form of an annuity, preferring instead to roll over benefits to an IRA. This would allow for investment opportunities that could build up the funds, providing for greater payouts for the couple. Alternately, the couple may want the larger benefits resulting from a single life annuity and they aren't concerned about receiving benefits after the participant's death.

 Strategy: *Beware of any waivers made in a prenuptial agreement. A prenuptial agreement to this effect isn't sufficient; the required waiver must be signed after one becomes a spouse.*

YOUR STATE AND RETIREMENT BENEFITS

Where you live when you collect benefits affects the tax you'll pay on this income. Under federal law, states are barred from taxing benefits on nonresidents. So, for example, if you earn a pension in New York but retire to Florida to collect your pension, New York cannot tax that income. The same is true for payments made to retired partners—the state in which the payments were earned cannot tax the income if the payments are made after the partner becomes a resident of another state.

States have varying rules on the extent to which pensions and retirement income are taxed. For example, a number of states exclude all government pensions. Some states exempt a portion of retirement benefits earned at private companies or through IRAs (e.g., Louisiana—$6,000; Michigan—$35,920 in 2006; New York —$20,000). About half the states do not tax retired military pay.

10

Investing in real estate

"*It is a comfortable feeling to know that you stand on your own ground.***"** —ANTHONY TROLLOPE

A GREAT DEAL OF WEALTH in this country has been created through real estate holdings. Home prices in the past few years have shot up as mortgage rates remain low and the stock market continues to disappoint. Even relatively modest investments in this asset, like the purchase of a home, can provide significant opportunities for generating wealth. And real estate investments need not be made only by an individual. You can invest in real estate and real estate–related securities through various publicly traded vehicles.

This chapter examines various types of real estate investments you may make, from personal residences and vacation homes to more sophisticated real estate investment trusts (REITs) and mortgage-based securities. There are also explanations of various funding mechanisms, such as mortgages and refinancing. And throughout the chapter, the tax rules that help make real estate investments worthwhile are considered.

YOUR HOME AS A TAX SHELTER

A home may be the single largest purchase you'll ever make. But, more importantly, it's the place where you'll live, probably for years to come.

Your home can also become your personal tax shelter and give you special tax considerations when you sell it.

Current write-offs for home ownership

Some costs of home ownership are currently deductible, while others are not. Current deductions reduce the out-of-pocket cost of these items.

> **Example:** If you claim a deduction for $10,000 of eligible costs—interest on your mortgage and real estate taxes—and you're in the 28% tax bracket, your out-of-pocket cost is only $7,200 (the value of the deduction is $10,000 x 28% or $2,800).

Caution: High-income taxpayers may lose some benefit from their home-related itemized deductions.

You can deduct as itemized deductions:

▶ **Mortgage interest** on your main home *plus* one other home (such as a vacation home). However, limits apply. For loans to buy a home ("acquisition indebtedness"), you can deduct interest on loans up to $1 million. For loans other than acquisition indebtedness ("home-equity loans"), you can deduct interest on loans up to $100,000. So, for example, if you obtain a $25,000 mortgage to buy your home, you can fully deduct the interest on the loan. Similarly, if you take out a home-equity loan of $25,000 to renovate your kitchen, interest on the loan is fully deductible. To qualify for deductible mortgage interest, the loan must be secured by the home (that is, you must risk foreclosure on the property if you fail to repay the loan).

▶ **Real estate taxes.** There's no dollar limit on this deduction.

▶ **Casualty and theft losses.** If your house is damaged by storm, fire or other casualty and you're not compensated by insurance, you can deduct your loss if it exceeds 10% of your adjusted gross income (after reducing the amount of the loss by $100).

You cannot deduct:

▶ **Homeowner's insurance**

▶ **Maintenance and repairs**

▶ **Utilities**

> *Strategy: Deduct allowable expenses and depreciation on your home if you use a portion of your home for business and meet IRS requirements, explained in this chapter. Or see IRS Publication 587,* Business Use of Your Home. *You will, however, have to recapture the depreciation when you sell your home. Depending on how long you use your home office, you may not be able to apply the exclusion of gain on the sale (see below) to the business portion of your home.*

Tax-free sales

When you sell your home, you may be eligible to exclude up to $250,000 of gain ($500,000 on a joint return). This means that your profit becomes tax free.

Eligibility: You must own and use the home as your principal residence for three out of five years preceding the date of sale. If you're married, only one spouse has to meet the two-year ownership test (that is, title can be held in the name of one spouse). The joint $500,000 exclusion can be claimed as long as both spouses satisfy the two-year use test and neither spouse has claimed the exclusion within the past two years. The two years don't have to be consecutive, and temporary absences, such as a one-month vacation, are disregarded.

If you have more than one residence, only one is a principal residence at any one time (determined by your use of it during the year). But you can claim an exclusion once every two years, so each home can ultimately entitle you to an exclusion.

> **Example:** You live in a home in Connecticut, your principal residence, for seven months and another in North Carolina for five months. But if, within the five-year period, you live primarily in the Connecticut home in years two and three and in the North Carolina home in years four and five, then either home exclusively is eligible for the exclusion. You can sell one and claim an exclusion. After two years, you can sell the other and claim another exclusion.

If you have to move before satisfying the two-year test because of a change in employment, for health reasons or other circumstances, you can prorate the exclusion for the period of time that you've satisfied the test. For example, if you are relocated after you have owned and used your home for one year, you can claim half the exclusion.

Tax-free borrowing

You don't have to sell your home to reap tax-free returns. If the value of your home has appreciated and/or you've paid down your mortgage, you can tap into the equity for tax-free funds. Of course, you'll have to repay the mortgage, which will cost you not only initial lending costs but also interest on the loan (discussed later in this chapter). However, with mortgage rates down, wrapping your existing mortgage into a new low-rate loan may not cost you much more each month than you're already paying (depending, of course, on how much you borrow and what the difference is between the old and new interest rates).

> **Example:** You bought your home eight years ago for $200,000, using a $160,000 mortgage. Since then, in this hot real estate market the value of your home has risen to $350,000 while the balance on your mortgage has declined to $150,000. There is potentially $200,000 of equity ($350,000 less $150,000) that you can extract from your home via a mortgage (although lenders may not necessarily let you borrow this entire amount).

MAKING THE DOWN PAYMENT

Home ownership can produce tax write-offs that reduce your ongoing costs. But how do you raise the capital needed to become a homeowner in the first place? Saving for a down payment can take years. Some are fortunate to have family to assist with a down payment, as either a gift or a loan. Others may qualify for a no-money-down mortgage. For others, special tax rules can help you raise the down payment necessary for home ownership.

No-money-down mortgages

You may be able to become a homeowner without a down payment. Some lenders are willing to make no-money-down mortgages. To qualify, you need a high income and a good credit rating. But qualifying for this mortgage will cost you in the long run. You'll pay 1% or more interest on the loan.

Sources of no-money-down mortgages include:

▶ **Bank of America** (888-293-0264)

▶ **Countrywide Home Loans** (800-669-6659)

▶ **GMAC Mortgage** (800-638-4622)

▶ **Wells Fargo Home Mortgage** (800-234-1625)

 Strategy: *Beware of no-money-down financing unless you expect to remain in your home for several years. If you sell earlier than a few years, you'll have to pay out-of-pocket broker fees. Unless the home's value has appreciated, you won't have paid down the loan sufficiently in a short time to cover this cost.*

Interest-free or below-market family loans

You may be able to borrow a down payment from a relative. Before you do so, make sure this won't invalidate your mortgage agreement. In some cases, the bank wants you to have the down payment outright (as savings or a gift) and may require a statement from you that funds from a relative are a gift and not a loan.

Assuming you need a loan and have a willing lender with favorable terms, understand the tax ramifications of your arrangements. Generally, if you obtain a loan at an interest rate below the rate that the IRS considers to be a market rate (this rate changes monthly and is posted on the IRS Web site at **www.irs.gov**), the lender is treated as receiving the amount of forgone interest (the difference between the market rate and interest actually received). This forgone amount of phantom income is called "imputed interest."

However, intra-family loans can be made *without* triggering attribution of this phantom income to the lender.

▶ **Loans up to $10,000** can be made as a "gift loan" without imputing income to the lender. This dollar limit applies to the total amount of loans between the parties.

▶ **Loans up to $100,000** can be made as a "gift loan" without the lender having to recognize income as long as the borrower's net investment income—from dividends, interest, etc., less related investment expenses—does not exceed $1,000. If net investment income exceeds this limit, then the imputed interest rules apply, but only to the extent of the borrower's net investment income.

 Strategy: *Put the terms of an intra-family loan in writing. Include repayment terms, interest rate (if any) and other conditions. A promissory note will enable the lender to claim a bad debt deduction if the borrower fails to repay the loan. Without such written evidence, the IRS may argue that the loan was a gift, not a loan.*

Penalty-free IRA withdrawals

If you're under age 59½, withdrawals from IRAs generally are subject to a 10% penalty. But you can withdraw from your IRA up to $10,000 to buy your first home. First-time home-buying expenses include a down payment, closing costs and other related expenses only if you have not owned a home within the past two years. The funds must be used within 120 days following withdrawal, but if the deal falls through, the funds can be rolled back into the IRA so long as the repayment takes place within that 120-day period.

There are, however, drawbacks to tapping into your IRA:

▶ **IRA withdrawals are taxable.** Even though you may escape the 10% penalty, you'll still pay ordinary income tax on the withdrawal, leaving you only the net (after-tax) amount for home-buying purposes.

▶ **Withdrawals reduce your retirement savings opportunities.** Because the withdrawn funds cannot be replaced, you lose out on tax deferral.

▶ **The $10,000 limit is a lifetime cap** on penalty-free IRA withdrawals for home-buying purposes.

 Strategy: Use this IRA penalty exception to avoid mortgage insurance limits. Generally, if you put down less than 20% of the purchase price, the lender requires you to carry mortgage insurance—called private mortgage insurance (PMI)—which adds additional cost to the loan. By increasing your down payment, you may save more on mortgage interest than you would have earned from your IRA investment.

Hardship distributions from 401(k) plans

If you participate in a company 401(k) plan that permits hardship distributions, consider turning to the plan for a down payment on your home. To qualify for this distribution, you have to show the plan administrator that you can't raise the money in any other way.

There are also drawbacks to taking a hardship distribution from your 401(k) plan:

▶ **If you're under age 59½,** you'll owe both regular income tax and a 10% early distribution penalty on the distributions.

▶ **You're barred from contributing** any part of your salary to the plan for the 12 months following the distribution.

▶ **You lose out on the opportunity to build up your retirement savings in the plan.**

Tax credit for first-time home buying in the District of Columbia

A special tax credit of up to $5,000 can be claimed by first-time home buyers in Washington, DC. A tax credit reduces your taxes dollar for dollar.

Example: You qualify for the full credit, and your tax liability for 2007 is $7,250. You can reduce the amount of taxes you owe by $5,000, leaving you with a tax liability of only $2,250.

If the amount of the credit exceeds your tax liability (with certain adjustments), you can carry forward the excess amount to offset your liability in a future year.

You're treated as a first-time DC homeowner if you haven't owned another home in Washington, DC, within one year of the date of purchase. However, the credit phases out for higher-income taxpayers, so your eligibility depends on your modified adjusted gross income for the year of purchase. *Note:* This tax break is set to expire at the end of 2007 unless Congress extends the law.

FINDING A MORTGAGE

Most people don't have the cash to pay for their house in full. Instead, they finance the purchase by obtaining a mortgage to cover a substantial portion of the cost of a home (generally, 80% of the cost). In shopping for mortgages, there are a number of features to explore.

Type of mortgage

There are two basic types of mortgages (as well as a hybrid of the two):

▶ **Conventional mortgages** provide for a fixed interest rate and a fixed monthly payment. During the earlier years, payments are largely interest. As the mortgage matures, payments are largely principal.

 Strategy: When interest rates are rising, lock into a fixed rate. For a modest charge, which may be merely a deposit, you can lock in a rate for 45 days, 60 days or other term while your mortgage application is processed.

▶ **Adjustable rate mortgages** (ARMs) provide an interest rate that adjusts according to a set formula. There are one-year adjustables where the rate changes annually, three-year adjustables where the rate is fixed for the first three years and adjusts annually thereafter, or any other variation that incorporates an interest rate that adjusts according to changes in current interest rates. *Caution:* Make sure there's a cap on the maximum interest rate adjustments (for example, no more than 2% per year with an overall cap at 12% interest). *Extra caution:* Stay away from ARMs with negative amortization, where your principal balance *increases* under certain conditions. Make certain the mortgage specifically states that there's no amortization of any kind.

▶ **Convertible mortgages.** These start out as ARMs but can be converted to a fixed term at your option. But because you usually pay a premium for this type of mortgage (for example, slightly higher introductory rates) be sure you understand what you're getting.

 Strategy: Use an ARM only if you can't afford a conventional mortgage. Otherwise, opt for a fixed-rate loan. Although the introductory rate can mean very low mortgage payments, when the rate adjusts, the payments may become unmanageable unless your income has increased sufficiently.

Term

How long will the loan run? Today most conventional mortgages run for a 30-year term. You can, however, obtain a conventional mortgage for almost any term you select. For example, you can opt for a 15-year mortgage.

It's a basic rule that the shorter the term, the larger the monthly payments. If you can make larger monthly payments, a 15-year mortgage will cut substantially the total amount of interest you'll pay on the loan. If you can't manage the larger payments required for a 15-year mortgage, inquire about a 20-year or 25-year loan, which may be feasible for you.

Caution: In most cases, stay away from 40-year mortgages. Although the monthly payments may be slightly lower than those on a 30-year mortgage, the amount of additional interest you'll pay over the term of the mortgage is huge. If, however, this is the only way to qualify for a mortgage, it may be worthwhile in order to gain home ownership; you can refinance for a shorter-term mortgage later on.

Interest rate

Mortgage interest rates in the marketplace change, usually from week to week. Your rate generally is the market rate at the time you close on the mortgage or as of another date on which you've locked in the rate. Use the following chart to see how much a loan will cost you in monthly payments.

The cost of monthly mortgage payments per $1,000 borrowed on a conventional 30-year mortgage

Rate	Term of the mortgage			
	15 years	20 years	25 years	30 years
5%	7.91	6.60	5.85	5.37
5.5%	8.18	6.88	6.15	5.68
6%	8.44	7.17	6.45	6.00
6.5%	8.72	7.46	6.76	6.33
7%	8.99	7.76	7.07	6.66
7.5%	9.28	8.06	7.39	7.00
8%	9.56	8.37	7.72	7.34
8.5%	9.85	8.68	8.06	7.69
9%	10.15	9.00	8.40	8.05

How to figure monthly payments: Divide your mortgage by $1,000 and multiply by the number in the row and column that correspond to your interest rate and mortgage term.

> **Example:** If you obtain a $200,000 mortgage at 6% for 30 years, your monthly payments for the next 30 years are $1,200 ([$200,000 ÷ $1,000] x 6.00).

Points

Points are charged by lenders to offset interest rates. One point equals one percent of your mortgage. *Rule of thumb:* The higher the points paid up front, the lower the interest rate you'll pay.

> *Strategy: Pay points to achieve a lower rate mortgage if you expect to recover those points within three to five years. Generally, one point can lower your interest rate by as much as ½ of 1% (for example, from 7% down to 6.5%). But if you expect lower rates in the future, keep the cash in reserve to refinance your mortgage when rates drop.*

If the bank gives you a choice to pay points in exchange for a lower interest rate, make sure you receive at least a 0.25% reduction of interest for every point you pay.

To determine whether to accept points or use the money you would pay for points to reduce the amount of the loan you need, use the Mortgage Points Calculator at **www.dinkytown.net/java/MortgagePoints.html.**

Special features

If you borrow more than 80% of the cost of the home (i.e., your down payment is less than 20% of the cost), you'll probably be required to carry private mortgage insurance (PMI) to cover the difference. The cost of PMI is figured into your monthly payments. For 2007 only (unless Congress extends the break), those with adjusted gross income of no more than $100,000 can claim an itemized deduction for PMI on mortgages obtained after 2006.

> *Strategy:* Make sure to drop the mortgage insurance once the equity in your home is greater than 20% of its value. Equity is increased by paying off part of the principal of your mortgage. Equity also increases when home prices rise.

Accelerating payments

Additional payments can shorten the term of a mortgage significantly, speeding up the equity buildup and saving thousands of dollars in interest. Obviously, the higher the interest rate, the more dramatic the savings.

> **Example:** You have an outstanding 6.5% 30-year mortgage taken two years ago. The original loan balance of $210,000 is now $205,149. If, instead of making a payment of $1,329 once a month, you make a payment of $665 every two weeks (resulting in one additional payment per year of $1,329), you'll reduce the term of the mortgage by eight years and two months and save more than $75,000 in interest.

Accelerate payments simply by sending in additional amounts with each mortgage payment you make. Most mortgages have no prepayment penalties. You don't need permission to make additional payments of principal. But ask your mortgage company for forms required with your additional payment so your payments will be credited properly.

> *Strategy:* Check your annual mortgage statement to make sure that additional payments have been credited to principal and not applied to escrow or attributed to some other purpose.

Accelerate payments through a mortgage acceleration program that may be offered by your mortgage company. There is usually a small fee for arranging the accelerated payments (for example, $300 up front and $5 with each payment). This additional cost may be well worth the expense. If you lack the discipline to make additional payments on your own, then using the program enables you to save thousands of dollars in interest over the life of the loan.

Tax treatment of mortgage payments

The tax laws favor home mortgages by allowing interest payments as itemized deductions. At the end of each year, the lender will send you a statement showing the amount of interest you've paid for the year; it sends a copy of this statement to the IRS as well.

Interest on a mortgage to buy or build a home—called "acquisition indebtedness"—is deductible on loans up to $1 million. Interest on other home mortgages—called "home-equity loans"—is deductible on loans up to $100,000. Thus, interest on loans up to $1,100,000 can be fully deductible. In both cases, however, the mortgage must be secured by the home.

Points

If you pay points—a type of up-front interest charge expressed as a percentage of the mortgage (for example, one point is 1% of the mortgage)—to obtain a mortgage to buy or build your home, deduct the points in the year you pay them. The closing statement for your home will identify the amount of points you've paid.

 Strategy: *Amortize mortgage-interest points over the term of the mortgage. Deduct them in equal amounts over the term, instead of writing them off in the year of payment. Choose this strategy if you won't benefit from a current write-off. For example, if you obtain the mortgage late in the year and your itemized deductions would not exceed the standard deduction, you'll be able to receive a tax benefit from them in future years by amortizing them.*

Shopping for a mortgage

In the old days, you would probably get your mortgage from the neighborhood bank where you had your savings and checking accounts. Today, there's usually little reason to be restricted to this one lender. You can shop around for the best terms, such as the lowest interest rates, few if any points and low closing costs.

 Strategy: *Consider shopping for a mortgage before you find the home you want. By prequalifying for a loan, you may be in a better position to negotiate the purchase price of a home—an edge that may be particularly useful in a tight real estate market.*

To shop for a mortgage online:
- ▶ Interest.com **(www.interest.com)**
- ▶ Lending Tree **(www.lendingtree.com)**
- ▶ MortgageExpo.com **(www.mortgageexpo.com)**

WHEN TO REFINANCE

If you have a high interest rate mortgage and the rates have come down, or if you have an adjustable rate mortgage and you want to lock into a fixed-rate loan, you may want to refinance your mortgage. This means obtaining a new loan to pay off the old one.

Should you refinance?

Some experts suggest that when there's an interest rate differential of at least two percentage points—for example, your loan is 8% and the current rate is 6%—it may pay to refinance. But a drop in the interest rates may not be enough to justify refinancing. Usually expect to recover your refinancing costs within about 18 months. Also anticipate remaining in your home for

some time to come. For example, if you plan to sell in three years when your children go to college, it probably doesn't make sense to refinance.

Costs of refinancing can include:

▶ **Points,** which are up-front interest charges.

▶ **Bank attorney's fees** (typically several hundred dollars).

▶ **Title and mortgage insurance updates.**

▶ **Mortgage recording taxes.**

▶ **Escrow costs** for property taxes and homeowner's insurance. If you refinance with a new lender, you probably have to put a certain amount into the lender's escrow account to cover your property taxes and homeowner's insurance. But this isn't lost money; it's used for your benefit. And you'll recoup your escrow balance from your old mortgage.

 Strategy: To save expenses, refinance with your existing lender. The lender may waive certain costs. But if the lender has sold your mortgage, then refinancing with the lender is like starting from scratch and can entail the same costs as using a new lender.

Tax treatment of points on refinancing

Individuals who have high interest mortgages may want to refinance for a lower rate. As I explained earlier, the lender may charge "points," a type of up-front interest charge, to bring down the rate on the mortgage—the greater the points, the lower the interest rate. One point equals one percent of the mortgage amount.

Points on refinancing are deductible, but the question is *when* you can claim the deduction. Points incurred to refinance the outstanding balance of an old mortgage are not immediately deductible. Points paid on acquisition indebtedness are deductible immediately. Instead, they must be amortized (deducted in equal amounts) over the term of the new mortgage.

 Strategy: If you are refinancing a mortgage that you've already refinanced so that you have been amortizing the points on the refinance, don't forget to deduct your remaining points in the year of your second refinancing. For example, if in 2005 you refinanced your original mortgage and paid $1,200 in points on a 30-year mortgage, you can deduct $1,180 if you refinance again in 2007 (you only deducted $40 in 2005 and in 2006).

CUTTING YOUR PROPERTY TAXES

If your home is overvalued or there's an error in the tax records, you may be paying more in property taxes than you should. According to the International Association of Assessing Officers, more than 50% of homeowners who challenge assessments get them reduced. But you must act to get a reduction; your city or town won't volunteer to check that your assessment is correct.

Check your current assessment

At your town or county assessor's office, check on the description of your property—its size, the description of your home and whether any personal property is included in the home's assessment.

Review comps in your area

The assessment of your home is based on its value, which, in turn, is based on a comparison with other homes in your neighborhood. Compare the assessment of your home with the assessments of homes you believe have similar value. Find similar homes by checking recent home sales in your area.

Obtain an appraisal of your home

If you think the town has overstated the value of your home, get your own appraisal. Use only an appraiser with the right credentials. *Cost:* Between $400 and $500.

List special factors affecting value

Your home's location may affect its value. If you are on a busy street with heavy traffic, the value would be less than if you were on a quiet cul-de-sac. Location near a highway is another negative factor. Look for changes that may have occurred since your home was last assessed (for example, a newly constructed mall or highway near your home).

 Strategy: Take advantage of special exemptions that entitle you to property tax reductions. Your local tax assessor's office can provide you with a list of exemptions. Exemptions may be available for senior citizens, veterans and the legally blind or disabled persons. States may create limited exemptions for owner-occupied homes (for example, New York's STAR program). See if your home qualifies for exemptions for historic properties or rehabilitated properties.

File for an assessment reduction

Each year, localities conduct hearings for assessment challenges. Gather all your information and present your case. Make sure you find out the rules, such as what you'll need to present and when you must appear. Failure to follow these rules can mean waiting another year for a contest.

REMODELING

Remodeling is a way to get the home you desire without moving. You'll enjoy the results for as long as you remain there. While comfort is often the primary motivator in renovating, your efforts should add to the value of your home so that you'll be able to recoup some or all of your investment when you sell.

Remodeling is expensive due to high demand for contractors and the high cost of lumber and other materials. Before you sink a lot of money into remodeling your home, make sure it's a wise decision. Here are some dos and don'ts for remodeling:

Do...

▶ **Select the right project.** Understand which projects are likely to recoup your investment when you sell. *Examples:* Kitchens and bathrooms are the best projects. Swimming pools, especially in the Northeast, are the least likely to hold their value.

▶ **Keep general standards of good taste in mind.** For the permanent aspects of a project—tile, appliances, etc.—use neutral colors that have general appeal. For the aspects that can readily be changed —paint, wallpaper, window treatments—you can deviate from the basics if you prefer, as a buyer can easily make changes.

▶ **Make energy-saving improvements.** Save both utility costs and taxes by making your home more energy efficient. There are federal tax credits for adding insulation, storm windows, solar energy and other energy improvements (but the credits only apply for a limited time). There may be state incentives as well, including income tax and sales tax breaks and special financing arrangements.

Don't...

▶ **Overdo it.** You don't want your house to be the highest valued home in the neighborhood, because it's unlikely you will recover your investment when you sell.

▶ **Do it yourself only if you can do it right.** You may be able to repaint or wallpaper, but adding a bathroom or a skylight may require the skills of a professional.

▶ **Overextend yourself.** Make sure you know the cost, time and effort entailed.

To learn about home remodeling—cost, project suggestions, other ideas—check out: **www.building online.com, www.build.com, www.thisoldhouse.com, http://doityourself.com, www.nari.org** (National Association of the Remodeling Industry) and **www.remodeling.hw.net** (*Remodeling Magazine*'s cost vs. value report).

VACATION HOMES

Y ou may buy a vacation home for fun—a ski chalet in Aspen or Stowe or a beachfront condo in Vero Beach. But don't overlook financial considerations when deciding to own a vacation home. You may be eligible for certain tax breaks that can make such ownership even more attractive.

Current tax write-offs

If you use your vacation home solely for yourself and your family, your deductions are limited to the same as those for your main home:

▶ **Mortgage interest within limits.** For loans for a second home ("acquisition indebtedness"), you can deduct interest on loans up to $1 million. For home-equity loans, you can deduct interest on loans up to $100,000. For example, if you obtain a $25,000 mortgage to buy your home, you can fully deduct the interest on the loan. To qualify for deductible mortgage interest, the loan must be secured by the home (you risk foreclosure on the property if you fail to repay the loan).

▶ **Real estate taxes.** There's no dollar limit on this deduction.

▶ **Casualty and theft losses.** If your vacation home is damaged by storm, fire or other casualty and you're not compensated by insurance, you can deduct your loss if it exceeds 10% of your adjusted gross income after reducing the amount of the loss by $100.

Caution: Buying a time-share in a vacation home doesn't entitle you to claim any tax breaks. A time-share isn't ownership in real estate; it's merely the right to use the property for a certain period of time.

Renting out your vacation home

If you don't use your vacation home all the time and don't mind having someone inhabiting your home, you may be able to claim special tax breaks for renting your home to strangers:

▶ **Rentals of less than 15 days per year.** All rent receipts are tax free in this case. For example, if you rented out your home in Miami for one week for Super Bowl XLI in 2007, you don't have to report the payment you received. However, you can't claim any deduction for maintenance or for expenses other than those that can be deducted by any homeowner—mortgage interest, real estate taxes and unreimbursed casualty losses.

▶ **Rentals of at least 14 days or 10% of the days rented in the year.** If your personal use of the home exceeds 14 days or 10% of the number of days the home is rented during the year, whichever is greater, you must report your rental income. However, you can claim deductions to the extent of this rental income. *Result:* You cannot claim rental losses unless they result from deductions that any home-owner can claim (mortgage interest, real estate taxes and casualty losses). But if your personal use is less than 14 days or 10% of days rented, your losses aren't limited by the vacation home rules. Instead, they're limited by the passive loss rules. Generally, this means that rental expenses are limited to rental income and other passive activity income; however, in the year you sell the home, losses become fully deductible.

 Strategy: Have your rental agreements reviewed by a tax professional when planning to rent out your vacation home. For example, if you place your beachfront condo with a leasing agent, make sure you understand what you can and cannot deduct.

Selling your vacation home

Your vacation home is a capital asset. If you sell your vacation home for a profit, your gain generally will qualify for favorable capital gains tax rates.

 Strategy: Convert your vacation home into your main home. If you sell your main home and make your vacation home into your main home, you can qualify for the $250,000/$500,000 home-sale exclusion as long as you meet the ownership and use requirements discussed in this chapter.

If you sell your vacation home at a loss, you won't be able to write it off. A loss on the sale of a vacation home is a nondeductible personal loss; only business and investment losses are deductible.

MULTIFAMILY HOMES

Buying a multifamily home, such as a two-family house, may be a way for you to own your own home. The tenants' rents offset your mortgage payments and other costs.

Strategy: *Make sure you carry the adequate homeowner's insurance to protect your personal areas of the house and the rental portions. For example, if your tenant slips in the hall, you want your homeowner's policy to cover any liability claims against you.*

Selling your multifamily home

When you sell your home, only the portion of the home used as your personal residence can qualify for the home-sale exclusion. The other portion is business property, and any gains on the sale would be taxed.

▶ **Depreciation recapture.** When you sell your home at a profit, the gain on the rental portion of the home qualifies as long-term capital gain (assuming you owned the home for more than one year). However, only a portion of this gain is taxed at the 20% capital gains rate. Depreciation that you've claimed on the rental portion of the home must be "recaptured" (taxed) at a 25% rate. Any gain in excess of this depreciation recapture amount is then taxed at 20%.

HOME OFFICES

Today, millions of Americans use their homes to conduct business, as telecommuters, for after-hours assignments or to run their own business. Using a home for business requires you to examine certain legal and tax issues.

Zoning

Are you allowed to conduct business from your home? Local zoning regulations will provide the answer. Check with your local zoning board for clarification. For example, you may be allowed to use your home for business but may be restricted from putting up any sign for the business.

Insurance

Will your homeowner's policy cover your business needs? Make sure the policy provides property protection for damage or theft of business property and liability protection in case business visitors are injured on the premises. You may need to obtain a rider to your homeowner's policy to be sure you have the necessary protection. Or, you may want to buy a separate business policy—typically a few hundred dollars a year—to cover home-office-related concerns.

Tax write-offs

Can you deduct the costs of maintaining your home office? The tax laws require that the office generally be used as your principal place of business. This is defined as using a home office for administrative or managerial tasks, such as bookkeeping and scheduling, if there is no other fixed location for performing these tasks. If you're an employee, business use of a home office must be for the convenience of your employer (for example, there's no company office for you to use).

Impact on a home sale

Using a portion of your home as a home office won't limit your ability to claim the home-sale exclusion. You can use the exclusion for gain on the entire home, including the home-office portion. However, you are required to "recapture" depreciation claimed on your home office when you sell the home. Depreciation claimed on or after May 7, 1997, is subject to recapture—it's taxable at a 25% tax rate.

INVESTING IN REAL ESTATE INVESTMENT TRUSTS (REITs)

If you want to invest in real estate without buying individual properties, do so through real estate investment trusts (REITs). These are publicly traded companies that invest in real estate, acquiring, leasing and managing realty such as shopping malls, office complexes, apartments and hotels. This investment is similar conceptually to a mutual fund. By investing in a REIT, you obtain:

▶ **Professional management.**

▶ **Diversification.**

▶ **Liquidity.** Unlike individually owned property that can take time to sell, you can opt to sell your REIT holding at any time.

By law, REITs are required to pay out 95% of their income, so they are ideal for producing income for investors. You may also realize capital gain or loss on your investment when you sell your holding.

As with any investment, read the prospectus carefully before you invest. Check out the REIT's properties and load charges, if any. The highest-yielding REIT may not necessarily be the best investment. Look for the creditworthiness of the managers and the occupancy rates for the properties. Instead of buying a REIT directly, you can buy shares in a real estate mutual fund that invests in REITs. Examples:

▶ CGM Realty Fund (**www.cgmfunds.com**, 800-345-4048)

▶ Columbia Real Estate Equity Fund (**www.columbiafunds.com**, 800-338-2550)

▶ Van Kampen Real Estate Securities Fund (**www.vankampen.com**, 800-421-5666)

MORTGAGE-BASED INVESTMENTS

Instead of investing in real estate, consider investing in mortgages related to real estate. As a group, these investments are referred to as mortgage-backed securities (MBSs) or mortgage pass-through certificates. At present, the MBS market is more than $4 billion. Generally, you buy an interest in a pool of mortgages or mortgage-backed securities, giving you a pro rata share of the cash flow from the mortgages. Your share of that cash flow is taxed as ordinary income.

165

Types of MBSs

The largest segment of the MBS market is based on Fannie loans (agency obligations of Fannie Mae, Freddie Mac and others are discussed in Chapter 6). MBSs include:

▶ **Collateralized mortgage obligations (CMOs)**—bonds collateralized by mortgages or mortgage-backed securities. See page 86 for more information.

▶ **Real estate mortgage investment conduits (REMICs)**—fixed pools of mortgages on which multiple classes of interests are issued to investors. *Note:* Today, CMOs and REMICs are often used interchangeably, with REMICs in greater use.

▶ **Stripped mortgage-backed securities (SMBSs)**—mortgage securities in which the underlying MBS is separated from principal and interest payments.

Strategy: *Take a miscellaneous itemized deduction for your share of the expenses for the mortgage-backed securities. For example, you may also be allocated a share of the REMIC's expenses. If so, you can deduct your share as a miscellaneous itemized deduction subject to the 2% of adjusted gross income floor.*

11

Collecting antiques

❝*Have nothing in your houses that you do not know to be useful or believe to be beautiful.*❞ —WILLIAM MORRIS

COLLECTING, WHETHER IT'S BOTTICELLIS or Beanie Babies, can provide both personal enjoyment and a solid investment. Hunting for the items and displaying them can be fun, and you may also reap financial rewards if you decide to sell your collections. But owning antiques and collectibles has its drawbacks.

Despite high prices on the buying end, don't be fooled into believing that antiques and collectibles are your avenue to financial success. The occasional story about someone finding a rare piece of pottery at a flea market or an old master at a garage sale is not the norm. Financially speaking, antiques and collectibles shouldn't be the cornerstone of your financial plans. But, with some planning and a good understanding of the antique and collectibles marketplace, you can view collections or special items as an attractive addition to an overall financial plan.

This chapter explains the ins and outs of collecting from a financial perspective and how to find bargains. It explains the tax consequences of selling items and how you can turn your collecting passion into a profitable business. It also explains special concerns for online auctions from both buyer and seller perspectives and special insurance concerns for valuable collections.

Estate planning for your collection is discussed in Chapter 20.

WHERE TO BUY OR SELL ANTIQUES AND COLLECTIBLES

The Antiques Roadshow, PBS's highest-rated show, celebrated its 10th anniversary and demonstrates the interest that Americans have in collecting and preserving items from the past. By far, the most common way to acquire an antique—technically, something over 100 years old—or a collectible, is as a family heirloom handed down from generation to generation.

But, there are numerous other ways to find items and as many ways to sell them. *Where* you hunt for or sell your items will often influence their prices.

Popular places to buy or sell antiques and collectibles

There are many ways to locate antiques and collectibles or sell them:

▶ **Antique shows.** Single-day or weekend events in cities nationwide. *Note:* With the advent of online auctions, the number and quality of antique shows has diminished considerably.

▶ **Antique stores.** A term that's often used quite liberally to cover both the stores on New York's Madison Avenue as well as junk shops around the country.

▶ **Auction houses.** Christie's and Sotheby's are the two most well-known houses. But there are numerous auction houses nationwide. Many of these specialize in certain types of antiques—furniture, porcelain, jewelry, etc.

▶ **Consignment shops.** Antique and collectibles stores stocked with items on consignment (the items aren't owned by the store owner but by outsiders who place items for sale and give the store owner a commission on the sale).

▶ **Estate sales.** When heirs don't want items or the estate needs to raise cash, items may be sold, typically through an auction-type process.

▶ **Flea markets.** There are thousands nationwide. Some local markets are held weekly. Larger markets attracting dealers from across the nation generally have limited dates, such as set weekends each year.

▶ **Garage and yard sales.** Homeowners eager to clean house may pack a yard with numerous items. Sometimes neighbors get together to host multifamily sales; they jointly advertise the sale, but each homeowner sells his or her own items.

▶ **Online auctions.** Amazon, eBay, Yahoo! and other online auction sites let you browse thousands of items daily from the comfort of your home. Online auctions are discussed in greater detail later in this chapter.

▶ **Thrift shops.** Generally run by charities, they sell items that have been donated.

Working with dealers

Dealers who sell collectibles can be a great resource for helping you locate items, evaluate what you've found and even resell items later on. In working with dealers, keep certain things in mind:

▶ **Don't assume that dealers know everything about the items they deal in.** Dealers, no matter how reputable, can be fooled by reproductions. And not all dealers may put in the time required to learn about the items they sell.

▶ **Don't assume that dealers are always working in your best interests.** They may undervalue items you want to sell in order to acquire bargains for themselves.

Getting appraisals

Before sinking any big bucks into an antique or collectible or selling a family heirloom, make sure you know what you've got. Do your own research at the library or online. If you can't find out an item's value through your own research, get the opinion of a qualified appraiser.

The type of appraiser you should use depends on the item you want appraised. You may be able to use a local appraiser (ask at a local antique store or, in the case of jewelry, a local jewelry store). For expensive works of art, furniture and other valuable antiques, contact Sotheby's or Christie's. If you can't locate the appropriate appraiser through your local phone directory, obtain a referral through:

▶ American Society of Appraisers (**www.appraisers.org**, 800-272-8258)

▶ International Society of Appraisers (**www.isa-appraisers.org**, 206-241-0359)

General rules for buying

Before you invest substantial sums in collectibles, make sure you understand what you're doing:

▶ **Buy the best you can afford.** Good items usually hold their value and even appreciate, whereas the prices of more common items generally don't move up.

▶ **Check condition.** While the key to real estate is location, location, location, the key to collectibles is condition, condition, condition. The most serious impact on price is the condition of an item. Damage, which may result in your being able to purchase the item at a reduced price, will also depress any price you're likely to receive on a resale. Items can be professionally restored, but this is expensive and still brings down the selling price.

▶ **Know what you're buying.** The best advice you can take is to "buy the book" first. There's a book available on almost any type of item you're interested in collecting. The book not only explains what to look for in these items but may also provide some price guidelines to get you started. *Caution:* Price guidelines are only guidelines; remember that prices change all the time.

▶ **Set limits.** Collecting can become a mania, eating up not only your time and attention, but also investment dollars you may need for the future. Decide in advance how much you have to spend on your collection and stick to it.

PROFITING FROM ANTIQUES AND COLLECTIBLES

Making money with antiques and collectibles is *possible* but not a certainty. Investing money in antiques and collectibles should be driven primarily by your enjoyment of the process and of owning the items, not your expectations of financial gains. Ask yourself, "If this item has no value, would I still want to own it?" If the answer is, "Yes, I'd enjoy owning it," then buy it, assuming you think the price is right. But if you're only buying an item to make money from a future sale, think twice before forging ahead.

Become an educated collectibles consumer

You must become a savvy shopper to be able to spot a bargain when you see it. General collector guides include:
- ▶ **Kovel's Antiques and Collectibles Price List** (800-571-1555)
- ▶ **The Lyle Official Antiques Review** (800-631-8571)
- ▶ **Warman's Antiques and Collectibles Price Guide** (800-258-0929)

There are also national trade papers—*Antiques and the Arts Weekly* (203-426-8036) and *Maine Antique Digest* (207-832-4888)—that can provide you with breaking news on collectibles—what's hot, recent sale prices, schedule of antique shows and auctions and more.

As the old Wall Street adage goes, to make money in the stock market you need to buy low and sell high. In the collectibles market, this means buying at *below* retail prices.

 Strategy: *Don't rely on price guides for determining value. Although the guides may be a good starting point, you need to consider many other elements—how old the guide is (prices change), recent sales of similar items and the state of the economy. High-priced antiques and collectibles are usually the first investments to be hit when the economy declines.*

Risks in buying antiques and collectibles

Buying valuable items is no guarantee that you'll make money in the long run. There are serious drawbacks that impede your ability to use antiques and collectibles as moneymakers:

▶ **Price.** There are no guarantees that the money you spend for a collectible will be returned on its sale. The price of antiques and collectibles can rise or fall, depending on normal market factors, such as supply and demand. Demand for items hinges largely on the public's taste.

The popularity of a particular antique or collectible is the driving force behind its price. Standard, expensive antiques, such as artworks, porcelain and silver flatware, generally hold their value and aren't usually subject to the whims of the marketplace. But other types of collectibles—for example, Beanie Babies and Pez dispensers—come in and out of favor. One type of collectible may be "hot" for a while, with prices soaring, only to be quickly replaced by another "hot" collectible. For example, remember when metal wastebaskets were the rage?

▶ **Liquidity.** Unlike stocks and bonds that can be readily sold, antiques and collectibles require finding just the right buyer. Despite online selling options, it's not always easy to locate this buyer. It's been estimated that 60% of listings on eBay don't sell. It may take you considerable time, effort and expense before a sale results.

▶ **Reproductions.** When items become popular antiques and collectibles, reproductions may not be far behind. Just about every type of antique or collectible—from Tiffany lamps to Nippon porcelain—can be copied. Import laws and other regulations are often lax, and the market can become flooded with fakes. The presence of reproductions can cause severe problems for your collection. Not only may you be fooled into paying full price for something that's worth far less, but, if reproductions abound, collectors may steer clear of a particular collectible. For example, certain silver patterns originally produced many years ago are being recast, and collectors can't determine whether items for sale are originals or recasts. *Result:* There's little or no market for these patterns. Those who've invested thousands of dollars in such collections can do little but sit and enjoy them, because virtually no one is interested in buying them.

▶ **Resale costs.** Unless you sell the items yourself—at a garage sale, flea market, online auction or otherwise—you may need to use a dealer or other middleperson to make a sale. This is especially so when you want to sell expensive antiques—rare books, art, coins and stamps. Using a dealer cuts substantially into your profits. The dealer also wants to make a profit, so the portion of the sales price that you receive may be far less than what the item sells for. In fact, sometimes dealers take as much as 40% of the proceeds, which means you may not even recoup your investment in the item sold.

 Strategy: Buy before items become hot. To paraphrase Barry Halper, who amassed the largest-ever collection of baseball memorabilia, the key to collecting is to start before anyone else has an interest in the items, and sell when everyone has an interest in them.

How profits are taxed

Tax law looks unfavorably on sales of collectibles. Although gain on the sale of most capital assets, such as stocks and mutual fund shares, is taxed at no more than 15%, gain on the sale of collectibles held more than one year is taxed at 28%.

Note: If you're a dealer in antiques or collectibles, the items are treated as your inventory. This means that gains are really ordinary income, not capital gains. Whether you're a dealer is a question of fact. If you hold items primarily for resale and you turn them over as quickly as possible, you're probably a dealer. If you buy and hold for the long term, you're probably only a collector.

TURNING YOUR HOBBY INTO A BUSINESS

If you buy and sell items, not for your own collection but as a means of making money, collecting what you love can become a profitable business. This is so even if you only carry on this activity on a part-time basis.

Taxwise, if you can demonstrate a profit motive for your collecting activities, you can treat your expenses as deductible business expenses. If your expenses exceed your business income, you can use your loss to offset your income from other sources (e.g., interest and dividends). To be in business:

▶ **Register your business name** with your city or county (e.g., "doing business as" the name you select).

▶ **Open a separate business bank account** and don't commingle your personal funds with these business funds.

▶ **Keep good books and records** for the business.

▶ **Obtain a sales tax resale number** so you can collect sales tax on items you sell (where required) and avoid paying sales tax on items you buy to resell.

If you fail to demonstrate a profit motive, expenses are not deductible as business expenses. They may be miscellaneous itemized deductions—but only to the extent of your income from the activity and only to the extent that all miscellaneous itemized deductions exceed 2% of adjusted gross income. The tax law provides a presumption of a profit motive. If you can show a profit in three out of five years (two out of seven years for horse-related activities), you're presumed to have a profit motive. If you fail to meet this test, you can still demonstrate your profit motive by showing that you conducted the activity in a businesslike manner.

 Strategy: *Write a business plan for your collectibles activity as you would for any other type of business, outlining how you plan to make a profit. Writing the plan will help you focus on how you intend to become profitable.*

ONLINE AUCTIONS

Millions of people buy and sell antiques and collectibles on eBay and other online auction sites. There are over 230 million registered users on eBay alone. More than 1.3 million people make a full-time living on eBay! So there's certainly money to be made in this way. Keep in mind, however, that money can be lost as well. Whether you go online as a buyer to build up your collection or a seller to make money or simply to "trade up," here's what you need to know:

If you're buying online

Buying online is basically no different from buying in a retail store, at a flea market or at an auction you attend in person. The wise words are *buyer beware*, that is, know what you're buying. Because you're buying online, you'll have to rely on photos and the seller's assurances about an item's authenticity and condition.

▶ **Payment method.** Generally, sellers are paid by check, which usually must be delivered within a week or 10 days of the auction's close. Most online auction sites now accept online payment through PayPal. Some dealers accept payment by credit card. If you're buying an expensive item (several hundred dollars or more) and the dealer does not accept credit cards, consider using an online escrow service such as Tradenable.com, which holds your payment until you have received and inspected the item.

▶ **Shipping costs.** Make sure you understand who bears the cost of shipping and insuring the item. The buyer usually pays this cost.

▶ **Return policy.** Check whether the seller will refund your money if you're not satisfied. Reputable sellers will always do so if the item turns out to be different from what it was purported to be (for example, it is sold as "mint" condition but turns out to have obvious damage). Understand any time constraints that apply to the refund policy.

 Strategy: *Check the seller's previous track record, looking for good and bad comments. This information can be found at most sites. It just may help you avoid dealing with an unreputable seller.*

If you sell online

Make sure to provide all the information necessary to fully describe your item and to allow buyers to contact you. Photographs are usually essential to getting top dollar for your items.

▶ **Set a reserve.** This is the minimum price you will accept for your item. It means that you won't sell for less than this minimum.

▶ **Understand the cost to you.** As a seller, the site may charge a listing fee (for example, a few pennies per item), as well as a commission on the sale. This, too, may be modest.

> **Example:** Amazon.com Auctions and eBay each have a listing fee for posting the item. And each requires a payment from the seller if the item sells. If the item fails to sell, it's possible to relist it on these sites without an additional listing fee.

▶ **Respond promptly.** When prospective or successful buyers submit questions about the item or you, provide the information as quickly as possible.

▶ **Work with an online escrow company.** Payment isn't disbursed to you until the buyer receives the goods. The buyer can pay by credit card even though you don't have merchant authorization for the card; eBay's escrow company for this purpose is **www.escrow.com**.

To learn about online auctions in general, check out **www.vendio.com.** To participate in online auctions, check out the following general auctions (then click on the category of collectibles of interest to you):

▶ Amazon.com Auctions **(www.auctions.amazon.com)**

▶ Collectors Universe **(www.collectors.com)**

▶ eBay **(www.ebay.com)**

▶ Yahoo! Auctions **(http://auctions.yahoo.com)**

There are also smaller auction sites devoted to limited categories of collectibles. Examples:

Coins...

▶ Superior Galleries **(www.sgbh.com)**

Pottery, porcelain and glassware...

▶ Just Glass **(www.justglass.com)**

▶ Pottery Auction **(www.potteryauction.com)**

Stamps...

▶ Greg Manning Auctions **(www.gmauctions.com)**

Don't like the auction format? You can list items at fixed prices through various sites, including eBay and Craigslist **(www.craigslist.org)**.

INSURING COLLECTIONS

Safeguarding your collections is important for both personal and financial reasons. You may have put significant time and love into amassing your collections. There may also be a large investment at stake.

Just because your collection is in your home, don't assume that damage or theft of these items is covered by your homeowner's policy. Typically, homeowner's insurance has certain limitations or exclusions. For example, on a deluxe-plus homeowner's policy, you only have coverage for the following:

▶ **Coins and bank notes** (numismatic property)—up to $200

▶ **Jewelry, watches and precious and semiprecious stones**—thefts up to $2,500 ($1,000 per item)

▶ **Rugs**—thefts up to $10,000 ($2,500 per item)

▶ **Silverware, pewterware and goldware**—thefts up to $2,500

▶ **Stamps** (philatelic property)—up to $1,000

▶ **Trading cards, comic books and Hummels**—up to $1,000 (but no more than $250 per item)

Amending homeowner's coverage

You may be able to adequately insure your antiques and collectibles by obtaining a rider to your homeowner's policy. The cost of additional coverage varies with the items to be insured. Generally, you'll have to list each item to be included in this special coverage, along with proof of cost and an appraisal or other determination of value.

Separate coverage

To protect your collection from damage or theft, consider obtaining a separate policy. This coverage isn't cheap (it's usually a fixed cost per $1,000 of coverage) but for valuable items it may be worth the expense. What's more, the coverage generally covers items in transit as well as items out on consignment.

 Strategy: *Reduce insurance coverage as you sell items from your collection. Otherwise, you'll overpay.*

12

Windfalls

❝*Do not be overly elated by good fortune. Remember how easily it can change.***❞** —AESOP

YOU MAY BE FORTUNATE and receive unexpected money suddenly. A rich uncle may remember you in his will or name you as the beneficiary of his million-dollar life insurance policy. That dollar lottery ticket may pay off handsomely or you may successfully answer all of the questions on *Who Wants to Be a Millionaire*. On the other hand, you may be unfortunate—for example, the victim of an accident—and receive money through an insurance settlement or legal action.

If you receive money through inheritance, the lottery or otherwise, your sudden wealth presents both opportunities and potential problems. You have a chance to build your good fortune into a solid financial base, providing yourself and your family with financial security. But sudden wealth and the decisions it brings can be overwhelming. New responsibilities go along with newfound wealth.

This chapter explains what to do when receiving certain windfalls to maximize your financial opportunities. It also discusses how to avoid pitfalls that can result from windfalls. And it tells you how to find missing assets—that is, how to create windfalls for yourself and your family.

DON'T TURN "EASY COME" INTO "EASY GO"

Sudden wealth does not necessarily mean sudden financial brilliance. The more money you have to manage, the more complex it may become. Hasty and ill-advised actions can dissipate your wealth as quickly as you receive it. Use a commonsense approach to handling newfound wealth:

Don't...

▶ **Go on a spending spree.** You may spend more than you should and live to regret it. *Rule of thumb:* Splurge with no more than 1% of your windfall.

▶ **Quit your job or make other lifestyle changes immediately.** You need to look at the big picture before making any drastic moves. The size of the windfall, your age and how you plan to live out the rest of your life must all be taken into account. You may find that the windfall isn't large enough to replace the income from your job. Or you may discover that managing your new assets can become a full-time job.

▶ **Listen to the advice of nonfinancial people.** Your barber or neighbor may mean well, but may be uninformed about money matters.

▶ **Make investments without first developing a financial plan.** For example, you may put money into an annuity. If you later decide it wasn't the best investment for you, you'll have to pay surrender charges and possibly tax penalties to get out of it.

▶ **Give your money away all at once.** Although a windfall may enable you to help family, friends and charitable causes, a rushed gift may not be wise. You may leave yourself short of funds needed in future years. Even if you can afford to give money away, you may needlessly incur gift taxes that could have been avoided by careful planning. And you may not be able to claim full charitable contribution deductions unless your philanthropic transfers are carefully crafted.

▶ **Ignore the tax bite on the windfall.** Although inheritances and recoveries for personal physical injuries are largely tax free, other windfalls are taxable at combined federal and state tax rates up to about 36%. And keep in mind that even though some windfalls are subject to automatic withholding—for example, lottery payments are reduced by a 25% withholding tax in 2003—this may not be enough to cover your actual tax liability.

Do...

▶ **Take things slowly.** You don't have to make decisions all at once. *Rule of thumb:* Wait at least six months before making any major decisions about what to do with your money.

 Strategy: Park your cash in a money market fund until you decide how to invest for the long term. You'll earn a higher interest rate than a bank account. Don't put your money in a noninterest-bearing checking account or you'll miss out on an income opportunity.

▶ **Deal with immediate issues.** Use a windfall to pay off debts (other than a home mortgage). Go through the motions necessary to receive your windfall, filing papers in court or taking other required action.

▶ **Get expert assistance.** You may want to meet with a financial planner and a tax professional to develop a comprehensive financial and tax plan. What you spend on professional assistance may actually save you money in the long run if it helps you avoid costly financial mistakes. Financial experts are discussed in Chapter 2.

▶ **Protect yourself.** Now that you have a valuable nest egg, look into increasing your insurance as quickly as possible, especially umbrella policies for added liability protection ($5 million or more) and life insurance for new estate-planning needs.

 Strategy: Get an unlisted phone number if your windfall is publicized. All states except Delaware are permitted to make public the names of lottery winners. Big lawsuits and inheritances—matters of public record—may be covered by the media. Protect yourself from being bombarded by financial propositions and pleas for charity.

INHERITANCES

According to some statistics, the current older generation is poised to pass on more than $3 trillion in inheritances. This tax-free windfall presents great opportunities. If you're a lucky heir, an inheritance can provide you with financial security for the rest of your life. If the inheritance is substantial, make sure you proceed as you would with any windfall to avoid dissipating your new wealth, as discussed earlier in this chapter.

Tax aspects of inheritances

Generally, your inheritance comes to you income tax free. So, if you inherit 100 shares of X stock from a grandparent's estate, you're not taxed when you receive the shares.

When you sell inherited property, you can use a "stepped-up" basis to determine your gain or loss. This means that your basis is the value of the property used for estate tax purposes (generally the value of the property on the date of the decedent's death, but it may be six months later if the executor so elects). When you sell the property, your gain (or loss) is measured from the value of the property for estate tax purposes. And you're automatically treated as having held the property long term, regardless of how long the decedent owned the property or how long you held it.

> **Example:** You inherit 100 shares of IBM from a parent who paid $40 a share. On the date of your parent's death, the stock was trading at $100 a share. The estate is settled 10 months later and you receive the stock. You immediately sell the stock for $120 a share. Your profit is $20 a share ($120 minus $100).

Starting in 2010, the stepped-up basis rule is scheduled to be replaced by a carryover basis rule—you inherit the property *plus* the decedent's basis for that property. *Result:* When you sell, you'll report gain if the property has appreciated over the decedent's basis. Of course, the carryover basis rules may never take effect—they're tied to the repeal of the federal estate tax, which may or may not occur. And even if the carryover basis rules do apply, there's a generous exemption, so you may still be able to enjoy a stepped-up basis for some or all of your inheritance.

Taxable inheritances

Certain types of inheritance *don't* come tax free. As the beneficiary, you're liable for the income tax on these items. These items collectively are called income in respect of a decedent (IRD). Taxable inheritances include:

▶ **Annuities.**

▶ **EE and I bonds:** All accrued interest may be taxable to the beneficiary if the interest isn't reported on the deceased individual's final income tax return.

▶ **Qualified retirement plan benefits,** including 401(k) plans.

▶ **Traditional IRAs,** and Roth IRAs that fail to satisfy certain requirements to make the earnings tax free.

▶ **Other income in respect of a decedent** (for example, collection of a sole proprietor's accounts receivable).

Although you aren't taxed when you receive the right to an inheritance—for example, when savings bonds are retitled in your name as the beneficiary—you are taxed when you actually receive the income—for example, when the bonds are redeemed or reach their final maturity date.

Example: You inherit a parent's $100,000 IRA and opt to take distributions over your life expectancy. You'll pay tax on the distribution you take each year from the IRA.

If you must report an inheritance as taxable, you may be able to claim a special deduction for the estate tax attributable to the item. This is a miscellaneous itemized deduction, so you must itemize your deductions and not claim the standard deduction to benefit from this write-off. This deduction is *not* subject to the 2% of adjusted gross income floor.

 Strategy: Claim this deduction when you report the IRD even if you didn't pay the estate tax and even if the estate has not yet paid the tax.

Refusing bequests

Should you ever refuse a bequest? The answer is sometimes yes, if you're already financially secure. Accepting an inheritance that won't enhance your lifestyle or financial security can complicate existing estate plans. If you disclaim an inheritance that you're entitled to, the property passes automatically to the next heir who would have received it by the decedent's will. You would thereby avoid gift (or estate) tax in transferring the property to the next in line.

Example: Your parent leaves property to you, but you don't want the inheritance. Under the terms of your parent's will, that property passes to your child if you die before your parent. By making a disclaimer, you're treated as having died before your parent, so your child receives what would have been your inheritance.

 Strategy: Make a qualified disclaimer of an inheritance to avoid making a gift of the bequest to the party who ultimately receives it. Do so by notifying the executor in writing that you don't want your inheritance. Don't accept any benefit from it. You must act within nine months of the decedent's death.

FINDING "LOST" MONEY

You may be sitting on a windfall without even knowing it. According to one statistic, one in eight Americans owns unclaimed property in the form of bank accounts, inheritances, prizes and the like. *Total value:* More than $400 billion. Here are some examples of the more common types of unclaimed money:

▶ **Bank accounts.** Checking and savings accounts may become dormant, and money orders and cashier's checks may go uncashed. Check with your state's unclaimed-property office. Some states have online listings that you can check for your name or the name of a relative (see below).

▶ **Dividends.** Cash dividends on stock may be returned to the issuing companies if checks are undelivered.

▶ **Inheritances.** If you believe you were entitled to a bequest from a deceased relative, check the probate records for the county in which the relative lived. This is a matter of public record. You don't need anyone's permission to look.

▶ **Insurance.** When a person dies, relatives may not know of the existence of an old policy.

▶ **Lottery winnings.** Many prizes go unclaimed; Powerball, a 20-state lottery, puts the figure at about 12% of all prizes. Generally, you have between 180 days and one year from the date of the drawing to claim your prize.

*Strategy: If you go to the trouble and expense of buying a lottery ticket, be sure to check whether you've won. You can check winning numbers online at sites such as **www.lottery.com**. Keep your tickets safe, because lottery commissions won't pay prizes without them.*

▶ **Pensions.** You may have earned a pension years ago; perhaps the company subsequently went out of business or terminated the plan. You can find out about any pension benefits you may be entitled to through the Pension Benefit Guaranty Corporation (PBGC); its Web site is at **www.pbgc.gov**. If the plan folded because it couldn't meet all its obligations to participants, you may be entitled to a minimum monthly pension paid by the PBGC. However, this applies only to benefits in defined-benefit plans and other plans subject to what's known as minimum funding requirements. It doesn't apply to 401(k) and most other defined-contribution plans.

▶ **Safe-deposit boxes.** When annual rental fees are not paid, boxes are sealed. After some time, the contents may be held as unclaimed property.

▶ **Social Security benefits.** The payment of Social Security benefits isn't automatic. Benefits are paid out only if claims are made. Elderly individuals entitled to benefits may never have submitted claims. And, when a person dies, a spouse is entitled to a small death benefit—if a claim is made.

▶ **Tax refunds.** The payment of tax refunds isn't automatic—you must request a refund on a return filed within certain time limits. In November 2006, the IRS was looking for 95,000 taxpayers who were owed refunds totaling approximately $92.2 million. To see if one of these checks is yours, call the IRS special refund hotline at 800-829-1954 or use the "Where's My Refund?" feature at **www.irs.gov**.

▶ **Union benefits.** Unions may provide life insurance policies or other benefits for members which relatives may not be aware of.

▶ **Utility deposits.** When people move, they often fail to request a refund of deposits they've made to electric companies, telephone companies and other utilities.

▶ **Veteran's benefits.**

Lost assets

Every state except Hawaii has an online search engine to check for lost assets. Generally, assets are placed in the custody of the state where an owner was last known to reside. It's generally a good idea to check not only the state in which you now live, but every state in which you've ever lived; those states may not have your current address. To find your state's site, go to **www.webcentive.com/unclaimed_links.html.** Other resources for starting your search:

▶ **Missing Money** provides direct links to lost money listings in these states: Alaska, Arizona, Colorado, District of Columbia, Florida, Idaho, Kansas, Kentucky, Louisiana, Maine, Massachusetts, Missouri, Montana, New Hampshire, New Jersey, North Dakota, South Dakota, Vermont, West Virginia and Wisconsin. North Carolina, Oklahoma and Tennessee records will be available soon. Visit **www.missing money.com.**

▶ **ACS Unclaimed Property Clearinghouse** offers a free search; go to **www.acsupch.com.**

INSURANCE SETTLEMENTS AND LEGAL ACTIONS

Accidents and legal actions can result in million-dollar awards from insurance companies and other responsible parties. The money is usually intended to cover future medical costs resulting from the incident in question. The settlement may also cover future living expenses, especially when injuries from an accident prevent employment.

Insurance settlements are not always paid out in a lump sum. Instead they may be "structured settlements" in which money is doled out over time. There may be court-imposed limits on how the money can be used, especially when the funds are for minors. For example, investment of settlement funds may be restricted to US government securities only.

 Strategy: *Convert a structured settlement to cash by selling it. Businesses that pay up-front cash for payments to be received over time are described on page 182.*

Reporting insurance settlements

Money received as damages for a physical injury or illness is tax free. But other awards—for example, for pain and suffering, for property damage or for punitive damages—are taxable.

Generally, personal injury actions are handled by attorneys on a contingency fee basis. If they win, they recover a portion of the award, typically one-third. Reporting taxable damages when contingency fees are involved can be confusing. The way to proceed depends on state law:

▶ **Where state law gives attorneys certain rights** in these situations, then plaintiffs need only report their net awards (these damages less attorney's fees).

▶ **Where state law does not create these rights for attorneys,** plaintiffs must report the entire award. They can deduct legal fees as a miscellaneous itemized deduction, but doing so can trigger alternative minimum tax (miscellaneous itemized deductions aren't deductible for AMT purposes). The alternative minimum tax is discussed in Chapter 15.

LOTTERY PRIZES AND OTHER GAMBLING WINNINGS

Gambling is entrenched in our society. Religious organizations sponsor bingo, states conduct lotteries and Native Americans build casinos. Even though the odds may be slim, millions of Americans routinely gamble. When Lady Luck smiles, make the most of it.

 Strategy: Don't count on winning a jackpot to secure your financial future. The odds are highly against you. For example, the 2000 Powerball jackpot of $295 million had odds of more than 80 million to one. The 2000 California lottery paying $87 million had odds of 41 million to one. Instead, rely on sound financial principles.

Lottery winnings

The first American lottery took place in 1612 when the English worked to raise funds for the Jamestown settlement in Virginia. Today, 40 states and the District of Columbia use lotteries to raise revenue netting $42.4 billion in ticket sales annually. Payouts from lottery jackpots are made in one of two ways: As a lump sum or in installments over a fixed number of years, generally 20 or more. If the payout is made in a lump sum, winners are given the current value of the prize. *Rule of thumb:* You would receive about half the face amount of the award if you took it in a lump sum; for instance, a $3 million pot would mean a $1.5 million lump-sum payment. Whether you would receive more or less than half the face amount would depend on the lottery's installment period. If the installment period is less than 25 years, you would receive more than half of the jackpot as a lump sum. If the period is more than 25 years, you would receive less than half as a lump sum.

Which is the better financial choice, installment payments or a lump sum? Generally, the lump sum makes more sense if you can invest the money wisely. The installment payments are figured using a conservative rate of return, say 6%. If you can beat that rate of return, then you'll recoup more over the installment period through your lump sum than you would have received through installment payments.

Lottery winnings are subject to automatic federal income tax withholding of a flat 25% in 2007. Thus, if you opt to take a jackpot in a lump sum, the half of the face amount you're due to receive is reduced by nearly another one-third for taxes.

> **Example:** One lottery jackpot of $42 million was paid in a lump sum of $22.7 million. But after withholding, only $16.3 million was actually paid out to the winner. And another $2 million is still owed in taxes; withholding does not necessarily cover the entire tax bill.

Up-front cash

If you win a jackpot payable over a number of years, you can cash in by selling your right to receive payments to a commercial enterprise. Obviously, you lose a portion of your winnings this way, but you gain immediate access to a lump sum. Such enterprises include:

▶ Atlantic Financial (**www.megawealth.com**, 800-559-2900)

▶ Peachtree Settlement Funding (**www.lumpsum.com**, 866-864-6888)

▶ Singer Asset Finance (**www.singerasset.com**, 800-670-6777)

Tax rules on gambling winnings (and losses)

The tax rules on gambling winnings and losses aren't in your favor. Heads the IRS wins, tails you lose.

Winnings: You must report your winnings in full. You can't offset your winnings by netting out your losses. *Caution:* Gambling winnings are reported to the IRS. You receive a copy of what's reported on Form W-2G, *Certain Gambling Winnings.*

What's reported? Generally, winnings of $600 or more that are at least 300 times the wager. For keno games, winnings of $1,500 or more are reported. For bingo games and slot machines, the reportable amount is $1,200 or more.

As mentioned above, winnings are subject to a withholding of federal income taxes at the rate of 25% in 2005 (28% for keno, bingo and slot machines). This can be claimed as a credit when a return is filed, but it may not be sufficient in some cases to cover a winner's tax liability for the year.

 Strategy: If you win big, review your estimated tax payments for the year. Despite automatic withholding, you may need to increase your estimated tax payments to avoid penalties.

Winnings are also subject to state and local income taxes. Does moving to a low-tax state after winning a big jackpot make sense as a means of avoiding state income tax? One man from Ohio tried this, moving to Florida, a no-income-tax state, after his lottery winning. But an Ohio court ruled that he still owed state income tax to Ohio, the place where the money was earned.

Losses: You can deduct your gambling losses as a miscellaneous itemized deduction, but only to the extent of your winnings.

Example: If you win $1,000 but lose $5,000 in the same year, your deduction is limited to $1,000 (you can never deduct the other $4,000).

The deduction for gambling losses isn't subject to the 2% of adjusted gross income limit. But you can't use this deduction if you claim the standard deduction.

 Strategy: Save all your losing lottery tickets, horse bets and other evidence of what you gambled. The losses you can report aren't limited to the type of winnings you report. For example, if you win $1,000 on your one and only lottery ticket for the year but lost $1,000 in bingo, you can deduct the bingo losses.

Help for compulsive gamblers

Gambling can get out of hand for some people, wiping out savings and leading to debt. For help with compulsive gambling, contact your local chapter of Gamblers Anonymous or visit **www.gamblersanonymous.org**.

TAX REFUNDS

Can you receive a windfall from taxes? If you pay more income tax (through wage withholding, automatic withholding on certain income and estimated taxes) than you owe, you're entitled to a refund. Depending on how much you have overpaid, you may view your refund as a windfall.

 Strategy: Don't celebrate a tax refund. You've simply made an interest-free loan to the government, something you're not required to do. Figure your withholding and estimated taxes more carefully to avoid a refund and ensure that payments are sufficient to avoid penalties.

As mentioned earlier, each year, the federal government keeps millions of dollars in overpaid income taxes because taxpayers fail to make refund claims. Similarly, states are sitting on millions of dollars in state income tax refunds. If you overpaid your federal and/or state income taxes, you may be entitled to a refund. *Caution:* To claim a tax refund, you must act within certain time limits explained below. If you don't, you'll lose out forever.

When to make a claim

Generally, you have three years from the filing of your original return or two years from the date the tax was paid, whichever is later. The clock starts on the actual date of filing, not the due date.

> **Example:** Your 2006 income tax return's due date is April 16, 2007. If you file your return on March 1, 2007, you have until March 1, 2010 to file your refund claim of overpaid 2006 income taxes. If you obtain an automatic filing extension and file on July 1, 2007, you have until July 1, 2010, to file your refund claim.

If a refund relates to worthless securities or a bad debt, you have seven years to file an amended return as your refund claim. And if you are considered "financially disabled" (suffering from a physical or mental illness or condition that makes you unable to handle your financial matters), the time limits are suspended for the period of disability. However, there's no suspension of the time limits if a spouse or other person is authorized to act on your behalf (for example, under a durable power of attorney).

States may have different time limits for filing refund claims, so ask your state tax department for its rules.

How to make claims

You must file a return to make a refund claim. This is so even if you're not otherwise required to file a return (for example, if your income is below the filing threshold).

Amended returns: If you file your return and later discover you have overstated income or omitted write-offs you were entitled to, you can file an amended return within the time limits outlined above. Use IRS Form 1040X, *Amended US Individual Income Tax Return,* for this purpose. *Caution:* Weigh carefully the refund you expect against the possibility of having the IRS question other items on your return. Don't request a small refund at the risk of an audit.

SHARING YOUR WINDFALL

Just because you receive unexpected money doesn't mean you have to keep it. You can spread your new-found wealth around, giving to family and friends and favorite charities. Helping out family, friends and favorite causes is a lofty ideal. The reality is that of big lottery winnings, only about 5% goes to charity and only about 20% to family and friends. The psychology of parting with money plays a key role in deciding whether to make gifts. Some may feel poor despite a large windfall and be reluctant to give much away. Others may simply have no experience with gifting and need to learn the benefits and mechanisms—something financial advisers can teach them.

Charitable giving, including setting up private foundations to dole out substantial amounts, is discussed in Chapter 15. Giving to family and friends is discussed in Chapter 19.

13

Employee benefits

❝*A good workman is never overpaid.***❞** —Proverbs

EMPLOYERS ARE UNDER NO LEGAL or moral obligation to offer benefits, but many do as a means of attracting and keeping good employees. When the company bears the cost of medical coverage, retirement savings and other benefits, you are relieved of these burdens and can put your money to work elsewhere. Many employee benefits, called fringe benefits or perquisites (perks), are tax free.

Today, employee benefits can make up a nice chunk of a compensation package. Your employer may be able to obtain these benefits at better prices than you would be able to command.

This chapter explains how employee benefits can save you money, even if they're partially taxable. It lists the various types of fringe benefits that enjoy special tax treatment. Use this list to assess what your company offers or to evaluate future job prospects. Retirement plans, among the most valued employee benefits, are explained in Chapter 8. Special employee benefit rules and other issues for company owners are discussed in Chapter 14.

HOW EMPLOYEE BENEFITS SAVE YOU MONEY

When a company pays for a benefit on your behalf, you save substantially. You don't have to come up with cash to pay for the benefit on your own. Depending on the item, this may free up more than just the cost of the benefit since you would have to cover the expense with after-tax dollars.

> **Example:** Assume you were in the 28% tax bracket. If you wanted to pay for life insurance, a nondeductible personal expense, and the premiums were $1,000 a year, you would have to earn about $1,400 to have the $1,000 after taxes to cover the premiums.

There's an added benefit to company-paid expenses. Often the company can command lower prices than you would have to pay for the same benefit.

> **Example:** The company can provide group term coverage at substantially lower premiums than individual term coverage, with the same death benefit.

Even if the employer-paid benefit is taxable to you, it's still a big money saver. Your cost is limited to the tax on the value of the benefit.

> **Example:** Assume you're in the 28% tax bracket. If your company pays for financial planning, a taxable benefit, and you avail yourself of $1,000 in assistance, your cost for receiving this benefit is only $280 ($1,000 x 28%).

Some benefits may be exempt from income tax but still subject to employment taxes, including Social Security and Medicare taxes. If so, then your cost for these benefits can be no more than 7.65% of the value of the benefits.

 Strategy: *If you can afford it, negotiate for employer-paid benefits in lieu of increased compensation, such as an annual pay raise. The company would not pay any more than the compensation it already agreed to pay, but you'll benefit on an after-tax basis.*

TAX-FAVORED EMPLOYEE BENEFITS

What type of benefits does the tax law favor? Some benefits incur no income tax or employment taxes. Some benefits have limits on what is tax free. Some benefits are exempt from income tax while subject to employment tax. *Note:* The tax treatment of these benefits can change from year to year. Fringe benefit restrictions for owners are discussed in Chapter 14.

Here's a rundown of the most common types of employee benefits—in alphabetical order—and how to take advantage of them:

Adoption assistance

Your employer may reimburse you or pay directly for your cost of adopting a child under a company-sponsored adoption assistance program. In 2007, you aren't taxed on amounts up to $11,390 if your adjusted gross income (AGI) is no more than $170,820, regardless of your filing status. The exclusion is phased out for AGIs between $170,820 and $210,820. The benefit is fully taxable if AGI exceeds $210,820.

Athletic facilities

Use of a gym, tennis courts or other athletic facilities on company premises is tax free. But company-paid membership to health clubs, golf or tennis clubs or other sporting facilities is a taxable benefit.

Bonuses

You're fully taxed on any bonus you receive, just like additional pay. But if you agree in advance to defer the receipt of the bonus until some future time (such as retirement), this deferred compensation generally isn't taxed until you receive it. However, it is still subject to Social Security and Medicare taxes in the year it's earned.

Company car for personal use

Your company may allow you to use a car it owns for business and your personal purposes. If a company-owned car can be used for personal purposes, you are taxed on this benefit. But the resulting tax cost is far less than what it would actually cost you to drive your own car. The cost to you is only the tax on what the employer reports. Your employer can choose to:

▶ **Report the actual value** of your personal use, or…

▶ **Assume that the car** is used 100% for personal purposes and treat the entire benefit as compensation.

Personal use can be figured in several ways. One way is to base it on what's called the annual lease value (ALV) of the car, a figure taken from IRS tables.

> **Example:** Assume that you use a $30,000 company car for personal time one-quarter (25%) of the year. The ALV of a $30,000 car is $8,250, and the taxable benefit to you is only $2,063 (25% of $8,250).

> *Strategy: Deduct your business use of a company car if your W-2 form reports 100% of the car's use as personal. You can deduct any business use of the car as a miscellaneous itemized deduction subject to the 2% of adjusted gross income floor. For example, you can deduct business use based on the IRS standard mileage rate (48.5¢ per mile in 2007).*

▶ **Reimbursement for business use of your car.** If you use your own car on company business, you may be reimbursed by your employer. Reimbursement can be arranged on a tax-free basis if made under an "accountable plan." Even if your company doesn't tell you that it's using an accountable plan, you'll know it because you'll be required to substantiate business travel to your employer within 60 days of the travel and return any excess reimbursements no more than 120 days after the expense was paid or incurred. Reimbursement in excess of business expenses is taxable to you. *Note:* You can't deduct your car expenses if they are reimbursed by your employer under an accountable plan.

If reimbursement is made to you under a nonaccountable plan, then it is reported as income. You can then claim business use of your car as a miscellaneous itemized deduction, subject to the 2% floor.

▶ **Commuting costs.** Reimbursement for your commuting costs is taxable. Commuting costs are personal expenses. *Exceptions:* Reimbursements for commuting (up to the value of a one-way trip that exceeds $1.50) only when you work beyond normal hours and it's considered unsafe for you to use other means of transportation. *Also:* Public transportation passes, discussed on page 193.

Company stock

If you're given company stock, you're taxed on the benefit. But if the stock is subject to restriction or a substantial risk of forfeiture, you aren't taxed until the restriction or risk is lifted.

> **Strategy:** *Immediately report the receipt of company stock or other restricted property as income. You'll pay income tax only on the current value of the stock or property. Future appreciation will be converted into a long-term capital gain, which is taxed at a lower rate. Ask your tax adviser about a Section 83(b) election to report this income.*

Dependent care assistance

If your employer reimburses you or pays directly for the cost of dependent care, you aren't taxed on up to $5,000 of this benefit. *Caution:* If you receive this tax-free benefit, you can't claim a dependent care credit with respect to the same expenses.

> **Strategy:** *Participate in an employer-sponsored flexible spending arrangement (FSA) for dependent care costs if available and if your employer doesn't pay directly for dependent care. You agree to a salary reduction contribution to the FSA, which is used to reimburse you for dependent-care expenses. While this arrangement means that you are paying for dependent care, you'll be able to do so with pretax dollars.*

Disability insurance

Employer-paid disability insurance is a tax-free fringe benefit. But if you become disabled and receive disability benefits, they'll be taxable to you.

> **Strategy:** *Arrange for additional compensation in lieu of employer-paid disability insurance. If you pay for your own disability insurance, should you need to receive benefits, they'll be tax free. And when you leave the company, you can continue your coverage.*

Educational assistance

Employer-paid college courses are tax free up to $5,250 annually, whether job related or not. The exclusion applies to both undergraduate- and graduate-level courses. There's no dollar limit for educational assistance that's job related. Job retraining is tax free as well, even if you no longer work for the company.

Also, if you work for a college or other educational institution and receive a discount on tuition, you're not taxed on this benefit.

Group term life insurance

Your employer may provide term life insurance, typically double your annual salary. This benefit is tax free up to $50,000. If you receive additional coverage, the excess is taxable according to an IRS table that imputes income based on age (without regard to the actual cost of additional coverage). This IRS table results in only a modest taxable amount for excess coverage. The following table, based on IRS figures, shows what you would have to pay tax on for each additional $1,000 of coverage. You don't have to figure your taxable amount each year; it's included on your W-2 form.

Annual cost per $1,000 of group term life insurance

Your age as of the end of the year	The annual cost per $1,000
Under 25	$ 0.60
25–29	0.72
30–34	0.96
35–39	1.08
40–44	1.20
45–49	1.80
50–54	2.76
55–59	5.16
60–64	7.92
65–69	15.24
70 and older	24.72

Example: Assume you're 54 years old and your employer pays for $100,000 of coverage. You're not taxed on the first $50,000 of coverage; your additional income from the excess coverage for the year is only $138 ($2.76 x 50).

Health and accident insurance

Employer-paid health coverage isn't taxable to you, except to the extent it covers a domestic partner. Reimbursement of medical expenses under a company medical reimbursement plan is tax free as well.

Since health costs have skyrocketed, some employers have cut back or eliminated medical insurance as a benefit. Instead, you may be asked to share the cost or pay it entirely. If the company carries group medical coverage, the cost is lower than you would pay if you bought similar coverage individually.

▶ **Flexible spending arrangements (FSAs).** Employers may offer the option of participating in an FSA to cover uninsured medical costs. You agree to contribute a certain amount to the plan on a pretax (salary reduction) basis. You can then submit receipts for noncovered medical costs—for example, eyeglasses, hearing aids and the deductible portion of prescription drugs—for reimbursement. At the start of each year, project what you might spend throughout the year and then agree to a salary reduction of that amount as your contribution to the FSA. *Caution:* FSAs have a use-it-or-lose-it feature. If you don't spend everything you've contributed by the end of the year (or within a 2½-month grace period if the plan has adopted it), you forfeit what remains.

 Strategy: Participate in flexible spending arrangements to cover medical insurance if this option is open to you. For example, premium-only FSAs let you pay for coverage at group rates on a pretax basis. You agree to reduce your salary in the amount of the premium.

Annual physicals paid by your employer are also tax free, whether or not they're covered by insurance.

▶ **Health reimbursement arrangements (HRAs).** Employers may contribute a set dollar amount, say $3,000, to a special account that you can tap to pay medical costs not covered by insurance. You aren't taxed on the contribution nor when you tap into the account. If you don't use up the money in your account, you can carry it forward to be used in a future year.

▶ **Long-term-care insurance.** Increasingly, companies are offering this insurance to cover nursing home costs that aren't covered by Medicare or other health insurance. This insurance is treated as health and accident insurance—tax free to you if paid for by your employer.

Health savings accounts (HSAs)

Companies looking for ways to cut their growing cost of health coverage for employees may buy high-deductible health plans (coverage designed for catastrophic rather than routine medical needs). These plans, first authorized on January 1, 2004, can be supplemented with savings-type accounts called a health savings account and are funded with tax-deductible contributions by employers or employees. The following chart shows the requirements for 2007:

Type of coverage	Minimum annual deductible out-of-pocket expense limit	Maximum contribution
Self-only coverage	$1,100/$5,500	$2,850
Family coverage	$2,200/$11,000	$5,650

Those age 55 or older can make an additional $800 contribution to an HSA in 2007 ($900 in 2008 and $1,000 starting in 2009). You can tap into the account to cover your uninsured medical costs completely tax free. If you use the money for any other purpose, the distributions are taxable. What's more, if you're under age 65, you'll owe a penalty on the distribution.

 *Strategy: If your employer does not offer health coverage, you can buy your own high-deductible health plan and set up an HSA. Your deduction for contributions to the HSA can be claimed even if you don't itemize your other deductions. For details on insurers offering this type of coverage and trustees of HSA accounts, go to **www.hsainsider.com**, **www.hsafinder.com**, and **www.ehealthinsurance.com**.*

Housing

If you're given housing on your employer's premises (for instance, if you work in a hotel and get a free room), you're not taxed on this benefit as long as you must accept it as a condition of employment.

However, subsidized housing—off the premises—is not a tax-free benefit.

Incentive stock options

Companies are permitted to grant a certain amount of incentive stock options (ISOs) each year. You're not immediately taxed when you receive them nor when you exercise the options to acquire stock. But the exercise of ISOs gives rise to an adjustment to income. The adjustment, which is added to your other income for alternative minimum tax (AMT) purposes, is the difference between the value of the stock acquired via the option and the amount you actually paid for it.

 Strategy: Talk to a tax adviser about timing the exercise of ISOs to avoid triggering the AMT. Generally, you'll want to exercise a certain amount of ISOs each year to avoid bunching the AMT adjustment into a single year. AMT strategies are discussed in Chapter 15.

All future appreciation on the stock can be treated as a long-term capital gain if you meet two requirements—you must not sell the stock until you've owned it more than one year from the time the options are exercised, *and* more than two years from the date the options were granted. If you fail to meet either of these holding requirements, the appreciation will be treated as ordinary income and taxed at a higher rate. If you sell the stock within a year of exercising the ISO, your gain, if any, is ordinary income for regular income tax purposes, but there's no AMT adjustment in this case.

Note: You are allowed to increase the basis of the stock acquired through an ISO by the amount of any AMT adjustment when you exercised the ISO. This can be a big tax saver.

Interest-free loans

If you borrow money from your employer and pay no interest (or a very low rate of interest), the interest that was waived is treated as additional income. This is measured by IRS interest rates published monthly and depends on the term of the loan (short-term, mid-term or long-term).

Example: You have an interest-free, short-term loan of $10,000. The IRS short-term loan rate for the month you first borrow the money is 6% per year. If that amount is outstanding for the entire year, you'll be taxed on $600, the interest you weren't charged but should have paid under tax rules.

Strategy: Deduct the interest as investment interest if you use the proceeds to make investments other than tax-free municipal bonds. You can use your net investment income (investment income less investment expenses for the year) as an itemized deduction.

Meals

There is such a thing as a free lunch. Free meals on your employer's premises are tax free. For example, if you work at a restaurant, your meals there aren't taxable. But any meal allowances (meals that aren't furnished in kind) are taxable.

Meals at company cafeterias that are employer-subsidized may be tax free (you aren't taxed on the discount).

Moving expenses

If your employer covers relocation costs for a job-related move, you're not taxed on this benefit. There's no dollar or income limit. Moving expenses are tax free whether your employer pays them directly or reimburses you.

Nonqualified stock options

Like ISOs, no tax results from the grant of these options. However, the difference between the option price and the value of the stock at the time of exercise is taxed as ordinary income. Any future appreciation is taxed as a long-term capital gain as long as the stock acquired is held more than one year. There are some differences in tax treatment depending on whether the stock is publicly traded or privately held.

Parking

Your company can provide you with free parking. The exclusion is limited to $215 per month in 2007. Parking is valued according to its regular commercial value in the same or nearby locations. If you opt for cash in lieu of free parking you are taxed on cash received.

Retirement plans

Contributions made by an employer on your behalf to 401(k) and other qualified retirement plans are discussed in Chapter 8.

Sick pay

If you're entitled to a certain number of paid sick days, the pay is fully taxable.

Similarly, if you're paid for any time off under the Family Medical Leave Act (FMLA) for the birth or adoption of a child or to care for a sick child, spouse or parent, the pay is taxable. Employers subject to the federal FMLA are *not* required to pay for any covered leave time.

Tax, legal, investment and other counseling

If your employer pays for you to receive professional tax and/or investment advice, you're taxed on the employer's cost for the benefit.

 Strategy: Deduct the amount of the taxable benefit as a miscellaneous itemized deduction, which is subject to a 2% of adjusted gross income floor. Tax advice and investment-related expenses, including counseling, are tax-deductible items that can offset the additional compensation reported to you.

You're not taxed on certain employer-related benefits provided outside the scope of medical coverage—substance and alcohol abuse counseling, counseling for other addictions and marriage counseling.

You're also not taxed on certain in-house assistance paid by your employer. For example, free electronic filing for your income tax return.

And you're not taxed on employer-paid retirement planning services for you and your spouse if your employer maintains a qualified retirement plan. There's no dollar limit on this exclusion.

Transit passes

If your employer gives you monthly commuter transit passes or tokens, you're not taxed on up to $110 per month in 2007. If the passes cost more, only the excess is taxable to you.

If you have a choice between transit passes and cash and you opt for the cash, then you're taxed on this benefit.

The same is true of employer-provided commuter van transportation, called van pooling. The same dollar limit applies. If you use both transit passes and van pooling, the dollar limits apply to both benefits combined.

If you pay for transit passes, you may be able to do so on a pretax basis. Ask your employer whether this option is available to you. This is done through a salary reduction agreement in which you consent to forgo a set amount (limited to the monthly dollar limits). *Bonus:* This salary reduction *isn't* made on a use-it-or-lose-it basis. You can carry forward any amount you haven't spent until you use it up.

Vacation pay

Most companies offer paid vacation time. Remember that all vacation pay is taxable.

ROUNDUP OF TAXES ON EMPLOYEE BENEFITS

Use the following chart to see if your benefits are free from income and/or Social Security and Medicare taxes:

Employee benefits in 2007—income and FICA tax treatment

Benefit	Income tax	Social Security and Medicare taxes
Adoption assistance	Tax free up to $11,390 if AGI is below a threshold	Not exempt
Athletic facilities	Tax free for facilities on company premises; taxable for paid memberships to outside facilities	Taxable benefits are not exempt
Awards	Generally taxable (awards for length of service or safety achievement are tax free within limits)	
Bonuses	Taxable	Not exempt
Company car for personal use	Taxable	Not exempt
Company stock	Taxable	Not exempt
De minimis benefits (e.g., Christmas hams, occasional personal use of company copier, occasional meal money or carfare home)	Tax free	Exempt
Dependent care assistance	Tax free up to $5,000	Exempt
Disability insurance	Premium payments tax free (but benefits are taxable)	
Education assistance	Tax free up to $5,250; tax free without limit for job-related courses	Exempt if tax free
Employee discounts	Tax free	Exempt
Free parking	Tax free up to $215/month	Exempt
Group term life insurance	Tax free for coverage up to $50,000 (excess coverage taxed according to IRS table)	Exempt up to $50,000 of coverage
Health and accident insurance	Tax free	Exempt
Health reimbursement arrangements	Tax free	Exempt
Health savings accounts (HSAs)	Exempt	Exempt
Housing	Tax free if on premises for convenience of employer and condition of employment	Exempt
Incentive stock options	Tax free at grant and exercise (but may be subject to AMT on exercise)	
Interest-free loan	Taxed on interest not charged	Not exempt
Meals	Tax free if on premises for the convenience of employer	Exempt
Moving expenses	Tax free if employee could have deducted expenses had he/she paid them	Exempt

(continued on next page)

Employee benefits in 2007—income and FICA tax treatment (cont'd)

Benefit	Income tax	Social Security and Medicare taxes
No-additional-cost benefits (e.g., free flights to airline employees, reduced phone charges to telephone company workers)	Tax free	Exempt
Nonqualified stock options	Taxable if value is readily ascertainable (otherwise, taxable when exercised)	
Retirement plans	Contributions are tax free (distributions are taxable)	Exempt
Tax and investment counseling	Taxable	Not exempt
Transit passes and van commuting	Tax free up to $110/month	Exempt
Vacation pay	Taxable	Not exempt

DON'T OVERINDULGE IN THE COMPANY'S CAFETERIA PLAN

Cafeteria plans aren't meal tickets. They're a menu of fringe benefits that you can choose from to cover your personal needs. Some benefits are tax free; others are taxable. Selecting benefits you *don't* need can leave you short of benefits you could use, and may entail needless taxes. Since your overall benefit dollars are limited, you want to opt for the benefits that will do you the most good—items you would otherwise have to pay for on your own.

> **Example:** If you're younger than age 40, you probably don't want to opt for long-term-care insurance.

COORDINATING BENEFITS FOR WORKING COUPLES

If you and your spouse work for separate employers, you should coordinate your benefit selections to optimize protection at the lowest cost.

Compare company health plans

Coverage differs substantially from company to company:

▶ **If each employer offers noncontributory coverage**—that is, if it doesn't cost you a thing—then obviously keep both health plans.

▶ **If one or both plans requires you to pay for coverage,** choose one plan. A noncontributory plan may not be the cheapest if it has high deductibles and lots of exclusions that you must pay for out of pocket. In assessing cost, take into account deductibles, required co-payments and the extent of coverage. Regardless of cost, make sure the coverage is the kind you want. For example, make sure the plan provides the type of maternity care, psychiatric coverage and other benefits you may need.

Example: One employer may provide company-paid HMO coverage, while the other may provide a more flexible company-subsidized plan. If you don't want to use the HMO doctors in your area, then you would opt for the other plan even if you or your spouse will have to pay for some portion.

Other factors: Consider job stability in selecting a health plan. If one spouse anticipates a job change, then the family may be better off with health coverage from the other spouse. Also consider each company's record on health coverage. Some companies routinely make changes or increase costs to the employee. A change can mean a whole new network of doctors or a group you may not prefer.

Compare other benefits

Two-earner couples should assess other benefits too. For instance, some employers now provide home computers and cell phones as a benefit. If a couple needs only one of these items, don't accept both. Instead negotiate for other benefits, such as extra time off.

Don't duplicate automatic coverage

If your company automatically pays for a particular benefit—for example, dependent care assistance—then your spouse should not select this coverage at his or her company. He should instead opt for other benefits, such as additional life insurance.

NEGOTIATING TIPS FOR JOB HUNTERS

When the job market is tight, qualified individuals can negotiate better compensation packages. Here are ways to get the best deal:

▶ **Signing bonuses.** They're not just for star athletes. If you're going to change jobs, ask for a cash payment up front. Aim for a cash replacement of what you're giving up—years of vesting in a qualified retirement plan, special perks of the old job (such as built-up vacation time), a year-end bonus.

Example: If your old job gave you four weeks of paid vacation and now you'll have to start building from two weeks, include compensation for those two lost weeks.

▶ **Vacation time.** Companies have firm policies that relate vacation time to seniority. But it doesn't hurt to ask if you can get the same number of weeks you had before.

▶ **Relocation assistance.** If you'll have to move to take a new position, ask that your new employer foot the bill. Moving expenses were discussed earlier in this chapter.

14

All about owning a business

"You have to have your heart in the business and the business in your heart." —Thomas J. Watson

IF YOU OWN OR HAVE an interest in a business, you have a unique opportunity to enhance your financial future. It's been estimated that two-thirds of the millionaires in the US are small-business owners who take small salaries, live modestly and build their wealth over time. If you own a business, you can have a direct impact on improving company profits and enhancing your compensation package. The business can provide benefits, not only in the form of salary but also in retirement plan benefits, fringe benefits and special write-offs that can turn your business into your own tax shelter.

If you own a business, consider how to maximize your profits through savvy operations and minimize income taxes on business income through such strategies as income shifting. You also want to minimize your future estate taxes through special transfer techniques for business interests. And when you leave the business, you'll be looking for ways to get every dollar out and to pay as little as possible in taxes.

This chapter discusses ways to increase your company's bottom line—to build your business and enhance what you can take from it. It also explores ways to use your business to add to your wealth. And it examines strategies for minimizing income, gift and estate taxes.

INCREASING YOUR PROFITS

No matter how large or small your business, there's always room for improving your bottom line. The stronger and more profitable you make your business, the better your personal financial well-being. You'll be able to take more from the business in salary and other benefits and, if you desire, sell the business at a greater profit. To increase profitability, remember the "three Ps":

▶ **People**

▶ **Pricing**

▶ **Products**

People

People's productivity is an important factor in improving company profits. Look for ways to increase it by eliminating tasks that aren't necessary or useful. For example, don't waste man-hours compiling information that will never be used. Don't incur overtime costs that aren't absolutely required.

Pricing

Whether your business sells a product or a service, what you charge dictates what you earn. Overcharge and you'll lose sales. Undercharge and you'll lose out on money you could have earned. Know what the market will bear by keeping an eye on your competition and on your customers' comments.

Products

It's basic advice, but offer only products that have a market. Eliminate products or services that aren't productive or profitable for the company. Carrying inventory you'll never move or trying to market services that no one wants is a waste of company resources and a profit drain. Focus on products and services that are stars; put marketing money behind your winners and cut out your losers.

 Strategy: *Get rid of inventory that is not saleable. Consider donating excess inventory to charity. C corporations can claim an enhanced donation, the cost of the inventory plus 50% of the unrealized appreciation in the goods. For help with arranging donations of your inventory, see Gifts In Kind at* **www.giftsinkind.org**. *Or write down inventory that's become obsolete by offering it for sale before the end of the year.*

Other ways to increase profits

If your company has investments, look for ways to optimize your after-tax returns. For example, it may be better for the company to invest in stock rather than income-producing investments such as bonds. *The reason:* C corporations can claim a dividends-received deduction on stock dividends. If the corporation owns less than 20% of another corporation, only 30% of dividends are taxed (70% are tax free). If the corporation owns 20% or more of another corporation (but not 100%), then only 20% of the dividends are taxable. For wholly owned corporations, there's a 100% deduction on received dividends.

GOING ONLINE

What does having a Web site mean to your business? Is it a marketing tool to enhance the public's knowledge of your company? Is it an alternative point of sale? Is it your company's main connection with the public? Different companies may use the Internet in different ways.

Web sites are a two-way street

When someone clicks onto your site, make sure he or she leaves behind information you can use to build a database for future sales. For example, offer rewards for completing an online questionnaire. Then use the information to hone your marketing strategies. But don't ask for too much information. This will only lower the number of responses.

 Strategy: Assure the customer that information he provides will be kept confidential. Many consumers prefer not to have personal information sold to other companies, and may be reluctant to supply information without assurances of confidentiality.

Special concerns

Before your products or services were available online, your business may have been confined to the state in which you're located. But on the Web, you're now effectively operating in all 50 states. This raises new issues for the company:

▶ **Promotions and contests** must meet legal requirements in all 50 states.

▶ **Taxes get more complicated:** Do you have to charge sales tax if you sell to someone in another state? If you sell there, are you now liable for state income tax there as well? Cybertax is a whole new area of tax law that's both confusing and potentially costly. Make sure you discuss your Web business with a knowledgeable state and local tax professional.

Insure against liabilities

A Web site opens you up to a new range of liabilities that require special insurance coverage, sometimes called "cyber coverage." Don't expect your existing liability policy to cover:

▶ **Copyright and trademark infringement claims.** For example, if you link to another site and there are copyright problems on that site, you could be brought into a lawsuit on infringement claims.

▶ **Misinformation resulting in liability.** For example, if you post information that someone relies upon and it turns out to be wrong, causing injury, you could be held liable for damages.

▶ **Confidentiality breaches.** For example, if someone hacks into your site and obtains customer credit card information, you could be held liable.

 Strategy: Review your Web exposure with a knowledgeable insurance person, and amend existing coverage or take on a separate policy to cover Web-related issues. Monitor your site carefully to eliminate problems.

Going public

If you're thinking that your online business can be the next dot-com darling of Wall Street, think again. During 2000, nearly 200 dot-coms went bust, including such well-known companies as Auctions.com and even Value America, an old-time dot-com that had been public since 1996.

Of course, if you've hit upon something that the public really wants, you may be a welcome newcomer to "the street." EBay, Yahoo! and YouTube are dot.com superstars. Think about how your business is organized from a legal standpoint. The right kind of organization can facilitate a public offering. If you're now a limited liability company, you'll have to convert to a corporation. If you're an S corporation, you'll have to terminate the S election when it's time to go public. Lay the groundwork now for your future plans.

INCOME SHIFTING FOR TAX SAVINGS

When your business is profitable, your salary and other compensation can put you into a high tax bracket. Income taxes can be saved within a family when interests in the business are shifted to relatives in lower tax brackets. Income shifting can be accomplished on a tax-free-gift basis.

Sharing interests in your business

Generally, you want to keep your business interests within the family to maintain control over the business. Interests can be given to a spouse, but this won't shift income since a couple's combined income is reported on a joint return.

You can give interests to parents who are receiving assistance from you. This can enable you to provide support without writing out a check each month. As business owners, they can receive income from the company in the form of dividends or other payouts. However, they can't be paid any compensation unless they provide services to the company.

Interests can also be given to children. Children under age 18 at the end of the year are subject to the so-called kiddie tax, a mechanism that largely defeats the opportunity for income shifting before they turn 18. Under the kiddie tax, unearned income (such as dividends) over a set dollar amount ($1,700 in 2007) is taxed to the child at the parents' top marginal rate. So, if you are in the 35% tax bracket in 2007 and give shares in your company to your 12-year-old child, no meaningful income shifting results since unearned income over $1,700 is taxed at your top tax bracket.

 Strategy: *Hire your child to work in the business. All earned income is taxed at the child's marginal rates. Hiring your child is discussed later in this chapter.*

Once a child is 18, all income is taxed at the child's tax rate. The result of transferring business interests to the child is that more after-tax income remains in the family.

Ways to give away interests

In gifting interests in your business, the following considerations need to be addressed:

▶ **Keeping control.** You don't want to lose your control over the company.

▶ **Gifting to minors.** In most cases, children under the age of majority (generally 18 or 21, depending on state law) can't own shares directly. However, shares can be held by a custodian under the Uniform

Gifts to Minors Act (UGMA) or the Uniform Transfers to Minors Act (UTMA). Alternatively, shares can be placed in a trust for the benefit of the child. Using a trust means that you can, under the terms of the trust, delay or prevent your child from getting his or her hands on the shares on reaching majority.

▶ **Preserving the business organization.** If the company is an S corporation, there are limits on the number of shareholders (100) and on the types of owners (only certain trusts can hold shares).

Gifting business interests for income shifting

If you want to give away shares that will be shielded by the annual gift tax exclusion—$12,000 annually per recipient in 2007, or $24,000 if a spouse consents to the gift—you can use special valuation discounts, discussed in greater detail in Chapter 20. These discounts are allowed because of certain conditions—a lack-of-marketability discount if the company isn't public, a minority-interest discount for interests given to a minority owner (even if the family together owns a majority of the company) and a built-in gains tax discount for the tax that would have to be paid if appreciated company assets were sold (even if the business has no plans to sell). These discounts enable you to give away *more* than $12,000 worth of the business annually with no tax cost.

> **Example:** Your closely held corporation owns $100,000 worth of property so that the company is valued at $100,000. If you can show that valuation discounts totaling 40% are applicable, then you could make a gift of $20,000 ($20,000 x 60% = $12,000). For a 33% discount, $17,900 of property could be transferred under the $12,000 gift tax exclusion ($17,900 x 67% = $11,993).

> **Strategy:** *Obtain a qualified appraisal to determine the business value and help fix the size of the interests you wish to give away. This appraisal can be costly, but if you want to maximize your gifts, you'll need precise information.*

> **Strategy:** *File a gift tax return to report gifts for 2007 you consider to be worth no more than $12,000. If you do, the IRS has only three years to question your valuation of shares and the discounts you've claimed. But if you file no return, the IRS has an indefinite period to challenge your valuation discounts.*

YOUR BUSINESS AS A TAX SHELTER

Your first and primary concern in running a business is to make it viable so that it can continue to grow, enabling it not only to pay your salary but also to carry the payroll for your workers. If you've been successful—that is, the business is fiscally sound and has a bright future—you may want to look for ways that the business can be used to enhance your personal wealth without diminishing the fiscal soundness of the business.

Salary

The law sets no dollar limits on what you can take from your business as compensation in the form of salary, bonuses, etc. Public corporations have a $1 million deduction limit on compensation to top brass. But as a practical matter, payments to you are limited by what the business can afford and what it can deduct:

▶ **What the business can afford.** When you take money out of the business, as compensation or benefits or otherwise, you need to weigh the impact on the business. Can the business afford what you want? You don't want to put your business in peril by taking out more cash than its cash flow can support.

▶ **Deductibility.** The deduction for compensation is based on what is "reasonable." This depends on what your services are worth to the business. If you want to maximize payments to yourself, special factors—such as your handling multiple jobs for the company—should be carefully documented in the corporate minutes.

 Strategy: Consider a salary payback agreement to protect the company. If the IRS determines that your compensation is unreasonable, it will disallow a deduction for the portion that it deems excessive. A salary payback agreement converts the excess portion into a loan you must repay. Since you've included the excess payment as income on your personal return, you'll be able to deduct any repayment to the company. Having such an agreement can create the impression that you believe your compensation to be unreasonable.

▶ **Hire your spouse and children.** Putting relatives on the payroll can mean more income for your family. As long as they perform work for the company and their compensation is reasonable for their work, the business can deduct payments to them.

Hiring your spouse also bulks up retirement benefits if your spouse is a full-time employee eligible to participate in a company retirement plan. And travel expenses for you and your spouse can be fully deductible. Generally, the cost of spousal travel isn't deductible, but if your spouse is an employee, it becomes a legitimate business expense. Further, by having earnings, your spouse builds up his or her own Social Security benefits.

Hiring your children can mean tax-free income to them and a deduction for your business. They can earn up to the standard deduction amount without any income taxes. In 2007, the standard deduction for singles is $5,350, so wages up to this limit are completely free from income taxes. The business deducts their wages, reducing the income on which taxes must be paid.

Example: If you're a sole proprietor and pay your teenager $4,000 in the summer to perform office work, you can deduct this payment on your Schedule C. If you're in the 28% tax bracket, the salary is costing you only $2,880 out of pocket; the other $1,120 is your tax savings from the deduction.

If your business is unincorporated, wages to your child under the age of 18 are free from employment taxes as well—a savings for both you and your child.

 Strategy: Fund Roth IRAs for your children from business wages. Even if they spend their wages on entertainment or college, you can give them what they need to fund their Roth IRA (100% of compensation up to the $4,000 limit for 2007). For example, if they earn $1,500, you can put this amount into a Roth IRA to build up their tax-free retirement savings.

Retirement benefits

You can set up a qualified retirement plan for your business. You cannot discriminate against your rank-and-file employees; you must include them in the plan under certain conditions. But you can design a plan that skews contributions and benefits in your favor. For example, you may want to use a defined-benefit plan if you're more than 20 years older than your employees so that you get the majority of company contributions to the plan.

If your spouse works for the business, you can each have retirement savings, providing substantial retirement income for the family. Even if your spouse earns only a modest amount, you can make a contribution to the company plan on your spouse's behalf.

You need to work with a pension professional to tailor a plan to your company's profile. Retirement plans are explained in Chapter 8.

You can also set up nonqualified plans to supplement or supplant qualified plans in order to amplify your benefits. For example, you may consider using deferred-compensation arrangements to shift income to retirement years and postpone income tax on the payments until receipt.

Fringe benefits

You can let your company pay for many of your personal expenses—a car, life insurance, dependent care and more. However, many fringe benefits must be provided to your employees as well if the company wants the write-offs and you want to avoid reporting income. Fringe benefits are explained in Chapter 13.

Caution: Certain fringe benefits cannot be provided to sole proprietors, partners, members in LLCs and more-than-2% S corporation shareholders on a tax-free basis. This is because certain tax-free benefits are limited to "employees," and these owners aren't considered employees for this purpose. Fringe benefits that are not tax free to owners include:

- ▶ **Adoption assistance.**
- ▶ **Dependent care.**
- ▶ **Education assistance.**
- ▶ **Free parking** (other than on a trip away from the regular office).
- ▶ **Medical coverage.** If the business pays the owners' medical insurance, the cost of the insurance is taxable on this benefit. Then they can claim an offsetting deduction on their personal income tax returns. Premiums are 100% deductible as an adjustment to gross income.
- ▶ **Transit passes.** While employees can exclude up to $110 per month in 2007, the exclusion is limited to $21 per month for these owners.

INTEREST-FREE LOANS FROM YOUR BUSINESS

Taking money out of your business in the form of loans can be favorable to both you and the company because:

▶ **You get cash that's not taxable.** If you had taken the funds as salary or a dividend, the money would be ordinary income.

▶ **The business is not diminished by the loan** since it's carried on the balance sheet as such.

From your perspective, if the loan carries little or no interest, your repayment obligations are minimized. However, under rules governing below-market loans, low or interest-free loans create income for you. You're treated as receiving the interest that should have been charged but was not. This is referred to as "forgone interest." The rate that should have been charged is the IRS interest rate, adjusted monthly, for the term of the loan (short-term, mid-term or long-term), called the applicable federal rate or AFR.

Example: You borrowed $25,000 from the company as a demand loan on an interest-free basis, and it remained outstanding for all of 2006. Since the blended interest rate for all of 2006 was 4.71%, you would have imputed income of $1,178.

▶ **Safe harbor.** There's no imputed or phantom interest if the loan does not exceed $10,000, as long as the main purpose of the loan isn't tax avoidance.

From the company's perspective, imputed interest is taxable, but the company may or may not be entitled to an offsetting deduction. If you're an employee of your company, then the company can treat the imputed interest as additional compensation and claim a deduction for it. But if you're merely a passive shareholder, the imputed interest is viewed as a nondeductible dividend payment, leaving the company with imputed income from the interest it should have charged but did not.

★ **Strategy:** *Fully document the loan terms, and specify any loan security. Include details of the loan in the corporate minutes. Sign a promissory note with a stated rate of interest and repayment terms. Adhere to the terms of the note (for example, make timely payments of interest and any required principal). If you fail to follow formalities, the IRS may question whether the arrangement is in fact a loan and not a disguised dividend.*

From your perspective, you're taxable on the imputed interest, either as compensation if you're an employee of the business or as dividend income if you're a passive owner. You *may* be able to claim an off-setting interest deduction. It depends on what you use the loan proceeds for:

▶ **If you use the proceeds for investments,** you can deduct imputed interest on the loan as investment interest to the extent of your net investment income (investment income less investment expenses).

▶ **If you use the proceeds for personal purposes**—say, to take a vacation, redecorate your home or pay for your child's wedding—the interest is nondeductible.

▶ **If you use the proceeds to buy a home** *and* the loan is secured by the residence, you can deduct the interest on a loan up to $1 million.

HANDLING YOUR COMPANY'S TAXES

The taxes your company pays determine the real profit it makes. So, to boost your profits, you need to minimize your federal, state and local taxes. Look for ways to reduce:

▶ **Income taxes.**

▶ **Employment taxes.**

▶ **Sales and use taxes.**

Good accounting

From a business as well as a tax standpoint, you need to know exactly how your company is doing. The only way to know is to keep good books and records. To that end:

▶ **Work with an accountant**. This is discussed in Chapter 2.

▶ **Use quality record-keeping software**, such as *QuickBooks Pro* (**http://quickbooks.intuit.com**) or *One-Write Plus* (Peachtree Software, **www.peachtree.com/onewrite**).

Record keeping for taxes is explained in IRS Publication 583, *Starting a Business and Keeping Records*, which can be found at **www.irs.gov**.

Avoiding audits

Maximizing your tax options can sometimes lead to tax troubles—IRS audits that can result not only in additional taxes but also in penalties and interest. To avoid potential problems, know what the IRS thinks about your type of business. The IRS has published its audit guides—manuals used by IRS personnel to conduct audits—on its Web site (**www.irs.gov**). There are about three dozen guides so far; if your industry hasn't yet been focused on, it may well be featured in a future guide.

Avoiding personal liability for company taxes

If your company fails to pay income tax withholding and the employees' share of Social Security and Medicare taxes, you can be held 100% personally liable for the payment. This is so even if the company is incorporated or a limited liability company that otherwise provides protection from personal liability. This penalty applies to a "responsible person"—that is, someone with authority to sign checks and direct payments by the company.

SIDELINE BUSINESSES

You don't need to have a full-time business to enhance your income and enjoy certain tax advantages. You may be able to:

▶ **Build up Social Security benefits.** If you don't have a salary at least equal to the maximum Social Security wage base ($97,500 in 2007), you won't be able to collect the maximum Social Security benefits.

But if your sideline business is profitable, you can add to your future benefits by paying additional Social Security taxes now.

▶ **Build up retirement savings.** Whether or not you're covered by a company retirement plan through full-time employment, you can start your own retirement plan for your sideline business, as long as it's profitable. Not only will this produce more retirement income for you in the future, but you'll obtain a valuable current tax deduction for your contributions to the plan. Retirement plan options are discussed in Chapter 8.

▶ **Convert nondeductible personal expenses into deductible expenses.** You may be able to take advantage of certain fringe benefits—that is, have your business pick up the tab (and deduct it). You may also qualify to claim a home-office deduction if you use a portion of your home for business (see below).

Limit on losses

If your sideline business isn't profitable, you may not be able to deduct losses in excess of income from the sideline activity. You can deduct all of your losses only if you have a reasonable expectation of making a profit for the business. The way you carry on your activity—how businesslike you are—can be a good indication of your profit motive.

 Strategy: Conduct a sideline activity in a way that demonstrates a profit motive. Write a business plan. Carry on the activity professionally. Use a separate business bank account, maintain good accounting and records and use business methods that will make you profitable.

You can rely on a presumption that you have a profit motive by showing that your business made a profit in three out of five years (two out of seven years for horse-related activities). But to claim this presumption you must file a special form with the IRS, which almost guarantees that your return will be audited at the end of the presumption period.

WORKING FROM HOME

Millions of individuals run full-time or part-time businesses from home. This can save you time and expense, because you don't have to commute.

Using your home for business can enable you to write off expenses. In addition to items you're already deducting (mortgage interest, real estate taxes and casualty losses), you can deduct:

▶ **Depreciation.** This is a noncash deduction; you're writing off the purchase price of the business portion of the home without any current cash outlay.

▶ **Rent,** if you lease your home.

▶ **Maintenance and repairs.**

▶ **Cleaning costs.**

▶ **Utilities for the home office,** including electricity, gas or oil, and water.

Collectively these expenses are taken as a single home-office deduction. To qualify for write-offs, your home office must be used regularly and exclusively for business. It must also be:

▶ **Your principal place of business.** This generally is where you earn your money or where you keep your books and perform other administrative tasks (assuming there's no other fixed location for doing these tasks).

▶ **A place to meet** clients or customers on a regular basis.

The tax rules for claiming a home-office deduction are explained in IRS Publication 587, *Business Use of Your Home*, at **www.irs.gov**.

WHEN YOU SELL A BUSINESS

The sale of a business can be the single most important financial transaction of your life. It's the culmination of all your efforts over the years, and you want to be sure you make the best deal possible. The money from the sale of your business may be your primary retirement income and protection for your family's financial security.

Selling the business to family members

If your child works in the business, you may have a built-in buyer. The same may be true for grandchildren. Structure the sale of the business to a child for your financial advantage using three key methods:

▶ **Outright sale**. Your child (or the company) buys out your interest in a lump sum. You receive all of the proceeds from the sale at once and report gain in the year of the sale.

Strategy: Make the transaction a part-sale/part-gift if you can afford to forgo some of the sale price. Make a gift of a portion of the business to your child and sell him or her the balance. Alternatively, you can give a portion of the business and have the corporation redeem the balance of your shares. This part-sale/part-gift technique may help bootstrap the transaction.

▶ **Installment sale**. Your child makes payments to you over time, a portion of the sales price plus interest on the installment payments.

Advantages of an installment sale...

▶ **You receive an income stream** over the period of the installment sale.

▶ **Gain, and the taxes on the gain, are deferred.** You report gain when you receive installment payments.

Strategy: Have any outstanding installment obligations canceled at your death as an additional inheritance to your children. They will receive the canceled obligations as a tax-free inheritance. It's possible to structure the installment sale to include self-canceling installment notes (SCINs) to avoid estate taxes. Careful wording is necessary to exclude the canceled notes from your estate. Work with a knowledgeable attorney to draft the sale.

Disadvantages of an installment sale...

▶ **You run the risk that your child won't make payments.** Although the payments may be secured by the business, there's the risk that your child may run the business into the ground.

▶ **You don't have use of all the money at once.** If you plan to start a new business, this could be a drawback.

► **Private annuity.** You can sell the business in exchange for a private annuity. The annuity payments are figured according to your life expectancy. A part of each annuity payment represents capital gain for the sale of the business. From your perspective, a private annuity has both advantages and disadvantages.

Advantages of a private annuity...

   ► **You save on estate taxes.** Since the annuity terminates at death, there is nothing to include in your estate.

   ► **You defer income taxes.** Gain is spread over the remainder of your life, with a portion of each payment representing capital gain.

   ► **Gift taxes are avoided** as long as the business is properly valued to ensure that you're selling, not giving, the business to your child.

Disadvantages of a private annuity...

   ► **Valuation can be difficult.** A careful appraisal of the business is necessary so that payments can be structured to avoid any gift tax.

   ► **Payments are unsecured.** In order to achieve the desired tax results, your child's obligation to make payments can't be secured by the business or otherwise. You must rely on your child's promise—and ability—to pay.

   ► **You must pay professional fees to set up the private annuity.** Appraisal fees to determine the value of the business, attorneys' fees to draft the arrangement and accounting fees to compute the annuity payments can add up to thousands of dollars.

Inside buyers

If you don't have a child or relative who'll buy the business, perhaps there are other "insiders" who can do so.

   ► **Partners or co-owners.** If you have co-owners, it's generally advisable to work out a buy-sell agreement to obligate them to buy out your interest under certain conditions. If you retire or you become disabled, the terms of the agreement may force them to pay you for your interest.

 Strategy: Plan for funding the buy-sell agreement. How are your co-owners going to raise the capital needed to buy out your interest? It may be possible to structure the arrangement so that payment comes from the business itself or through special buy-out insurance.

► **Employee stock ownership plans (ESOPs).** If your business is incorporated as a C or S corporation, then this qualified plan can buy you out. You sell your shares to the ESOP.

Strategy: *Defer recognition of gain from the sale of your shares to an ESOP by reinvesting the proceeds in other securities—stocks and bonds issued by US corporations. Use this deferral if you have held your shares for at least three years prior to the sale and, immediately following the sale, the ESOP will own at least 30% of each class of the corporation's outstanding stock or 30% of the total value of the corporation's stock. Deferral continues as long as you hold the replacement securities. If you hold them at death, your heirs get a stepped-up basis to their value at that time, and avoid any income tax on the appreciation built up over your lifetime. This deferral option applies only if the business is a regular C corporation. It can't be used for an S corporation.*

Sale to outsiders

If you don't have a child to sell your business to, and you don't have co-owners or employees ready and willing to buy out your interest, you'll need to look outside the business for a buyer. In working out a deal with outsiders, follow some simple strategies:

▶ **Work with professionals.** Finding the best buyer means getting the best price. To do this, it's generally a good idea to work with a business broker or, for larger businesses, an investment banker. Although you'll pay for their assistance, you should net more in the long run. Then enlist the services of an accountant and an attorney to go over the details. How you structure the sale will affect what you'll keep after tax.

▶ **Elect S corporation status.** If your company operates as a regular C corporation, you can eliminate the potential double taxation on the sale of the business if you elect to be taxed as an S corporation. In this way, the proceeds are taxed only to you as a shareholder and not to the corporation as well. *Caution:* Double tax isn't eliminated if there are built-in gains—appreciated assets at the time of conversion. These gains are taxed to the corporation if they're sold within 10 years of the S election.

▶ **Take payments over time.** You can structure the sale as an installment sale, requiring so much down with payments over time. This allows you to report gain over the period in which you receive the installment payments.

 Strategy: *Weigh the tax benefits of accepting a payout over time against the possibility of the company (or its owners) failing to make good on all its promises. You may wish to accept a lower purchase price up front rather than a higher price to be paid out over time. Remember that money in hand can be invested, perhaps making up the difference in proceeds.*

▶ **Be realistic.** While the business may currently be the focus of your life, this personal relationship does not necessarily translate into value when it comes time to sell.

Give yourself the time needed to find the right buyer. Don't expect overnight success; start marketing the company well before the time you wish to depart. But don't neglect the business operations while you focus on the sale, or you could diminish the value of the thing you're selling.

▶ **Walk away when it's over.** You may structure a sale to provide you with an ongoing relationship with the business as an employee or a consultant for a set number of years. You receive compensation from your services separate and apart from the proceeds of the sale. But whether or not you continue an association with the company, don't expect new owners to duplicate your management style or keep things the same. Be prepared emotionally to let go.

15

Taxes, taxes and less taxes

The United States has a system of taxation by confession. —SUPREME COURT JUSTICE HUGO BLACK

ALTHOUGH THE TAX CONSEQUENCES of various financial actions are included in many other topics throughout this book, there are some tax concepts that don't fit neatly into these areas. You need to see the big picture of taxes—how they can reduce your current income and your estate in the future.

This chapter is concerned primarily with income taxes imposed by the federal government. You may also be subject to state and local income taxes.

This chapter focuses on some general strategies for increasing wealth by keeping Uncle Sam's share of your income at a minimum. It explains the difference between investing with pretax dollars and after-tax dollars. It discusses ways to shift income so that family income is maximized. It also explains how giving property away can actually provide you with substantial benefits. It tells you how to stay out of trouble with the IRS, and how to find tax information online.

211

IT'S NOT WHAT YOU EARN, BUT WHAT YOU KEEP

Tax planning can increase your income and your wealth. This is because what you have to spend or invest depends not only on what you make but also on what you pay in taxes. By cutting taxes, you have more funds available to do the things you want to do.

Investing after-tax dollars

Most personal savings must be made with after-tax dollars. In other words, you must earn a salary and pay tax on that salary, and then you can invest what's left. The only way to have money to invest is to *not* spend it on something else. Often this requires saying no to certain things, like buying a new wardrobe or purchasing a new car.

For many, a sizable portion of monthly income is devoted to the repayment of debt. If debt can be reduced or eliminated, it means more after-tax income is available for investing.

Investing pretax dollars

The tax law does encourage certain investments on a pretax basis. These include deductible IRAs and 401(k) plans, and SIMPLE plans funded through salary reduction arrangements. By taking advantage of these opportunities to invest money that's never been taxed, you can optimize your return.

> **Example:** In 2007, you contribute $15,500 to your company's 401(k) plan on a salary reduction basis. Your W-2 form doesn't include this as income so you don't pay income tax on it. The full $15,500 is invested and can compound, undiminished by taxes, while you're in the plan. In comparison, if you had invested after-tax dollars, you would have only $11,160 to invest (assuming you're in the 28% tax bracket). If that $11,160 were to earn 8% annually, each year those earnings would be reduced by the taxes owed, so compounding would not be on the full 8% return.

However, there's a price to pay for investing pretax dollars. Although dollars aren't taxed when the funds go into the plan, they are taxed when they come out. You are taxed upon withdrawals from these investment vehicles. And not even death wipes out the tax obligation on these savings plans. Whatever remains in these accounts on your death will eventually be taxed to your heirs.

WHAT'S YOUR TAX BRACKET?

The income tax system is based on graduated tax rates in 2007 of 10%, 15%, 25%, 28%, 33% and 35%. A portion of income is taxed at the lowest rate. Once the limit for that rate is met, the next taxable dollar of income falls into the next tax bracket. Generally, the term "your tax bracket" refers to the highest tax bracket to which your income is subjected. This is because planning impacts the top dollar you earn.

Example: In 2007, you're single with taxable income of $55,000. The first $7,825 is taxed at 10%, then up to $31,850 is taxed at 15%, the excess over $31,850 is taxed at 25%. It's common to say you're in the 25% tax bracket even though the bulk of your income is taxed at lower rates.

TAX-FREE INCOME ITEMS

The tax law provides a host of items that are never taxed. Since they're not diminished by being taxed, their value is increased. These tax-free income opportunities include:

▶ **Gain on the sale of your main home.** You can exclude up to $250,000 of gain ($500,000 on a joint return) if you've owned and used your home as your main residence for at least two of the five years preceding the date of sale.

▶ **Roth IRAs.** All earnings on your contributions to a Roth IRA can be withdrawn tax free as long as the account has been open for at least five years and withdrawals are taken after age 59½, on account of disability, to cover first-time home-buying expenses (up to $10,000 per lifetime) or to pay medical expenses or health insurance premiums.

 Strategy: If eligible, contribute to a Roth in order to start the five-year holding period. The holding period begins at the start of the year to which the contributions relate. For example, if you make a Roth IRA contribution for 2007 on April 15, 2008, the five-year period is calculated from January 1, 2007.

Now, 401(k) plans may allow you to designate your salary reduction contributions as Roth 401(k) contributions—after-tax contributions that will give rise to tax-free distributions later on.

▶ **Interest on municipal bonds.** Interest paid on state and local municipal bonds isn't taxable for federal income tax purposes. Whether the interest is taxable for state income tax purposes varies from state to state. (See page 87 for a chart on the taxability of municipal bond interest by state.)

▶ **Certain capital gains.** Tax on long-term capital gains can be avoided if assets are donated to charity. You get a charitable contribution deduction for the value of the assets at the time of the donation and never have to pay income tax on the appreciation you have realized. Tax on gains is also avoided on assets held until death. *The reason:* Heirs receive a stepped-up basis for inherited property. This means their basis for determining their future gain or loss is the estate tax value of the property—generally the value of the property on the date of death. So all appreciation up to that point is never taxed.

▶ **Child support payments.** Amounts you receive for the support of a child aren't taxed to you or to the child.

▶ **Inheritances.** If you receive property as a bequest, you're not taxed on this receipt. However, once the money is invested or property is sold, you are then taxed accordingly.

▶ **Life insurance.** If you receive proceeds from a life insurance policy upon the death of the insured, the payments are tax free. Accelerated death benefits from a life insurance policy paid to someone who is terminally ill are also tax free. But only a limited amount of accelerated death benefits paid to someone chronically ill is tax free.

▶ **Tax-free fringe benefits.** Personal items paid for by your employer may qualify for tax-free treatment. For example, employer-paid medical insurance isn't taxable to you. Certain fringe benefits, however, have dollar limits on the tax-free amounts or impose income requirements for obtaining tax-free treatment. Fringe benefits are discussed in Chapter 13.

▶ **Military benefits.** Many of the payments and services furnished by the federal government to members of the military and their families are tax free. For details see IRS Publication 3, *Armed Forces' Tax Guide,* at **www.irs.gov**.

▶ **Damages.** Compensatory damages received in actions for personal physical injury or illness are tax free. However, punitive damages arising out of these actions are taxable, as are all other types of recoveries. Worker's compensation is also tax free.

▶ **Income of those not required to file a return.** If someone's income is so low that he or she doesn't have to file an income tax return, then it's tax free. For example, if your child, age 5, receives interest on a savings account of $500 for the year and has no other income, this income is tax free since it's fully offset by the child's standard deduction amount ($850 for 2007). Income earned by your widowed parent who's at least 65 years old isn't taxable until it exceeds a specified level ($10,050 in 2007).

INCOME SHIFTING

A key strategy for reducing taxes on family income is shifting some income to relatives in lower tax brackets. Since they pay lower income tax there's more after-tax income for the family as a whole. As income tax rates decline, income shifting remains an important tax-saving strategy even though the savings may not be as great as when rates were higher.

Keep in mind that you can't merely give away the right to receive income. You must actually gift the income-producing property. For example, you can't simply assign to your child the right to collect interest on a bond you own. You have to transfer ownership of the bond to your child to shift the income to him or her.

In deciding how much property to shift to children, keep special tax rules in mind. Children under the age of 18 at the end of the year are subject to the kiddie tax, a mechanism that largely defeats the opportunity for income shifting. Under the kiddie tax, unearned income (such as dividends) over a set dollar amount ($1,700 in 2007) are taxed to the child at the parent's top marginal rate. So, if you are in the 35% tax bracket and give a corporate bond to a child who is 12 years old, interest income over the limit is taxed to your child at 35%, yielding no tax savings for the family.

But once a child is 18, all income is taxed at the child's tax rates. The result of transferring business interests to the child is that more after-tax income remains in the family.

Consider giving appreciated assets that you've wanted to sell. In this way, your child can sell the assets and pay the capital gains tax on the sale. Presumably, your child will pay a lower tax rate than you would.

> **Example:** You want to sell stock now priced at $10,000 that cost you $2,500 several years ago. Your tax cost would be as much as $1,125 ($7,500 gain x 15% capital gains tax). But if you give the stock to your child who then sells it, the gain may be zero, depending on the child's other income, or $375 ($7,500 gain x 5% capital gains tax), assuming the child is in the 10% or 15% tax bracket. *Note:* In 2008 through 2010, those in the 10% or 15% tax bracket pay zero tax on long-term capital gains and qualified dividends.

▶ **Advantages of income shifting.** Obviously, a key reason for income shifting is to reduce income taxes. *Another reason for gifting assets to family members:* To reduce the size of your estate, potentially lowering your estate taxes.

▶ **Disadvantage of income shifting.** Once you give away property you can't get it back. You lose control over the property and can't recoup it even if you were to need it in the future.

GIVING TO GET

Whoever said it's better to give than to receive must have had federal tax rules in mind. This is because the law provides substantial write-offs for donating money and property to charity.

Cash donations are deductible as itemized deductions. Your benefit from the deduction depends on your tax bracket. This benefit, in effect, reduces the after-tax cost of making the donation.

> **Example:** You donate $1,000 to your favorite charity. If you're in the 28% tax bracket, your deduction saves you $280. This means the donation cost you only $720 to make.

Donations of appreciated property held more than one year have an added tax benefit. Not only can you deduct the value of the property at the time of the donation, but you can also avoid capital gains tax on the appreciation.

> **Example:** You donate $1,000 of appreciated stock to your favorite charity. You paid $200 for the stock five years ago. If you're in the 28% tax bracket, your deduction saves you $400 ($280 for the deduction plus $120 in capital gains tax you would have to pay if you sold the stock).

Property doesn't have to appreciate for you to deduct it. For example, you may wish to donate your used car or old clothes to charity. Obviously, these items have declined in value since you acquired them. But you still get a tax benefit from their donation and avoid the inconvenience and expense of selling them.

▶ **The deduction for a car** depends on its value. For donations valued up to $500, you can rely on the car's blue book value adjusted for condition and mileage (visit *Kelley Blue Book* at **www.kbb.com**). For cars valued over $500, the deduction is limited to what the charity receives for it on a sale if there is no substantial use by the organization before the sale. You must obtain a written acknowledgment from the charity of the donation within 30 days of the contribution. *Important:* The same rules apply to donations of boats.

▶ **The deduction for used clothing and household items** is also the lower of your cost or their fair market value. A deduction generally can only be claimed for items in good used condition or better. Determine fair market value using IRS Publication 561, *Determining the Value of Donated Property,* by visiting **www.irs.gov**.

Before you write a check or donate property, make sure the charity meets two criteria. First, make sure it's approved by the IRS so that your donations will be tax deductible. You can check on the status of a charity by going to **www.irs.gov** or by checking IRS Publication 78, *Cumulative List of Organizations*.

You also should make sure that the charity you've selected really serves charitable purposes and doesn't just funnel funds to the organization's officers in the form of high salaries and other expenses. You can check how much of a charity's collections are used for its exempt purposes (and how much is used for administration) by checking with:

▶ American Institute of Philanthropy (**www.charitywatch.org**, 773-529-2300). Ask for a sample copy of their *Charity Rating Guide*. Postage and handling is $3.00.

▶ Better Business Bureau Wise Giving Alliance (**www.give.org**, 703-276-0100). Request its free *Better Business Bureau Wise Giving Guide.*

▶ Charity Navigator (**www.charitynavigator.org**). View top ten lists related to charities.

Limits on charitable deductions

Your adjusted gross income limits how much of your donations you can write off in the current year:

▶ **50% limit.** This limit applies to cash gifts to most charitable organizations (such as the United Way, Cancer Care, the Heart Fund, hospitals, universities and governments).

▶ **30% limit.** This limit applies to capital gains property (held more than one year) donated to the organizations described above. It also applies to cash and other property donated to other groups (private nonprofit operating organizations, veterans' organizations, fraternal societies and nonprofit cemeteries).

▶ **20% limit.** This limit applies to capital gains property donated to nonoperating private foundations.

Deductions in excess of these AGI limits can be carried forward for up to five years.

Appraisals and tax forms: To claim the deductions you're entitled to, you will need certain substantiation. For example, starting in 2007 donations in any amount must be accompanied by a written acknowledgment from the organization, a bank statement, or other approved means.

Noncash contributions over $500 but not over $5,000 must be listed on IRS Form 8283; if the property is worth more than $5,000 (or $10,000 for closely held stock), an appraisal summary must be attached to the return. Property donations over $20,000 require a full qualified appraisal. *Warning:* The failure to obtain the necessary substantiation and appraisals can result in the loss of a deduction even if the donation is bona fide.

Sophisticated charitable giving

Here are ways to give to charity and continue to enjoy a benefit from what you have given:

▶ **Charitable remainder trust.** You retain an income interest for life, and the charity gets whatever remains in the trust at your death. So you enjoy the income from the property for as long as you live. You can claim a current tax deduction for the value of the charity's remainder interest, determined by IRS tables.

▶ **Charitable gift annuity.** Your donation entitles you to receive annuity payments for the rest of your life. You claim a current deduction for the value of the gift (what the charity receives less the value of your annuity). The charity does all the work of setting up and administering the annuity; there's no charge to you. *Note:* A portion of each annuity is taxable. When the annuity is funded with appreciated assets, the taxable portion is part ordinary income and part capital gain.

Strategy: Consider making donations for a deferred gift annuity, also called a deferred payment gift annuity. Contribute now and claim a charitable deduction now (the contribution is the difference between the value of the annuity based on IRS tables and the value of the donation). But the annuity doesn't start until some specified date in the future—for example, at age 65. By deferring the start of the annuity, you increase the payments you'll eventually receive. Warning: *Enter into this arrangement only with a well-established charity that has a deferred gift annuity program—for example, the Salvation Army or the UJA-Federation of New York. The charity needs to be there when you're due to start collecting your payments.*

▶ **Private foundations.** For those with substantial wealth, private foundations allow donations to be managed by donors and funneled to selected organizations. Again, a current tax deduction can be claimed for donations to the foundation even though funds may not be disbursed for charitable purposes until some time in the future.

 Strategy: Name yourself and/or members of your family to the foundation's board of directors. By working for the foundation, you can receive a salary for your services.

▶ **Donor advised funds.** Instead of setting up your own foundation, consider making contributions to commercial funds that allow you to direct your contributions toward specific charities or causes. While you can *advise* on how your donation is to be used, you cannot *require* this application. Commercial funds include:

▶ **Fidelity Charitable Gift Fund** (**www.fidelity.com** or **www.charitablegift.org**, 800-682-4438), which requires a $5,000 minimum contribution.

▶ **Schwab Charitable Fund** (**www.schwab.com**, 800-746-6216), which requires a $10,000 minimum contribution.

▶ Vanguard Charitable Endowment Program (**www.vanguard.com** or **www.vanguardcharitable. org**, 888-383-4483).

Estate tax savings

Charitable giving not only saves income taxes but also can have a beneficial effect on estate planning. You can reduce the size of your estate on a tax-deductible basis, saving income tax now and estate tax in the future.

While this tax savings may no longer be important for those with estates under the increasing exemption amount (explained in Chapter 20), it continues to be significant for those with larger estates. And, after 2010, current estate tax rules are scheduled to take effect so estates that may be exempt in the next several years may again become taxable at that time.

Alternatively, you can delay your charitable giving until your death. Bequests to charity are also deductible for estate tax purposes. So, for example, if you leave $10,000 to your favorite charity under the terms of your will, your estate can deduct that amount, saving $4,500 to $5,000 in estate taxes (depending on the year of death) on the bequest if your estate is in the maximum estate tax bracket.

You can optimize your charitable giving by coordinating your philanthropic goals with your family concerns.

 Strategy: Leave your deductible IRA to a charitable group. Since the charity doesn't pay income tax on this asset and the asset is deductible for estate tax purposes, the charity effectively receives the full value of the IRA. By comparison, your family would pay income tax on the IRA and the asset would be subject to estate taxes, effectively reducing the value of this asset by as much as nearly 75%.

AVOID THE ALTERNATIVE MINIMUM TAX TRAP

The tax law is set up so that taxpayers will pay at least some *minimum* tax regardless of the write-offs they claim. To ensure these minimum payments, there is an alternative minimum tax (AMT), with rates of 26% and 28% depending upon the amount of AMT income. However, while the AMT was intended to trap high-income taxpayers, it now includes many middle-income individuals, an estimated 4 million in 2005 and 2006. And with the decline in the regular tax rates, it's estimated that as many as 30 million taxpayers may be subject to the AMT by 2010, without a change in the law. Here are some of the triggering items and how to plan around them:

Incentive stock options (ISOs)

If your employer grants you ISOs, you're not taxed when you exercise the options. However, the spread between the option price and the fair market value of the stock on the date of exercise is an adjustment to income for AMT purposes.

 Strategy: *Time the exercise of ISOs so as not to trigger the AMT. In other words, don't exercise them all in the same year, but spread the exercise over several years.*

Note: For 2007 through 2012, there is a refundable tax credit for those with long-term AMT credits resulting from the exercise of ISOs.

Private activity bonds

Interest on bonds issued by states and municipalities for certain private purposes—to build a stadium, for instance—is exempt from regular income tax but is not exempt from the AMT. These bonds generally pay a slightly higher rate of interest than other municipal bonds in view of the potential tax factor.

 Strategy: *Sell private activity bonds and replace holdings with other municipal bonds to avoid AMT liability on the interest. When you purchase municipal bonds, make sure they're AMT-free.*

Itemized deductions

Deductions that serve to reduce your regular tax may, in fact, trigger the AMT. For instance:

▶ **Medical deductions** can reduce AMT only to the extent they exceed 10% of adjusted gross income.

▶ **Mortgage interest on a home-equity loan** may not be deductible for AMT purposes. Only interest on a loan to buy, build or substantially improve a principal residence is deductible for AMT purposes.

▶ **State and local taxes** aren't deductible for AMT purposes. But if you received a refund of these taxes that you reported as income, it's a negative adjustment to AMT, reducing your AMT liability.

 Strategy: *Don't prepay state and local taxes to reduce your regular tax if it results in AMT liability.*

▶ **Miscellaneous itemized deductions** aren't deductible for AMT purposes.

If you are subject to AMT

If you are subject to this tax despite all of your planning, then take advantage of the relatively low rates you'll have to pay (no more than 28%). Accelerate income into the current year so that it's taxed at the 28% rate if you ordinarily are in a higher tax bracket.

▶ **Sell Treasury bills** that would ordinarily come due in the following year, provided you're not losing more on the sale than you're gaining in AMT savings.

▶ **Cash in CDs** prior to maturity, weighing the cost of any early withdrawal penalties.

▶ **Take steps to accelerate income** from a sole proprietorship (for example, bill customers early so payment is received before the end of the year).

▶ **Take a bigger bonus** from a closely held corporation, as long as total compensation remains within "reasonable" limits so the corporation can deduct the payment.

Strategy: *Check for eligibility for an AMT credit. Items that don't permanently reduce your tax but only affect the timing of the tax, such as the adjustment for incentive stock options, can give rise to a minimum tax credit.*

ESTIMATED TAXES

Federal income taxes are made on a pay-as-you-go basis. Don't wait until you file your return to pay your entire tax bill. You're required to pay a certain amount through withholding or quarterly estimated taxes. If you fail to meet the minimum, you'll be subject to penalties (the penalty rate changes quarterly).

Minimum estimated tax requirements

Generally, you must pay at least 90% of your current tax liability or 100% of the prior year's liability to escape penalty. Payments are the total of withholding on wages, withholding on other items (such as gambling winnings) and your quarterly estimated tax payments. Your total payments must cover:

▶ **Regular tax liability**

▶ **Alternative minimum tax**

▶ **Employment tax** on household employees

▶ **Self-employment tax** for self-employed individuals

However, if your adjusted gross income in the prior year exceeded $150,000 (or $75,000 if married filing separately), then you can't rely on the 100% prior year safe harbor. Instead, you must pay at least 90% of the current year's tax liability or 110% of the prior year's liability.

> **Example:** You're single, and in 2006 you pay $20,000 in income tax. Your 2007 liability is $25,000. To avoid estimated tax penalties in 2007, your withholding and estimated tax payments must total at least $20,000 (100% of the prior year's liability of $20,000 because it is less than $22,500, which is 90% of the current liability of $25,000). But if your adjusted gross income in 2006 was more than $150,000, then your required payments in 2007 would be $22,000 (110% of the prior year's liability of $20,000 because it is less than $22,500, which is 90% of the current liability of $25,000).

Quarterly payments

Don't miss the deadlines for making any required quarterly estimated tax payments. Payments for the current year are due April 15, June 15, September 15 and January 15 of the following year.

Voluntary withholding

You can avoid the need to make quarterly estimated tax payments by requesting that withholding be taken from certain payments as follows:

Voluntary withholding

Item	Withholding rates
Pensions	Additional withholding (above mandatory amounts) at the rate applicable to mandatory withholding
Social Security payments	7%, 10%, 15% or 25% (your option)
Unemployment benefits	10%
Wages—additional withholding over required amounts	Rate applicable to your other wage withholding

MANAGING TAX PAYMENTS

An illness in the family, unemployment, an unexpected income item (such as phantom income from a tax shelter investment) or just bad fiscal management can leave you short of funds to pay your taxes. Don't panic, but act to minimize interest and penalties that would otherwise result.

Pay as much as possible as quickly as possible

Interest accrues on underpayments at a rate that adjusts quarterly. There are also underpayment penalties if certain minimum payments have not been made on time. Tap into your other resources—borrow from family or friends if necessary—to pay your taxes.

 Strategy: *Don't use your credit card to pay your taxes. While this is now permissible on American Express, Discover, MasterCard or Visa simply by calling 800-2PAYTAX or 888-PAY1040, you'll pay a convenience fee of nearly 2.5%, plus interest to the credit card company—possibly at a rate of 21% or more annually. The frequent-flier miles or other benefits earned on the card for this charge probably aren't worth the cost to you.*

Use a home-equity loan to pay your taxes in an emergency. The rate you'll pay is probably lower than what you would pay on a commercial loan or credit card. And the interest on a loan up to $100,000 is deductible. But don't use this borrowing option lightly; you're putting your house at risk.

 Strategy: *File your return on time even if you can't pay your full tax bill. This will avoid any late-filing penalties: Half of 1% per month on the outstanding tax balance up to 25%.*

Ask for an installment agreement

This will allow you to spread your payments over time. You won't avoid interest and penalties, but you'll have breathing room to satisfy your tax responsibilities. The 0.25% penalty under an installment agreement is half the usual penalty on late payments. Interest changes quarterly.

You can request an installment agreement by filing IRS Form 9465, *Installment Agreement Request.* Attach it to your return or, if you have already filed the return, send it to the IRS service center where that return was filed. To obtain the form, call 800-829-1040 or download it from **www.irs.gov**. There is a fee for obtaining an agreement.

▶ **If you owe no more than $10,000,** you can take up to three years to pay off your tax bill. This agreement is automatically granted upon your request if you meet certain requirements.

▶ **If you owe more than $10,000 but not more than $25,000,** you'll probably be allowed to pay off your debt over five years. This option isn't automatic, but simplified IRS procedures typically grant your request and don't require any liens on your property.

▶ **If you owe more than $25,000,** you can usually work out an agreement with the IRS to pay over time. You propose what you can pay monthly and negotiate from there.

Note: A partial payment installment agreement can be obtained under special circumstances.

Make an offer in compromise

If you're in dire financial straits and additional time won't help you to pay off your tax liability, the IRS may be willing to accept a settlement of less than the full tax owed. You must prove that making the full payment would impose a substantial economic hardship—in other words, that you need your assets and income for your basic living needs. You must make partial payment with your offer (a 20% upfront nonrefundable payment for a lump-sum offer or all partial payments pending a periodic payment offer). And it will cost you a $150 fee for getting the agreement. To see if you are eligible to make an offer, complete Step 1: Is Your Offer in Compromise "Processable?" in Form 656, *Offer in Compromise* at **www.irs.gov**.

HOW TO AVOID A TAX AUDIT

No one wants a tax audit. It can be scary, time consuming and costly. You can wind up owing not only additional taxes but also substantial interest and penalties, plus professional fees if you use an accountant or other tax professional to represent you. Even though audit rates have been quite low in recent years, someone is still being audited, and you don't want that someone to be you. You need to avoid calling attention to your return, and simple strategies can help you do this.

▶ **Avoid mathematical errors.** IRS computers will pick up these mistakes and call attention to your return. If you manually prepare your return, check and double check your math. Nearly 25% of all hand-prepared returns contain simple math errors. *The most common error:* Taking the tax from the wrong column of the tax table for one's filing status. To avoid math errors, use computer software to prepare your return. Software cuts math errors to less than 2%.

▶ **Report information as you receive it.** The IRS computer-matching program can detect discrepancies between items reported to it on Forms W-2, 1098, 1099, etc. If you believe that reported items are incorrect, first ask the issuer to make a correction. But if that hasn't been done by the time you file your return, first list the item *exactly* as it was reported on the form. Make the adjustment you believe to be correct. For example, say you have a joint bank account with your sister. The bank reports all the interest to you under your Social Security number. Report the full amount of interest on your return, then subtract the amount of interest belonging to your sister.

▶ **Watch for audit red flags.** Deduct every item you're entitled to. But be aware that the IRS has models for what is deductible based on adjusted gross income (AGI). The chart on page 222 reflects the averages for 2004 returns. If your AGI falls into a certain category but you've claimed larger write-offs than the average for this category, your return may be flagged. This doesn't mean you have a problem, if you have the proof to back up your deduction. But if you're unsure about certain write-offs, you may wish to err on the side of caution based on the averages.

Average itemized deductions*

Adjusted gross income	Medical	Taxes	Interest	Charitable donations
$ 15,000–$30,000	$ 6,229	$ 2,761	$ 6,664	$ 1,969
$ 30,000–$50,000	5,324	3,592	6,933	2,132
$ 50,000–$100,000	6,125	5,808	8,310	2,663
$100,000–$200,000	9,811	10,528	10,949	4,130
$200,000 and over	31,332	38,143	19,721	19,014

*This table reflects 2004 returns, the most recent year for which statistics were available.

▶ **File separate returns.** If you're married but have concerns about your spouse's financial affairs, you can avoid problems by filing a separate return. It may cost you more in taxes than you would pay by filing jointly, but you may save money in the long run by avoiding an audit.

▶ **Complete all return information.** Answer all the questions on the return. For example, answer "yes" on Schedule B if you have a foreign bank account. Attach all Form W-2s as well as any Form 1099s showing income tax withholding. Sign and date the return.

▶ **File amended returns sparingly.** There are many good reasons for filing an amended return—perhaps you overlooked a deduction, a retroactive change in the law created a new opportunity, etc. But weigh the tax refund you may receive against the tax cost you could incur if the IRS were to audit your return. Filing an amended return invites greater scrutiny of the tax positions you have taken.

Working with a tax professional

If you've done what you can to avoid an audit but face one anyway, make sure to select the right professional to represent you. While you're not required to have a representative—you can speak for yourself if you prefer—it's generally *not* a good idea to forgo representation. You may say or do something that creates additional problems.

▶ **Accountant or enrolled agent.** Use this type of tax professional if the audit involves simple mistakes or questions about record keeping or basic interpretations of the tax law. Accountant-client privilege protects disclosures relating to federal civil tax matters only. It does not apply to mere tax preparation, to state tax matters (unless the state creates a privilege), federal criminal matters or other federal matters, such as SEC filings.

▶ **Attorney.** Use a tax attorney if there is *any* possibility that the IRS may raise charges of fraud, which is a criminal offense. Only an attorney can keep your disclosures confidential. There is no such protection for disclosures you make to accountants and other tax professionals when it comes to criminal matters.

 Strategy: Use an attorney who can hire an accountant to work on your tax matter. In this way, disclosures to the attorney's agent—the accountant—are protected under attorney-client privilege.

See Chapter 2 for a more detailed discussion of tax professionals.

GETTING TAX INFORMATION ONLINE

If you want information on taxes or to get an answer to a question, you don't need to consult a tax professional. You can usually find the answer online. The number of online tax resources for obtaining information, tax forms and other materials is enormous and many of them are quite good.

IRS Web site (www.irs.gov)

Use this site to obtain tax forms and publications to help you prepare your return and resolve your tax questions. You can even complete certain forms online by entering your personal information. The forms can then be printed for filing. But the site isn't limited to tax preparation help.

▶ **Tax developments.** *e-News For Tax Professionals* is the IRS's online newsletter for anyone who's interested in the subject, and you can subscribe to it free of charge. It alerts you to the latest tax developments. You can also access weekly Internal Revenue Bulletins that contain IRS rulings and other pronouncements. For the latest news, go to **www.irs.gov/newsroom**.

▶ **Problem solving.** The IRS conducts problem-solving days in different cities throughout the year. These days are listed at **www.irs.gov.** You can also find out how to contact your local Problems Resolution Office for help with issues you have been unable to resolve on your own, as well as find out about free IRS assistance for the elderly, blind and hearing impaired, through your local IRS office.

National accounting firms

Big firms maintain Web sites. While much of the information online is geared toward marketing, you also can find valuable information.

▶ Deloitte **(www.deloitte.com)**. You'll find the latest developments on federal, state and local taxes.

▶ KPMG **(www.us.kpmg.com)**. Get great links to other tax sites.

▶ PriceWaterhouseCoopers **(www.taxnews.com)**. Learn about the latest tax news and information.

Tax research

If you want to find information on your own—for instance, how to file a case in the small-case division of the US Tax Court without using an attorney, how to run down a court decision or how to find an article on a tax subject—there are many places to look.

▶ BarbaraWeltman.com **(www.barbaraweltman.com)**. See tax and financial ideas for small businesses.

▶ CCH Inc. **(www.cch.com)**. Legislative highlights.

▶ BottomLineSecrets **(www.bottomlinesecrets.com)**. Search for articles on specific tax topics.

▶ Cornell Law School **(www.lawschool.cornell.edu)**. Search for decisions from federal and state courts.

▶ IRS.com **(www.irs.com)**. Find links to tax information.

▶ Tax and Accounting Sites Directory **(www.taxsites.com/state.html)**. Find links to state tax information and forms.

▶ TRAC, a data gathering organization associated with Syracuse University **(http://trac.syr.edu/tracirs)**. Find out about audit risk based on your income, location and other factors.

▶ US Tax Court **(www.ustaxcourt.gov)**. This site contains Tax Court decisions, filing procedures for small tax cases and other court-related information.

16

Debt is not bad

❝*Private credit is wealth.*❞ —ANONYMOUS

DEBT IS A NORMAL PART of financial life. People borrow money to buy a home or a car or to finance a business. They also use credit cards as a convenience to pay for things they want or need. Debt, in and of itself, isn't a bad thing. But if it's handled poorly and not monitored closely, debt can lead to financial ruin.

To manage debt properly, understand how your credit rating can affect your ability to borrow and the interest you'll pay. You also need to avoid increasing debt needlessly, how to pay it down and how to get out of debt. Credit cards can too easily be abused, without good understanding of the consequences.

This chapter explains the uses and abuses of credit and debit cards and discusses various sources of borrowing other than from traditional banks. And it provides guidance for managing debt and dealing with it when you've become overwhelmed. Borrowing for home mortgages is discussed in Chapter 10.

YOUR CREDIT RATING

Your credit rating is a history of how you've met your financial obligations. If you've paid bills regularly and repaid loans on time, you have a good credit rating. If you're consistently late or fail to pay bills, your credit rating is bad. Here's what your credit rating can affect:

▶ **Your ability to borrow money.** A lender doesn't want to advance funds to someone who's not likely to repay the loan or who has a history of making late payments.

▶ **Your rate of interest to borrow money.** Those with a good credit rating command more favorable rates from lenders than those with a questionable rating.

▶ **Whether you get a job.** Increasingly, employers check the credit rating of prospective employees and may be reluctant to hire those with unfavorable reports. The federal Fair Credit Reporting Act permits employers to use consumer credit information in making an employment determination.

Getting a good credit rating

How do you ensure a good credit rating? You need two things—debt and a good payment history. If you've never borrowed money or paid a utility bill, you don't have *any* credit history, good or bad.

To establish a good credit rating you need to borrow money and/or pay bills in your own name. Borrowing money doesn't only mean taking a bank loan to buy a car or a home; it also includes using a credit card to make purchases or cash advances. Bill-paying includes rent and utilities.

Of course, you need to make good on your obligation to repay your debt or to pay what you've promised to pay. With credit cards, you must make timely payments of at least the minimum amount.

 Strategy: *If you're married, don't use joint credit cards. Your credit history can be adversely affected by your spouse's record. If you have joint cards, remove your name from the existing account, and ask for a separate credit card application. Be responsible for your own credit history.*

Checking your credit rating

You may think that you have a good credit history, but don't rely on assumptions. Request a copy of your credit report, by phone or online, from any of the three major credit reporting bureaus:

▶ Equifax (**www.equifax.com**, 800-685-1111)

▶ Experian (**www.experian.com**, 888-397-3742)

▶ TransUnion (**www.transunion.com**, 877-322-8228)

You can obtain your credit report once a year at no cost. But if you want to see your report more frequently, there's a $9 charge (certain states are less). If you've been turned down for credit or denied a job because of your credit report, you're entitled to a copy of your report at no charge. *Strategy:* Monitor your credit report to detect not only potential identity theft, but also to alert you to key changes in your rating that may be problematic. Use a monitoring service, such as Equifax Credit Watch (**www.econsumer. equifax.com**), which costs $12.95 per month.

Finding your credit score: Your credit rating boils down to a specific score, called a FICO score (after the company that devised it). Your FICO score lets you know precisely where you stand—whether you're viewed as a good credit risk or not. A bank may set a FICO score threshold for offering its preferred mortgage rates. If your rating is below the threshold, you may still be able to get a mortgage but may have to pay a higher rate.

The FICO score ranges from 300 to 850; the higher your score, the better your credit rating. Good credit and favorable loan terms generally apply to those with a score of 720 or higher; a high-risk person is someone with a score below 600 who may have difficulty obtaining credit or, if he or she can get it, will pay higher interest rates for it. Find out your score at MyFICO **(www.myfico.com)**.

Correcting mistakes in your credit report

If the information in your credit report is correct, it can't be changed. But errors can be corrected or removed by taking these steps:

▶ **Review your credit report.** Check statements for accuracy. For example, the report may show that you filed for bankruptcy five years ago when, in fact, you never did. The report may have confused you with someone with the same name. Typically errors occur because of "Jr." or "Sr." added to your name. For example, your dad's debt may appear on your credit report, or vice versa. If you explain a mistake, the reporting agency must investigate further and correct errors on your report.

▶ **Write the credit bureau about any errors you find.** Explain why the information is not correct. The Fair Credit Reporting Act requires incorrect information to be removed from your report if not completely accurate or if it can't be verified within 30 days. Negative information must be removed within seven years (10 years in the case of bankruptcy).

▶ **Add an explanation to your report.** If the information is correct but you think that a further explanation is needed, request the bureau to include such explanation. For example, if the report shows late payments but you were late only because of a period of unemployment or hospitalization, have this explanation included in your report.

▶ **Improve your credit rating.** If you find unpaid balances on your credit report, pay them as promptly as possible. While they will remain as late payments, they will no longer be delinquencies.

 Strategy: If current information is in error, contact the appropriate creditor to submit new information. Anything a creditor has included in your credit report can be corrected by that creditor.

Caution: Don't pay someone who promises to clean up your credit report by changing information that's correct. Correct information—no matter how harmful to your credit rating—can't be changed, and doing so is illegal.

CREDIT CARDS—GOOD NEWS AND BAD NEWS

Credit cards are a convenience which allow you to spend without carrying cash around. They can help you establish a good credit rating to get a home mortgage or other loans. They enable you to make installment repayments over time. Credit cards function like a line of credit, allowing you to spend up to a certain fixed dollar limit. The credit card company determines your credit limit by your credit rating.

The ease of using "plastic" can lead to financial disaster. According to recent figures, the average credit card debt in this country is now about $8,900, but can be much higher, depending on age and location. Individuals carry an average of 2-3 credit cards. The Federal Reserve Board estimates that consumers now devote one third of their income to paying credit card debt.

Finding the best credit cards

Credit card applications find their way into your mailbox on a regular basis. But not all credit cards are the same. Terms and conditions vary widely.

▶ **Fees.** Many cards have no annual fees. Others charge $20 and up. For example, the American Express Gold Card carries a $125 annual fee and the American Express Platinum Card has a $395 annual fee. For most people, the perks or extra benefits don't justify the cost. People who travel frequently on business may take advantage of these benefits, but others won't gain anything other than the prestige of a gold or platinum card.

Strategy: Look for a no-fee card offered as part of a package deal. Banks, for example, may offer a senior banking package that includes a no-fee credit card. Brokerage firms may give credit cards to investors with "wrap accounts," but with an annual fee.

▶ **Interest rate.** Rates can range up to 21% or more annually. An annual rate of 18% means interest is accruing at 1½% per month! Some cards offer a very low introductory rate to entice you to transfer account balances from higher-interest cards. *Caution:* There may be dollar limits on what you can transfer. And you may be charged for interest on the transfer from the very first day. While the low rates offered by some credit card companies may be appealing, you may need to look for another low-rate card at the end of the introductory period—typically six months—or wind up paying a high rate after that.

▶ **Billing cycle.** Most credit cards are on a 25-day billing cycle. This cycle operates as a grace period. If you pay your outstanding balance within the cycle, you don't incur any interest charges. *Caution:* Credit card companies aren't required to offer this grace period. Avoid credit card offers that don't mention a grace period.

▶ **Other charges.** Read the fine print of your credit card agreement to learn about other fees and penalties you may owe. For example, some cards charge a fee for cash advances.

Strategy: Don't carry more credit cards than you really need. Usually a single card from each type of major issuer—MasterCard, American Express, etc.—is sufficient. This will keep temptation down by minimizing your credit limit.

Types of credit cards: There are several kinds of credit cards:

▶ **Bank cards** (MasterCard, Visa, Discover)

▶ **General credit cards** (American Express, Carte Blanche, Diners Club)

▶ **Proprietary cards** issued by companies for use only at their stores or facilities (Sears, Staples, Saks, Chevron)

Strategy: *Use credit union credit cards available to members of a credit union and their families. They typically carry a lower rate of interest than commercial credit cards.*

Repayment

Making only the minimum payment each month can keep you in debt for more than 11 years! You must pay *more* than the minimum to reduce the outstanding balance and get out of debt.

Pay off old debt before incurring new debt. This isn't always easy to do—emergencies do arise. But postpone discretionary purchases until you pay off the existing balance on your credit cards or at least bring it down substantially.

 Strategy: *Mail your credit card payment at least one week prior to the due date. If your payment is just one day late, it can trigger a penalty of $25 or more.*

DEBT CARDS

Debit cards are made out of the same plastic as credit cards, but they're different in many ways. Debit cards function like credit cards by letting you purchase goods and services without cash on hand. But debit cards are tied to your bank account, and the amount you can charge is limited to what's in your account.

Advantages:

▶ **You can't spend more than you have.** You can't get into debt by using your debit card, unless your account has a line of credit that you tap into.

▶ **You can easily obtain a debit card** even if your credit rating prevents or limits your using a credit card.

▶ **Debit cards are a convenient alternative to checks.** You don't need to carry checks. You can access your funds when you travel, eliminating the need to carry travelers' checks.

Disadvantages:

▶ **There's no grace period for payment.** The funds are immediately subtracted from your account.

▶ **They do not have the same transaction protection as credit cards.** For example, if goods purchased with a debit card aren't delivered, you still must pay for them. In contrast, you can contest such charges on a credit card.

▶ **If someone gains access to your card,** he or she can deplete your bank account.

Smart cards

A variation on the debit card is the smart card, or store-value card. This isn't tied to your bank account; instead, it's purchased for a fixed amount and used only for a limited purpose. The amount you pay for the card determines what can be charged to the card. *Examples:* Phone cards, college campus cards, store gift cards and smart cards from various merchants (e.g., Starbucks).

BORROWING FROM FAMILY OR FRIENDS

Need a quick loan? You may want to turn to family or friends for some money. Keep certain points in mind when borrowing from someone you know.

Relationships

Money can cause trouble in friendships. If you borrow money, make sure that the lender can afford to do so—that if you don't repay the loan it won't affect the person's standard of living. See that your lender understands the risk of the loan—why you need the funds, and whether there's a chance you may be unable to repay it.

Terms

Among family members, money transactions tend to be informal. But it's a good idea to clarify certain issues up front:

▶ **Interest rate.** Are you required to repay the loan with interest? Will the interest be less than the current bank rate?

▶ **Repayment period.** Are you expected to pay back the loan within a set time? Is the loan payable on demand (meaning that payment is open-ended unless the lender calls the loan)?

▶ **Other terms.** Do you provide any collateral for the loan? Under what conditions can you reclaim your collateral before the loan is fully repaid? What happens if you default on payment?

Strategy: Always put the loan terms in writing as a formal promissory note or loan agreement. In the event of default, your lender will be able to deduct the outstanding balance as a short-term capital loss. Without a note, the IRS may charge that the lender was making a gift, not a loan.

Low-interest or interest-free loans

If the interest rate is below what the IRS deems the going market rate, there may be tax consequences to both the borrower and the lender. The market rate, called the "applicable federal rate" or AFR, depends on the period of the loan: Short-term (up to three years, or payable on demand), mid-term (more than three years but not more than nine years) or long-term (more than nine years).

▶ **The lender is treated** as receiving interest equal to the rate that should have been charged.

▶ **The borrower is treated** as having paid interest equal to the rate that should have been charged.

Small gift loans: Even if the loan carries a below-market interest rate, there is no imputed interest if the loan does not exceed $10,000 (and if the loan isn't used to purchase interest-producing assets such as stocks or bonds).

Large gift loans: Loans up to $100,000 may also be free of imputed interest as long as your net investment income is $1,000 or less. For example, if you borrow $25,000 from a relative or friend for a down payment on a home and your net investment income doesn't exceed $1,000, there's no imputed interest even if the loan has a zero interest rate. If your net investment income is over $1,000, then imputed interest is limited to your net investment income (the difference between your investment interest and your investment expenses).

OTHER BORROWING SOURCES

You don't need a relative with deep pockets to find a lender. And you don't have to go to a bank and obtain a loan that depends on your credit rating. You have a number of options for raising cash in a hurry, without regard to your credit rating.

Line of credit on your bank account

You don't have to ask for a loan each time you need money. Set up a line of credit on your bank account and tap into it by writing a check or using an ATM card on the account. The amount of credit available depends on your credit rating and other factors.

Advantages:

▶ **The application process is simple,** requiring only the completion of a short bank form.

▶ **You borrow only what you need,** and you maintain your borrowing power by repaying your loans.

▶ **You repay the loan like a credit card**—paying at least a minimum amount each month, plus interest, or paying in full at any time.

Disadvantages:

▶ **Since it's so easy to use,** it's also easy to get into debt.

▶ **Interest rates on your credit line vary**—the bank will advise you of changes in interest rates.

Home-equity loans

Home-equity loans are available in two ways—you can borrow a fixed amount or establish a line of credit. For example, you may borrow a flat $50,000. Alternatively, you may obtain a $50,000 line of credit, drawing it down as needed. Home-equity loans are second mortgages on your home and, like a primary mortgage, the loan is secured by the property. The lender has the right to foreclose if you cannot make the required payments. Both types of home-equity loans share many of the same features.

Advantages:

▶ **You can usually borrow up to 80% of the equity in your home.** If your house is worth $300,000 and you have a mortgage of $160,000 remaining, you can borrow $112,000 (80% of $140,000).

▶ **Interest may be fixed at a relatively low rate.** Often there is a very low introductory rate (for example, for the first six months of the loan). Thereafter, the interest rate may vary in relation to the prime rate or other benchmark. Or you may lock into a low rate for the term of the loan.

▶ **Interest on a home-equity loan** up to $100,000 is fully deductible if you itemize deductions, even if you use the money for personal things.

Disadvantages:

▶ **You must apply for the loan** by completing a loan application form with personal financial information. Often this includes tax returns for the prior three years. Many companies selling home-equity loans advertise the simplicity of the process, but be aware that the process is not always simple.

▶ **There may be closing costs and other fees** for obtaining the loan (for example, a mortgage recording tax). Some lenders waive all fees provided the line of credit remains open for at least two years.

▶ **Generally you must repay the loan in level payments** within 15 years. However, there may be an initial period—say five or 10 years—before the loan converts to a fixed-payment loan.

▶ **You put your home at risk if you don't repay the loan.** The lender has the right to foreclose on the mortgage and sell your home if you can't keep up the payments on the home-equity loan.

 *Strategy: Look online for home-equity loan opportunities. Companies like Ditech.com (**www.ditech.com**) and Lending Tree (**www.lendingtree.com**) sell home-equity loans. Before accepting an online loan, compare the rates and other terms with those offered by neighborhood banks.*

First mortgages on your home, also called "acquisition indebtedness," are discussed in Chapter 10.

Margin account loans

Use your investments as a source of borrowing without using your principal. You can arrange for a "margin loan" from your brokerage account.

Advantages to margin loans:

▶ **The loan is easy to arrange.** You don't need to fill out any forms, other than to sign a margin account agreement spelling out the terms and conditions of your borrowing.

▶ **You can borrow up to 50% of the value of your securities** (and 90% of Treasuries). So, for example, if the stocks and bonds in your brokerage account are worth $100,000, you can borrow about $50,000 just by asking.

▶ **You control repayment.** You can pay it back as quickly or as slowly as you choose. However, interest continues to accrue on your outstanding balance.

▶ **The interest is deductible** if you use the proceeds of the loan to buy or carry your investments. In this case, interest is deductible to the extent of your net investment income (from interest, dividends, etc., less investment expenses). Investment interest in excess of your net investment income can be carried forward indefinitely and used in future years.

Disadvantages:

▶ **The interest rate isn't fixed.** It varies as frequently as the prime rate varies.

▶ **If the value of your account drops, you'll get a margin call.** You'll be asked to pay the shortfall in value. If you don't have outside cash for this purpose, part of your account holding will be sold to satisfy the call, even if the market rallies the next day and the value of the account rises again.

Life insurance loans

If you have a life insurance policy other than a term policy, you build up a cash surrender value. You can borrow against this equity in your policy.

Advantages:

▶ **The loan is easy to arrange.** You merely call the insurance company and request the loan. Often it's processed within 24 to 48 hours.

▶ **Interest rates on life insurance loans may be attractive.** Older policies carry very low rate terms; newer policies usually charge a going rate much like margin account loans.

▶ **Repayment terms are within your control.** You are not required to repay any particular amount of the loan at any particular time. You determine when and to what extent you repay the loan. Of course, interest continues to accrue on your outstanding loan balance.

Disadvantage:

▶ **Any portion of the loan, including interest,** that's not repaid is an offset to the death benefit your beneficiary will receive. So, if you have a $100,000 life insurance policy and borrow $10,000, your beneficiary will receive only $90,000 if the loan has not been repaid at the time of your death.

Retirement plans

If you participate in a 401(k) or other company-sponsored retirement plan, you may be able to borrow from the plan. The plan is not legally required to permit loans, but you'll find that many plans do.

Advantages:

▶ **The loan is easy to arrange.** Merely contact the plan administrator and request the loan. Once you sign a loan agreement, you'll receive a check for the amount of the loan, often within a few days of your initial request.

▶ **You can borrow up to 50% of your account balance,** up to a maximum of $50,000.

▶ *Interest rates are very modest, typically* 1% to 2% above the prime rate. *Bonus:* The interest you pay is credited back to your own account so you're really paying interest to yourself.

▶ **Repayment can be handled through payroll deductions.** This automatic payment method ensures repayment and avoids the temptation to use the money elsewhere.

 Strategy: Deduct the interest on a loan used to buy a home. If you use the loan to buy a home, the loan is secured by your home, and if you're not a "key employee" (e.g., a company officer earning over a set limit—$145,000 in 2007), you can deduct the interest as mortgage interest.

Disadvantages:

▶ **You must repay the loan in level payments** over no more than five years (or any reasonable period if the loan is used to buy a principal residence).

▶ **If you leave employment without repaying the loan,** it's treated as a taxable distribution.

▶ **Your account is not growing** on the funds you have withdrawn.

Strategy: Take a short-term loan from your IRA. Although borrowing from an IRA is prohibited, you can take a distribution for the short-term. As long as you replace the funds within 60 days, this arrangement is treated as a tax-free rollover. Caution: You can make only one rollover in an IRA account each year.

Credit card borrowing

If you don't have any other resources, you can use your plastic to obtain a cash advance.

Advantages:

▶ **The loan is easy to arrange.**

▶ **You can borrow up to your credit limit** on each card you have.

▶ **You can repay the loan as quickly** or as slowly as you wish.

Disadvantages:

▶ **Interest rates can be high.**

▶ **Credit card debt can spiral out of control** and put your financial health in jeopardy.

Find information about credit cards at Bankrate.com (**www.bankrate.com**).

STUDENT LOANS

If your child is headed to college, you may need a student loan to cover expenses. Fortunately, there are many government-sponsored and private sources of funding to assist you.

 Strategy: Before borrowing, explore all scholarships or grants available. This education assistance need not be repaid. No matter how favorable loan terms may be, they're not as attractive as free money! See chapter 18.

Finding out about student loans

Locating the right loans and loan application process can be confusing. Some loans are limited to families with low income. Other loans are more widely available. Interest rates and repayment terms vary widely.

Many high schools have programs for parents about the college application process, including student loans. College placement offices in high schools also contain materials to assist you.

To learn about student financial aid options, view materials and articles through the Federal Student Aid portal from the Department of Education (**http://studentaid.ed.gov/PORTALSWebApp/students/eng lish/index.jsp**). Two key commercial guides are:

▶ ***College Money Handbook*** (Peterson's Guides)

▶ ***The Scholarship Book*** (Prentice-Hall)

Online sources of information about financial aid, including scholarships and loans, are:

▶ The College Board (**www.collegeboard.com**)

▶ FastWEB (**www.fastweb.com**)

▶ FinAid (**www.finaid.org**)

▶ Octameron Associates (**www.octameron.com**)

The federal government's Direct Loan program: Three types of loans are available through the Direct Loan program:

▶ **Direct Stafford/Ford loans** (subsidized loans) are available to those in financial need. Starting July 2007, the amount generally is limited to $3,500 for the first undergraduate year, $4,500 for the second year and $5,500 for the third and fourth undergraduate years (limits are higher if parents can't qualify for Direct PLUS loans, below). Graduate students' borrowing limit is $20,500 (only $8,500 of which is subsidized).

▶ **Direct Stafford/Ford loans** (unsubsidized loans) are available without regard to financial need. The student is responsible for the payment of all interest charges on these loans.

▶ **Direct PLUS loans** are made to parents of dependent children and graduate students. Loan limits are up to the cost of attendance, less any other financial aid.

Note: Direct Consolidated Loans are merely a combination of two or more federally sponsored education loans. This is a repayment plan rather than a type of loan.

Other loan sources: You're not limited to borrowing under the Direct Loan program. Consider:

▶ **Federal Perkins Loans** to low-income undergraduate and graduate students. No repayment is required while the student is in school. Interest, at a very low rate, accrues during this time and for nine months following graduation. There is a 10-year repayment period.

▶ **Bank loans from commercial institutions.** Most banks provide loans to students and their families for higher education at lower interest rates than other commercial loans.

Strategy: Look for a bank loan that will be sold to the Student Loan Marketing Association (Sallie Mae). These loans encourage prompt repayment by refunding all but $250 of the loan origination fee if the outstanding balance is repaid within 24 months. For repayment within 48 months, the interest rate drops by 2%. And if the repayment is automatically debited from your bank account, you'll receive an immediate reduction of 0.25% off the interest rate. For further information about Sallie Mae loans, call 888-272-5543 or visit **www.salliemae.com**.

Strategy: Consider the federal work-study program as an alternative to borrowing. On- or off-campus employment, often at minimum wage, can supplement scholarships, grants and loans. Bonus: The student gains valuable work experience as well.

Loan application process

To apply for student aid, which includes loans, you'll be required to complete the Free Application for Federal Student Loan Aid (FAFSA). You can obtain the FAFSA form in several ways:

▶ From the student's high school guidance or college office.

▶ From the US Department of Education (**www.ed.gov,** 800-433-3243).

How much aid (in the form of scholarships, loans, work-study, etc.) you'll receive depends on your (and your child's) financial information. This information gives rise to your expected family contribution (EFC)— what you are expected to devote of your assets and income to the payment of college costs. Here are some guidelines to keep in mind:

▶ **5.65% of your assets** are presumed to be available for the payment of college expenses. Funds in your retirement accounts are ignored. Your income is also taken into account.

▶ **35% of the assets in your child's name** (20% starting July 1, 2007) are presumed to be available for the payment of college expenses. Earnings are also factored in. Funds in 529 plans are not counted as the child's assets even though the plan account is in the child's name.

Repayment

Federal student loans are usually repaid in monthly installments over a period of up to 10 years; the term depends on the amount borrowed. Extended repayment terms of up to 30 years are available under certain conditions. Income contingent repayment plans base the monthly required payment on income and provide for repayment in up to 25 years.

Commercial loans have their own repayment terms spelled out in the loan agreement. But all loans, government or commercial, can be repaid as quickly as you desire, cutting interest costs that would otherwise accrue.

 Strategy: *Explore debt forgiveness options. If your child works in certain locations— for example, an Indian reservation or the inner city—for a set period of time, some or all of the loan may be forgiven.* Bonus: *This debt forgiveness isn't taxable income.*

Tax treatment of interest

While interest on consumer debt (other than a home mortgage) isn't deductible, a special rule allows for a limited write-off of student loan interest. You can deduct interest up to $2,500 per year. This deduction is an "above-the-line" deduction that can be claimed whether or not you itemize other deductions. It applies only to qualified higher-education expenses—tuition, fees, supplies, room and board—at a qualified higher-education institution attended on at least a half-time basis.

Caution: The full $2,500 deduction can be claimed only if your adjusted gross income is below a certain level—$55,000 for singles or $110,000 on a joint return in 2007 (a phase-out of the $2,500 limit applies to income up to $70,000 for singles and $140,000 on a joint return). But if the loan was taken out in the student's name, he may have a modest AGI in the first several working years and be able to deduct interest on his loans.

MANAGING DEBT

Living with some debt isn't necessarily a fatal financial flaw. But you need to act to avoid *increasing* your debt.

▶ **Don't skip a month's payment,** even if your credit card company makes this offer to you. Skipping a payment doesn't stop interest from accumulating.

▶ **Avoid zero-interest financing programs.** You may see tempting ads for "no interest for 12 months." If you fail to pay the entire balance at the end of the zero-interest period, you'll owe interest backed in from the beginning of your borrowing, typically at rates as high as 21%.

▶ **Don't take on debt you don't need.** You may have to reassess your standard of living and make changes if you can't avoid new debt each month. Do you really need another sweater? Should you buy such an expensive gift for a friend? You may have to modify your standard of living to keep debt under control.

Caution: If spending is a compulsion or an addiction which has put you into unmanageable debt, you may need professional help. A spending compulsion can indicate a personality disorder requiring special counseling or medical assistance. To locate the best help, start by talking to your family doctor. If you have a relative or friend with a spending compulsion, talk that person into getting help before debt problems mount up.

GETTING OUT OF DEBT

Debt is easy to get into but difficult to get out of—Americans now owe $1.7 trillion in credit card debt. This is because of the interest that compounds on unpaid amounts, requiring an ever increasing portion of available income just to service this debt. Thus, it's important to take control of debt and reduce it to manageable proportions.

 Strategy: Use your savings to pay off debt, and use future dollars to rebuild savings. If you're paying 15% or more as interest on your credit card, you're probably not earning anywhere near that on your savings. Pay down your debt first. Save later.

Warning signs of debt that's out of control

Having some debt is a normal part of financial life. *Rule of thumb:* Spend no more than 20% of your monthly after-tax income (your take-home pay) on all consumer debt other than your home mortgage. Add up your car loans, student loans, credit card debt and other loan payments to see if you are well within this comfort zone.

If things get out of control, you need to take special action before matters get worse. How can you tell if you're in so deep that you need assistance getting out? In addition to exceeding the 20% rule, here are some other warning signs that things are out of control:

▶ **You're making only your minimum payments** each month.

▶ **You use one credit card to pay off another.**

▶ **You don't know exactly how much you owe.**

▶ **You're near your credit limits** on your cards.

▶ **You're late in paying,** or you skip payments on some bills (including basic living expenses such as utilities or rent).

▶ **You have to tap into savings** to pay your bills.

▶ **You're receiving calls from creditors** or collection agencies about overdue bills.

If you find that more than one of these signs apply to you, you're in—or at least getting into—financial trouble. Take action immediately.

 Strategy: *Get your spending under control to head off or reduce debt problems. If you have a spending problem (e.g., you use shopping to fill an emotional void), join Debtors Anonymous (781-453-2743 or* **www.debtorsanonymous.com***).*

Working your way out of debt

It took you a long time to get into the financial fix you now find yourself in. It will take you equally long, or longer, to get out of debt. Here are some steps to follow if your debt is larger than you'd like it to be:

▶ **Determine how much monthly income you have to pay your bills.**

▶ **List all your current obligations.**

▶ **Make a budget,** incorporating a repayment plan. Devote a greater share of your budget to the debt with the highest interest rate to pay it off more quickly.

 Strategy: *Cut up your credit cards (or put them away in a safe place if you know you won't touch them). This will prevent you from taking on any more debt that will complicate your financial life.*

Online debt reduction planning

Use online resources to set up and manage your own debt reduction. These include:

▶ Quicken's Debt Reduction Planner (**www.quicken.com/planning/debt**).

Debt consolidation

You can reduce your debt by reducing your interest charges. This can be done in two ways:

▶ **Find lower-rate credit cards.** Transfer the outstanding balances from high-rate cards to low-rate cards. Often credit cards have introductory offers with low interest for the first six months or so. If you use this type of card for reducing your interest rate, then you'll have to find a new low-rate card at the end of the introductory period.

▶ **Take a home-equity loan.** If you own a home with value greater than its outstanding mortgage, you can roll all of your outstanding debts into one loan secured by your home. A home-equity loan is a second mortgage on your home. Home-equity loans typically carry lower interest rates than credit cards and other debt.

As a rule of thumb, figure that you can borrow up to 80% of the equity in your home. This is the value of your home, less any existing mortgage.

> **Example:** Your home is worth $250,000 and your mortgage balance is $110,000. You can probably borrow as much as $112,000, which is 80% of the difference.

Bonus: The interest on home-equity debt up to $100,000 is deductible on your income tax return (interest on other consumer debt is not deductible, with the exception of limited interest on student loans). *Caution:* Taking a home-equity loan to pay off debt puts your home at risk. If you go into default, the lender can foreclose on the mortgage and you'll lose your home.

Working with a credit counseling agency

If you can't do it alone, you can find assistance in resolving your credit problems from a credit counseling agency. An agency can help you work out a repayment plan to satisfy your debts as an alternative to bankruptcy. (Under new federal bankruptcy law, a person must obtain credit counseling before seeking bankruptcy protection.) The agency can also provide counseling and education on debt management.

Repayment plan: The agency works with you and your creditors to arrange a repayment schedule. This repayment plan does not reduce the amount of your overall debt. But it does keep creditors and collection agencies from hounding you. It can also avoid garnishment of your wages, a process you probably don't want to involve your employer in. And it can help provide you with a model for better handling your debts in the future.

Both nonprofit organizations and for-profit companies offer this service. I advise people to stick with a nonprofit organization.

Before you agree to work with an agency, make sure you understand:

▶ **Whether credit counselors are certified.**

▶ **Whether the agency is accredited.** The National Foundation of Credit Counseling (NFCC) provides accreditation to agencies that use certified counselors and meet other criteria.

▶ **The costs to you** for any services you take advantage of.

To find a credit counseling agency near you, call the NFCC at 800-388-2227 or go to **www.nfcc.org.**

HANDLING COLLECTION AGENCIES

If you're late in paying your bills, creditors may turn over the task of collection to collection agencies. These agencies are prohibited from using abusive debt collection practices, as defined by the Fair Debt Collection Practices Act. These include:

▶ **Calling at inappropriate hours of the day.** Generally calls must be made after 8 am and before 9 pm.

▶ **Communicating with third parties without your consent.** This includes communications with your employer.

▶ **Threatening violence.**

▶ **Using obscene or profane language.**

▶ **Publicizing your delinquency,** other than notifying a credit reporting bureau.

▶ **Refusing to stop contact with you** after you notify the agency in writing that you refuse to pay the debt and wish contact to cease.

If you believe you've been the victim of an abusive collection practice, contact your local or state consumer protection agency. You may be entitled to collect actual damages (for example, injury to your reputation, plus up to an additional $1,000).

BANKRUPTCY

Bankruptcy is a last resort to curing your financial woes. What it is, what it can and cannot do, is often misunderstood. Bankruptcy is a court process in which your debts are settled, often for pennies on the dollar. You're left with certain assets allowed by law. Creditors have an opportunity to contest the proceedings.

Bankruptcy will:

▶ **Stop creditors from hounding you.** Once you file for bankruptcy, creditors are prohibited by law from contacting you. Their only recourse is to meet you in court.

▶ **End your responsibility for repayment.** The court applies your assets (after allowing you to keep exempt assets) toward your debts. Any excess amounts are forever wiped out.

Bankruptcy won't:

▶ **Give you a fresh start.** Bankruptcy history will stay on your credit report for up to 10 years. This can make it difficult for you to borrow money—to obtain a mortgage or a car loan, for instance. If you are able to obtain credit during this period, it's likely to be at higher interest rates than you would pay if you didn't have bankruptcy on your credit report.

▶ **Absolve you of certain personal responsibilities.** Bankruptcy won't wipe out your obligation to pay alimony or child support. Additionally, most tax obligations survive bankruptcy.

Bankruptcy—the different options open to you and what it means to your financial picture—is further discussed in Chapter 23. To determine whether bankruptcy is an appropriate solution to your debt problems, contact a lawyer who specializes in bankruptcy proceedings. For help in finding an attorney, see Chapter 2.

17

Budgeting

"*Annual income twenty pounds, annual expenditure twenty pounds ought and six, result misery.*" —CHARLES DICKENS, *David Copperfield*

SOME INDIVIDUALS NEED A ROAD MAP to manage their money. Money burns a hole in their pocket, with the result that there isn't enough to take care of all of their needs. Bills may go unpaid, resulting in damage to their credit rating. Funds are unavailable for savings and investment, leaving them short of money to do the things they want and with little income for retirement.

Most of these people can benefit from budgeting their money. By putting spending on a strict diet, they can limit their outflow of funds and maximize what's available for long-term needs. If you're one of these people, then budgeting may be a solution to your financial woes.

This chapter discusses how budgeting can help you manage your money more effectively. You'll learn how to make a budget. You'll see how to set up automatic payment programs, such as online bill paying, to help manage monthly obligations. Finally, you'll learn how to stick to it so you can achieve your financial goals.

WHY BUDGET?

Some people have the ability to allocate their funds to pay bills on time and systematically set aside money for long-term needs. They live within their means and don't overspend. Others may require guidelines for their spending and saving.

You may benefit from careful budgeting if the following statements describe your situation:

▶ **You're always short of cash** at the end of the month.

▶ **You constantly dip into savings** to meet ordinary living expenses.

▶ **You lose sleep over your spending.**

▶ **You don't save a set percentage of your earnings regularly** (ideally, 10% of after-tax income).

You don't have to be in debt to use a budget. All businesses—including the most profitable ones—use budgeting to handle their expenses and track their profitability. So why not follow suit and use a budget for your family finances? Having a budget can produce some positive results in your financial and, perhaps, your personal life.

Financial benefits of budgeting

A budget puts you in control of your money. You decide in advance how you'll spend it. Your financial life will become organized. You'll know where your money is going, you'll have records of what is happening to your income and expenses, and you'll be able to make financial plans, both short term and long term.

Attitudes and handling of money

Money can create a range of relationship problems, including being a leading cause of divorce. By communicating with a spouse about how family funds are spent, you can avoid conflicts over money.

 Strategy: Make sure both partners fully understand the family budget. If one spouse handles bill paying and banking, the other spouse should know about the finances. This will allow the spouse to handle matters if the need arises.

With a budget, you'll also free up more time for things other than paying bills and worrying about money. By having a game plan for your spending from month to month, you won't have to go over the same ground each billing cycle. True, it will take added time to set up and get used to working with a budget. But once you do, you'll be able to take that extra time to the bank!

A budget isn't a financial straitjacket. It need not limit what you do. Rather, it's a mechanism to free up money so you can do more with the time and money you have.

SPECIAL CONCERNS FOR TWO-INCOME COUPLES

Having two paychecks presents an opportunity to multiply family resources—increasing savings and investments and ensuring a brighter financial future. But a couple needs to work together for financial harmony. They may have different attitudes toward money—one may be a spender and the other a saver, for instance. Some issues to resolve include:

▶ **Methods for handling the family budget.**

▶ **Attitudes toward savings.** While talking may not change attitudes, it can lead to an understanding—and some compromises regarding what portion of each paycheck will be saved.

▶ **Responsibility for banking, bill paying, etc.** Although one person may be primarily responsible, the other should be familiar with the family's financial records and be able to act if the primary person cannot do so.

There are three ways to handle a family budget. The right choice depends on a couple's personal preferences, which can be affected by age, level of income and prior marital experiences. These methods include:

▶ **Separate pots.** In this method, each earner keeps his or her finances separate, and contributes to common expenses, such as rent and utilities. But each pays for his or her personal expenses, like clothing and entertainment.

 Strategy: Determine what portion of common expenses each earner is responsible for. A 50–50 split may make sense when incomes are roughly equivalent. But, it may be unfair to share payment of joint expenses equally if one spouse earns considerably less than the other.

▶ **Joint pot.** In this method, the resources of both earners are pooled together. Funds are then disbursed from this common pot.

▶ **Separate and joint pots.** In this method, a hybrid of the other two, a portion of each earner's funds is kept separate and a portion is commingled in a joint pot. Common expenses are paid from the joint funds, and individual expenses come out of the separate funds.

 Strategy: Agree on which expenses are common expenses and which expenses are separate. Some expenses are clearly one or the other—for instance, housing costs are joint expenses while health club memberships and haircuts are separate items. Some expenses can be debated—for example, education costs for one spouse.

WHAT'S IN A BUDGET?

A budget is simply a spending plan that you can follow to keep your money matters under control. No matter how much or how little income you have, there's a budget that will suit your needs. Budgets typically are drawn on a monthly basis, even though some income may be received and some expenses may be payable quarterly, annually or at other intervals. For budgeting purposes, put your income and expenses on a monthly basis if they aren't ordinarily that way.

Example: Your life insurance premium, payable annually, is $3,600. For purposes of budgeting, figure this expense at $300 per month. Obviously, in order to have the necessary funds to make the annual payment, you must actually set aside the $300 each month so that there will be $3,600 available to pay the premium.

Spendable income

In preparing a budget, you're deciding how to allocate your income to meet your financial obligations. Income for this purpose means *spendable* income. Generally, this comes from the following sources:

▶ **After-tax take-home pay.** What you have to spend isn't your gross salary, it's your paycheck. This is the money you have left over after subtractions are made for income tax withholding, FICA taxes, contributions to 401(k) and other employee benefit plans, and other amounts taken from your salary.

▶ **Interest and dividends.** If you have money in a bank account, you can spend interest without eroding your nest egg. Similarly, if you have dividend-paying stocks, you can spend the cash dividends as income. Of course, you will lose the benefits of compounding interest and reinvesting dividends.

▶ **Social Security benefits.** Whether you have all or only part of your benefits to spend depends on whether your benefits are taxable. For federal income tax purposes, they may be tax free, 50% included in income or 85% included in income, depending on your total income (including tax-free interest on municipal bonds). Benefits may or may not be exempt from state income tax. The taxation of Social Security benefits is explained in Chapter 1.

▶ **Other sources.** You may receive cash gifts for birthdays, anniversaries, graduations or holidays. Gifts are tax free, meaning that what you get is what you have to spend. Miscellaneous items may also give you income along the way—for example, a winning lottery ticket (for other than the grand prize). Generally, you can't count on these miscellaneous items and you shouldn't factor them into your budget.

Strategy: Don't factor in your principal (savings) unless you plan to use it up in your lifetime. Tapping into your bank account or investments for ordinary expenses will undermine your financial security. But if your primary source of income is your investments, you may use a portion of principal for paying regular expenses. For example, you may want to draw out 10% of your money market fund each year for retirement income. A portion of this withdrawal will be earnings, but the balance will be principal.

Expenses

Expenses include everything you spend money on or allocate funds for, including money you set aside for savings and investments. Expenses generally fall into two categories: Fixed expenses, which remain fairly constant from month to month, and variable expenses, which are irregular or occasional.

Strategy: Keep a record of what you spend in a month. Use a notebook to jot down every expenditure you make, from your coffee at Starbucks to your rent or mortgage payment. This is the only way you'll learn where your money is going.

Fixed expenses: These expenses are the backbone of your budget. They recur each month and are more or less the same in amount from month to month. You can't avoid them or reduce them without some radical changes in your lifestyle (for example, moving to a less costly location to reduce your rent, as explained in Chapter 19). Fixed expenses include:

▶ **Housing: Rent or mortgage payments** (including principal and interest). As a rule of thumb, your housing costs should not exceed more than one-quarter of your income. However, in today's housing market it's not uncommon for some—typically younger people just starting out—to spend one-third or more of their income on housing.

▶ **Utilities.** Electricity, gas, oil, water and telephone charges are treated as fixed expenses. You may also incur monthly charges for cable TV, Internet access or a cell phone. Usage may differ each month, but you'll have a utility expense each month.

 Strategy: *If your utility company allows you to make a fixed payment each month, this will help your budgeting. For example, the electric company can analyze your usage, determine monthly payments and make adjustments at the end of the year.*

▶ **Insurance.** Homeowner's insurance, car insurance, health insurance and other insurance costs are a constant presence in your budget. Some types of insurance are paid monthly (such as health insurance), but others may be paid annually, semi-annually or quarterly. These must be viewed as payable monthly for budgeting purposes.

▶ **Savings.** Although no bill collector will appear at your door if you don't divert funds into savings each month, failure to do so can have serious long-term consequences. Treat savings as a fixed monthly expense so that money will be set aside and not used for any other purpose.

▶ **Food and personal items.** In addition to supermarket expenses, add in monthly out-of-pocket costs for prescription drugs, over-the-counter medicine and other personal items. *Note:* Some budgets put food and personal items into the variable expense category.

▶ **Transportation.** Factor all transportation costs into your budget. These include car loan or lease payments, gas, oil, tolls, parking and public transportation costs (for example, a monthly commuter train ticket). *Note:* Some budgets put car expenses into the variable expense category.

▶ **Loan repayment.** Student loans and other personal loans typically carry a monthly repayment schedule. (Home mortgages are accounted for in housing costs, and car loans are part of transportation costs.) Another key component of loan repayment may be credit card payments on outstanding balances. Paying down credit card balances and getting out of debt are discussed in Chapter 16.

▶ **Other fixed expenses.** Depending on your personal situation, you may incur other regular expenses each month. For example, you may be paying alimony and/or child support. You may have tuition bills each month for your child's private school or college. You may have babysitting and other child-care costs or owe a fixed allowance to your child.

Strategy: *Be sure to review extra expenditures for items not otherwise specified as a fixed or variable expense. Add them to the appropriate category as "other" fixed expenses or "other" variable expenses.*

Variable expenses: These expenses are discretionary items—items over which you have control. In some cases, they may appear sporadically. Variable expenses include:

▶ **Clothing.** The cost of clothes and shoes as well as dry cleaning, alterations and other related costs are a variable expense.

▶ **Personal items.** Hair care, health-club membership and country club dues can all fit within this category of personal care. Also include here expenditures for subscriptions to newspapers and magazines.

▶ **Entertainment costs.** This is a broad category that encompasses eating out, going to the movies, buying lottery tickets and other fun things. Be sure to factor into your budget the cost of vacations.

▶ **Gifts.** Birthdays, anniversaries, holidays and other occasions call for gifts to be given to family and friends. *PriceGrabber* predicted that the average family in the US would spend about $1,200 in the 2006 Christmas season alone.

 Strategy: *Use nonmonetary ways to remember family and friends and reduce or eliminate gifts from your budget. Offers of personal services—babysitting for neighbors, for instance—can be as valued as a costly store-bought item. So too are handmade gifts—baked goods, knitted sweaters—that cost you the materials plus your loving labor.*

▶ **Charitable contributions.** Whether you make weekly contributions to the church collection plate or write periodic checks to your favorite causes, be sure to factor into your budget a projection of your total expenditures in this category. Include any dues you pay to belong to religious organizations.

 Strategy: *Volunteer your time—a cost-free donation to your favorite charity—and reduce or eliminate charitable contributions from your budget while still giving. Your free services may be valued by the charity just as much as—or more than—your cash donations.*

▶ **Other variable expenses.** Any item that defies categorization should be included here. For example, fees you pay to an accountant or a financial planner should be included in this part of your budget.

What about spending money—extra cash to buy a cup of coffee or to catch a cab? You can choose to create a "miscellaneous" category under fixed or variable expenses to cover this expense. It's probably better to treat it as a variable expense, even though you may view it as a fixed amount each month, because it's an expenditure that's within your control to reduce or eliminate.

SETTING UP A BUDGET

Once you marshal your income and expenses, you can then put together a budget to manage your money. The budget operates much like a company's balance sheet—your income should equal your expenses.

You can make your budget manually, using the following worksheet. Be sure to adapt it to reflect any special items you have each month.

If you're in the fortunate position of having your income exceed your expenses, then simply boost your monthly savings allotment. But if you find your expenses outstrip your income, you need to make adjustments.

Your monthly budget

Income		Totals
Interest, dividends, other investment income	$	
Salary (take-home pay)	$	
Social Security benefits	$	
Other income	$	
TOTAL INCOME		$
Expenses		
Fixed expenses:		
Food and personal items	$	
Housing (rent or mortgage payment)	$	
Insurance	$	
Loan repayment (and other debt service)	$	
Savings	$	
Transportation	$	
Utilities	$	
Other	$	
Variable expenses:		
Charitable contributions	$	
Clothing	$	
Entertainment	$	
Gifts	$	
Personal care and personal items	$	
Other	$	
TOTAL EXPENSES		$

Software

Use financial software to set up and manage your budget. The budget can be integrated with bill paying and investments. Try:

▶ Quicken and Quicken Deluxe (**www.quicken.com**)

▶ Budget Central (**www.tuliptreepress.com**)

▶ Moneyclip (**www.dacomp.com/dlmclip.html**). This is a shareware product that's free to use, once you pay a registration fee.

Online budgeting

You can make your budget using online calculators. Sites to check out for this purpose:

▶ Choose to Save (**www.choosetosave.org/ calculators/**)

▶ iFigure (**www.ifigure.com/money/budget/ budget.htm**)

BUDGETING SYSTEMS

O nce you know the numbers, you need to devise a system to put your budget into practice. In the old days when people were paid in cash, the envelope method was the system typically used for budgeting. Take-home pay was placed on the kitchen table and divided into envelopes for the family's expenses—rent, the grocer, the telephone company, etc. But today most people receive their income by check or direct deposit to their bank accounts, so the envelope method is impractical. But there are several other budgeting systems you can use:

Checkbook system

All your income is funneled into a single checking account, from which all your expenses are paid, including your check to your savings account or other investment vehicle.

Each month you balance your checkbook, not only to ensure that there have been no errors in banking (for example, no check was paid for more than you intended) but also to make sure your budget is still on track.

 **Strategy:** *Use the "memo" line on each check to note the item's category in your budget. This will help you track disbursements for a particular category.*

Software system

Put your checkbook into high-tech gear by using home finance software as your budgeting system. For example, using *Quicken* to print your checks is both a record saver and budget manager. When checks are written, funds are debited from the accounts you set up—housing, automobile, groceries, etc. Then you can check the status of these accounts whenever you want. At regular intervals—at least once a year—you can review your accounts and revise your budget if necessary. Software options are discussed above.

You'll find a listing of other family financial management software—some freeware, some shareware and some commercial—from ZDNet Downloads (**http://downloads-zdnet.com**).

Online system

New technology makes it possible to handle bill payments entirely online. Your bills are sent directly to the online bill-paying company, which then pays them. Online bill paying can be especially useful to frequent travelers who may not be home to pay bills on time. Unlike online banking, which may allow you to pay bills online from a particular bank account, online bill-paying companies can pay bills from any of your accounts. Other features:

▶ **There is a free introductory period**, typically three months.

▶ **You can make automatic payments** for recurring bills.

▶ **You can print or download bills** sent to the online company.

▶ **Bill-paying information can be downloaded** to your money management software (*Quicken, MS Money* or *Excel*).

Examples of online bill-paying companies:

▶ Quicken.com (**www.quicken.com**). Then click on "Bills & Banking," then "Pay Bills." Enroll in Quicken Bill Pay to manage and pay your bills online—either through your Quicken software or over the Web.

▶ PayTrust (**http://pmb.paytrust.com**).

▶ Status Factory (**www.statusfactory.com**).

▶ Yahoo! Bill Pay (**http://finance.yahoo.com/bp**).

 Strategy: Make sure your online bill-paying company offers insurance against unauthorized transactions. Many use Travelers Safe Web® to provide insurance up to $100,000 per loss.

LIVING WITHIN A BUDGET

Setting up a budget is a futile exercise if you don't follow it. But living within a budget can be difficult for just about anyone in view of the ups and downs of daily life. For instance, a sudden major repair to your home can throw your budget out of whack, requiring you to devote more of your income to loan repayment (if you won't be using your emergency fund or other savings for the repairs).

Create an emergency fund

Build up a reserve fund for emergencies, such as an illness that keeps you out of work, unemployment that cuts off your paycheck or a sudden expense such as a new roof or uninsured medical costs. *Rule of thumb:* Your reserve should equal at least three months of your normal expenses. For example, if your monthly expenses are $3,000, your savings in reserve should be at least $9,000. Some financial advisers suggest a reserve fund equal to six months of expenses. The size of your emergency fund also depends on whether you're a two-income household in which one income can carry you through the loss of the other because of layoffs, illness or otherwise.

Strategy: Put emergency funds in a money market account. The funds can earn a high return, and there won't be any penalties for tapping into the reserve if you need to do so.

Plan for major purchases

Don't let the need for a new car throw your budget out the window. Plan for the replacement of major items like a car, household appliances, etc. Set aside funds to be used for these purchases.

 Strategy: Keep your car and major appliances longer than originally planned. You'll save thousands of dollars in the long run. In assessing whether to keep a car or buy a new one, consider the addition of new car payments to your budget vs. increased repair costs for keeping the old car (especially if it's off warranty). Consider buying an extended warranty for the car, past the manufacturer's warranty. You'll pay a fixed price for repairs needed to keep the car.

Other major purchases include taking a vacation, paying for a child's wedding, buying a home or starting a business. Also, factor in the need to include savings for your retirement in your budget (8% to 10% of your take home pay is advisable although very difficult to achieve).

Reduce your debt

The less money you spend each month on interest payments on existing debt, the more money you'll have for other purposes. The way to cut this interest expense is simply to reduce your debt. Make larger monthly debt service payments to bring down your balances more quickly. This may mean forgoing discretionary items in the interim.

 Strategy: Pay off debt before building up savings. The interest from a savings account or other investment is likely lower than the interest rate you're paying on the debt. Once you've eliminated your debt, focus on your savings.

Bring your budget in line

How do you know whether you're spending too much on a particular category in your budget, such as clothing? There's no absolute way. But you can compare your spending with national averages. Here's what the federal government says the average household spent in 2003 from its budget:

- ▶ **Housing**—33%
- ▶ **Medical care**—6%
- ▶ **Grocery bills**—13%
- ▶ **Transportation**—19%
- ▶ **Clothing**—4%
- ▶ **Personal insurance and pensions**—10%

By comparing your spending with the national averages, you might learn where changes need to be made. For example, if you're spending considerably more on food than the national average, you might want to look at the reasons why. Maybe you're buying too many convenience foods, which are more costly than preparing meals yourself. If you're spending a lot more than the national average on clothing, maybe you need to forgo designer labels bought at retail in favor of knockoffs purchased on sale.

Review your budget regularly

Evaluate how your budget is working for you. Are you constantly falling short of cash even though your budget says you shouldn't? Do you have extra funds you haven't budgeted for?

There's no such thing as too much review. By all means, look things over each month to see if you're on track. At the very least, you should review your budget:

▶ **Once a year.** Do a year-end "audit" of your budget and make changes for the new year. Some expenditures may increase on January 1. For example, your rent may go up or the utility company may adjust the monthly payments under your budget plan.

▶ **When your marital status changes.** Marriage, death of a spouse or divorce has a clear impact on your budget. Can two live as cheaply as one? A change in marital status can affect both your income and your expenses. Use these changes to trigger a review of your budget.

▶ **When your family status changes.** According to the US Department of Agriculture, it will cost a middle-income family more than $190,000 to raise a child born in 2005 to age 17, and that doesn't include a college education. In 2005 (the latest figures available), it took a two-earner couple earning between $43,200 and $72,600 between $10,220 and $11,290 to feed, house, clothe and otherwise provide for a child for that year (depending on the age of the child, where the family lived and the family's income level).

 *Strategy: Review your budget when there's a birth, adoption or death of a child or when your child leaves home. Use an online calculator to determine what the cost of raising a child means to you (**www.babycenter.com/costofchild**).*

▶ **When you have a change in employment.** A raise, a bonus, retirement or the loss of a job has a clear impact on your income and may also affect certain expenses. Again, use a change in employment as a time for reviewing your budget. Also review your budget when a spouse adds (or subtracts) a second income for the family.

Strategy: *Assess the impact of a second income on the family. While it may mean another paycheck, it also can mean added expenses—child care, transportation, income and employment taxes, housekeeping and other costs. Whether it makes sense for a spouse to work depends on many factors, not just economic ones. Be sure to consider the complete financial impact of being a two-earner couple.*

Education 18

> **"*Knowledge is power.*"** —Francis Bacon

EDUCATION IS AN ESSENTIAL TOOL for getting a good job, living a productive life and achieving one's full potential. Today, higher education can be an extremely costly undertaking—easily exceeding $100,000 at a private college or university. For newborns who will enter the Ivy halls in 18 years or so, the cost is hard to imagine! For many consumers, paying for education isn't limited to the undergraduate experience—it may include primary and secondary school, prep school or graduate work.

If you have young children or grandchildren—or expect to have them—you'll want to get an idea of what a good education will cost. This will enable you to plan for ways to pay this expense so it doesn't put you in the poorhouse or burden you (or your child) with heavy debt.

Fortunately, there are tax-advantaged ways to save for an education that make it easier for families to put money aside for this important expense. But even if your savings run short of what's needed, there are ways to make paying for education just a little easier.

This chapter helps you determine what kind of expense you're facing and what payment alternatives are available. It also focuses on some key savings vehicles designed especially for education costs and tells you how to pay them in ways that make the government your paying partner. Borrowing to pay for higher education is covered in Chapter 16.

HIGHER EDUCATION COSTS

Agood education doesn't come cheaply. The cost of four-year private colleges already tops $100,000. And that's only tuition, fees and room and board. Incidental expenses—travel, a computer, spending money—can easily add thousands of dollars to the total bill. And if you have more than one child, your costs multiply accordingly.

To see what you can expect to pay for college, use a college savings calculator—plug in the child's age and other factors to project what it will probably cost. Then you can see what you'll have to save on a regular basis if you want to fully cover this expense and what you'll have to earn on the money to reach your goal. Sites for online college savings calculators may be found at the end of Chapter 1. Keep in mind that college expenses have increased at significantly greater rates than increases in the Consumer Price Index. According to the *College Board's Annual Report on Trends in College Pricing 2006,* the average college tuition at a public institution for the 2006–2007 year increased by 3.7% over the previous year. (The price is up 35% from five years ago).

Once you get over the sticker shock of college tuition and related costs, consider your alternatives for paying the way. You don't have to pick just one way—you can combine methods to more effectively cover the costs. Here are some alternatives for paying higher education costs:

▶ **Free or low-cost schools.** Not everyone has to own a Mercedes, and the same is true for higher education. The cost of state institutions for in-state residents in many cases is a bargain. And there are a number of schools that offer a top-notch education for free—including the four US service academies.

▶ **Borrowing.** There are many ways to borrow for higher education purposes (tax breaks for repayment are discussed in Chapter 16). Some loans are available only to those of low or moderate income, but many loans, including some federally sponsored loan programs, are open to everyone regardless of income. You can find out about college loan programs at:

▶ Octameron Associates **(www.octameron.com)**

▶ Collegeboard.com **(www.collegeboard.com)**

▶ Department of Education (federal financial aid) **(www.ed.gov)**

▶ FastWeb (scholarship search) **(www.fastweb.com)**

▶ Fin Aid (general information) **(www.finaid.org)**

 Strategy: Use funds from your traditional IRA or 401(k) plan penalty free to pay for your child's higher education even if you're under age 59½. But you'll have to pay ordinary income tax on this distribution and you'll be eating into your own retirement savings in the process.

 Strategy: Take a home-equity loan to pay for education costs. The interest on a home-equity loan up to $100,000 is tax deductible, and reduces the cost of repayment. And the interest on this type of loan may be highly favorable.

▶ **Save.** A key way to pay for college is to start saving well in advance. A parent can set aside funds in his or her name or can gift money to a child—in a custodial account under the Uniform Gifts to Minors Act or the Uniform Transfers to Minors Act, or in a trust. Generally, greater savings can be achieved by putting money in a child's name. *The reason:* A child over the age of 18 pays tax at his tax bracket, which is probably lower than the parent's tax bracket—leaving more funds after tax to pay for school. *Caution:* Putting funds in a child's name in a custodial account or trust can adversely affect the ability to qualify for financial aid, so if there's going to be a need for aid, it may be preferable to save in the parent's name (savings in 529 plans does not adversely affect financial aid eligibility). Only 5.64% of assets in a parents' name are deemed to be usable to pay for education (and a home, retirement savings and certain other assets are excluded), while 35% of students' assets (20% starting July 1, 2007) are to be used for this purpose. Some key tax-advantaged saving strategies are discussed later in this chapter.

▶ **Gifts.** Some children may be fortunate enough to have grandparents who can help pay for their education. A direct payment of tuition—not only for college but for any level of schooling—is gift tax free. There's no dollar limit on this opportunity. The rules on these direct gifts are explained in Chapter 20. *Caution:* Don't count on gifts to pay for school—the donor's circumstances may change and leave you high and dry, so consider your other payment options carefully.

▶ **Scholarships.** A child may be eligible for free money—funds that don't have to be repaid. There are scholarships awarded for need and others for merit—athletic, musical or scholastic abilities.

Financial aid

To obtain just about *any* type of financial aid—with income limits and with no such limits—you must complete the Free Application for Federal Student Aid (FAFSA). You can obtain the form through your child's high school guidance counselor or college office, or call the Department of Education at 800-433-3243 or download it at **www.ed.gov**. Click on "Financial Aid" and then click on "Finding Financial Aid." Scroll down to "Applying" and click on "Completing the Free Application for Federal Student Aid (FAFSA)." You may also need to complete the College Scholarship Service Financial Aid PROFILE Application, an additional form required by many private institutions. There is a modest charge for processing this application.

 Strategy: Complete and submit the financial aid form by the deadline—set by each of the colleges of your choice. The deadline may be well before an acceptance (or rejection) letter has been received.

 *Strategy: Don't fall victim to the financial aid and scholarship scams that abound. You can find aid or grant information yourself with just a little effort—for free—at your local library or through your child's high school college or guidance office. Or search online for financial aid and scholarship opportunities through reputable Web sites such as FinAid (**www.finaid.org**).*

COVERDELL EDUCATION SAVINGS ACCOUNTS

Coverdell education savings accounts, formerly called education IRAs, allow you to save for your child's or grandchild's education in a tax-advantaged way. While contributions are *not* tax deductible, there are significant benefits to these savings accounts:

▶ **Earnings aren't taxed currently.** This allows for tax-free compounding within the account.

▶ **Investment decisions are within your control.** You decide how to invest the contributions—in mutual funds, zero coupon bonds or otherwise.

▶ **Withdrawals used for qualified higher education purposes** are tax free.

Contribution limits

The contribution limit on behalf of a beneficiary is $2,000 per year. Contributions are not limited to your child or grandchild. They can be made on behalf of anyone under the age of 18 (or older if the child is a special needs beneficiary who requires more time to complete his or her education because of a physical, mental or emotional condition, including a learning disability). For example, you may contribute to a Coverdell education savings account for the benefit of your niece or nephew. But contributions can only be made by someone with modified adjusted gross income (MAGI) within set limits. A full contribution can be made only by singles with MAGI up to $95,000 (a phased-out contribution for MAGI up to $220,000) and by married couples filing joint returns with MAGI up to $190,000 (a phased-out contribution for MAGI up to $160,000).

 Strategy: Make a gift of funds to someone with a modest MAGI if your MAGI is too high to allow you to make direct contributions to a Coverdell education savings account. In this way, that person can contribute the funds to your beneficiary. (Remember that you can give up to $12,000 gift tax free annually to anyone you choose.)

Employers, trusts and other entities are now permitted to make contributions. If your employer does so as an employee benefit, it's additional compensation to you. But the tax on this compensation is really minimal. For example, your employer gives you the option of taking $1,000 of your bonus as a contribution to a Coverdell education savings account for your child. If you're in the 28% tax bracket in 2007, you'll pay just $280 in taxes—and the money will be out of your reach, building up for the benefit of your child.

 Strategy: Have your employer make an education savings contribution on your behalf if your income is too high for you to make a contribution on your own. There is no income limit imposed on employers or other savings entities making contributions.

Setting up Coverdell education savings accounts

These are custodial accounts for the benefit of a child under the age of 18. Many banks and other financial institutions already offer these accounts. Expect to see greater availability—with increased investment options—with the increased contribution limit.

 Strategy: If you are saving for a child under age 13, invest in growth mutual funds that have a long time horizon to grow. But if the child is within five years of college, consider switching some of the funds into fixed-income investments—for example, zero coupon bonds. In this way, you'll be sure to have the money available when you need it.

Just like IRA contributions, contributions to Coverdell education savings accounts for 2005 can be made until the due date of your tax return.

Example: You have until April 15, 2008, to make a contribution to a Coverdell education savings account for 2007. This gives you the time you may need to see if your MAGI falls within eligibility limits.

Strategy: Contribute as early in the year as possible if you are sure to meet the MAGI eligibility limits. If you make a 2007 contribution in January 2007, instead of waiting to the deadline of April 15, 2008, you'll gain about 15 months of additional tax-free compounding on your investment.

Tapping into Coverdell education savings accounts

Coverdell education savings account funds can now be used for a wider range of education expenses. Funds can be withdrawn tax free to pay for qualified higher education costs—tuition, fees, books and equipment (and room and board within certain limits). They can also be tapped for primary and secondary school—both public and private. Thus, they can be used to pay for religious day schooling or even home-schooling expenses. And they can be used to pay for academic tutoring, the purchase of a computer, software (other than games) and Internet access, school uniforms, transportation and extended-day programs.

 Strategy: Don't use Coverdell education savings account funds to pay for primary and secondary school expenses if you have other funds for this purpose. Leaving the funds in the account until college will allow for greater investment growth.

If the beneficiary (other than a special needs beneficiary) doesn't use the funds for college by the age of 30, the funds automatically become taxable *and* subject to a 10% penalty. This can be avoided by rolling over the Coverdell education savings account to a similar account for a family member—for example, a younger sibling.

529 PLANS

Nearly every state has college savings programs (called 529 plans after the section in the Internal Revenue Code that governs them) to help you save for a child's or grandchild's education. There are two types of programs:

▶ **Prepaid tuition plans**—where you prepay for this expense so that you know that the cost of tuition will be covered. Some states offer their own prepaid tuition plans. More than 250 private institutions have joined the Tuition Plan Consortium (**www.independent529plan.org**) to offer a prepaid tuition plan for private colleges and universities.

▶ **Savings programs**—where funds are invested by professional fund managers, such as Fidelity and TIAA-CREF, for the child's benefit. The funds available to pay for higher education costs depend on the manager's performance. *Caution:* There are no investment guarantees here—you can lose money.

 Strategy: Find the plan with the best investment options and lowest fees. More than a dozen plans are open to contributors regardless of their state of residence. For example, you may wish to investigate New York's program, which is administered by The Vanguard Group, and compare it with the program in your state.

Find out about 529 plans at individual state Web sites and at program managers' Web sites, including:

▶ Fidelity (**www.fidelity.com**)

▶ New York's program (**http://nysaves.uii.upromise.com**)

▶ TIAA-CREF (**www.tiaa-cref.org**)

Strategy: Save for education by spending money with Upromise, Inc. (www. upromise.com). This program channels a percentage of what you pay to certain companies—Avis, ExxonMobil, McDonald's and more than 100 national companies, 8,000 restaurants, 10 hotels and 400 online retailers—to the 529 plan of your choice. Other family members can also sign up—there's no charge for enrolling— and contribute to the same account for your child.

Though contributions to a 529 plan are not deductible for federal income tax purposes and you can't control investment decisions, they offer several important advantages:

▶ **Earnings aren't taxed currently.** This allows for tax-free compounding within the account— producing more money to pay for college.

▶ **There are no income limits on contributors,** so anyone with the funds to contribute can do so.

▶ **Withdrawals used for higher education purposes** are tax free.

▶ **Favorable treatment for financial aid.** Funds in 529 plans are not counted as student assets for the federal financial aid formula (FAFSA is explained on p. 255) even though the accounts are in the student's name.

▶ **You retain control over the funds** until they are used by the beneficiary. You can withdraw them if you need them, but you'll pay a penalty plus ordinary income tax on the earnings generated by your contributions.

 Strategy: If you can afford it, contribute to both a Coverdell education savings account and a 529 plan in the same year for the same beneficiary (assuming eligibility to make education IRA contributions). This double savings program can amount to a sizable education fund for your child.

 Strategy: Check for state tax breaks that may be available to you. For example, New York allows residents who contribute to the state program to deduct for state income tax purposes up to $5,000 ($10,000 per couple) each year.

To compare state plans, visit Saving for College **(www.savingforcollege.com)**.

US SAVINGS BONDS

Savings bonds—Series EE or I—are an easy way to save a little—or a lot—of money in a safe, secure investment. And if you've got higher education on your mind, there's also a tax break to sweeten the pot. Interest on bonds redeemed to pay higher education costs for yourself, your spouse or your dependents is tax free if you meet certain requirements:

▶ **You (and not your child) must own the bonds.** Grandparents may not exclude interest on their bonds unless a grandchild qualifies as their dependent. You must be at least 24 years old when you purchase the bonds.

▶ **Your MAGI must be within set limits that are adjusted annually for inflation.** For 2007, the range for singles is between $65,600 and $80,600 ($98,400 and $128,400 on a joint return).

EMPLOYER-PAID EDUCATION ASSISTANCE

Many companies encourage workers to pursue their education by paying some or all of the cost of attendance. If you take advantage of this opportunity, you can exclude up to $5,250 in employer-paid education assistance each year. The courses do not have to be job related to qualify.

If your employer pays for job-related courses, you can exclude *any* amount of assistance from your income —for undergraduate, graduate or other courses.

TAX BREAKS FOR PAYING HIGHER EDUCATION COSTS

If you're paying out-of-pocket for higher education costs, Uncle Sam may give you a hand—in the form of tax breaks for your payments. There's a special deduction (whether or not you itemize your other deductions) and an itemized deduction. And there are two tax credits. But you have to choose carefully—you can't take a double benefit for the same expenses, so weigh your options carefully.

Deductions

The federal government encourages the pursuit of higher education. There's an above-the-line deduction for higher education on 2007 returns. The deduction is up to $4,000 of expenses paid in 2007. Thus, if parents are in the 25% tax bracket in 2007 and pay at least $4,000 in expenses, the deduction will save them $1,000 in taxes. The tax break may not be substantial for some taxpayers, but many will appreciate any help in paying for education.

Note that you can only claim the deduction if you have an AGI up to $65,000 for singles and $130,000 on a joint return. A single parent with AGI over $65,000 but under $80,000 (married parents with AGI over $130,000 but not over $160,000) can deduct up to $2,000 in college costs. Even one dollar of excess AGI prevents the claiming of this deduction. The education deduction only runs through 2007 unless extended by Congress.

 Strategy: *Claim the deduction when the income limits prevent you from claiming a tax credit. But if you're eligible for either tax break, you'll probably save more by claiming a tax credit.*

If you take courses to maintain or improve your current job skills or are required by your employer or state law to take courses, you can deduct the expense as a miscellaneous itemized deduction to the extent that such costs exceed 2% of your AGI. But you can't deduct the cost of education leading to a new trade or business. There's no dollar limit to this write-off if courses meet the test for deductibility. What's more, deductible costs include not only course fees but also books and travel to and from the course.

Tax credits

Two different tax credits are available for education costs:

▶ **Hope credit**—100% of the first $1,100, plus 50% of the next $1,100 of qualified higher education costs for each student enrolled at least half time in the first two years of college, for a top credit of $1,650.

▶ **Lifetime learning credit**—20% of the first $10,000 of qualified higher education expenses, for a top credit of $2,000 per taxpayer (regardless of the number of students for whom expenses have been paid).

There are, however, income limits for claiming the credit. The credit phases out in 2007 for MAGI between $47,000 and $57,000 for singles ($94,000 and $114,000 on a joint return). Thus, a parent may be barred from claiming the credit if his income is too high.

> *Strategy:* Let the child claim the credit by waiving the dependency exemption if the child has tax liability that can be offset by the credit. For example, if a child has capital gain distributions from mutual fund investments and a parent is subject to the phaseout of the dependency exemption because of his income, waive the exemption (or what would have been the exemption but for the phaseout) and let the child claim the credit.

An education credit may be claimed in the same year in which distributions are taken from a Coverdell education savings account. However, the credit may not be based on expenses that have been paid with Coverdell education savings account distributions.

SCHOLARSHIPS, FELLOWSHIPS AND GRANTS

Students can obtain financial assistance, often without regard to financial need, through scholarship, fellowship and grant programs. These types of assistance are the best form of education financing because they do not have to be repaid (although some require work such as teaching or research, or a certain job commitment following graduation).

Finding grants

Grants are "free money" because they do not have to be repaid. Grants, scholarships and fellowships are usually awarded based on need and/or on academics or other talents. This type of assistance is available through schools as well as on the state and federal level. Federal grant programs include:

▶ **Pell Grants** is a needs-based grant for undergraduate study (with some exceptions). For the 2006–2007 academic year, the Pell Grant limit was $4,050 per year.

▶ **Academic Competitiveness Grants** up to $750 for the first year of undergraduate study and $1,300 for the second year for those with a GPA of at least 3.0. This grant is in addition to any Pell Grant Award.

▶ **National SMART Grant** up to $4,000 for each of the third and fourth years of undergraduate study in physical, life or computer sciences, mathematics, technology or engineering or in a foreign language determined critical to national security. This grant is in addition to any Pell Grant award.

Military

Those pursuing a military career, veterans and their dependents may qualify for certain education assistance programs through the federal government. The Montgomery GI bill covers about three-fifths of the average cost of a college education. Other education resources include the Armed Forces Tuition Assistance (TA) Program for enlisted service members and the Veterans' Educational Assistance Program (VEAP). For information about education benefits, visit the GI Bill Web site (**www.gibill.va.gov/GI_Bill_Info/benefits.htm**).

19

Lifestyle changes

❝*...the ever-whirling wheele of Change.*❞ —EDMUND SPENSER

C HANGES IN YOUR LIFESTYLE—marital status, where you live, spending habits—can have a significant financial impact on you, positively or negatively. Some changes reduce your standard of living while others improve it. You may increase living costs. Some changes can mean shared financial obligations, and others mean doing it on your own.

The size of your home and its location have a big impact on your monthly spending. Events in your life may lead you to change where you live, increasing or decreasing your costs. Changes to your marital status also affect your financial position.

This chapter explains how to view lifestyle changes in a financial context. You'll see how moving can reduce your monthly expenses and create a nest egg that will provide income for you if you opt to downsize. It also shows how upscaling can add to your monthly expenses in many ways. You'll see how changes in your marital status can impact your finances and tax obligations, and you'll find suggestions for managing these changes.

261

DOWNSIZING

Empty nesters and other individuals may want to increase their spendable income by cutting their housing expenses. Selling a home that's too large for your needs and moving to a smaller, less expensive one can help you increase your savings by adding the profit from the sale of your home. And going forward, your monthly expenses can be greatly reduced.

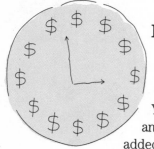

Building a nest egg

Tax rules favor the sale of a personal residence. A gain of up to $250,000 (or $500,000 on a joint return) is completely tax free as long as you've owned and used your home as your main residence for at least two of the five years preceding the sale. Your sale proceeds, after you pay off any remaining mortgage, broker's commission and other selling expenses, can go into savings. This, in turn, can be invested to produce added income for you.

Example: You and your spouse bought your home many years ago for $50,000. Over the years, you've put in another $50,000 to remodel the kitchen, add a new roof, replace a boiler and make other improvements. When your mortgage is down to $10,000, you sell the home without a broker for $350,000. Your gain of $250,000 ($350,000–$100,000) is tax free. After paying off the mortgage, you have $340,000 to invest. Assuming you can earn a 7% after-tax return on this income, you'll have $23,800 in new income each year. If you rent a condo for $800 a month, this income will cover your rent and still leave you $14,200 in spendable income—more than $1,100 per month.

If you use your sales proceeds to buy a smaller home, you'll still have money to generate additional income.

Example: In the example above, if you decided to purchase a condo for $150,000 you would have a nest egg of $190,000 ($340,000–$150,000). If you had a 7% after-tax return, you would have $13,300 in new income each year.

Reducing other housing costs

Downsizing not only frees up money and cuts your main housing cost—mortgage payments or monthly rent—but also reduces related housing costs down the line. Some expenses that will be reduced by downsizing:

▶ **Insurance.** The less costly your home, the less homeowner's insurance you require. This applies to the renter who insures only the contents of a leased residence.

▶ **Repairs and maintenance.** Lawn maintenance, snow removal and items of daily upkeep for a homeowner will be lower for a smaller home (whether a renter saves on these items depends on his or her responsibilities under the terms of his lease).

▶ **Utilities.** With less space to heat or cool and illuminate, you'll save on electricity, gas, oil and other utilities, whether you own or rent.

GOING UPSCALE

If you've received a substantial amount of money, perhaps through a large inheritance, a lottery jackpot, an initial public offering (IPO) of a new venture or the sale of a successful business, you may be able to afford a richer lifestyle. Before making any drastic changes in your lifestyle, consider the following:

▶ **Take things slowly.** Sudden wealth can create a feeling of euphoria that clouds one's ability to make sound financial decisions.

 Strategy: Factor in all of the costs of a scaled-up lifestyle. For example, a more expensive home means more expensive upkeep in the form of property taxes, landscaping and housecleaning bills. You may also want other accoutrements of a more expensive lifestyle.

▶ **Get financial advice.** Receiving a large amount of money may lead you to believe that you can afford to live better than your resources can actually support. Seek the assistance of financial professionals to determine how much you can afford for a house and to resolve other lifestyle issues. You should also discuss investments, insurance and other changes that come with increased wealth. Financial professionals are discussed in Chapter 2.

RELOCATING

Whether you're a retiree looking for warmer climates or an employee willing to relocate for a better job, keep in mind that it's cheaper to live in some localities than in others, because of differences in housing prices and the overall cost of living. *Caution:* Weigh the financial factors against your personal preferences. For example, while you may save money by relocating, this can mean moving away from family and friends.

Cost of living

How much is it going to cost you to live in the new location compared with your present one? Factors include:

▶ **Housing prices.** The prices of homes, as well as rents charged for rental properties, vary widely across the country. There even may be big variations within the same county. Check with local real estate agents to determine home values in a prospective location.

▶ **Food, gasoline and other expenses.** Like home prices, the cost of food, gasoline for your car, utilities to heat and cool your home and other expenses vary widely in different locations. Again, check on costs in your prospective area.

Strategy: If you're thinking of moving, subscribe to the local newspaper. You'll see the ads for real estate and products and services in the area. And you'll get a good idea of what's happening in that locality. Are people moving in? Are people leaving the area? A short-term subscription—three months or less—will give you a complete picture of the area.

If you're relocating because of a change in employment, you can see how your new salary will affect your standard of living. Use the online relocation salary calculator at **www.homefair.com**. And you can figure what moving your household goods and effects will cost you by using Realty.com's The Moving Calculator™ at **www.homefair.com/homefair/calc/movecalcin.html**.

Taxes

The cost of living includes the taxes you'll pay in your new location. Some states—California and Hawaii, for example—are known as high-tax states because of high income tax rates. Others—like New Hampshire and Nevada—are called low-tax states because they have no sales tax (New Hampshire) or no income tax (Nevada). Before making a move, explore *all* of the taxes you'll have to pay. For example, you may want to know whether Social Security benefits are exempt from state income tax. For state-by-state tax information, visit the Retirement Living Information Center, Inc., at **www.retirementliving.com**.

▶ **Property taxes.** If you plan to buy a home, find out the property tax rate in the area you're considering. If you plan to rent, then this isn't a key consideration, but it does impact you indirectly because the landlord will factor in his property taxes in the rent he charges.

 Strategy: Find out about property tax breaks to which you may be entitled. Many localities provide cuts for seniors, veterans and other categories of homeowners.

▶ **Sales taxes.** All but five states—Alaska, Delaware, Montana, New Hampshire and Oregon—have sales taxes. Many states also have county sales taxes, including Alaska. But the sales tax rate isn't the only thing to think about; the tax base matters, too. For example, Connecticut has a 6% state sales tax but exempts all clothing under $50. Illinois taxes prescription drugs while other states exempt them from sales tax. States also have sales tax "holidays" where tax is waived, typically on back-to-school clothing. Check on tax rates and tax bases for any state at **http://thestc.com/strates.stm** or at **www.town-usa.com**.

▶ **Income taxes.** All but eight states—Alaska, Florida, Nevada, South Dakota, Tennessee, Texas, Washington and Wyoming—have some income taxes. Some have local income taxes as well—for example, residents of New York City and Yonkers, New York, also pay a city income tax.

States with the highest income tax rates: California, Hawaii, Idaho, Iowa, Maine, Minnesota, Montana, New Mexico, North Dakota and Oregon. Washington, DC, also imposes a high income tax rate.

▶ **Estate taxes.** Although you won't be paying this tax when you die, your estate will be burdened with it, reducing what's left for your heirs. Many states impose a "pick-up tax" equal to the federal credit for state death taxes. However, some states still have estate taxes exceeding the credit limit, and others impose inheritance taxes directly on heirs. Estate taxes are discussed in Chapter 20.

To learn about all of the taxes in the state you're considering, check out the state's home page. Find it online through your state's home page, the Federation of Tax Administrators at **www.taxadmin.org**, or The Retirement Living Information Center at **www.retirementliving.com/RLtaxes.html**.

Intangibles

Relocating isn't only about money. You have to take other factors into account. These include:

▶ **Climate.** Maybe during those snowy winter months you dreamed of sunshine and warm weather, and now you plan to move to a warmer climate. Make sure you'll be comfortable with the heat and humidity of the summer months. Check out the rainfall and other factors such as hurricanes and tornadoes. And check to see what localities are prone to earthquakes, mud slides or wildfires so you won't be devastated by these events.

▶ **Recreation.** If you're an opera buff or an art fan, then a rural location that lacks concert halls and museums may not suit your taste. Look into sports facilities, sports teams, the arts and other recreational activities in your new location to see if they match your interests.

▶ **Education.** If you love to learn and plan to continue doing so, check on local colleges and other educational facilities in the new location. *Note:* Local colleges can also serve your cultural needs with special on-campus events.

▶ **Health facilities.** If you're comfortable with your own doctors and rely on them regularly, moving can be a traumatic experience. Finding replacement doctors may be difficult. The availability of qualified medical care is uneven throughout the country. If you have special needs, check out the assistance available in your proposed new home.

▶ **Crime.** If you're used to a relatively safe environment, make sure your prospective location isn't crime-ridden. By scanning the local newspapers, you'll see what's happening in that area.

Be sure to factor in the cost of moving. To get an idea of what it can cost you to move—interstate or locally—use The Moving Calculator™ at **www.homefair.com/homefair/calc/movecalcin.html.**

KEEPING CARS LONGER

A new car is often considered a luxury that you may want to forgo in the quest for financial security. Keeping a car for a few extra years can result in considerable savings. More Americans are doing so—the median age of cars on the road is now 8.6 years, up from 5.9 years in 1979. Of course, age isn't everything—mileage and the condition of the vehicle are really the factors that make a car "old."

Projecting car costs for the next three years

Expense for three years	Your old car	A new car
Acquisition costs (down payment, plus monthly payments x 36, plus sales tax)	$ 0	$ _____
Maintenance costs (repairs)	$ _____	$ _____
Gasoline* for three years	$ _____	$ _____
Insurance for three years	$ _____	$ _____
TOTAL COST	$ _____	$ _____
Less trade-in value**	$ _____	$ _____
TOTAL NET COST	$ _____	$ _____

*For comparison purposes, base estimates on $2.00 per gallon (or any other price you select), your average miles driven in a year and your gas mileage. If the old and new cars get about the same miles per gallon, then ignore this factor.

If you own the car, estimate trade-in value by using current figures in the *Kelley Blue Book* (www.kbb.com**). Add anticipated mileage for three years.

Decide if it makes more sense to maintain your old car or to buy a new one. The average new-car price in 2006 was around $28,000. First make sure that the old car is still safe. Consider the time required to service an old car and whether you will have patience for visiting the repair shop. Expressions like "nickel and diming" and "throwing good money after bad" often describe our efforts to keep an old clunker on the road. Generally, it's not a sound financial decision to make repairs that cost more than the car's trade-in value.

Strategy: Buy an extended warranty policy if you keep an old car beyond the manufacturer's warranty. You'll pay several hundred dollars, depending on the coverage and the length of the warranty, but this will insure against the unexpected cost of major repairs. You may receive solicitations in the mail for an extended warranty. Or ask your car dealership for a referral. Bonus: Extended warranties are transferable. If you decide to sell the car, the extended warranty is a key selling point. You'll probably recoup the cost of the warranty when you sell the car.

GROWING YOUR FAMILY

Having children can be a source of joy and fulfillment for you. But it can impose a serious and ongoing financial cost for the family. In some cases, it can mean going without for yourself to provide for your children. Understand what it takes to bear (or adopt) and raise children:

▶ **Housing.** Adding to your family can create a need for more space, requiring you to move to larger quarters. A bigger home means greater expenses all around (see "Going Upscale" on page 263).

▶ **Health costs.** Adding a child to a health insurance policy can convert a single or couple policy to a higher-cost family policy.

Strategy: Check your health insurance policy before starting a family to determine prenatal and postnatal coverage. You may want to add coverage before a pregnancy to keep out-of-pocket costs down.

▶ **Education.** Although free public school is available to everyone, opting out of the public school system may be desired for religious reasons or because of poor public school standards. The cost of private school—without school vouchers—can be high.

▶ **Employment impact.** Your employer may allow time off for maternity leave or for the adoption of a child. Under the federal Family Medical Leave Act (FMLA), you may be entitled to up to 12 weeks of *unpaid* leave for these events if your employer is subject to FMLA or a similar state law.

California has become the first state to mandate *paid* leave under its Paid Family Leave Insurance (PFL) Program. Workers have a certain amount withheld from their paycheck and contributed to the program. They can tap into it (up to $882 a week in 2007) when they're on approved leave.

Strategy: Check state or private disability coverage for maternity leave. You may receive disability pay for eight weeks (or some other period) if you have a baby. This pay, however, may be a fraction of what you would have received by remaining on the job.

Longer-term impact on employment

Beyond the maternity leave, being a parent can profoundly impact employment. Some parents decide to leave the workforce to become stay-at-home parents, eliminating a paycheck from the family coffers. But 60% of those with children under the age of six work outside the home. Some parents may opt for limited work arrangements—part-time work, flextime or job sharing—which reduces their income.

Weigh the financial cost of a reduced or eliminated paycheck against the benefits to be gained, both personal and financial. Your personal involvement with your child may be your paramount concern. From a financial perspective, staying home means saving on child-care costs, which can be expensive for quality day care arrangements.

What you pay for day care, of course, depends on the type of arrangement you opt for—live-in help, a professional nanny, neighborhood babysitters or a child-care center. It also depends on where you live. For example, you'll pay twice as much in Boston as you will in Dallas. Expect to pay a yearly salary anywhere from $4,000 to more than $20,000 for full-time day care (45 hours a week). The cost can be offset somewhat by claiming a tax credit, as discussed below.

Tax write-offs

Uncle Sam rewards you for having children by allowing you to claim certain write-offs or other tax benefits. Here's what to look for:

▶ **Dependency exemption** for providing more than half of the cost of supporting a child ($3,400 in 2007).

▶ **Child tax credit** of up to $1,000 for a child under age 17 if your income is below set limits.

▶ **Education credits** for paying certain higher-education costs if your income is below set limits.

▶ **Dependent care costs.** You may be able to claim a credit of $600 to $1,050 for one child and $1,200 to $2,100 for two or more children if you incur child-care costs so you can work (the maximum credit is determined by your level of income). If your employer pays for dependent care, up to $5,000 in such a benefit is tax free to you, regardless of your income.

▶ **Adoption costs.** You may claim a credit of up to $11,390 in 2007. If your employer pays for adoption costs, this same amount is tax free to you.

 Strategy: Watch the impact of increasing the number of family members on your alternative minimum tax (AMT) liability. Claiming a large number of exemptions for big families can trigger AMT, even if income and other write-offs are modest.

POSTDIVORCE FINANCES

Following a divorce, some individuals—typically women—may find their income and assets cut severely. Others who receive large financial settlements may be better off than before. Either way, divorce certainly means a change in how you handle your money and your investments. For example, if you've been a homemaker, a divorce may lead you to get back into the job market or return to school so you can hone your marketable skills. Following divorce, you may relocate to a different home in the same town or to a new location entirely. The changes in your income and assets following divorce present new challenges. Here are some actions to consider for putting your future finances on a firm footing:

▶ **Take stock of your financial status.** What are your current sources of income? What assets do you now own? Are you better off or worse off? Will your new financial status mean a change in your standard of living?

> *Strategy:* Buy health coverage under your former spouse's COBRA coverage if you don't have other health coverage. This will enable you to pay group health insurance rates for up to 18 months following the divorce. To find out about COBRA health coverage, talk to the human resources or benefits department at your former spouse's place of employment.

▶ **Set new financial goals,** both short term and long term.

▶ **Set up a budget.** This is important if you lack experience in handling money—for example, if your former spouse handled the family finances. It's also vital if your resources are limited. Budgeting is discussed in Chapter 17.

▶ **Review your postdivorce holdings.**

▶ **Establish your own credit if you haven't already done so.**

> *Strategy:* Work with a financial professional to reorganize your financial life. Financial professionals are discussed in Chapter 2.

Alimony and child support

If you are awarded alimony or support payments and/or child support, factor in these payments to the income you have for living expenses and other needs. Remember that alimony or support payments are taxable to you, so you have only the net amount after tax to spend as needed. In contrast, child support payments are tax free, so the full payments can be used for living expenses.

On the other hand, if you are making alimony payments to a former spouse, it can be deducted on your tax return. This deduction, which can be claimed regardless of whether you itemize your other deductions, reduces the out-of-pocket cost of making alimony payments. For example, if you're in the 35% tax bracket and pay $24,000 in alimony for the year, it's really costing you only $15,600 because it's saving you $8,400 in taxes.

Today, alimony payments generally run only for a limited number of years following divorce. Three to five years is typical (although payments may be for life for long-term marriages or older spouses). And child support payments generally end when your child reaches maturity, finishes college or otherwise attains some specified status. If you are the recipient of these payments, you need to make long-term plans for obtaining other income when these resources dry up.

If you've been out of the workplace for a number of years, make plans to learn the skills that will enable you to jump back in if you want or need to. In most cases, computer literacy is now a must. Regardless of your age, there are numerous ways to gain the skills you want. Resources include:

▶ **Community colleges,** which offer a wide range of computer and other courses at modest prices.

▶ **Adult education courses.**

▶ **Special training programs.** For example, you may qualify for "retraining" as a displaced homemaker or as a senior citizen. Many states, including Alaska, Illinois, Louisiana, Maine, New York and Washington, offer displaced homemaker programs to provide free or low-cost training, special financial aid, counseling and preemployment skills training (résumé preparation, interviewing, etc.).

Qualified retirement plans and IRAs

You may be awarded a share of your spouse's retirement accounts as part of your property settlement. You can roll over the funds from a qualified retirement plan or an IRA to your own IRA. Then invest the funds to maximize your personal retirement savings. See Chapter 8 for ideas on how to do this.

 Strategy: Fund an IRA based on your alimony income even if you don't work. You can build up your retirement savings by contributing up to $4,000 in 2007 to a deductible IRA or, if eligible, a Roth IRA (plus an additional $1,000 if you're 50 or older by the end of the year).

The family home

If you receive the family home in a property settlement, you may, depending upon finances and personal choice, decide to stay in the home or sell it. Often those who are financially able to do so remain in the home, at least until children from the marriage finish school. But there's usually no requirement as to where you live.

If you receive sole possession of the home but continue to share ownership, you may be obligated under the terms of the divorce decree to sell once the children have left home. This arrangement is sometimes necessary because there aren't enough family assets to be divided in any other way. *Potential problem with this ownership arrangement:* Although your former spouse is still an owner, it may be difficult to force any contributions toward taxes, maintenance or other home costs unless you wish to run to court all the time. And when the children have grown, you may be forced from your home unless you can raise the money to buy out your former spouse's interest for what the home is worth at that time.

Tax rules on selling the family home: Gain on the sale of your main home is tax free up to $250,000 while you're single, as long as you've owned and used the home as your main residence for at least two of the five years preceding the date of sale. If your spouse held title to the home before the divorce but you now have ownership, you can include in your period of ownership any time that your former spouse owned the home. But you must personally satisfy the two-year use requirement to claim the $250,000 exclusion.

If you continue to be a co-owner of the home but your spouse has sole occupancy, you can still claim the $250,000 exclusion for your portion of the gain when the home is sold. The period of occupancy by your spouse is treated as your own occupancy in this case. As long as you meet the two-year ownership requirement, the exclusion is yours.

Strategy: *Claim an exclusion of up to $500,000 of gain on the sale of your home if a new spouse meets the two-year occupancy requirement by the date of sale. Even if the home is in your name alone (or in joint name with a former spouse), you would be eligible for the $500,000 on a joint return.*

REMARRIAGE

When you remarry, not only does your family change, but your finances change as well. There are more people to consider in making money decisions, including a new spouse and perhaps children from a prior marriage. There may also be responsibilities for parents on one or both sides of the aisle.

Remarriage may mean that there are more resources available for the family to spend or invest. You need to take a comprehensive look at your new family's finances so that no one is shortchanged.

Prenuptial agreements

Before you marry, you may want to draw up a contract with your fiancé to spell out the financial terms and arrangements that you'll live by. In the past, these agreements were used mainly by wealthy individuals. Today, they're commonly used by those who remarry and have assets and children from former marriages that they want to protect.

 Strategy: *If your fiancé waives any rights in your company pension plan, make sure he signs a required waiver after the marriage. The tax law requires a spouse to make a written waiver, and since a fiancé by definition isn't a spouse, the prenuptial agreement doesn't satisfy the requirements of a written waiver.*

Beneficiary designations

 Following remarriage, revisit any beneficiary designations you've made on life insurance policies, retirement plans, IRAs, annuities or other assets containing beneficiary designations. This is especially important where the designation was made generically to "my spouse." You may not want assets payable to a former spouse, so you need to specify the name of the person you want the assets paid to.

Strategy: *When you remarry, execute new beneficiary designations and retain these forms with your important papers. Ask the appropriate party—the insurance company, bank, investment firm, etc.—for a new form. Make a new designation appropriate to your new marital status.*

Marriage penalty

People marry for love, companionship, religious beliefs and other personal reasons. But before rushing off to remarry, make sure you understand the tax implications of your decision. As the tax law now stands, there's a penalty imposed on couples who both work and have income. No, it's not a separate tax that married people have to pay. It's just that married people pay more tax than they would pay if they remained single (even if they lived together).

Example: In 2007, you have income from salary and investments of $175,000 and your partner has income of $60,000. You're both in your 50s, and neither of you has any dependents. If you remain single and claim the standard deduction, your combined federal income tax would be $50,167 ($40,930.75 for you and $9,236.25 for your partner). But if you got married, even on December 31, 2007, your joint tax liability for 2007 would be $50,975, or $808 more than if you hadn't married.

 Strategy: *Marry before the end of the year if only one spouse has income. In this case, marriage is a tax bonus because the couple will pay less tax overall. But if both people have income, consider postponing marriage until the start of the next year to avoid the marriage penalty for at least one year.*

Congress has ameliorated the marriage penalty by doubling the standard deduction for joint filers to twice that for singles and by increasing the 15% tax bracket for joint filers to twice the amount for singles. But there are still inequities in the tax law. For example, whether you are single or married filing jointly, you can use only $3,000 of capital losses to offset ordinary income.

For articles on personal and other issues related to marriage and remarriage, visit the Smart Marriages Web site **(www.smartmarriage.com)**. Remarriage also raises a number of estate planning issues. These are discussed in Chapter 20.

SUDDENLY WIDOWED

Widows (and widowers) may come into sudden wealth. They also may be emotionally vulnerable. Unfortunately, sometimes they lack money management and investment experience, if the deceased partner handled all of their financial affairs.

Go slowly

Don't make any major financial decisions—selling the house, putting money into an annuity, etc.—until six months to a year after the death of a spouse. Often a person is in emotional shock for several months afterward and has difficulty thinking clearly about his or her choices. Financial mistakes can be made easily.

Understand your new status

If you've been married for a number of years, finding yourself suddenly single can be a daunting experience.

The tax law may continue to view you as "married" for a limited time by allowing you to claim special status as a surviving spouse. If you support a dependent child, you can file a joint return (using favorable joint return tax brackets and the standard deduction for married filing jointly) for two years following the year of your spouse's death.

Example: Your spouse dies in 2007 and you haven't remarried. If you have a dependent child, you can file as a surviving spouse in 2008 and 2009.

Strategy: *File as head of household when you become ineligible for surviving spouse status. As long as you continue to provide more than half the cost of a household for a dependent, use head of household tax brackets and the standard deduction. These are both more favorable than the brackets for other single taxpayers.*

Get professional help

If you lack the sophistication or experience to handle your money matters, turn to someone who can help you. An adult child may be able to provide assistance. Better yet, pay a professional—a financial planner, an accountant or other professional—to help you with your financial affairs. Financial professionals are discussed in Chapter 2.

Estate planning

THIS COUNTRY IS ABOUT TO WITNESS the greatest wealth transfer ever, estimated by some prominent scholars to exceed $41 trillion in the period from 1998 to 2053. In fact, in 2004, about $295 billion passed from one generation to the next. You have worked a lifetime to build up your estate. Whether it's a fortune or only a modest sum, you don't want Uncle Sam to get the lion's share of it. Although the estate tax will be phased out over the next decade, you may still need to take action. Take taxes into account in planning your estate, because even though the federal estate tax burden is decreased, there are state tax death taxes to consider. And, taxes aside, you want to make sure your assets are distributed according to your wishes.

This chapter explains what's involved in estate planning—the property you need to think about and the problems you need to anticipate. It discusses ways to ensure that assets wind up in the hands of your intended heirs and the importance of estate planning to save taxes. There's also planning for incapacity due to illness, accident or another condition.

WHERE THERE'S A WILL...

A will—which may be a simple or complex legal document—may be your last voice on earth. Let it speak clearly so that family members won't have to guess your intentions, bicker among themselves about bequests or be hit with unnecessary costs.

Despite the importance of having a will, according to a survey by FindLaw, only about 44% of Americans actually have one. If you die intestate—in other words, without a will—state law dictates who will manage your estate and how your assets will be divided. And you will lose opportunities for tax-wise bequests.

 Strategy: *Work with an attorney to draw up your will to ensure that your will complies with state requirements. Save on professional fees by doing the legwork yourself. Think about what you want your will to say. Collect all necessary information for your attorney. Alternatively, you can use software to prepare your will—for example,* Quicken Lawyer 2003 ***(www.quicken.com)*** *or* Willmaker ***(www.nolo.com).*** *But if you use software, have an attorney review your will to make sure you haven't overlooked anything.*

Think about what you want to include in your will. To help you avoid overlooking important details, here are some points to consider:

Executor

This is the person who quarterbacks your estate. The person may be called a personal representative instead of an executor, but the job remains the same. He or she marshals your assets, pays your debts, files your tax returns, distributes your assets according to your wishes and winds up your affairs.

The executor can be a relative—your spouse, child, niece—or a financial institution, typically the trust department of a bank. You can have more than one executor, something quite common for those with two children. Name an alternate executor to serve if your first choice declines or is unable to serve.

Generally an executor is entitled to fees for his or her services; state law typically fixes these fees based on the size of the estate. But you can negotiate other fees—something you may want to do if you select a financial institution to act as executor—or provide that your executor serve without fees.

 Strategy: *Ask the person you want to name as your executor whether he or she would be willing to serve. It would upset your plans if the person declined the appointment after your death.*

Bequests

These are the shares in your estate that you leave to named beneficiaries—your spouse, your children, charities and others. You can make various types of bequests, including:

▶ **Specific bequests.** Leaving your grandfather's watch to your son, 100 shares of IBM to your daughter or your collection of baseball cards to your best friend are examples of specific bequests. Generally, gifts to charity are made as specific bequests—for example, $10,000 to your religious institution or alma mater.

▶ **Unspecified bequests.** You may leave portions or percentages of your estate without specifying which assets should be used to satisfy this bequest. For example, you may leave one-quarter of your estate to each of your four children.

▶ **Residuary estate.** Whatever remains in your estate, after specific bequests and the payment of administrative costs and estate taxes, is your residuary estate. Typically, to designate a residuary bequest, you'll see language in a will such as "I leave all the rest, residue and remainder of my estate…"

Note: Since your assets are constantly changing, wills typically don't mention specific items. However, specific assets are mentioned if you make specific bequests. Residences or other real estate as well as closely held businesses may also be highlighted.

Trustee

This is the person who manages the property in trusts that are set up under the terms of your will. Since the trusts may go on for many years—well beyond the settlement of your estate—select someone who you expect to be able to serve for a long time. This person can also be the executor. If this person is also a beneficiary of your trust, you'll need a cotrustee because the trustee-beneficiary is prevented from making decisions that can affect him or her.

Like an executor, a trustee is entitled to fees for services based on the size of the trust.

Guardian

If you have minor children, generally under age 18 or 21 (depending on state law), you'll want to designate someone to take responsibility for them in the event of your death. Generally, the other parent is the natural guardian. But if you and that parent should die in a common disaster—a plane crash, car accident or house fire, for instance—or the other person can't assume parental responsibility because of illness or otherwise, you'll need a third party to act.

Your designated guardian is responsible for both the person and property of your children. You can, however, have different guardians for each purpose, one to raise your children and the other to manage their property.

 Strategy: Name a backup guardian in case your first choice can't act when his or her services are needed. Also, if you designate a couple to act as guardians—for example, your sister and brother-in-law—make sure your will is clear about whether one can act alone. Consider what happens if the couple divorces.

Pets

If you have a beloved dog, cat or other pet, be sure to give thought to how best to ensure their continued care after your death. Who will take care of your pet and how will veterinary bills and other costs be covered? Consider setting up a trust for this purpose. The funds in the trust are set aside for pet care. Currently, 38 states including Alaska, Arizona, Colorado, Florida, Iowa, Michigan, Montana, New Mexico, New Jersey, New York, North Carolina, Oregon and Utah, allow pets to be named beneficiaries of a trust and provide for enforcement of the terms you provide. California, Missouri and Tennessee permit trusts for the benefit of pets, but do not enforce the terms if the trustee you select fails to implement them. Check with your local humane society for details.

Other clauses

Fine-tune your will by including directives that will prevent problems:

▶ **Tax clauses.** If your estate is large enough to be subject to federal and/or state taxes, who's going to pay? Each beneficiary for his share of the taxes? Your executor for all taxes from probate assets? A tax clause can clarify who pays estate taxes.

▶ **Simultaneous death.** If you and a beneficiary die under circumstances in which it's impossible to determine who died first—for example, in a car crash or plane crash—state law sets up a presumption on the order of death, which you can change if you wish. You may want to presume not to survive your spouse if you have more assets than your spouse, so that passing assets from your estate to hers will enable her to take advantage of her exemption amount ($2 million in 2007 and 2008). But if you each have about equal estates, then you would want the presumption to be that you each survived the other, thereby preventing assets from passing into each other's estates and incurring administrative costs.

Executing a will

Executing a will means signing it in accordance with state law. Make sure you have the required number of witnesses, generally two. Also make sure they meet state requirements—for example, they can't be beneficiaries under your will, they can't be related to you (relatives are potential beneficiaries if your will is ruled to be invalid) and they may have to be over age 18 or 21.

 Strategy: *Videotape the will signing if there's any question about your competency (or that of your witnesses). Pictures often speak louder than words about legal competency.*

Revoking a will

If you've already made a will and want to make a new one, you must revoke the old one. You can do this either by tearing up the original will or by including a revocation clause in your new will, stating that you revoke all prior wills.

WHAT'S YOUR "ESTATE"?

When you die, your estate is the total of every asset you own or have an interest in. There are two types of estates; the second is broader and includes the first:

▶ **Your probate estate** includes assets passing under the terms of your will (or, if you fail to have a will, under your state's laws of intestacy). These are assets solely in your name that don't pass automatically to a named beneficiary.

▶ **Your taxable estate** includes every asset you own or have an interest in. These include all probate assets as well as assets passing automatically by operation of law. These so-called "outside" assets include life insurance, IRAs and qualified retirement plan benefits, annuities and jointly owned property.

To plan effectively for passing on your assets and saving taxes, you need to know the full extent of your estate. The following worksheet can be used to compile a list of your assets. Enter the value of the assets using what you believe they're worth today. Asset values can fluctuate from day to day, but you need some reference point. If you're not married, obviously you don't need to include assets in your spouse's column. And, even if you own assets jointly with someone—a brother or daughter, for instance—you can skip the last column as well; assets jointly owned with someone other than a spouse are includible in the estate of the first owner to die, except to the extent the other owner paid for the asset.

Asset worksheet

Asset type	My assets	My spouse's assets	Jointly owned assets
Annuities	$	$	$
Automobiles	$	$	$
Bank account			
Checking	$	$	$
Savings	$	$	$
Boat	$	$	$
Bonds			
Corporate	$	$	$
Munis	$	$	$
Savings bonds	$	$	$
Treasuries & agency bonds	$	$	$
Business interests			
Partnerships	$	$	$
Proprietorships	$	$	$
LLCs	$	$	$
S corporations	$	$	$
C corporations	$	$	$
Cash	$	$	$
Collectibles and antiques	$	$	$
Computers & electronic equipment	$	$	$
Home			
Main	$	$	$
Vacation	$	$	$
Household furnishings	$	$	$
Furs	$	$	$
IRAs			
Roth	$	$	$
Traditional	$	$	$
Jewelry	$	$	$
Life insurance	$	$	$
Medical savings accounts	$	$	$
Mutual funds	$	$	$
Qualified retirement plan benefits	$	$	$
Real estate (other than homes)	$	$	$
Stocks	$	$	$
Stock options			
ISOs	$	$	$
Nonqualified	$	$	$
Other assets	$	$	$

Liabilities

For tax purposes your estate isn't made up solely of your assets. You must, of course, reduce assets by liabilities. Here are some of the liabilities you may have:

- ▶ **Credit card debt**
- ▶ **Margin loans**
- ▶ **Mortgage on your main home or vacation home**
- ▶ **Mortgage on investment/rental property**
- ▶ **Personal debt** (for example, money you owe to a friend)
- ▶ **Retirement plan loans**
- ▶ **Other liabilities**

Note: Loans on your life insurance policies are not treated as liabilities since they need not be paid back. They merely reduce the proceeds payable to your beneficiary.

Financial inventory

Recording assets and liabilities not only helps you plan your estate, but serves as a vital reference to your heirs in locating assets after your death. To complete your financial inventory, add the following:

▶ **Account numbers** for bank and brokerage accounts and policy numbers for life insurance policies and annuity contracts.

▶ **Location of assets** (for example, where you keep deeds, stock certificates, insurance policies and the key to your safe-deposit box).

▶ **Name and phone number of financial advisers** (your accountant, attorney, stock broker, insurance agent, etc.). Also include the name and number of your employer's human resources department so your heirs can locate any employee benefits, including qualified retirement plan benefits.

▶ **Passwords and user IDs** for access to online bank and brokerage accounts, ATM cards, computer security systems, seller accounts (e.g., eBay and Amazon) and entry gates at communities and storage facilities.

Strategy: Let your heirs know where to find your financial inventory—for example, in a home safe. You may also want to leave a copy with the attorney who holds your will.

WHAT'S THE POTENTIAL TAX BITE?

As the federal laws now stand, more than half your estate might be lost to estate taxes. The top federal estate tax rate in 2007 through 2009 is 45%. In 2010 the federal estate tax is repealed. But in 2011, the old rates are scheduled to reapply unless Congress makes repeal permanent—with a top rate of 55%. If you pass assets to grandchildren or other heirs that skip a generation, there may also be a generation-skipping transfer tax to consider.

Strategy: Review your current estate plans with an estate planning professional in light of the sweeping changes in federal estate and gift tax rules. You may need to revise your will or other documents or use new strategies to take advantage of the changes in the next decade.

How much is estate tax free?

Not every person's estate needs to be concerned with estate taxes. For federal estate tax purposes, you can pass tax free up to $2 million in 2007. The exempt amount increases to $3.5 million in 2009 (there is no estate tax in 2010—the $1 million limit is set to reapply in 2011). Of course, some states impose taxes on smaller estates, so even if you're exempt from federal estate tax, there may be a state death tax on your assets. You need to consider your state's death tax laws.

For married couples, the exemption amount is effectively doubled. This means that a married couple can pass on to children up to $4 million in 2007.

 Strategy: *Married individuals should use their tax-free allotments fully. Make sure that the first to die doesn't waste the exemption amount by passing all assets directly to the surviving spouse. Bypass (or credit shelter) trusts or other strategies are necessary to utilize each spouse's exemption amount.*

Once you know the size of your estate, you can calculate your federal estate taxes using online calculators, such as Fidelity (**www.fidelity.com**). Click on "Planning & Retirement," then scroll down to "Estate Planning."

For links to other estate planning resources, visit **www.estateplanninglinks.com.**

Most states have their own estate or inheritance taxes, and many estates exempt from federal estate tax may still owe a state-level tax. To find out about death taxes in your state, call your state department of tax or revenue or click on its Web site.

General methods for reducing estate taxes

If your estate is larger than the exemption amount, what can you do to avoid or minimize the tax bite? Consider directing property to certain individuals or by making gifts while you're alive.

▶ **Marital bequests.** If you're married, you may pass assets in a qualified way to your surviving spouse, entirely tax free. There's no dollar limit to the tax-free amount that can pass to a surviving spouse. *Caution:* If your spouse is *not* a US citizen, in 2007, the marital deduction is limited to $125,000, unless assets are placed in a qualified domestic trust (QDOT). This is a trust that has a US trustee and meets certain other requirements. If a QDOT is used, then an unlimited amount can effectively be passed tax free to a spouse who's not a US citizen.

▶ **Charitable bequests.** Property left to charity is exempt from estate tax. There's no limit on the size of the charitable deduction that can be claimed by an estate to reduce or eliminate its taxes. Charitable bequests are discussed on page 281.

▶ **Lifetime gifts.** The more assets removed from your estate during your lifetime, the smaller your estate will be when you die. Giving away property in tax-wise ways can cut your estate without any current tax cost to you. Lifetime gifting is discussed later in this chapter.

▶ **Life insurance trusts.** Use an irrevocable trust for your life insurance policy. As long as you don't have an interest in the trust, the proceeds aren't included in your estate. Caution: If you already own a life insurance policy and transfer it to the trust, you'll have to outlive the transfer by three years to keep the proceeds out of your estate. Life insurance trusts are discussed in greater detail later in this chapter.

Special rules for IRAs (other than Roth IRAs), qualified retirement plans and other income

In addition to estate tax on these items, there may be an income tax burden on the beneficiary because you've never been taxed on these items. When your beneficiary inherits them, they become taxable.

 Strategy: *Claim an offsetting income tax deduction for the portion of federal estate tax payable on income in respect of a decedent. This is a miscellaneous itemized deduction not subject to the 2%-of-adjusted-gross-income floor. The beneficiary claims this deduction even though it's paid by the estate. It can even be claimed* before *the estate actually pays it, as long as the liability for the tax is certain.*

CHOOSING YOUR HEIRS

Commonly, all assets are left to a spouse with the assumption that he/she will then pass on to children after the spouse's death.

But this bequest scheme may not be wise in all circumstances; it may result in unnecessary taxes. And not all your possible heirs may need or even want an inheritance.

A wealthy child

If your child is already wealthy, leaving him assets may complicate his estate planning without improving his standard of living or quality of life. Consider forgoing bequests to such a child in favor of needier relatives.

 Strategy: *Talk to a child you plan to disinherit to avoid family discord and the possibility of hurt feelings.*

Children in different situations

One child may work in your family business while the other does not. If you're leaving the business to the working child, you'll want to find ways to provide for the other child so that there's no friction between the siblings. For example, you may name the nonworking child as beneficiary to your life insurance policy or IRA.

A disabled child

If your child is developmentally or physically impaired and receives government assistance, don't leave anything directly to the child. Instead, consider a supplemental-needs trust to provide the things that government benefits don't cover—a birthday party, for instance, or a trip to DisneyWorld.

Alternatively, you can leave funds to your other children or relatives with the informal understanding that they will use the funds for the benefit of your disabled child. *Caution:* There are no checks or balances on this method. The funds can wind up being used in other ways and can even be attached by your child's creditors.

Strategy: Don't leave assets to someone in a nursing home who's receiving Medi-caid. Your bequest will be used merely to supplant government benefits and won't necessarily improve the person's care or standard of living.

Disinheriting your relatives

You aren't required by law to leave *anything* to a child or other relative, except for a spouse. State law creates minimum spousal bequests, and if you don't leave that minimum amount, your spouse can demand it. But if you want to disinherit a child, a sibling or anyone else who would inherit from you if you didn't have a will, there's nothing to prevent you. Just make it clear in your will *why* you're doing so—a helpful strategy if the disowned relative tries to overturn your will. In some cases, it may be advisable to use a "contestability" clause, disinheriting anyone who challenges your will.

GIVING TO CHARITY

If you're so inclined, you can give your assets to charity. Whether you do so during your lifetime and claim an income tax deduction or at your death for an estate tax deduction, the results are the same. You'll cut the size of your estate by the amount of your gift, you (or your estate) will save on taxes *and* you'll benefit your favorite organization or cause.

You can, of course, make outright gifts by check or via the transfer of stock, bonds or mutual fund shares.

Strategy: In planning which assets to give to charity, select appreciated assets, such as stock, held more than one year. You'll receive a current deduction based on the asset's current market value and you'll avoid capital gains tax on the asset's appreciation.

If you have substantial assets to give to charity, you can take advantage of a number of sophisticated options that can benefit both you and the charity.

Charitable remainder trusts

This type of trust lets you keep an income interest for life, with the assets remaining in the trust passing to the charity at your death. You claim a deduction for the present value of the charity's remainder interest, which is figured using IRS tables. Alternatively, you can set up a charitable remainder trust under the terms of your will, naming some individual, such as your spouse or child, as the income beneficiary. Again, your estate enjoys the charitable contribution deduction. *Caution:* The trust must be set up either as a charitable remainder unitrust or a charitable remainder annuity trust that meets certain strict guidelines on payouts and other matters. Work with a tax professional who can set up the trust for you.

Strategy: During your lifetime fund the trust with appreciated assets to gain a double tax benefit. Not only will you enjoy a charitable contribution deduction, but you'll avoid capital gains tax on the asset appreciation.

Gift annuities and deferred gift annuities

Instead of setting up your own trust, you can achieve the same results—a lifetime income and a gift to charity after your death—with a gift annuity. Certain major charitable organizations, such as the Salvation Army and the United Jewish Appeal, have programs for gift annuities. You contribute a certain amount and are guaranteed to receive a fixed income for life.

You can increase your income stream by deferring its receipt. For example, if you're in your 50s, you can contribute now to an organization's charitable gift annuity program that will start paying you an income when you're 65. Since the charity has the funds to invest for several years before paying you income, it can maximize that payment.

Pooled income funds

Another variation on the charitable remainder trust is the pooled income fund. Instead of having your own trust, you make your contribution to a fund that bases your lifetime income on your share of the pooled funds. Unlike the charitable remainder trust, which has costs for setup and administration, there are no costs for contributing to a pooled income fund. What's more, the money is professionally managed so it's possible for the fund to pay out favorable returns. Your income from the fund varies from year to year, depending on the fund's investment performance.

Private foundations

If you have substantial assets to pass on to charity, consider a private foundation. The foundation is required by law to give away at least 5% of its asset value to tax-exempt organizations of your choosing.

Donor advised funds

Instead of setting up your own foundation, you can contribute to a fund that lets you suggest how your contributions should be directed. By law, the fund can't be compelled to use the money as you suggest, but in most cases, a donor's wishes are followed.

▶ **Community trusts.** Community trusts—many of which have been around for many years—let you name the causes you would like to benefit.

▶ **Commercial funds.** Funds such as Fidelity's Charitable Gift Fund, Schwab's Fund for Charitable Giving and Vanguard's Charitable Endowment Group permit you to list the organizations you wish to benefit. Each fund has its own minimum donation requirements, so check with the fund for details (see Chapter 15).

GIFTS TO MAKE NOW OR LATER (BY INHERITANCE)

For the past 25 years, the federal estate and gift tax law has been a unified scheme—with the same exemption amounts and tax rates. But this situation was changed by The Economic Growth and Tax Relief Reconciliation Act of 2001. The lifetime gift tax exemption is $1 million compared with a $2 million exemption for estate tax. The gift tax exemption rises no further (even though the estate tax exemption will increase to $3.5 million in 2009). The top tax rate on gifts is now 45%. When the estate tax is repealed in 2010, the gift tax remains—but at a rate equal to the top individual income tax rate of 35%.

Using your annual gift tax exemption

In addition to a lifetime exemption amount, there is an annual exclusion. For 2007 you can give away up to $12,000 for each beneficiary you select. For example, if you have three children and give them each $12,000 this year, you can give away $36,000 completely tax free. If you repeat the process each year for 10 years, you've given away $360,000 with no gift tax cost.

Married couples can double the size of gifts to a beneficiary, even if the subject of the gift belongs to one spouse. All that's necessary is for the other spouse to consent to "split" the gift. A signature on the annual gift tax return is all that's required to show this consent.

Making gifts to state qualified tuition plans

Today all states offer state-sponsored college savings plans (referred to as 529 plans after the section in the Tax Code creating them). More than a dozen states have no residency requirements for participation, so everyone has an opportunity to use a 529 plan. Depending on the state's plan, contributions of $100,000 or more per beneficiary may be permitted. These contributions can be made in a lump sum or in any amount desired each year (unless a fixed dollar limit is reached). Details of 529 plans are explained in Chapter 18.

Advantages of lump-sum contributions: You can reduce your estate by large amounts in one fell swoop. For example, if you have four grandchildren and the money to make large gifts, you can contribute $100,000 to a 529 plan for each beneficiary, or a total of $400,000.

What's more, this gift can be *entirely* gift tax free. *Reason:* You can elect to treat the gift as having been made ratably over five years. So, if you're married and your spouse consents to the gift, a $100,000 gift is treated as having been made over five years at $20,000 per year, an amount fully protected by the annual gift tax exclusion. With the annual exclusion at $12,000 in 2007, a 529 plan contribution of $60,000 ($12,000 x 5) is gift tax free.

 Strategy: Check state income tax deductions if you are planning gifts to 529 plans. For example, in New York, a resident can deduct up to $5,000 in contributions each year ($10,000 per married couple). Compare the state income tax benefit for annual contributions with the estate tax benefit of larger lump-sum gifts.

Using an IRA (other than a Roth IRA) for charitable giving

You can't give your IRA away while you're alive, unless you withdraw the money and pay taxes on it and gift away what's left. But if you're planning to leave money to charity, consider naming a charity as the beneficiary of your IRA instead of using other assets for your charitable bequest. Your estate will get a deduction for the value of your IRA. And since the charity is a tax-exempt organization, it won't have to pay income tax on your IRA funds. This means that less of your assets will be eroded by taxes.

 Strategy: *Leave assets other than your IRA (or other income in respect of a decedent) to your family members. These other assets, including Roth IRAs, don't entail any income tax costs to them.*

CREDIT SHELTER TRUSTS

A credit shelter trust, also called a bypass trust, is attractive to many people. This type of trust allows you to provide for your spouse for his or her lifetime; at your spouse's death, property passes to your named beneficiaries. The assets passing into the trust are included in your estate but are shielded from tax by your exemption amount—$2 million in 2007. So, when your spouse dies, the assets remaining in the trust are not included in your spouse's estate. The point of the credit shelter trust is to subject enough assets to tax in the estate of the first spouse to die in order to make use of, and not waste, the exemption amount.

Example: Assume you die in 2007 with an estate of $2 million and your spouse also has $2 million in his own name. If you pass your estate to your surviving spouse using the marital deduction, your estate will escape estate tax entirely. But if your spouse dies in 2008, the estate will be worth $4 million, or more if the assets appreciate. Had you put your $2 million into a credit shelter trust for the benefit of your spouse, that amount would pass the tax hurdle in your estate. That $2 million would be protected from tax by your exemption amount—$2 million. Thus, when your spouse died, only $2 million—his own assets—would be includible in his estate (and would be tax free because of the exemption amount).

 Strategy: *Make sure that each spouse owns assets in his or her own name. Where assets are all jointly owned, divide them into separate accounts. Each spouse should have sufficient assets in his or her own name to fund a credit shelter trust.*

 Strategy: *Where an estate has a credit shelter trust, the income beneficiary should tap into trust principal only after using up other assets. Since these assets are already tax-proof, don't use them unless absolutely necessary!*

Strategy: Review existing credit shelter plans. As the estate tax exemption rises, your estate may not be large enough to fully fund a credit shelter trust and *provide your spouse with a bequest. For example, if your estate is $2 million and your will provides that your credit shelter trust be funded for the maximum federal exemption amount,* all *of your estate would pass into this trust in 2007 (when the exemption amount is $2 million), leaving no other assets to pass directly to your spouse. In this case, you would probably want to limit your credit shelter to a dollar amount or make other provisions.*

QTIPs

If you're married, you may want to consider leaving property to your spouse in trust rather than in an outright bequest. Perhaps you want to protect an inheritance for children of previous marriages as well as make sure that your current spouse is taken care of after your death. To accomplish both with optimum tax effect, use a qualified terminable interest property (QTIP) trust. A QTIP trust provides lifetime income interest to your spouse. After your spouse's death, the assets remaining in the trust pass to your children, grandchildren or other beneficiaries. The trust qualifies for the marital deduction in your estate, so its assets are exempt from your estate and not taxed at that time. The assets may be taxable when your spouse dies.

The QTIP trust must comply with tax law requirements in order to achieve the desired tax result. But there's great latitude in ensuring the well-being of your spouse. For example, in addition to the income, which is automatically paid to your spouse, assets in the trust can be used for the health, maintenance and support of your spouse.

DYNASTY TRUSTS

If you want to provide for your heirs and their heirs, do so with a trust. Its terms will guide how your assets are used for many years. Assets placed in the trust are taxed once—as a gift or for estate tax purposes, depending on when the trust comes into existence. Thus, assets can be passed from generation to generation without additional estate taxes (although there may be a generation-skipping transfer tax).

Example: Assume you put $1 million into a dynasty trust that earns 7% annually. If no distributions were made, at the end of four generations— approximately 80 years—there would be almost $900 million in the trust. In comparison, if assets were transferred from generation to generation in outright gifts, there would be only about $35 million after four generations. Estate taxes would have eroded the rest and diminished the value of compounding returns.

Time limits

In the past, state law generally required a trust to end no later than 21 years after the death of a specified beneficiary, someone living at the time of the trust's creation. This old English rule was called the rule against perpetuities. Today, about half the states—Alaska, Arizona, California (90 years), Colorado, Delaware, Florida (360 years), Idaho, Illinois, Louisiana, Maine, Maryland, Minnesota, Missouri, Nebraska, Nevada, New Jersey,

New York, Ohio, Rhode Island, South Dakota, Texas, Virginia, Washington (150 years), West Virginia and Wisconsin—have partially or fully done away with this rule, allowing trusts to run almost indefinitely, have extended the allowable term, or allowed trusts to be reformed.

 Strategy: *Include trust terms that can adapt to changing times. Give the trustee latitude to handle special circumstances, now and in the future. And provide a method for selecting successor trustees; your original trustee won't live forever.*

Caution: Setting up and administering these trusts may not come cheap. Legal fees can run from $5,000 up, depending upon the complexity of the trust.

QPRTs

If you own a home—your main residence or a vacation home—you have an opportunity to transfer it to your children or other beneficiaries at greatly reduced transfer tax cost. The tax law allows a qualified personal residence trust, or QPRT, for this purpose. In a nutshell, you give away your home but retain the right to live in it for a set period, generally 10 to 15 years. The cost of the gift is the value of the home reduced by the value of your retained interest, determined by IRS tables.

The longer your term interest, the smaller your gift tax cost. *Caution:* If you die before the end of the stated term, the value of your home is includable in your estate, as if you hadn't set up a QPRT. But your only loss would be attorney's fees and administrative expenses to create the trust.

Advantages: You transfer an asset for a fraction of the tax that would result upon your death. You continue to have the use of your home for a set period of time. Perhaps that's all the time you expect to need in the home because you plan on relocating. There may be no out-of-pocket gift taxes to be paid since any gift tax can be offset by your exemption amount.

 Strategy: *Balance the term of the trust against your gift tax cost. The longer the term of the trust—the time you're allowed to use the home without question—the smaller the gift (and the lower the gift tax cost). But if the term is too long, you may die before it's over and your transfer tax savings will evaporate.*

If you don't want to live in the home, you want to relocate or you need to move to a nursing home—your trust can sell the home. The trust effectively converts to a grantor-retained annuity and trust (GRAT). The cash is invested to pay you an annuity for the remainder of the trust term, and the assets then pass to your child when the trust term ends. *Caution:* If you put a vacation home into a QPRT, your trustee can't claim the home-sale exclusion to avoid tax on gain from a sale of the home. This exclusion applies only to a main home. The trust can claim the exclusion as long as you meet the two-year ownership and use requirements (see Chapter 10).

Disadvantages: At the end of the trust term, you no longer have an absolute right to live in the home. You'll have to lease it from the new owner—your child or other person you've chosen. And, of course, there are costs involved in setting up and running the trust—appraisal fees for determining the current value of the home, attorney's fees for drafting the trust and making a deed, recording fees for the deed, etc.

Strategy: *Adopt a wait-and-see approach to estate and gift tax changes before creating a QPRT. It may not be necessary if these transfer taxes are eliminated.*

IRREVOCABLE LIFE INSURANCE TRUSTS

If you carry life insurance, keep it out of your estate by having it owned by an irrevocable trust. Set up the trust and transfer the policy to it—once you do so, you can't get the policy back and the trust can't be changed after you set it up. As long as you live more than three years after the transfer, the proceeds of the policy collected by the trust after your death will be out of your estate—and not subject to tax. It may cost $2,000 to $3,000 to set up the trust, but the tax savings may be well worth it.

 Strategy: *Find out if your group-term life insurance (from an employer or through a professional or trade association) can be transferred to your trust. If so, complete any necessary transfer forms.*

 Strategy: *Set up an irrevocable life insurance trust before you buy any new life insurance and have the trustee buy the policy with your funds. That way, you never owned the policy. Upon your death, there would be no estate tax on the insurance proceeds.*

If you plan to transfer funds annually to the trust to cover the premiums using your annual exclusion, be sure to include a *Crummey* power in the trust document. This power requires that the beneficiaries of the trust (for example, your children) be notified of the additions to the trust and have the right to withdraw them within a set time (typically 30 to 90 days from notification).

 Strategy: *Be sure that the trustee keeps copies of all beneficiary notification forms to prevent the IRS from contending that the additions were taxable gifts to the trust.*

LIVING TRUSTS

You can set up a trust during your lifetime and retain full control over your assets. Living trusts are aggressively sold as probate-avoidance techniques. But there are other advantages of living trusts—and some disadvantages.

Living trusts can:

▶ **Pass assets** to your heirs when you die.

▶ **Consolidate your assets** for easy asset management while you're alive.

▶ **Save on administrative costs.** Since assets in the trust pass outside of your probate estate, there may be some cost saving for court filing fees and attorney's fees.

Living trusts can't:

▶ **Avoid estate taxes.** Since you retain the right to revoke the trust and recoup your assets while you're alive, the assets in the trust are includable in your estate. You can, however, use any tax device that's available under a will, such as a marital deduction or charitable deduction.

▶ **Avoid administrative costs.** While there may be a cost savings at the time of death, there are generally larger up-front costs for setting up the trust (several thousand dollars, depending on complexity) and for transferring assets into the trust.

USING FAMILY LIMITED PARTNERSHIPS (FLPs)

Individuals who own businesses or substantial assets—real estate or sizable investment portfolios—can cut estate taxes while retaining control over these assets by setting up family limited partnerships (FLPs) and giving away limited partnership interests to family members. You consolidate your assets in one entity, making management of assets easier.

 Strategy: Use a family limited liability company (FLLC) to accomplish the same goals as the FLP but obtain personal liability protection for all family members who own interests.

How FLPs work

Set up a partnership to which you transfer your assets. As a general partner, you hold all limited partnership interests. Give away the limited partnership interests, typically in amounts of no more than the annual gift tax exclusion so the transfers are tax free. In valuing limited partnership interests, certain valuation discounts can be claimed:

▶ **Minority interest discount.** Having a limited partnership interest means you can't demand distributions or control the management of the business, so a valuation discount is allowed.

▶ **Lack of marketability discount.** In a family-owned business such as a privately held company, there's a limited market for selling interests, even if such interests could be sold and were not subject to restrictions on selling to outsiders. A discount is allowed for this factor.

▶ **Built-in gain discount.** If the major asset of the partnership—for example, a building—were to be sold, tax on the resulting gain would lower the value of the partnership as a whole. The tax law recognizes a discount for this factor, even if no sale is contemplated.

 Strategy: You can give away $20,000 worth of assets if you claim a 40% discount. As long as this discount is reasonable under your circumstances, $20,000 worth of assets is fully shielded by the annual gift tax exclusion of $12,000 in 2007 ($20,000 reduced by 40% is $12,000). Or give away assets worth $16,000 using a 25% discount.

As general partner you keep control over the partnership, managing the assets and deciding when and to what extent distributions should be made. If you wish, you can continue to give away limited partnership interests until you retain only your general partnership interest.

Cautions

The IRS is vigilant in limiting or restricting the use of valuation discounts to reduce transfer tax costs. It may try to increase the amount of the gift to raise gift tax costs. Or it may effectively void the gift and include the property in the donor's estate. Here are some arguments the IRS has used and how to get around them:

▶ **Excessive valuation discounts.** The IRS may challenge the amount of discounts claimed. *To counter this challenge,* make sure your facts support your discounts. Keep in mind that *overall* (total) discounts should probably not exceed 40%.

▶ **Sham transfers.** Where the donor keeps control over the property that's gifted, the IRS may allege that in fact no gift has been made. For example, where a parent continues to treat FLP assets as his own, depositing FLP funds in his own account, the transfer may be disregarded and all FLP assets included in the parent's estate. *To counter this challenge,* respect the formalities of the arrangement. Set up separate FLP bank accounts and segregate FLP assets from personal assets.

▶ **Future interests.** The annual gift tax exclusion applies only to gifts of present interests. Where the general partner has such control over the partnership that the limited partners have virtually no real interest, the IRS may allege that this is a future interest not eligible for the exclusion. *To counter this challenge,* don't tie the hands of the general partner so that the limited partners have no real interest. For example, don't prevent him from making distributions.

ESTATE PLANNING FOR COLLECTIBLES

If you're a collector, the objects in your collection are probably quite precious to you regardless of their monetary value. Here are some things to think about when planning for their disposition:

Who's going to inherit your collection

Are you going to keep it together or divide it up? Decide in advance how you want it handled to avoid conflict among your heirs and to protect your collection.

Keeping your collection together: Find someone—your child, a museum—who wants your collection. If you leave your collection to one child, you'll need other assets to leave to your other children and relatives.

If you leave your collection to a museum, library or other nonprofit organization, make sure it will be treated as you want—displayed, maintained and cherished. To ensure the best treatment of your collection, you may enhance your bequest with cash for the care and protection of your collection.

Dividing your collection among your heirs: If you can't find an individual or organization to take your collection, you'll have to divide it among your children or other beneficiaries. You can be helpful by stating in advance how you want them to divide your collection. Consider the following:

▶ **Arrange for specific items to go to named beneficiaries.**

▶ **Allow sale of the collection,** with the proceeds divided among beneficiaries.

▶ **Allow selection of items by mutual agreement among beneficiaries** or by a system in which each beneficiary takes a turn in selecting one item until the collection is fully divided.

Other concerns

Make provisions for carrying costs related to your collection—shipping expenses to transfer your collection to your heir, insurance and other upkeep items.

If your collection passes to your beneficiaries (and not to a charity), make sure you think about the estate tax obligation. Valuable collections can trigger large estate taxes. If the taxes are borne by the estate, do not inadvertently disinherit an heir. The person who inherits the residuary estate will receive only what's left after estate tax.

 Strategy: *If your heir is responsible for the estate tax payment on his inheritance, leave cash or liquid assets to handle this obligation so he's not forced to sell his inheritance just to pay the tax.*

LIFETIME PLANNING FOR OLD AGE AND DISABILITY

Estate planning generally focuses on what happens to your property after your death. But you should also be concerned with having an accident or an illness that renders you unable to handle your affairs. Who will act for you? Who will speak for you? Your will doesn't address these lifetime concerns.

 Strategy: *Work with an "elder law" attorney who specializes in financial and other issues relating to old age and disability. For help in finding an elder law attorney in your area, contact the National Academy of Elder Law Attorneys (**www.naela.org**, 520-881-4005).*

Medical issues

The US Supreme Court has recognized that every adult has the right to determine his or her own medical treatment, including withholding treatment, even if it leads to death. The right to forgo artificial life support that controls breathing, feeding and hydration can easily be ensured by putting your wishes in writing. There are two basic types of written *advance medical directives*—living wills and health-care proxies (or medical powers of attorney). It's estimated that about 70% of those with illnesses such as cancer forgo artificial life supports.

▶ **Living will.** This document states the type of care you want or do not want. For example, it can express your desire *not* to be kept alive by extraordinary means (respirators, feeding tubes, etc.). It can also include your desire to die at home or to receive medications for pain.

▶ **Health care proxy/medical power of attorney.** This document designates someone—your spouse, your adult child, your best friend—to speak for you regarding medical care if you're unable to speak for yourself.

 Strategy: *Check state law to determine which document you need as an advance medical directive. If you maintain residences in more than one state, sign documents that will be recognized in each location. For example, if you have homes in New York and Florida, sign a health-care proxy for New York and a medical power of attorney for Florida. Make sure that the documents agree; name the same person to act on your behalf and authorize the same decisions regarding your care.*

Five Wishes Living Will: A new type of health-care proxy or medical power of attorney is the Five Wishes Living Will. This document, now recognized in 33 states and the District of Columbia, includes the same instructions about health care that ordinary health-care proxies contain but has an additional element. It incorporates your feelings about medical treatment and your loved ones.

> *Strategy: Obtain advance medical directives recognized in your state from a local stationery store or from the National Hospice and Palliative Care Organization (**www.caringinfo.org**, 800-989-9455). Obtain a copy of the Five Wishes Living Will for $5 from the Commission on Aging with Dignity, Box 1661, Tallahassee, FL 32302 (**www.agingwithdignity.org**, 888-594-7437). It's generally advisable to work with an attorney who can ensure that the document meets your individual requirements.*

For information about end-of-life care, including hospice and home care, see National Hospice and Palliative Care Organization (**www.caringinfo.org**).

States recognizing Five Wishes Living Wills

Alaska	Minnesota
Arizona	Mississippi
Arkansas	Missouri
California	Montana
Colorado	Nebraska
Connecticut	New Jersey
Delaware	New Mexico
District of Columbia	New York
Florida	North Carolina
Georgia	North Dakota
Hawaii	Pennsylvania
Idaho	Rhode Island
Illinois	South Carolina
Iowa	South Dakota
Louisiana	Tennessee
Maine	Virginia
Maryland	Washington
Massachusetts	West Virginia
Michigan	Wyoming

Financial issues

Who will handle your banking, pay your bills and oversee your investments if you become incapacitated? To avoid the need for court intervention, which can be time consuming, costly and embarrassing, there are two main ways to ensure that your money will be managed:

▶ **Durable power of attorney.** This form designates an agent to act on your behalf in money matters. You can empower your agent (called an attorney-in-fact) to sell your home (which may be desirable if you move to a nursing home), file tax returns, put in claims for retirement benefits and make all money-related decisions. Durable power of attorney is discussed in greater detail in Chapter 23.

Strategy: *Use a "springing" power of attorney to empower the agent only when you become incapacitated. Assuming state law permits, specify that the durable power of attorney "spring" into effect when two doctors certify your incapacity or some other criterion of incapacity is met.*

▶ **Living trust.** This is a trust set up during your lifetime; you retain the right to recoup the assets until you die or become incapacitated. You transfer ownership of your bank accounts, securities portfolio and other assets to the trust. You name a trustee to manage your assets in the trust, typically after you cease to serve in this function. Living wills are discussed in greater detail earlier in this chapter as well as in Chapter 23.

Strategy: *Set up a standby trust with its terms in place. Asset transfers will be triggered by your incapacity. The triggering event should be clear, such as certification of incapacity by two doctors. Make sure that you have in place the mechanism to fund the trust—for example, authorization of an agent, in a durable power of attorney, to transfer your assets to the trust.*

For additional information on issues related to becoming incapacitated, see Elderweb.com **(www.elder web.com).**

21

Secrets of staying out of money trouble

"*Be prepared.*"

—SCOUT MOTTO

S OME FINANCIAL PROBLEMS are caused by ignoring what you should be doing. Others are caused by scams. And some financial problems are out of your control, such as a former spouse not paying you child support.

You can avoid financial problems—identity theft, difficulties in financial accounts, scams—with some planning or by applying financial savvy. Think about the time and effort required to earn your money. Isn't it worth just as much time to take precautions to protect it?

This chapter explains how to prevent problems from arising and how to deal with them if they happen. You'll learn how to follow commonsense practices to avoid creating problems. You'll find out how to perform simple tasks on a monthly or other regular basis to prevent problems from getting out of hand. And you'll learn how to avoid being duped by unscrupulous sales pitches.

PREVENTING IDENTITY THEFT

One of the fastest growing crimes today is identity theft: Someone obtains your Social Security number, your date of birth or other personal information and uses it to get credit in your name without your knowledge or consent, pass bad checks or charge huge sums that will show up on your credit report. Here's how you can protect your identity:

▶ **Don't give out your credit card number to anyone** unless *you've* contacted *them* to obtain goods or services. For example, if someone calls or e-mails you to "update your account information," it could be a scam. Don't give out any personal information; request the caller to send you the paperwork and respond by mail. This will allow you to determine if a request is legitimate.

▶ **Guard your Social Security number with all your might.** Ninety-nine percent of all identity theft occurs by someone obtaining a Social Security number. Don't carry your card with you unless you have to. Make a photocopy of your medical or Medicare card and delete your Social Security number on it. Be suspicious if you don't receive your annual earnings report from the Social Security Administration (if someone intercepted it, they have your Social Security number).

▶ **Shred *all* of your bills and other paper containing personal information,** including all credit card applications you receive. The cost of a shredder, available at Staples, Office Max and other office-supply stores, is as little as $25.

▶ **Lock up your mailbox** to prevent someone from stealing your mail to obtain your personal information.

▶ **Look out for bills or replacements of expiring credit cards that don't arrive on time**—a missing bill or new credit card could mean that someone has intercepted your mail and changed the billing address.

▶ **Don't respond to phishing**—an official-looking (but bogus) e-mail asking for personal information, such as your Social Security number, bank account or date of birth. An identity thief uses this information to access your financial accounts and/or obtain credit in your name.

Keep your passwords and personal identification numbers (PINs) safe

Learning your password or PIN number is the key to opening your account information and using your ATM and credit cards, which is a form of identity theft. Some tips:

▶ **Avoid using your name,** your mother's maiden name, your Social Security number or your date of birth in any password or PIN you select.

▶ **Mix numbers and letters for passwords** and PINs.

▶ **Use special symbols and characters** in passwords and PINs.

▶ **Use different passwords** and PINs for different accounts.

 Strategy: *Change passwords and PINs frequently—at least once every six months.*

Immediately report what's lost or stolen

Lost credit cards can be canceled and new numbers easily issued. But if your wallet contains your driver's license—which includes your date of birth—an identity thief has all the information needed to take on your identity. Be vigilant of any financial activity being conducted under your name. Subscribe to a credit monitoring service at a cost of less than $10 per month. Or consider carrying identity theft insurance, which costs between $25 and $50 to obtain coverage between $15,000 and $25,000 of losses (including lost wages for time off needed to clear your identity). Carriers include American International Group (**www.aig.com**), Chubb Group of Insurance Companies (**www.chubb.com**), Encompass Insurance (**www.encompassinsurance.com**), Farmers Group Inc. (**www.farmers.com**) and Travelers Insurance (**www.travelers.com**).

To learn more about identity theft and how to avoid it, go to the FTC's Identity Theft site (**www.ftc.gov/bcp/edu/microsites/idtheft**).

CHECKING YOUR STATEMENTS

Even in today's highly automated society, mistakes on financial transactions easily occur. It's up to you to check all statements and transaction confirmations and catch and correct any errors.

Checking information

When you receive account information from your broker or mutual fund company—such as a confirmation slip showing a transaction or a monthly statement reporting what's in your account—go over it carefully. Make sure the information conforms with your understanding and your records. For example, if you receive a confirmation slip from your broker showing you bought 100 shares of X Corp. but you didn't place the buy order, correct the error immediately. *Caution:* The failure to make corrections in a timely fashion can make it more difficult to right any wrongs and could even result in permanent problems.

Correcting mistakes

If you find a problem on a confirmation slip or statement you've received in the mail, you can:

▶ **Call the customer-service number** that appears on the document. Every brokerage firm and mutual fund has a toll-free number for this purpose.

▶ **Call your broker** and ask him/her to follow up. If the problem isn't corrected promptly, call the branch manager.

BALANCING CHECKBOOKS

Banks often make errors in honoring checks and reporting deposits. For example, you write a $10 check but the bank debits your account for $100 instead, leaving you with $90 less than you thought you had. Or the bank may fail to enter a deposit you make on the first of the month on your statement, again leaving you short of the funds you expect.

The only way to detect an error is to balance your checkbook each month. This simply means comparing your checkbook entries with the monthly bank statement. In most cases, the reverse side of your bank statement provides a worksheet for making this comparison. Enter the total of the checks you've written and the deposits you've made, adjusting those figures for checks and deposits that haven't cleared yet and other charges to your account (e.g., per-check fees). Your final figure should match with the bank's figure. If it doesn't, check your math—often simple errors are the problem.

Personal financial software such as *Quicken* (**www.quicken.com**) and *MS Money* (**www.microsoft. com**) can perform this function automatically. If you use this software to write your checks, balancing your checkbook is easy.

Correcting problems

If you find an error on your statement, visit your bank's local branch or call customer service. Explain why you believe there's an error and request that it be corrected immediately.

If the bank's error resulted in additional charges or fees—for example, if its error caused your balance to fall below the required minimum, producing added monthly fees—make sure that the fees are dropped when the error is corrected.

If the bank has bounced your check in error, make sure that it rectifies the situation by waiving any fees or charges on your account and explaining its error to those who received your check. The bank should also be responsible for paying any fees or charges that another party incurred.

For more information about making complaints with respect to your bank accounts, visit Consumer Action Web site at **http://consumeraction.gov/banking.shtml**.

Safeguards

To avoid problems from mistakes or miscalculations in your account, an ounce of prevention may be worthwhile. Consider using certain safeguards so that your checks will never be dishonored—in other words, bounced.

► **Obtain overdraft checking privileges.** This is essentially a line of credit with a fixed dollar limit that you can tap into simply by writing a check. The interest rate fluctuates. There's no cost for having the overdraft privileges in place—you pay only when you use it. Having overdraft checking privileges will save you from incurring fees for writing checks that you might not be able to cover.

► **Link your checking account to another account.** If you have insufficient funds in the checking account to cover a check, your other account will serve as a backup.

► **Check your account balance regularly**—in person, by telephone or online. If the balance seems way out of line with your expectations, investigate further.

CHECKING CREDIT CARDS

Check your monthly credit card bill carefully. Make sure that what appears on the bill reflects your charges accurately and that all payments have been properly credited.

 Strategy: If you find a billing error, call the credit card company immediately. They will note the question on your account and send paperwork to process your complaint. Retain a copy of all correspondence until the matter is resolved.

The credit card company should respond to you within 30 days and, following an investigation, should make a correction within 90 days. You don't have to pay the amount in question during an investigation.

If you pay for something by credit card and don't receive goods or services, try to resolve the problem with the merchant. If you can't, you may be able to obtain a refund by getting a charge back to your account. If the sale is for more than $50 and the order was in-state or within 100 miles of your home, ask for the charge back by putting your request in writing. Even if the sale did not occur within these limits you can often obtain a charge back. As with mistakes in billing, call the credit card company. It may comply over the phone or send you a form so that you can make a formal written request.

Safeguards

If your credit card is lost or stolen, notify the credit card company immediately. State law provides you with automatic protection. Your liability for unauthorized use of your card is limited to $50, and there's no liability once you notify the credit card company.

For information on credit card protection companies, see Chapter 16.

HOW TO AVOID RIP-OFFS

Telemarketing scams are on the rise, especially against the elderly. The Federal Trade Commission estimates that there are about 140,000 telemarketing companies—and as many as 10% of them are fraudulent. One in six Americans is the victim of a telemarketing scheme each year. While most telemarketers represent legitimate companies, there are others that prey on the unwary. Don't fall for these top 10 frauds of 2005 (listed in order of frequency), identified by the National Consumer League's National Fraud Information Center:

▶ **Prizes, sweepstakes and gifts.** Contests require you to send money first in order to collect a prize or "free gift" (if you've won a prize or gift in a legitimate contest, there should be no charge to you).

▶ **Scholarships and grants.** You're falsely promised help to get government money and pay a fee for this "assistance."

▶ **Magazines and buyers clubs.** Subscriptions or renewals that are never mailed and buyers club memberships that give you nothing you couldn't obtain without paying the membership fee.

▶ **Credit card offers.** You're promised a credit card even if your credit is bad, if you pay an upfront fee.

▶ **Fake check scams.** You receive payment with phony checks and are instructed to wire money back.

▶ **Advance fee loans and credit protection.** Lenders charge fees up front for personal or business loans that never materialize or you pay for credit protection that doesn't exist.

▶ **Lotteries and lottery clubs.** You're told that you've won but must pay for help to collect winnings (often in a foreign country).

▶ **Work-at-home plans.** Kits that have exaggerated promises of financial rewards.

▶ **Phishing.** Calls from purportedly reputable source, such as banks, ask for personal information, such as Social Security number and date of birth.

▶ **Travel and vacations.** Free or discount travel offers never materialize.

Another scam is a charity asking for money for a nonexistent cause. Don't contribute to a charity unless you have confirmed its legitimacy. Find out whether the charity is an IRS-approved organization (**www.irs. gov**). Another scam involves shady credit-repair services. While there are certainly legitimate credit-repair services, there are many telemarketers making false claims or charging outrageous prices.

 Strategy: Don't compound your troubles by falling for another scam—help in correcting previous scams. Some unscrupulous telemarketers cheat you out of money and then offer to help recover it—for a fee. They sometimes call themselves "cost recovery operators."

Safety rules to avoid rip-offs

Understand your consumer protection rights and follow these simple rules to avoid telemarketing scams:

▶ **Don't agree to any advance payments** for credit repair or to obtain loans. Wait until you receive the goods and services before you make any payments.

▶ **Don't agree to any 90-day inspection** or 90-day return policy. After 90 days, it's too late to cancel bogus charges on a credit card bill. You might be stuck paying for the goods or services.

▶ **Don't give out your credit card number** to anyone who calls you unsolicited.

▶ **Don't give out your bank account number** to anyone who calls you unsolicited.

▶ **Don't talk to any telemarketer** calling before 8 am or after 9 pm—it's not legal for them to do so.

▶ **Ask for the name of the company** and the telephone number of the telemarketer.

If you buy something from a telemarketer, federal law grants you a guaranteed three-day cancellation period for any sale over $25. Key services covered by this rule:

▶ **Dance lessons**

▶ **Dating referral services**

▶ **Health-club memberships**

▶ **Weight-loss programs**

Some states have more liberal cancellation periods and extend the period for those age 65 and older. For example, North Dakota has a 15-day cancellation period.

If you've been victimized

If you have reason to think you've been victimized, contact your local or state consumer protection agency and/or your state attorney general's office immediately. You'll find the number in your local phone directory. The chances of recovering all of your money are slight, but the government may be able to catch the scam artists.

Also contact your local Better Business Bureau (listed in your local phone directory) and the National Fraud Information Center (NFIC) (800-876-7060) to report the scam so that others won't be victimized. You can also report a fraud to the NFIC online at **www.fraud.org/welset.htm.**

Preventing telemarketer calls

You don't have to answer any calls from telemarketers. Use Caller ID, a service available through your telephone company that enables your phone to display the caller's number and decide whether or not to answer the phone.

Screen your calls with a telephone answering machine. Telemarketers hang up when a message machine is on the other end.

Federal law allows you to request that you be added to a telemarketer's "do not call" (or "no-call") list. (Banks, insurance companies, charities, political organizations and others are exempt and may still call you.) When a telemarketer calls, you simply ask to be placed on the list. Keep notes on who calls you—jot the name of each company on a notepad near the phone. If you're called after asking not to be, you can sue in small claims court under the federal Telephone Protection Act and collect damages of up to $500 per violation.

For information about the National Do-Not-Call Registry from the Federal Trade Commission (FTC), visit **www.donotcall.gov** or call 888-382-1222.

Registration on the national list is free and lasts for five years.

 Strategy: *Put your cell phone number on the National Do-Not-Call Registry. Telemarketers have begun to solicit business through cell phones, even though it is illegal for them to do so and you pay for the unwanted call if you pick up.*

The majority of states have their own do-not-call lists which were in operation before the national registry. Some states are no longer accepting new entries—you will be directed to the federal registry. If you haven't yet signed on the national registry or your state's list, which should you use (assuming your state list is open)? Check to see how long you stay on your state's list. If it is longer than five years (the federal term), consider using the state's list.

No-call states

State	Number to call
Alabama	877-727-8200
Alaska	907-269-5100
Arizona	602-542-5025
Arkansas	501-682-1334
California	916-322-3360
Colorado	800-309-7041
Connecticut	860-713-6300
Florida	800-HELP-FLA
Georgia	800-282-5812
Hawaii	808-586-2636
Idaho	208-334-2400
Illinois	312-814-3000
Indiana	888-834-9969
Kentucky	800-671-7701
Louisiana	877-676-0773
Maine	207-626-8816
Massachusetts	866-231-2255
Mississippi	866-622-5567
Missouri	866-662-2551
Nebraska	401-472-2682
New York	866-887-5478
North Carolina	919-716-6000
Oklahoma	800-390-5708
Oregon	877-700-6622
Pennsylvania	888-777-3406
Tennessee	800-342-8359
Texas	866-896-6225
Virginia	804-786-2071
Wisconsin	866-966-2255
Wyoming	307-777-7841

 Strategy: *Check with your state's consumer protection agency to see whether you can use this additional protection to block all telemarketers from contacting you.*

Caution: You do not have to add your cell phone to the Do Not Call list because telemarketers are already prohibited from calling cell phones

Online scams

Junk e-mail (called spam) often includes scams—offers designed to entice you to part with your money. Online scams can be just as financially damaging as those by telephone. It's been estimated that losses resulting from online scams in 2005 exceeded $13.8 billion. Offers of get-rich-quick opportunities and other schemes are rampant. The National Consumer Fraud Information Center has identified the following as the top 10 online frauds in 2005, listed in descending order of frequency:

- ▶ **Online auctions**
- ▶ **General merchandise sales**
- ▶ **Nigerian money offers**
- ▶ **Fake checks**
- ▶ **Lotteries**
- ▶ **Phishing**
- ▶ **Advance-fee loans**
- ▶ **Adult services**
- ▶ **Work-at-home schemes**
- ▶ **Internet access services**

Follow the same approach you would on the telephone—take action to block spam, and don't fall for scams.

- ▶ ICSA Labs provides information on e-mail hoaxes (**www.icsalabs.com**).

- ▶ The Junkbusters site contains useful information on ways to keep spam out of your online mail box (**www.junkbusters.com**).

DIVORCE PLANNING

Financial settlements are usually a prime concern to both parties in a divorce. When emotions are running high, missteps can result in serious financial mistakes. One party can agree to terms in an effort to make a quick settlement without fully understanding the implications of those terms.

Family debt

Who's liable for debts incurred by one spouse or debts incurred jointly? A creditor can go after either spouse who is liable on a joint debt, such as a joint credit card, even if a separation agreement or divorce decree makes one spouse liable for the debt. The language of the separation agreement or divorce decree can give the spouse who pays the creditor the right to go after the other spouse for funds.

Strategy: *Take care of family debt before finally settling property matters. A spouse's promise to "take care of" a debt may be unreliable. Cancel joint credit cards so that one spouse can't obligate the other spouse to pay new debts.*

Alimony

Alimony or support obligations are typically payable on a monthly basis—directly to the former spouse or to a third party (for example, a landlord) for the benefit of a former spouse. In deciding whether to take alimony or a property settlement—if there's a choice—consider that alimony obligations can't be discharged in bankruptcy but property settlements can be. If you take a property settlement in installments, there's always the possibility that you won't receive all of them. If your former spouse gets into financial difficulty and declares bankruptcy, you're merely another unsecured creditor who's out of luck.

Child support

If you're having trouble collecting child support—because your spouse has moved to another state, for instance, or is simply a deadbeat parent—don't give up. You can still collect the money that's owed and intended to benefit your child by taking steps. You have several alternatives in how to proceed in the collection process:

▶ **Do-it-yourself.** In some cases, all that may be required is some persistence to make sure the checks arrive on time. But if you can't go it alone—for example, if you can't locate your former spouse— pursue your other options.

▶ **Hire an attorney.** This can be a costly option. Your time and perhaps lost wages for a court appearance as well as attorney's fees for handling the matter may add up to a significant sum. Weigh the amount to be recovered against the cost, financial as well as emotional, of pursuing your claims.

▶ **Use your state's social services.** For a modest charge (around $25), your state's social services agency can access a national Data Match system to track down a deadbeat parent. (Check your phone book for such listings as Child Services, DHR, HRS or Social Services; the agency's name varies from place to place.) While this method is inexpensive and you keep what you collect, it can be a lengthy process because of government red tape and bureaucracy. You may wait a year or more before you see any support payments.

▶ **Use a private collection agency.** There are companies that specialize in this type of debt collection. They are highly effective in collecting unpaid child support—some claim a 90% collection rate—but it will cost you. These companies keep 25% to 33% of whatever they recover. Examples of private collection agencies:

▶ SupportKids.com (**www.supportkids.com**)

▶ Child Support Network (**www.childsupport.com**)

▶ Child Support Intervention (**www.deadbeatparent.com**)

Like alimony, child support obligations aren't dischargeable in bankruptcy.

22

Record keeping

❝*Property has its duties as well as its rights.*❞

—THOMAS DRUMMOND

MOST OF US DON'T LIKE to keep records—it can be a boring and tedious process. However, good records are essential for financial and tax purposes, and they are the only way to know whether you're meeting your financial goals or whether to adjust your strategies. And records are necessary to properly process items such as insurance claims and tax returns.

You need to develop good record-keeping habits, systematically recording and retaining information necessary for financial purposes. Know what records can be discarded, so your home and workplace don't become cluttered with unnecessary papers.

This chapter shows how to keep records that will help you increase assets, support insurance claims and cut your taxes. It discusses what records you need to keep to track wealth and prepare income tax returns. It also discusses using computers to simplify your record keeping, particularly for your investments. And it explains how long to retain, and when you can dispose of, certain records.

INCREASING YOUR WEALTH WITH GOOD RECORD KEEPING

While many people don't enjoy the process, good record keeping can help you in a surprising number of ways. Record keeping can:

▶ **Tell you whether your investment strategies are working.** For example, you'll be able to track stock and mutual fund performance to see which nonperforming (or underperforming) investments you should sell.

▶ **Enable you to submit complete and accurate insurance claims** when your property is damaged or stolen, maximizing your insurance recovery.

▶ **Enable you to complete your tax returns.** With good records, you'll be able to claim more deductions, reducing your taxes and saving you money. And you'll have more protection against IRS questions in case your return is examined.

▶ **Enable your heirs to locate your property.** Poor records can prevent your heirs from locating all of your assets, and they eventually can become the property of the state. Even if your heirs know of the existence of assets, information about them may be incomplete—for example, they may know you have an account at a bank but not which bank and what account number. Getting this information can be time consuming and even costly if the estate's attorney is handling the matter.

RECORD KEEPING FOR INSURANCE PURPOSES

You may not think you have a considerable amount of possessions until you start to catalog them. For insurance purposes, it's a good idea to make an inventory of every item you own. This will allow you to submit a complete insurance claim if your property is damaged or stolen.

Making an inventory

Be systematic in making a record of the items in your home. Go room by room. Start at one side of the door and go around the room clockwise recording every item you see. Don't forget to open closets and drawers to note items you've stored there. Include items in the basement, attic and garage and on the patio and deck. Also include shrubs and garden decorations (for example, sculptures).

There are several ways to make an inventory, depending on how detailed you want to get and how much time you want to spend on it. The more details you can provide, the better. For example, it's helpful to include the model number, serial number, date of purchase and cost of each item. Some suggestions on how to make an inventory:

▶ **Use a camcorder** or digital camera to photograph every item in every room, paying particular attention to artwork or antique furniture.

▶ **Use an inventory spreadsheet** that comes with home finance software. These inventory outlines are useful in reminding you of the items you own. But they may not provide listings for all of your possessions, so you'll need to make additions.

▶ **Make your own inventory lists**—room by room, item by item.

Strategy: Update your inventory periodically—at least once a year. Add items as you purchase them—perhaps a new DVD player or microwave oven. Eliminate items that you've sold, given away or discarded.

Storing your inventory

Regardless of which method you use, keep your inventory in a safe place. A well-prepared inventory won't do you any good if there's a fire or other catastrophe in your home and your record is destroyed. Make sure you keep your inventory in a safe place. Some suggestions:

▶ **At home in a fireproof safe.**

▶ **In a bank safe-deposit box.**

▶ **With your insurance agent.**

▶ **Off-premises**—with a relative or friend, or at your office.

Strategy: Regardless of where you store your home inventory—for example, at home in a fireproof safe—keep a second copy in another location.

RECORD KEEPING FOR TAXES

Records are the proof that backs up positions you've taken on your tax returns. For certain deductions, such as most travel and entertainment expenses, records are mandatory; without them you can't claim write-offs you may otherwise be entitled to. Sometimes you can reconstruct information, but it's difficult and time consuming and not always complete or accurate. It's a far better strategy to maintain the records you need so you won't be caught short if the IRS or state tax authorities question your return.

Record-keeping methods

The records required for tax purposes, discussed below, can create clutter or become lost if you don't have a system for keeping them together. There are several tried-and-true methods for keeping tax records:

▶ **Shoebox approach.** Throughout the year, place in a box all the records you know you'll need. At year-end, sort your records into appropriate categories.

▶ **File folder approach.** Use an expandable 12-month file folder to slot records by month.

▶ **Three-ring binder approach.** Build a record keeper with a three-ring binder. Use dividers with tabs to separate items—stock transactions, charitable contributions, etc. Then, when tax time rolls around, add W-2s, 1099s and Schedule K-1s to your binder.

▶ **Computer plus.** If you use software to track your income and expenses—information you use to prepare your return—you must supplement it with paper records. These include canceled checks, receipts, sales slips and similar papers. Consider using the methods described on page 305 to hold your paper records.

> *Strategy: Put a copy of your completed tax return in a binder for a permanent record of your taxes for the year. Label the binder by the year. Keeping your tax records and tax return in one binder makes storage of tax information compact and easy.*

Records for preparing tax returns

Before you begin preparing your tax return (or providing information to an accountant for this purpose), you need to gather a wide range of records. If you know in advance what you'll need, you can easily put your records together and be ready to begin tax return preparation.

▶ **Old tax returns.** Review your old returns to remind yourself of items you might overlook, such as carryovers of unused capital losses, investment interest, charitable contributions, home-office deductions, etc.

▶ **Canceled checks and receipts.** Keeping computer records doesn't eliminate the need for certain paper trails—checks and receipts to back up claimed deductions such as unreimbursed medical expenses and employee business expenses.

▶ **Information returns.** Each year at the end of January you receive information returns of certain tax items—income and expenses—that are also reported to the IRS. These include W-2 forms to report salary and compensation; 1099s to report interest, dividends, IRA and retirement plan distributions and other types of income; and 1098s to report mortgage interest, student loan interest and tuition you paid. Later in the year you may receive other information returns—Schedule K-1s from partnerships, limited liability companies, S corporations and trusts or estates in which you have an interest.

▶ **Year-end brokerage statements.** These show the transactions you've made during the year so you can report them on your return. They also note margin interest you've paid and tax-free interest you've earned, both of which are reported on your tax return.

Tax returns

The tax law requires you to keep a copy of your return and all supporting records—receipts for unreimbursed medical expenses, canceled checks for small charitable donations, etc.—for at least three years, the normal time within which the IRS can audit your return.

The IRS can go back six years if it suspects that you understated your income by 25% or more, by under-reporting it or by overstating deductions. It can go back seven years if you claim a worthless security or a bad debt deduction. And there's no time limit if you failed to file a return (or the IRS thinks you failed to file) or if there's an allegation of fraud.

> *Strategy: Save all returns and proof of filing, such as certified receipts, forever. The returns don't take up much space. You'll be glad you have them if the IRS or your state questions whether you filed in a particular year.*

Asset records

Maintain your basis in assets you acquire so you can properly determine your gain (or loss) when you sell them. Include in basis:

▶ **What you paid for the asset.** To remember your cost basis, keep confirmation slips of all securities transactions, closing statements for real estate and sales receipts for other assets (for example, a receipt from an auction house for a painting you purchased at auction).

▶ **Improvements or additions** you made to the asset.

 Strategy: Include in basis all dividends you reinvest in stock or mutual funds. The failure to add these dividends to your basis can result in double taxation, once when you receive the dividends and again when you sell the asset and report too much gain.

Keep the asset records for as long as you own the assets *plus* the time limits outlined above—generally three years from the filing of your return.

 Strategy: Simplify your tax reporting by attaching to your tax return a computer-generated spreadsheet of your trades. The spreadsheet should segregate short-term and long-term transactions. Then, instead of listing each trade on Schedule D, simply enter your net trades for short-term and long-term transactions.

A record keeper for your US savings bonds may be found in Chapter 6.

Mandatory records

While records are generally required to claim deductions and other positions on your tax return, there are some write-offs that must be proved with specific types of records. These write-offs are subject to special substantiation requirements:

▶ **Charitable contributions.** You must obtain a written acknowledgment from the organization for any gift of $250 or more. A canceled check or bank statement is sufficient proof for claiming a charitable deduction for smaller gifts. You may also have to obtain appraisals for certain property donations (special rules apply to car and boat donations).

▶ **Car expenses.** You must keep note of your mileage, date of use and purpose when claiming a deduction for car expenses. Deductions may relate to business, charitable, medical or moving purposes.

▶ **Entertainment and travel expenses.** Business entertainment and travel costs must be supported by both receipts for the expense and a notation in a diary, expense account report or similar record of each entertainment or travel item's date, nature and purpose.

 Strategy: Don't save receipts for travel and entertainment expenses under $75 per item (other than lodging). Receipts are required for these expenses only if the cost of the item—for example, a business dinner—is $75 or more.

Additional information on record keeping for taxes can be obtained from the IRS **(www.irs.gov).** Check:

▶ **IRS Publication 463,** *Travel, Entertainment, Gift, and Car Expenses,* for details on record keeping for these write-offs.

▶ **IRS Publication 526,** *Charitable Contributions,* for details on records for donations.

▶ **IRS Publication 552,** *Recordkeeping for Individuals,* for details on what records to keep and how long to keep them for tax purposes.

RECORD-KEEPING SOFTWARE

Why be bent over your books, entering each detail of every financial transaction you make? Today you can use computer software to make record keeping fast and simple.

Software designed for personal finances allows you to:

▶ **Enter all of your income and expenses** so you can see your spending habits.

▶ **Track your investments** so you can see how they're performing.

▶ **Balance your checkbook** so you know what funds are available at all times.

▶ **Keep an inventory of your personal assets**—a valuable record for insurance purposes if items are stolen or destroyed.

Examples of personal finance software:

▶ MS Money **(www.microsoft.com)**

▶ Quicken **(www.quicken.com)**

Traders

If you make a large number of trades annually, record keeping can be a nightmare. Simplify it with special spreadsheets designed for frequent traders.

▶ **GainsKeeper** provides online tracking capability **(www.gainskeeper.com).** The annual cost ranges from $49 for up to 100 trades to $149 for 1,000 trades. You can increase your trade limit by purchasing "Trade Buckets" at any time.

▶ **TradersAccounting.com** provides a Trade Tracker spreadsheet that coordinates with *MS Excel* to provide an attachment that can be filed with a Schedule D to report gains and losses for the year **(www.tradersaccounting.com).**

 Strategy: *Protect your records from corruption with good virus protection software. Programs that offer online updates offer the best protection because you can routinely protect against new viruses.*

ONLINE SECURITIES RECORDS

With a computer and access to the Internet, you can organize and keep online records for your securities transactions.

Advantage of online record keeping:

▶ **It's easy to do.** Simply enter the information about your holdings and the site does the rest. This can include updating the value of your account, showing the percentage of change and maintaining a record of your basis.

Disadvantage of online record keeping:

▶ **It's possible to lose records.** Computer problems can wipe out your securities records, and records can be lost when changing software or other platforms. For example, if you change from AOL 4.0 to a newer version, your online records must be reentered manually (they don't automatically update to the newer version).

 Strategy: Keep backup for information posted online so that you can reconstruct records if online information is lost.

Sites for keeping online records

▶ **AOL** stock and mutual fund trackers (click on "Quotes").

▶ **GainsKeeper,** which offers online tracking capability for traders (**www.gainskeeper.com**).

You can download a "wizard" to enable you to keep track of your savings bonds on your computer. The wizard is available free from Treasury Direct (**www.savingsbonds.gov**).

WHAT YOU CAN DISCARD

Knowing *what* records to discard and *when* is as important as knowing what to keep in the first place. If you don't discard unnecessary items, records can inundate your home with clutter. Good record-keeping habits include not only keeping records but also getting rid of them in a timely and organized manner.

Each month

As you check your deposit slips against your bank statement you may discard the slips as long as the statement is accurate. Similarly, check receipts for credit card purchases against your monthly credit card statement. After your review is complete, discard the receipts unless you need them for another reason, such as returns, exchanges, warranties or tax purposes.

After one year

At the end of the year, you can discard monthly bank statements, credit card statements and brokerage firm statements. You can also discard reconciled checks that aren't needed for tax purposes.

 Strategy: Retain year-end brokerage and mutual fund statements to compare your portfolio's performance from year to year. They also contain important information for tax purposes—interest paid and tax-free interest earned during the year.

After sales

Hold receipts on big-ticket items, such as electronic equipment, until you sell, donate or trash them. The receipts may be necessary to validate warranties or for tax purposes.

Retain all records and receipts for home improvements for as long as you own your home. These records help to minimize gain on the sale of your residence and will reduce your tax if your gain otherwise exceeds the exclusion amount of $250,000, or $500,000 on a joint return. After the sale, treat these records as tax records and hold for the recommended periods.

23

Financial protection

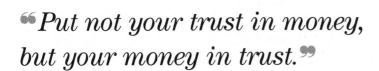

"Put not your trust in money, but your money in trust."

—OLIVER WENDELL HOLMES

AMASSING ASSETS is only one step in creating wealth. Holding on to your assets is equally important. Events that happen to you, your family or financial institutions can threaten or undermine your assets— for example, divorce, lawsuits, bank failure, infirmities that force you into a nursing home and personal bankruptcy.

But you can take advantage of certain financial protections to avoid property loss. Some protection is automatic, like FDIC protection for deposits within certain dollar limits. But other protections require action on your part.

This chapter discusses some circumstances and events that can adversely affect your wealth. It explains the protections to which you're automatically entitled. It also explains what steps to take for protection where there's no automatic protection available.

PRENUPTIAL AND POSTNUPTIAL AGREEMENTS

In the past, prenuptial agreements—contracts signed by a couple planning to marry—were only for the rich. Today, these agreements are used by any couple with assets (or who anticipate assets) they want to protect. For example, prenuptial agreements are for remarriages in which the parties have children from prior marriages. A parent will want to protect the financial future of his or her child, and protect himself or herself from repeating problems from previous marriages. They're also helpful where one or both parties have business interests including start-ups or technology companies. The future value of those interests are impossible to predict but are worth protecting in case of divorce.

For the terms of an agreement to be recognized, there are certain minimum legal requirements that must be satisfied:

▶ **The agreement generally must be fair and reasonable** to each party at the time it is signed and cannot violate state law—for example, by encouraging divorce. The agreement usually must also be fair and reasonable at the time of divorce or death of either party in order to be enforced.

▶ **Each party must make a complete and accurate disclosure** of his or her financial affairs, listing all assets and liabilities.

▶ **Each party should be represented by separate counsel** who can advise on the legalities.

 Strategy: Make sure to draw up the agreement before the wedding date. This will afford time for each party to consider the terms and conditions of the agreement and to discuss matters with a financial planner if desired.

Prenuptial agreement alternatives

Don't want to sign an agreement? Take alternative action to protect your personal assets:

▶ **Don't obtain joint credit cards.** These make each spouse fully responsible for his or her debts. One spouse can blemish the credit history of the other by unduly piling up debt and failing to repay it.

▶ **Keep assets acquired prior to the marriage** and any gifts and inheritances received during the marriage in separate accounts. Don't commingle these assets. It may be difficult if not impossible to prove what belongs to whom if the marriage breaks up.

CONTRACTS

What you don't know about the ramifications of a contract's terms can hurt you. Before you sign any contract that obligates you to pay something or do something, make sure you know what you're getting into.

 Strategy: Have an attorney review any contract you're considering. You'll pay a fee for the attorney, but this will protect you and perhaps save money in the long run.

▶ **Employment-related and business-related contracts.** If you're asked to sign a noncompete agreement as a condition of employment, make sure the terms—length of time and area of noncompetition—are reasonable. If you write a book for a publishing company, make sure you fully understand the royalty arrangement. If you co-own a business, make sure the terms of a buy-sell agreement among owners protect you and your family.

▶ **Home-improvement contracts.** You can inadvertently jeopardize your home if you don't understand the fine print in home-improvement contracts. For example, the contractor may place liens on your home unless the contract contains a lien release or lien waiver before any work is started.

▶ **Leases.** While landlords generally use standard lease agreements, there may be additional conditions on your lease. For example, the lease may shift to you the burden of making repairs, such as fixing a leaky pipe.

▶ **Premarital or postmarital agreements.** Make sure your attorney reviews the agreement from your perspective, especially if it was your partner's idea to have such an agreement in the first place. These agreements are discussed on the preceding page.

▶ **Real estate contracts for purchasing a home or other property.** Terms and conditions of real estate purchases are critical, so make certain you don't agree to things you didn't intend (for example, waiving the right to inspection or conditioning the closing on obtaining a mortgage).

Even after you've signed certain contracts, it may be possible to get out of any obligations you agreed to. Certain contracts are subject to "cooling off" periods—generally three days, but sometimes longer—in which you can cancel the contract without penalty. Contracts subject to this opportunity for review include:

▶ **Mortgage refinancing.** Even if you sign all the contracts at closing, you can still cancel within the cooling-off period. You can't accelerate the refinancing by waiving the cooling off period; by law the mortgagor (bank or finance company) can't give you the money before the cooling-off period has expired.

▶ **Personal contracts for health-club memberships,** dance lessons, dating referrals and weight loss programs. Cooling-off periods for these contracts are discussed in Chapter 21.

LOST OR STOLEN CREDIT CARDS

If your credit cards are lost or stolen, what's your legal liability for any charges that are made? Under law, you can be held liable only for $50 in unauthorized charges. Once you notify the credit card company, there's no further liability.

Caution: There's no dollar limit for losses on stolen or lost debit cards. Your accounts can be wiped out if someone obtains and uses your cards before you can cancel them.

> *Strategy: Photocopy every card in your wallet and note its toll-free number in case the card is lost or stolen. Keep this record at home. If you need to, you'll be able to contact every credit card company immediately.*

Credit card protection: You can carry special protection—a type of insurance—against unauthorized purchases. The cost for this protection is about $12 to $15 annually. From a financial standpoint it doesn't pay to carry the coverage, because your maximum exposure is only $50 per card.

But you can gain an important benefit from such coverage—freedom from the inconvenience of reporting each separate card loss. In case of loss, you make one phone call to the credit card protection company. And it can be an important protection for debit cards if the insurance extends to these cards. *Another benefit:* Emergency cash advances when you're away from home.

IDENTITY THEFT

What happens if you become one of the more than 8.9 million people (in 2006) who are victimized by this crime, the fastest growing crime in America, according to the Federal Trade Commission (FTC)? Like most victims, you'll probably spend about 40 hours and about $1,200 to clear your name. But you may be able to obtain some financial protection.

Credit monitoring services

A credit monitoring service alerts you within 24 hours of any changes to your credit file (for example, someone has made an application for a new credit card under your name). The annual cost for this service ranges from $40 to $120. Identity Fraud Inc. (**www.identityfraud.com**). Indentity Guard (**www.identityguard.com**). Privacy Guard (**www.privacyguard.com**). True Credit (**www.truecredit.com**).

Insurance

Purchase identity theft insurance—a new type of policy that helps victims with the cost of restoring their good name and credit. The insurance, which is usually just an add-on to your homeowner's policy, pays for the cost of fixing credit records, lost wages for time away from work to talk with credit bureaus and investigators, long-distance phone calls, attorney fees and other costs. Premiums for $15,000 of coverage with a $100 deductible range from $15 to $30 per year. American International Group (**www.aig.com**). Chubb Group of Insurance Cos. (**www.chubb.com**). Encompass Insurance (**www.encompassinsurance.com**). Farmers Group, Inc. (**www.farmers.com**). Travelers Property Casualty Corp. (**www.travelers.com**).

Note: Identity theft coverage is not currently available in all states.

FDIC PROTECTION FOR YOUR BANK ACCOUNTS

When a number of banks failed in the 1980s, depositors became acutely aware of protection—or lack of protection—for their accounts. Insurance-like protection is provided by the Federal Deposit Insurance Corporation (FDIC), a government agency formed to safeguard the deposits of member banks that go under (**www.fdic.gov**, 877-275-3342). Today, the FDIC has nearly $96 billion in reserves to cover accounts eligible in case of bank failure.

What's covered?

Federal deposit insurance covers deposits *only* in member banks—financial institutions that display an FDIC logo. If the bank is covered, all types of accounts within the bank, including savings, checking, NOW accounts, CDs and Christmas clubs, have protection. *Caution:* Not all online banks carry FDIC protection for depositors. Ask before transferring funds into online accounts—or at least understand your risk if you decide to transfer to an uninsured online bank.

What's not covered?

If you buy Treasuries through your bank, they're not FDIC insured, but they do remain your property if a bank goes under. You'll have to go through channels to recover them. The FDIC becomes a receiver for the bank and you present a receipt for the Treasuries to reclaim them or wait until they mature to receive the proceeds.

If you purchase stocks or bonds through a broker associated with the bank, your securities don't have FDIC protection. But they may have SIPC protection, discussed later in this chapter.

If two banking institutions merge, your accounts at each institution retain separate coverage—but only for six months after the merger. Certificates of deposit, however, continue separate coverage until their earliest maturity.

Limits

The basic limit for FDIC protection is $100,000 per depositor. Certain retirement accounts have protection up to $250,000. (The same protection limits apply to depositors in credit unions through NCUA, which is the National Credit Union Administration, a US Government agency.) You can't increase your limit by dividing your funds into different accounts within the same bank or using different branches of the same bank. However, deposits in separate categories of legal ownership enjoy separate insurance. Categories of ownership include:

▶ **Single accounts.** Custodial accounts under the Uniform Gifts to Minors Act or the Uniform Transfers to Minors Act are considered accounts of the minor, not the custodian.

▶ **Joint accounts,** as long as each owner has equal rights of withdrawal and has separately signed a deposit account signature card. Each owner is considered to have an equal share of the account, regardless of whose Social Security number appears on the account. *Note:* Community property law doesn't affect FDIC insurance, so an account in the sole name of one spouse is in the single account category even though the other spouse may have an interest in the account under state community property law.

▶ **Testamentary accounts** that show an intention to be passed on automatically at the death of the account owner. The beneficiary must be a certain relative—spouse, parent, sibling, child or grandchild of the account owner—and designated on the account. If so, then each beneficiary has full FDIC protection. Beneficiaries are deemed to have equal interests in the account. Each owner is insured up to the limit for *each* beneficiary of the account. *Examples:* Totten trust accounts, revocable trust accounts or "payable-on-death" accounts. You'll know if you have a testamentary account by the designations ITF, ATF or POD on your account statements or passbook.

> **Example:** One family, consisting of a husband, wife and three children—five people—can enjoy $800,000 of FDIC protection for their deposits:

▶ **Health savings accounts (HSAs),** which are tax-sanctioned accounts for medical savings, are treated the same as any personal account for FDIC purposes.

Account title	Amount deposited
Husband in trust for wife	$100,000
Wife in trust for husband	100,000
Husband and wife in trust for their three children	600,000
TOTAL	$800,000

If the beneficiary is other than one of the specified relatives, the account is treated as a single-ownership account of the depositor.

► **Irrevocable trusts.** Each beneficiary enjoys up to $100,000 in protection. This protection is separate from single-account or other category protection each beneficiary may enjoy.

► **Retirement accounts**—self-directed retirement accounts, such as IRAs, SEPs and other Keogh plans, have a $250,000 protection limit. IRAs and self-directed retirement plans are added together and treated as one category. For example, a self-employed individual with an IRA and a profit-sharing plan must add the balances for purposes of the $250,000 limit. Only IRA and Keogh time deposits made before December 19, 1993, are treated separately. Retirement plans generally receive "pass-through" coverage—each plan participant can enjoy up to the $250,000 limit. *Note:* Roth IRAs are treated the same way as traditional IRAs. Coverdell education savings accounts (formerly Education IRAs) are not treated like IRAs but rather as irrevocable trust accounts.

Deposits at different branches of the same bank are combined for purposes of determining your limits. But accounts at separate banks aren't added together for purposes of these limits. You can have the full coverage for accounts at each bank.

Calculating your limits online: You can figure your FDIC protection online using the Electronic Deposit Insurance Estimator (EDIE) at **www2.fdic.gov/edie.** You enter certain account information—what's on deposit and under whose name (not account numbers)—and then click on the calculator to find your limits.

Banking problems

If you have problems about your account that you can't resolve through your bank, contact your state's banking commissioner for assistance.

SIPC PROTECTION FOR YOUR SECURITIES ACCOUNTS

If you keep your stocks and bonds in "street name"—in other words, if you deposit your securities with a brokerage firm—what protection do you have if your broker absconds or if the firm goes out of business? The Securities Investor Protection Corporation (SIPC) is a nonprofit organization that provides insurance protection for customers of broker-dealers (brokerage firms) who are members of SIPC **(www.sipc.org).** Don't assume that your account is fully insured for all losses you may sustain.

What's covered?

If the firm that holds your account goes under, you receive all securities registered in your name plus a pro rata share of customer cash and securities held by the firm. In addition, you receive a maximum of $500,000 (including up to $100,000 for cash) to make you whole. Securities include stocks, bonds, mutual funds, certificates of deposit, notes and other interests registered with the Securities and Exchange Commission.

> **Example 1:** You own 10 different stocks held in street name worth $150,000, plus cash of $20,000. If the firm is a member of SIPC and fails, you'll receive cash of $170,000 (or a portion in securities).

> **Example 2:** Same as above, except your securities are worth $430,000, plus cash of $100,000. You'll receive $500,000 ($400,000 for the securities plus $100,000 for the cash). You'll lose $30,000 worth of securities.

Example 3: Same as above, except your securities are worth $560,000, plus cash of $150,000. You'll receive $500,000 ($400,000 for the securities plus $100,000 for the cash). You'll lose $210,000 ($160,000 for excess securities, plus $50,000 for excess cash).

If you have more than one account with the same firm, each account may enjoy protection up to the $500,000/$100,000 limits. Thus, if you have one account in your name and one with a spouse, each account is fully insured as long as each joint owner has authority to act with respect to the whole account. *Note:* Most brokerage firms carry insurance for your account far in excess of the SIPC limit—usually $10 million or more.

What's not covered?

If your account declines in value because of market fluctuations, you can't claim SIPC protection. That's a market risk not covered by SIPC.

Some investments made through a brokerage firm may not be covered by SIPC. For example, investment contracts that are not registered with the Securities and Exchange Commission aren't covered. This may include limited partnerships for real estate or oil and gas ventures.

Not all companies selling securities are covered by SIPC. The firm must be a member of SIPC; look for the SIPC symbol, which is similar to the FDIC logo. Mutual fund shares held by companies that exclusively sell mutual funds may not be members of SIPC, so these investments aren't protected if the mutual fund goes bad.

Caution: SIPC insurance won't protect you if your brokerage firm doesn't pay SIPC premiums. So even if a broker claims to have SIPC coverage for your account, don't assume this to be true.

POWERS OF ATTORNEY

Who's going to handle your money in case of disability or incompetence? Perhaps the simplest and least costly way to handle this contingency is a durable power of attorney. This document authorizes another person, called your agent or attorney-in-fact, to handle your financial affairs.

Who should be your agent?

Make sure the person you name is someone with two key qualities:

► **Financial savvy**

► **Trustworthiness**

Your agent will have virtually full authority over your investments, bank accounts and other assets. There are no checks or balances on what your agent does. If he makes errors in judgment or absconds with your funds, you may simply be out the money.

Usually a spouse empowers the other spouse to act as agent. This enables the spouse to sell a jointly owned home, file a joint tax return, file for retirement benefits on behalf of the incapacitated spouse and make other financial decisions.

Another obvious choice for agent is an adult child. If there are two or more children, you can have more than one agent. You can require that the agents act together, agreeing on any financial decision. Or you can empower each to act alone, so that one handles your banking, for instance, while the other makes investment decisions.

You can also name two agents outside the family to act singly (severally) or jointly on your behalf. It may be helpful to require joint action if there's any concern about competence or trustworthiness but you don't have another person who can act on your behalf.

 Strategy: *Name an alternate agent in the event that your first selection is unable to serve. For example, if you name your spouse but he or she is injured in a car accident with you, you'll want another person authorized to act.*

Scope of authority

What do you want your agent to do? If you want the broadest possible authorization, you must say so. In addition to the standard powers included in preprinted power of attorney forms, consider whether you want your agent to have the following authority:

▶ **Gift giving.** If you want your agent to be able to make gifts, be clear on the extent of this power. The power can be unlimited, meaning your agent can do whatever you would do if you were able to act. Or it can be limited by a benchmark, such as the annual gift tax exclusion, and to a certain class of people, such as your immediate family.

▶ **Retirement plans.** State whether you want your agent to make certain decisions relating to your accounts—naming beneficiaries, taking distributions, etc.

▶ **Tax matters.** Empower your agent to deal with the IRS and state tax authorities to sign tax returns, request refunds and challenge IRS audits.

Decide on payment

Usually if a family member or close friend acts as your agent, there's no payment for their services. But if your accountant or attorney handles your money, you'll probably pay professional fees. Agree in advance what this professional will charge—it generally shouldn't be the same as the hourly rate charged for regular professional services.

TRUSTS FOR ASSET MANAGEMENT

Trusts can be used for many different purposes. One of the key purposes is to have a financial management system. One easy way to create this system is with a revocable trust, often called a living trust because you set it up while you're alive and keep the right to recover the assets in the trust at any time.

Who should be your trustee?

You can serve as trustee of your living trust until such time as you become incapacitated or simply want to turn the job over to someone else. The party you name as your successor trustee should have two key qualities:

▶ **Financial savvy** to manage the assets you transfer into the trust. The more complicated the assets (for example, investment real estate), the more sophisticated your trustee needs to be.

▶ **Trustworthiness,** so assets are protected. You're giving your agent virtually unfettered authority over your investments, bank accounts and other assets. There may be no checks or balances on the actions of your agent. If he or she makes errors in judgment or absconds with your funds, you may simply be out the money.

 Strategy: *To check on the trustee's actions, require your trustee to provide an annual accounting to a court. It's a costly process, for which the trust pays, and generally makes sense only for large trusts.*

Usually a spouse empowers the other spouse to act as trustee, especially if the trust contains joint assets. This will enable the spouse to sell the assets titled to the trust.

Another obvious choice for your successor trustee is an adult child. If you have two or more children, you can have more than one trustee. Or you can use a trust department in a bank. Make sure the party you want to act as your trustee is willing to do so. Trust departments may have minimum asset requirements before they'll agree to act. If your trust is small, they may not be willing.

 Strategy: *Name an alternate trustee to act if your first selection can't do the job. Your trust may run for many years, and you want to be sure that there will be someone you're comfortable with at the helm.*

Consider naming two successor trustees. You can permit them to act alone, so either one can make decisions for the trust. Or you can require joint action for some or all decisions, a protection against a single trustee's mismanaging or otherwise draining the trust.

Decide on payment

State law provides a statutory fee schedule for trustees. The amount of the fees depends on the size of the trust. Usually if you have a family member or close friend act as your trustee, he or she will waive any fees. But if you have your accountant, attorney or a trust department act as trustee, they'll take the statutory rate unless you negotiate a reduced fee in advance.

 Strategy: *Coordinate your trust with your power of attorney. Clarify when your agent can act, and with respect to which of your assets, to avoid conflict with your trustee. Your agent and trustee can be the same person. Each is a fiduciary who must act according to his charge—the terms of your power of attorney or the language in your trust document.*

ASSET PROTECTION

Assets generally can be reached by creditors to satisfy debts, including any monetary judgments against you. But there are some assets that enjoy special protection. And there are some strategies you can follow to gain protection where you lack insurance or other measures of protection.

Protection for your assets can be achieved if the assets are no longer in your name—that is, if you transfer title to your assets. However, transfers to family members as gifts can be challenged as fraudulent—made solely to defraud creditors. Generally, if such transfers are made *after* there is a creditor claim—for example, after a lawsuit has been filed against you—then the transfer can be set aside so that assets are no longer protected. Thus, the key to asset transfers intended for asset protection is timing—the longer the time between the transfer and any claim against you, the more protected your assets will be from challenges.

Homestead protection

Those who live in Florida and Texas can protect fully their home from creditors' claims. Most other states, however, have only limited protection for personal residences. Under the 2005 federal bankruptcy law, no more than $125,000 of a homestead exemption can be claimed unless the debtor has resided in the state for at least 40 months prior to filing for bankruptcy.

 Strategy: *Apply for homestead protection if you move to Florida and intend to make it your domicile.*

Business interests

Make sure to protect your personal assets from the claims of business creditors. Special business entities limit creditors' claims to the assets of the business. You can achieve this protection by forming:

▶ **Corporations.** Whether your corporation is a regular C corporation or an S corporation that has elected pass-through tax treatment, all corporations offer protection from personal liability.

▶ **Limited liability companies (LLCs)**, special business entities formed under state law. All states and the District of Columbia allow one-person LLCs, so even if you're in business by yourself, you can achieve personal liability protection with an LLC.

Caution: You may become personally liable for your company's debts, regardless of its form of business organization, if you personally guarantee its debts. For example, if you obtain a business loan, you may be required to give your personal guarantee unless the business has assets sufficient to secure the loan.

Retirement benefits

Are IRAs and qualified plans benefits protected from the claims of creditors? If you get into financial trouble and lose your shirt, you may still be able to retain your hard-earned retirement benefits, even if you're forced into bankruptcy. Under the 2005 federal bankruptcy law, all funds in company retirement plans and rollover IRAs are protected in bankruptcy. However, contributory IRAs, including Roth IRAs, have protection only up to $1 million.

Education savings

Funds in Coverdell education savings accounts and 529 plans are usually fully exempt in the case of bankruptcy. However, contributions to such savings plans between 365 and 720 days prior to filing for bankruptcy are exempt only up to $5,000 per beneficiary—there is no protection for contributions made within one year of filing for bankruptcy.

Medicaid planning

The cost of long-term nursing home care is high, now averaging more than $70,000 annually and more than $140,000 in some localities. It's going higher every year. Elderly individuals with chronic illnesses, such as Alzheimer's disease, may be forced for health reasons into a nursing home, but Medicare and Medigap policies don't cover the cost of this long-term care. Except for the very wealthy who can afford nursing home costs or the moderately well-off who can afford to pay premiums on long-term care-policies that cover nursing home costs, these seniors may have to use up assets they've accumulated over a lifetime.

If assets (resources) fall below levels set by federal and state rules and income does not exceed set limits, these seniors can have their nursing home costs picked up by Medicaid, a joint federal and state program for those in need. Also, with some planning, assets can be transferred—and preserved for family members—without causing any loss of Medicaid eligibility. Generally, asset transfers must occur more than 60 months prior to making a Medicaid application.

 Strategy: *Consult an elder law attorney before there's any immediate need for nursing home care. For example, on the first signs of any chronic illnesses or conditions, it may be time to explore asset transfers as part of Medicaid planning.*

Asset protection through offshore accounts

Moving money offshore can provide protection from the claims of creditors. Certain places, including Switzerland, the Cayman Islands and the Cook Islands, are well known as tax havens because their laws generally protect foreign depositors from enforcement of US judgments.

Advantage:

▶ **Asset protection.** The main reason to have an offshore account is to protect your money from creditor claims.

Disadvantages:

▶ **Costs.** There may be sizable costs—more than $15,000—to set up and administer offshore trusts and accounts.

▶ **Investment returns.** You may not necessarily receive the same interest or other returns on your offshore funds that you could obtain for domestic investments.

▶ **Political risks.** While many tax havens have usually been stable, there's always a risk of a change in the political climate that could adversely affect deposits.

Note: If you have an offshore account with more than $10,000, you're *required* to inform the IRS and, in some situations, file additional returns.

In addition to the disadvantages listed above, also keep in mind that foreign accounts aren't necessarily creditor-proof. Here are some shortcomings to consider:

▶ **In some locations, trusts set up for yourself aren't necessarily judgment-proof.** Only trusts set up for someone else have this protection.

▶ **US courts can compel you to return offshore assets under certain circumstances,** and you would be subject to contempt penalties if you don't comply.

▶ **There may be minimum deposit requirements.** Even if you *want* to use an offshore account, you may not have enough assets to do it.

US alternatives to offshore accounts: Certain states, including Alaska, Delaware, Nevada, Rhode Island and Utah, have created special trust laws designed to provide asset protection without requiring you to go out of the country. For example, the so-called Alaska trust can be used not only for estate planning purposes to remove assets from one's estate, but also for asset protection purposes. You need a minimum of $10,000 in an Alaska bank and must use an Alaska trustee, such as an Alaska trust company. The Alaska trust is an irrevocable trust that enables the creator of the trust to be eligible for distributions, but creditors of the creator can't get at assets in the trust. *Caution:* The laws on these trusts are new so they're still untested.

IRS RELIEF

If you get into trouble with the IRS—you can't pay your tax bill, for instance, or you fail to file a return—don't ignore the problem. It will only get worse. Communication with the government is the best way to resolve problems and control costs for penalties and interest.

 Strategy: *Consult a tax professional when problems arise. Then the problems can be addressed promptly and in the most advantageous manner.*

If you get into tax trouble, you may find a way out by means of special relief provisions.

Innocent spouse rules

Married couples who file joint returns are jointly and severally liable for the tax, interest and penalties relating to those returns. This means the IRS can come after either spouse for the full amount. But one spouse may be responsible for underreporting income or overstating deductions on a return and the other spouse may be unaware of this situation. Since it would be unfair to make the "innocent spouse" pay the other spouse's taxes, there are several avenues of relief:

▶ **General innocent spouse relief.** This is available when an underpayment results from income omissions or overstated deductions by one spouse and the other spouse had no knowledge of it.

▶ **Separate liability for partial relief.** The liability is apportioned on the basis of each spouse's share of income and deductions. This relief is available only if the couple is divorced or separated or has lived apart for at least 12 months prior to the request for relief.

▶ **Equitable relief**—when one spouse is not eligible for either of the two other relief provisions but it would be unfair to hold that spouse liable for the tax. Unfairness exists when the couple is divorced or separated or hasn't lived together for at least 12 months, the innocent spouse had no knowledge of the tax due and holding the spouse liable would impose an economic hardship.

Requesting relief: Generally, a taxpayer has two years to request innocent spouse relief. The two-year period is measured from the date the IRS first notifies the taxpayer of collection activities relating to a joint return.

 Strategy: *In thinking about divorce agreements, consider including tax clauses that specify responsibility for the payment of tax by one or both parties. Such a clause does not bind the IRS or require it to go after the responsible spouse. But, the spouse will have a cause of legal action if he or she is held liable for the other spouse's share.*

Installment payment agreements

Like financing a car or other expensive item, the IRS lets taxpayers pay their taxes in installments if certain requirements are met. But paying taxes over time doesn't eliminate interest charges and late-payment penalties. It's shrewd to pay as much as possible as soon as possible to keep these costs down.

How to obtain an installment agreement depends on how much is owed:

▶ **If the amount owed is no more than $10,000,** a taxpayer is automatically eligible for an installment payment arrangement. The taxpayer has to make repayment within three years and meet other requirements.

▶ **If the amount owed is more than $10,000 but not more than $25,000,** the IRS has a streamlined procedure for obtaining an installment agreement. The grant is not automatic, but the IRS isn't too strict in allowing such agreements. The taxpayer has to make repayment within five years.

▶ **If the amount owed is more than $25,000,** a taxpayer must make a formal request and demonstrate a valid reason why there's a need to pay over time. The IRS *may* grant the request—all terms of the agreement can be negotiated. In 1999, the last year for which statistics were available, 62% of all installment agreement requests were granted.

Cost: There's a $105 fee for obtaining an installment payment agreement ($52 if payments are to be debited from the taxpayer's bank account). It's not paid separately; the IRS simply adds it into the repayment amount.

Offers in compromise

If a taxpayer believes that he'll never be able to fully pay his taxes at any time, and he wants to keep the IRS from seizing his property, the IRS may agree to settle his tax debt for pennies on the dollar. Generally, a taxpayer must show an economic hardship to qualify for this settlement—for example, he'll need to show that he can no longer earn a living because of a long-term medical condition or that his assets can't pay both his taxes and his basic living expenses.

A taxpayer must request an offer in compromise—it's not automatic—by proposing the amount he would be able to pay in a lump sum or in installments. The taxpayer must provide the reason why he can't pay and detailed financial information listing his income and assets. And he must pay a $150 fee for making an offer. In addition to the fee, offers must be accompanied by partial payment, which is nonrefundable: 20% for a lump-sum offer and all proposed installments for an installment payment offer.

 Strategy: *Before making an offer, see if it is "processable" by completing a worksheet in IRS Publication 656, Offer in Compromise at **www.irs.gov**.*

Resolving problems

If you have a tax problem that you can't resolve on your own, you may be able to get the IRS to help you.

If a problem has reached crisis proportions—the IRS is about to foreclose on your home, seize your bank account or garnish your wages in error—ask the Taxpayer Advocate for emergency help (find your local advocate by calling 877-777-4778). To stop the IRS's activity, file Form 911, *Application for Taxpayer Assistance Order*, downloadable from **www.irs.gov**.

BANKRUPTCY AS A LAST RESORT

For individuals facing severe financial difficulties, bankruptcy may be the only way to obtain a fresh start. Financial troubles develop due to a variety of reasons:

▶ **Personal problems**—illness or accident, unemployment, divorce and, commonly, excessive debts or spending.

▶ **Charitable and civic liabilities**—volunteering as a board member or trustee of a homeowner's association, political action group, religious group or other charitable organization.

▶ **Business problems.** Professional malpractice suits can wipe out a professional's life savings in an instant. Similarly, sole proprietors have complete exposure for actions arising from their business.

Strategy: *Have adequate insurance to protect yourself from bankruptcy. Before accepting a position on a board, check its directors and officers (D&O) liability coverage. If you're a professional—doctor, lawyer, engineer, architect—carry malpractice insurance. If you're a sole proprietor, consider incorporating or forming a limited liability company to obtain protection from personal liability.*

An individual who is unable to work his way out of debt even after credit counseling services (discussed in Chapter 16) may need to consider bankruptcy. Filing a petition will cease all collection actions by creditors, giving a person time to resolve debt problems. Filing the petition also stops any garnishment orders already in effect. Filing for bankruptcy can also reduce the amount of tax you owe. In a debt adjustment plan you can stop interest and penalties on all taxes you owe—even the ones that are non-dischargeable, making it easier to pay off your taxes.

Bankruptcy is a complex procedure that is now governed by the Bankruptcy Abuse Prevention and Consumer Protection Act of 2005. The bankruptcy process is started by filing a bankruptcy petition in federal court. There are two basic types of bankruptcy proceedings:

▶ **Repayment plan under Chapter 13 of the bankruptcy law.** Most individuals with a steady income must repay creditors using a structured repayment plan over a period of five years. At the end of the repayment plan, some, but not all, debts are discharged. Before seeking bankruptcy protection, consumers usually must obtain credit counseling.

▶ **"Fresh start" under Chapter 7 of the bankruptcy law.** A liquidation of a person's assets to give a fresh start is now possible only for those who meet a "means" test, which is a comparison of the debtor's income to the median income in the state in which the individual lives. Eligibility under Chapter 7 is stringent, so most consumers must use Chapter 13 relief (special rules apply to farmers, business owners and those in the military).

Bankruptcy does *not* end all of a person's debts. Nondischargeable debts include:

▶ **Alimony** (maintenance). **Note:** Bankruptcy can wipe out obligations in property settlements.

▶ **Bills incurred for luxury items.**

▶ **Child support.**

▶ **Debts arising from certain intentional actions**—drunken driving, fraud, malicious injury.

▶ **Federal and state income taxes.**

▶ **Secured loans.**

▶ **Student loans.**

Costs: Bankruptcy isn't free. There's a court filing fee to start the proceedings. A person seeking bankruptcy relief should consider hiring a lawyer for representation—an advisable strategy considering what's involved. And the court-appointed trustee who oversees the bankruptcy receives a statutory fee for his or her services, about 10% of the amount paid to creditors under a repayment plan.

24

Year-end planning

> **"***I'll work on a new and original plan.***"**

—W.S. GILBERT

FINANCIAL PLANNING isn't a onetime exercise. It requires constant monitoring of your investment performance and periodic changes to your goals and strategies. Regular reviews—perhaps monthly or quarterly—are certainly advisable. But be absolutely sure to conduct year-end examinations of your investments, taxes and other financial positions. This will enable you to make last-minute changes to reposition investments, save on taxes and have a long-range view of your financial position.

Year-end planning involves strategies for optimizing your tax situation for the current year and positioning yourself for more favorable investments and tax savings in the future.

Many of the ideas and strategies in this chapter have been mentioned elsewhere in this book. However, this chapter emphasizes the importance of annual reviews. It discusses investment decisions to consider before the close of the year, from both an investment and a tax perspective. It also discusses general year-end strategies for reducing current taxes and saving on taxes in the future. Tax strategies include those for your personal return as well as your business return.

IMPORTANCE OF YEAR-END PLANNING

Year-end planning is important from a financial and tax perspective. It gives the opportunity to modify your financial plans in light of market changes, your personal situation, tax law changes and other developments. It also lets you take steps to reduce current taxes.

You may have developed a routine for annual year-end planning, making the same decisions every year if they've worked for you. But, it's a shrewd move to start fresh each year so you don't overlook new opportunities.

 Strategy: *Plan a year-end visit with your financial professional—planner, accountant, broker, etc.—to review your financial position with someone who can offer advice. There may be new information about investment products, tax law changes or trends in the marketplace.*

Use this checklist to flag the need for year-end planning that will affect your present and future financial situation. Do comprehensive planning if any of the following situations applies to you now or will apply to you in the future:

Year-end planning checklist

Personal situation:

Did you get married? _____

Did you get divorced? _____

Did your spouse die? _____

Did you have a child (or adopt a child)? _____

Did your child move out of your home? Move back in? _____

Is your child going to private school? College? Graduate school? _____

Did you relocate? _____

Did you buy or sell a home? _____

Did you make charitable contributions? _____

Did you or a family member (spouse, child or parent) have health issues? _____

Work-related:

Did you (or your spouse) start working? _____

Did you (or your spouse) retire or get laid off? _____

Did you receive a big raise or a bonus? _____

Did new employee benefits become available to you? _____

Did you participate in a retirement plan? _____

Investment-related:

Did you buy or sell securities? _____

Did any of your investments become worthless (or did any loans you made go bad)? _____

Did you make other investments (real estate, collectibles)? _____

Did any of your CDs, bonds or Treasuries mature? _____

Steps in year-end planning

Year-end planning is a multifaceted task. You need to consider *all* aspects of your financial picture:

▶ **Review your insurance coverage.** For example, you may need to adjust the coverage on your home or want to eliminate collision coverage on your car. You may want to increase your life insurance coverage or drop it entirely. You may want to boost your disability coverage if your income has increased. Insurance coverage is discussed in Chapter 4.

▶ **Analyze your debt.** Look for ways to reduce or eliminate it. *Caution:* Watch out for holiday purchases that can insidiously boost your credit card debt. Debt reduction strategies are discussed in Chapter 16.

▶ **Review your investments.** You may want to change your portfolio holdings.

▶ **Review your taxes.** You may want to act now to minimize your taxes for the year, putting you in a better tax position for the coming year, especially in light of tax changes. For example, you may want to sell certain investments for tax results. Or you may want to make year-end charitable contributions to boost your itemized deductions. These strategies are discussed later in this chapter.

PORTFOLIO INVESTMENT STRATEGIES

Review your asset allocation goals. How much of your assets did you plan to hold in equities? In fixed income? In cash? Compare your year-end position with your goals to see how they match up.

▶ **If your portfolio is out of alignment,** consider selling some assets to get your allocation back in line. Keep tax results in mind in taking gains or losses (discussed below).

 Strategy: Rebalance your portfolio by directing new investments into the portion of your portfolio below its asset allocation target. For example, if you wanted to have 60% of your assets in equities and 40% in fixed income but your year-end holdings are $80,000 in equities and $40,000 in fixed income, your actual asset allocation is 67% in equities and 33% in fixed income. To rebalance, you can add $10,000 to your fixed income, putting your portfolio back to roughly a 60/40 allocation.

▶ **Even if your portfolio is within your targeted asset allocation,** you may want to alter that allocation in light of changes in your personal financial picture or in the market. For example, you may have taken an aggressive 80% equity/20% fixed income approach in the past few years. But with changes in the stock market, you might now wish to modify your asset allocation to 60/40 or some other mix.

Mutual funds

Watch purchases late in the year. While you may be investing in a good fund, you may be buying a tax liability. A fund may pay year-end distributions to shareholders of record on a particular date (usually in November). You'll pay tax on the fund's full-year capital gains distribution even if you held the fund for only a few weeks, as long as you are a shareholder on the fund's record date. The price of a fund generally drops following the record date, usually by an amount reflecting the distribution, so by waiting until after the record date to buy you'll pick up shares at a more favorable price and avoid a tax cost.

 Strategy: If you hold the fund in your personal account, call the fund manager or check the fund's Web site to find that critical record date. This isn't necessary if the fund is in a tax-deferred account such as an IRA. Don't wait until the record date to buy the fund if you believe the price of the shares may rise substantially in the interim.

PORTFOLIO TAX STRATEGIES

You may have already taken gains and losses on securities transactions during the year. You may also be sitting on other potential gains and losses, paper gains and losses that you can actualize before year-end. By reviewing both paper and actualized transactions, you can act to reduce taxes and reposition your portfolio in light of changing investment philosophies and market conditions.

To optimize your tax position for the year, understand key rules on capital gains and losses. These rules are explained in detail in Chapter 5. Here's a review of some key points you should keep in mind when reviewing year-end securities transactions:

▶ **Long-term capital gains**—gains on securities held more than one year—receive favorable tax treatment. The top tax rate generally is 15% (5% for those in the 10% or 15% tax bracket in 2007 and zero in 2008 through 2010).

▶ **Short-term capital gains**—gains on assets held one year or less—are taxed at the same rate as your ordinary income up to 35%.

▶ **Capital losses** can be used to offset capital gains, plus up to $3,000 of ordinary income. Losses in excess of these limits can be carried forward and used—up to these limits—in future years.

▶ **Losses cannot be taken** if substantially identical securities are purchased within 30 days before or after the date of sale.

Use the worksheet on the following page to lay out your transactions to date. This will help you determine whether you're in an overall gain or loss position. In preparing your worksheet, include:

▶ **Capital gains distributions from mutual funds** as long-term capital gains, regardless of how long you've owned the funds. Call the fund manager or check the fund's Web site to determine capital gains distributions that will be paid this year.

▶ **Your share of capital gains and losses** from pass-through entities, such as partnerships, S corporations or trusts, in which you have an interest. Unfortunately, your statements may not be available before year-end and you won't be able to factor these gains and losses into your tax picture.

▶ **Bad debts from nonbusiness loans.** These are automatically treated as short-term capital losses, no matter how long the loan was outstanding.

▶ **Capital loss carryovers from last year.** Short-term losses from last year are carried forward as short-term losses, and long-term losses from last year are carried over as long-term losses. Look at your tax return for last year to remind yourself of any carryovers.

Note: Keep in mind that the tax treatment of gains and losses from securities may be affected by gains (or losses) in other assets, including collectibles and unrealized depreciation on real estate.

After you complete the worksheet, review your paper gains and losses to see which ones you want to take to improve your tax position.

Worksheet for gains and losses on your securities transactions
Actualized short-term transactions

Description	Date acquired	Date sold	Cost (basis)	Sale price	Gain (loss)
			$	$	$
Nonbusiness bad debts					$
Short-term gains (or losses) from pass-through entities					$
Short-term loss carryover					$
TOTAL SHORT-TERM GAINS (OR LOSSES)					$

Actualized long-term transactions

Description	Date acquired	Date sold	Cost (basis)	Sale price	Gain (loss)
			$	$	$
Capital gains distributions					$
Long-term gains (or losses) from pass-through entities					$
Long-term loss carryover					$
TOTAL LONG-TERM GAINS (OR LOSSES)					$

Tentative gain (or loss) position

Short-term gains (or losses) $ _____

Long-term gains (or losses) $ _____

Net short-term or long-term gains (or losses) $ _____

Strategies for optimizing gains and losses

Is your net gain a short-term capital gain or a long-term capital gain? Is your net loss a short-term capital loss or a long-term capital loss?

▶ **If short-term gains exceed long-term gains,** take losses (short-term or long-term) to offset your gain (to prevent such gains from being taxed at ordinary income rates). Short-term losses first offset short-term capital gains and then can be used to offset long-term capital gains. Similarly, long-term losses first offset long-term capital gains and then can be used to offset short-term capital gains.

▶ **If long-term gains exceed short-term gains,** you have net long-term gains taxed at up to 15%. You can opt to report your gains at this favorable tax rate or offset gains by taking capital losses.

▶ **If you have net short-term or long-term losses,** offset them by any type of capital gains (but preferably short-term gains otherwise taxed at ordinary income rates), leaving $3,000 of losses to be used to offset ordinary income. If your capital losses exceed your capital gains plus $3,000 of ordinary income, the excess can be carried forward and treated as a capital loss—short-term or long-term—next year.

 Strategy: *Put investment opportunities before tax considerations. Don't let tax results drive your investment decisions. Keep the settlement date in mind when you take gains and losses. For gain purposes, you must sell at least three days before the final trading day of the year. For loss purposes, you can sell up to the last day of the year.*

Update basis records

As part of your year-end portfolio planning, update your records on the basis of stocks and mutual fund shares to reflect dividends and other distributions invested during the year. Your failure to make a basis adjustment can cause you to pay tax twice on the same money—once when you receive the distribution and a second time when you sell the stock or mutual fund shares and report more gain than necessary. Record-keeping methods are discussed in Chapter 21.

Reposition investments for tax impact

Use the proceeds from year-end securities sales to reposition your holdings not only for better returns but also for greater control over taxes in future years. Consider:

▶ **Investing in tax-efficient mutual funds.** This will minimize annual distributions that are reported as taxable income each year.

▶ **Buying municipal bonds for tax-free interest.**

▶ **Buying non-dividend-paying stocks that aim for appreciation.**
In this way, you report profits only when you sell your shares.

INCOME (AND DEDUCTION) STRATEGIES FOR PERSONAL RETURNS

You have *some* control over the income and expenses you have to report for the year. While many items occur automatically, others can be either kept in the current year or postponed to next year, whichever will prove more advantageous to you tax-wise.

Income strategies

As a general rule, you probably want to defer income to a future year if at all possible to postpone income tax and possibly produce other benefits. Deferral is an effective strategy if you are in a tax bracket above 15% since income deferred will be subject to a lower tax rate.

Don't *automatically* adopt a deferral approach. Look at your individual tax picture. Maybe your income this year is modest and you anticipate climbing into a higher tax bracket next year (for example, perhaps your nonworking spouse will be returning to the job market next year).

If you anticipate a year-end bonus, you may be able to arrange to receive it as deferred compensation. This postpones having to report the income in the year you earned it. And if your salary is already at the top wage base for Social Security purposes ($97,500 in 2007), then you'll save on these taxes as well. Deferred compensation is subject to FICA (Social Security and Medicare taxes) in the year you *earn* the income, not the year in which you receive it.

> **Example:** In 2007, when your regular compensation is $100,000, you also receive a $10,000 bonus. Since you've already paid your Social Security tax for the year up to the limit, you pay only the Medicare portion of the tax (1.45%) on the bonus. When you receive the bonus in a later year, there's no additional Social Security or Medicare tax at that time.

> **Strategy:** *Arrange for deferred compensation before actually earning the income. Consult your employer at the start of the year to ask for a deferred-compensation arrangement instead of a year-end bonus. You can't defer compensation once it's already yours.* Caution: *Don't defer compensation if you think that the company has financial difficulty. Since deferred compensation can't be a secured promise to pay, you must rely on the good faith of your employer to make good in the future.*

Make investments that won't pay off until next year. For example, after June 30, purchase a short-term CD or Treasury bill coming due the following year. The interest on these instruments will be reported in the year the investments come due.

Don't purchase mutual funds that have yet to pay their year-end distributions. Buying funds just prior to the record date means you'll pick up a full year's income from the fund, even if you own it for only a few weeks.

Caution: You can't postpone income merely by refusing to recognize it. For example, if you receive a check for interest or another type of income, you can't avoid reporting it this year simply by *not* depositing it or cashing it. As long as the income is within your control, it's your current income. And it will probably be reported to the IRS as income to you on a Form 1099.

Look ahead: By year-end it may be too late to make a significant impact on your income for the current year. But it's a great time to get ready for the coming year. Look for opportunities to reduce *reportable* income without cutting your actual income. Examples:

▶ **Contribute to a 401(k) or SIMPLE plan.** Save for your retirement on a tax-advantaged basis. You agree to a salary reduction that's contributed to the plan. For income tax purposes, the salary reduction isn't currently taxable.

▶ **Contribute to a flexible spending arrangement (FSA).** You may be able to pay for medical expenses or child-care costs on a tax-advantaged basis. If your employer has an FSA, you can contribute to the plan. The money is treated as if you never received it—it's not taxable to you. But you can use the money to pay for medical expenses or dependent-care expenses. Caution: FSAs have a use-it-or-lose-it feature. If you don't spend your full contribution, the money is lost; it doesn't carry over to the next year.

▶ **Reposition your portfolio.** You may want to shift investments to receive future tax-free or tax-deferred income rather than current income. Repositioning your portfolio is discussed earlier in this chapter.

▶ **Think about collecting Social Security.** If you will turn 62 in the coming year, you're eligible to commence benefits—at a rate that's lower than what you would collect at your full retirement age. But if you expect to continue working, collecting at age 62 can result in a loss of benefits if your earnings exceed a limit that adjusts annually ($12,960 in 2007). Whatever your age, if you expect to start collecting Social Security benefits next year, consider the impact that your income will have on the taxation of those benefits. This is discussed in Chapter 1.

Deductions

The flip side to income deferral is deduction acceleration. Again, as a general rule, you probably want to accelerate deductions to the current year where possible. For example, if you're in the top tax bracket and anticipate making charitable donations next year, do it now. You'll gain an additional tax savings of $50 by making your $10,000 charitable contribution deduction before the end of the year rather than waiting until next year. Be sure this approach makes sense for your individual tax picture.

Bunching deductions: Determine if your itemized deductions are more or less than your standard deduction amount.

If you're near but not over the standard deduction amount, consider increasing deductions to enable you to itemize. Alternatively, consider postponing deductions to next year when you may exceed the standard deduction amount (expected to be adjusted upward for inflation).

> **Example:** In 2007, you are single (under age 65 and not blind) and your itemized deductions to date total $5,000. You're thinking of making a $100 charitable contribution. Doing so in 2007 won't provide you with any tax benefit—your standard deduction exceeds your itemized deductions. If you postpone the donation to 2008, you may obtain a tax benefit at that time, depending on your itemized deductions and how much the standard deduction is adjusted for inflation.

If you bunch your deductions, consider alternating years, taking the standard deduction in one year and itemizing in the next. But keep in mind that the standard deduction can increase each year for inflation adjustments.

Standard deduction amounts

Filing status	2006	2007
Married filing jointly	$ 10,300	$ 10,700
One spouse 65 or older or blind	11,300	11,750
Both spouses 65 or older or blind	12,300	12,800
One spouse 65 or older and blind, other spouse 65 or older or blind	13,300	13,850
Both spouses 65 or older and blind	14,300	14,900
Surviving spouse	10,300	10,700
65 or older or blind	11,300	11,750
65 or older and blind	12,300	12,800
Head of household	7,550	7,850
65 or older or blind	8,800	9,150
65 or older and blind	10,050	10,450
Single	5,150	5,350
65 or older or blind	6,400	6,650
65 or older and blind	7,650	7,950
Married filing separately	5,150	5,350
65 or older or blind	6,150	6,400
65 or older and blind	7,150	7,450

Charitable contributions: If you itemize your deductions, consider stepping up your charitable contributions before year-end. Keep these tax rules in mind when making last-minute donations:

▶ **Mailing a check on the last day of the year** makes the donation deductible that year, even if the organization doesn't receive the check or deposit it until next year.

▶ **Charging a donation on your credit card** is deductible in the year of the charge, not in the year you pay the bill.

▶ **Authorizing a donation by phone or via online banking** is deductible only when the funds are disbursed to the organization, not when you make the call or input the information to your computer.

▶ **Pledges** aren't deductible until you actually pay them.

Strategy: Donate appreciated property—such as stocks, mutual fund shares, collectibles—that you've held more than one year to obtain a double tax benefit. Deduct the property's full value and avoid the capital gains tax on the appreciation. It can take several weeks to donate mutual fund shares, so don't wait until the last minute to start the process.

Medical expenses: Schedule and pay for elective medical procedures that aren't covered by insurance, such as laser eye surgery. Also consider new eyeglasses or stock up on contact lenses for the coming year. But do so only if your total unreimbursed medical expenses exceed 7.5% of your adjusted gross income (AGI). If they do not, such costs won't be deductible this year. It may be smart to postpone expenses that can possibly be deductible in the future, depending on your total medical expenses and AGI.

Miscellaneous deductions: Pay for items that may be deductible as miscellaneous itemized deductions if your total exceeds 2% of your adjusted gross income. Miscellaneous itemized deductions include:

▶ **Unreimbursed employee business expenses** such as small tools, union dues and professional dues.

▶ **Investment-related expenses,** including financial subscriptions, Internet access fees for online trading and fees for financial advice.

▶ **Tax-related costs** such as tax books, accounting fees and tax preparation software.

Retirement plan contributions: Make retirement plan contributions for the year. This means funding your IRA (if eligible to do so) or any self-employed retirement plans—profit-sharing, money purchase, defined-benefit, SEP or SIMPLE plans. Don't overlook an opportunity to contribute to an IRA on behalf of a nonworking spouse, if eligible to do so. While you can wait until the due date of your return to make IRA contributions for the prior year and the extended due date of your return to contribute to self-employed retirement plans, the earlier you contribute, the sooner you start earning tax-deferred income.

> **Example:** You have $3,000 sitting in a money market fund. You can make your 2007 IRA contribution as late as April 15, 2008. If you transfer the $3,000 from your taxable money market fund to your tax-deferred IRA, you'll reduce your current taxable income.

 Strategy: *Make Roth IRA contributions instead of deductible IRA contributions if you're eligible to make this choice. Although you'll lose a current deduction, you'll gain tax-free income over time, a far greater benefit.*

Alternative minimum tax (AMT)

The AMT was created to ensure that all taxpayers, especially wealthy ones, pay at least some tax even if they have substantial write-offs. It's now estimated by The Urban-Brookings Tax Policy Center that more than 3.4 taxpayers paid AMT in 2005, including those of modest means and could reach 29.5 million in 2010 without a law change. And as regular income tax rates decline over the next several years, millions more will become subject to the AMT. Thus you should consider the possibility of AMT and take steps to avoid it—or, if you can't avoid it, to benefit from its relatively low tax rates.

You may fall victim to the AMT, which results in a tax of up to 28%, if you have substantial itemized deductions, a large number of personal exemptions or various other income adjustments and tax preference items. Some, but not all, of these items are within your control. By watching the timing of certain transactions or investments, you can avoid or minimize your AMT exposure. Here are some ideas:

▶ **Don't prepay state and local taxes at the end of the year** if you (or your tax adviser) project you'll be subject to AMT. These taxes aren't deductible for AMT purposes, and you'll lose the benefit of the prepayment.

▶ **Switch out of municipal bonds that are "private activity bonds"**—bonds issued after August 7, 1987, used to build stadiums and to fund other nonessential public projects. While private activity bonds may pay slightly higher interest rates and the interest is exempt for regular tax purposes, having these bonds can trigger AMT.

▶ **Watch the timing for exercising incentive stock options.** The spread between the option price and stock price is treated as an adjustment to income for AMT purposes. So exercising a substantial number of ISOs in a single year can trigger AMT. Spread the exercise of ISOs over a number of years. Check for eligibility for the refundable credit related to previously-exercised ISOs.

Estimated taxes

You must pay a certain portion of your current year's tax liability on a pay-as-you-go basis, by withholding on your wages and other items and by quarterly installments of estimated taxes.

The final estimated tax payment isn't due until after the end of the year. But year-end is a good time to review your payments to figure your final payment. A shortfall can result in costly penalties. Generally, your estimated tax payments (including withholding on compensation, retirement plan distributions and other payments) must equal at least 90% of the current year's tax liability or 100% of the prior year's liability.

But if your adjusted gross income in the prior year exceeded $150,000 ($75,000 if married filing separately), then you can't rely on the 100% exception. You'll have to pay 110% of the prior year's tax liability.

In planning for estimated taxes, consider:

▶ **Asking your employer to increase withholding** on income or bonuses late in the year to avoid the need for estimated tax payments. No matter how late in the year, withholding is treated as made ratably over the year to avoid penalties for underpayment of estimated tax earlier in the year.

▶ **Taking year-end distributions from mutual funds into account** in figuring estimated tax requirements. These year-end distributions may not be received until January. If you don't know what the distributions will be, call the funds to inquire.

Looking ahead: If estimated taxes are a bother, avoid them in the coming year by increasing your withholding. You can have taxes withheld from the following payments:

▶ **Compensation.** File a new Form W-4, *Employee's Withholding Allowance Certificate,* with your employer to reduce your withholding allowances so that additional tax will be withheld. If you don't file a new form, your employer will withhold taxes based on the last one you filed.

▶ **Pensions and retirement plan distributions.** File Form W-4P, *Withholding Certificate for Pension or Annuity Payments,* to request additional withholding from payments you're receiving. Withholding from pensions and annuities paid on a regular basis—for example, monthly—is similar to wage withholding. Withholding on nonperiodic payments (such as a lump-sum distribution) is made at a 10% rate. In either case, you can request additional withholding.

▶ **Social Security benefits.** File Form W-4V, *Voluntary Withholding Request,* with the Social Security Administration requesting that it withhold taxes from your benefits at any of the following rates in 2007—7%, 15%, 25% or 28%.

 Strategy: Consider incorporating a sole proprietorship to avoid the need for estimated taxes. Compensation from your business is subject to withholding, whether or not you elect S corporation status. In deciding whether to incorporate, weigh other factors, such as the added complexity and the cost of operations.

BUSINESS STRATEGIES

If you own a business, even a sideline business, you may be able to take steps at year-end to minimize tax on business income—assuming you're on a calendar-year basis. Your ability to control your income and expenses to some extent depends on your tax accounting method.

Income strategies

If you have a cash basis business and want to postpone income, control year-end income by waiting until late December to send out invoices for work completed or goods shipped. You don't receive payment until the start of the new year. But don't consider doing this if:

▶ **There's concern about whether you'll receive payment.** Collect as soon as possible if your customer's credit is shaky.

▶ **You have business losses that can be offset with income.** Don't postpone income. Collect it as soon as possible and use it to offset your losses.

▶ **You expect next year to be even more profitable than this year,** putting you into a higher tax bracket. In this case, it's better to report the income currently when it may be taxed in a higher bracket.

Note: New laws now allow small inventory-based businesses to change from the accrual method of accounting to the cash method. Doing this means that you'll have control over your year-end income and deduction strategies.

Deduction strategies

If your business uses the cash method of accounting, bulk up year-end deductions by stocking up on supplies and paying all outstanding bills.

▶ **Equipment.** Equipment placed in service by the last day of the year qualifies for the first-year expensing deduction, up to $112,000 in 2007. This deduction is allowed even if the purchase is financed.

> **Example:** On December 31, 2007, you buy and place in service business computers costing $112,000 that you charged to your business credit card. You can elect to expense the $112,000 in 2007, even though you don't pay the credit card bill until 2008.

▶ **Retirement plans.** Set up a profit-sharing, money purchase or other qualified retirement plan no later than the last day of the year. You don't have to put even $1 into the plan at this time. You have until the extended due date of your return to fully fund the plan and claim a deduction.

> **Example:** If you're a sole proprietor who obtains a filing extension until October 15, 2008, you have until this date to make contributions to your profit-sharing plan for 2007, as long as you set up the plan by December 31, 2007.

Caution: If you have a defined-benefit plan or other plan subject to full funding requirements, contributions must be made no later than September 15, even if your return isn't due until a later date.

> **Strategy:** *Use your tax refund to fund your retirement plan. For example, say you're a sole proprietor with a profit-sharing plan. You obtain a filing extension until October 15. You actually file your return on May 1 and receive a refund on June 10, and you make your contribution that day. You can* claim *the deduction on your return filed on May 1 even though you didn't contribute until June 10.*

▶ **Accrual basis C corporations.** If the business is short of cash at year-end, the board can take action to reduce taxes currently. For example, the board can authorize a charitable contribution deduction by December 31 (the corporation's year-end date). As long as the contribution is actually paid by March 15 of the following year, it's deductible in the year of the authorization.

A similar approach can be taken for year-end bonuses. As long as they're paid by March 15, they're deductible in the year of authorization. But bonuses to more-than-50% owners are not deductible until actual payment is made. *Note:* S corporations taking this approach for owners can't deduct year-end bonuses or other payments until they're actually made.

Start planning for next year

Now's the time to think about next year. Decisions you make now can save you taxes in the future.

▶ **Review changes in the tax laws** to see which ones you may benefit from. Cost-of-living adjustments, scheduled law changes (such as expanded retirement plan and fringe benefit opportunities) and other developments may favorably impact your business decisions. Don't know what these changes are? Spend time with a tax professional—your business accountant, for example—to see how you can take advantage of these developments.

▶ **Review your form of business organization.** You may wish to change it as your business grows, or due to other reasons. Contemplating such changes now can enable you to act in a timely fashion. For example, if you're a sole proprietor who wishes to incorporate for personal liability considerations but you want to use the S corporation format for pass-through tax treatment, you'll want to incorporate at the start of the year and then elect S corporation status within the first two and a half months of the corporation's new year. If you miss this deadline, you'll have to wait until next year for S corporation status.

▶ **Adopt qualified retirement plans.** This will enable you to contribute to your own retirement savings and to attract and retain valued employees. The earlier in the year you act, the greater your range of options. For example, if you are a small employer and want to use a SIMPLE plan, even for yourself as the company's only worker, you can't wait until year-end. Notice requirements make it necessary to adopt the plan earlier in the year. SIMPLE plans and other retirement plan options are explained in Chapter 8.

▶ **Adopt employee benefit plans.** Consider switching from traditional health coverage to a high-deductible health plan and then make tax-deductible contributions to a health savings account (HSA), the funds of which grow on a tax-deferred basis and can be used tax free to pay uninsured medical costs—the result can be as much as a 40% cost savings for the business. Or consider using flexible spending accounts (FSAs) for your employees. This will enable them to funnel their pretax compensation into a plan to pay for medical expenses or dependent-care costs. You want these plans in place at the start of the year to allow employees to make monthly salary reduction contributions to the plan.

▶ **Plan your equipment purchases for the year.** Waiting until late in the year can limit your write-off options. For example, if you place in service more than 40% of your equipment in the final quarter of the year, a special depreciation convention kicks in to limit write-offs for those late purchases.

Index

344